INDIA'S
CONSTITUTION
IN THE MAKING

BY

B. N. RAU

Edited by

B. SHIVA RAO

Foreword by

DR. RAJENDRA PRASAD

President of India

ORIENT LONGMANS
BOMBAY CALCUTTA MADRAS NEW DELHI

ORIENT LONGMANS PRIVATE LTD.

17, CHITTARANJAN AVENUE, CALCUTTA 13

NICOL ROAD, BALLARD ESTATE, BOMBAY 1

36-A, MOUNT ROAD, MADRAS 2

KANSON HOUSE, 24/1, ASAF ALI ROAD, NEW DELHI 1

GUNFOUNDRY ROAD, HYDERABAD 1

17, NAZIMUDDIN ROAD, DACCA

LONGMANS, GREEN & CO. LTD.

6 & 7 CLIFFORD STREET, LONDON, W. 1

605/611 LONSDALE STREET, MELBOURNE C. 1

THIBAULT HOUSE, THIBAULT SQUARE, CAPE TOWN

LONGMANS, GREEN & CO. INC.

119 WEST 40TH STREET, NEW YORK 18, NEW YORK

LONGMANS, GREEN & CO.

20 CRANFIELD ROAD, TORONTO 16

First Published: May 1960

PRINTED IN INDIA

AT THE VASANTA PRESS, THE THEOSOPHICAL SOCIETY, ADYAR, MADRAS 20

FOREWORD

SRI B. N. RAU was a distinguished member of the Indian Civil Service who acquired varied experience in the many posts that he held in the course of a long judicial career. His intimate knowledge of law and exceptional talents led him ultimately to the highest post which a member of that service could hope for on the judicial side, namely a judge-ship in a provincial High Court. For a brief period after retirement he was Prime Minister, at a difficult time of transition, of one of the largest Indian States, Jammu and Kashmir.

All this seemed to be preparatory for the great work which brought him into close contact with me in 1946, the framing of India's Constitution by the Constituent Assembly. His subsequent work in the United Nations as India's permanent representative was among his outstanding contributions in a life full of significant achievements. Appropriately, he crowned his career with a term for two years as a judge of the International Court of Justice at the Hague.

By knowledge, experience and natural gifts he was the inevitable choice for the post of Constitutional Adviser to assist the Constituent Assembly in drafting India's Constitution. His first task, on assuming charge of the office in July 1946, was to collect and prepare, in a lucid and simple form, background material for the guidance of the members of the Assembly. Most of them were laymen without any legal training, while not many, even among those who had such training, could claim adequate equipment for the kind of specialised work involved in framing a constitution. The difficulty was not paucity of material so much as the selection and the proper interpretation of a vast mass of information scattered in the history, the constitutions, both written and unwritten, and the actual working of the constitutional machinery in many countries. He greatly lightened the task of the members of the Assembly with several brochures, papers and notes based on a careful study of different aspects of the constitutions and of the constitutional precedents of several countries and with a fairly complete draft of the Indian Constitution to form the basis for detailed discussions.

If Dr. B. R. Ambedkar was the skilful pilot of the constitution through all its different stages, Sri B. N. Rau was the person who visualised the plan and laid its foundation. He was superb in draftsmanship, endowed with a style which was at once clear, illuminating and precise—qualities which are indispensable in any document of legal or constitutional importance. He was not only deeply learned but careful and circumspect in regard even to the minutest details, so that any problem that he handled received full consideration from every aspect, thus eliminating, as far as possible, mistakes through misunderstanding or misinterpretation. The opinions which he gave on any controversial point that arose in the course of the discussions in the Constituent Assembly were full and judicious and based on a deep study of the subject. His services to the Constituent Assembly were highly appreciated even outside India, and the credit for preparing the framework of the Constitution of Burma goes to him in a large measure.

These qualities of his, which enabled the Constituent Assembly of India to complete its complicated labours in less than three years, were later utilised in the United Nations where his great services were recognised and his opinions highly prized and respected. Although no mean lawyer, he never indulged in legalistic arguments, but always took a broad, statesmanlike view of all questions which came up for consideration in the world organisation.

When the history of the Indian Constitution comes to be written, Sri B. N. Rau will occupy in it a significant place. Among the many stalwarts who played their part in the Constituent Assembly in the fulfilment of an extremely difficult undertaking, he distinguished himself by his erudition and detachment and his quietly persistent efforts.

Gathered in this volume are the notes and memoranda that he had originally prepared, either for the members of the Constituent Assembly or of its committees or for me as its President. A piece reprinted here appeared originally in *The Hindu*; some of the other papers had a somewhat restricted though practical purpose in view, since they were not primarily intended for the general reader. But even a casual glance through these pages will indicate how valuable they are for a better understanding of our constitution. The basic unity of the theme imparts to these essays, notes, memoranda and reports an integration which they would otherwise have lacked.

The volume, so welcome by itself, underlines the urgent need for further research, to bring together the scattered mass of background material and data which influenced and shaped thinking in the Constituent Assembly and has given to our constitution its present form and content. Such research is necessary, not only for the student of contemporary politics, but for a full understanding by future generations of our constitution and of the interplay of social forces and attitudes behind the prosaic work of legal draftsmanship.

I have, therefore, the greatest pleasure in commending the book to the public, and, in particular, to discerning readers who, in the very nature of things, must be comparatively few in number. My pleasure in doing so is all the greater as I look upon this as the discharge of a debt due to the memory of a guide, philosopher and friend in a task of such supreme national importance as the framing of the Constitution of India.

Rashtrapathi Bhavan, New Delhi
24th January 1960

PREFACE

THIS volume contains a selection from the papers relating to the making of India's Constitution of Sri Benegal Narsinga Rau (1887-1953) who was Constitutional Adviser to the Constituent Assembly through all the stages of its labours. One of the considerations which weighed with him in accepting a seat on the International Court of Justice at the Hague early in 1952 was the hope of utilising the court's winter vacations for writing an authentic story of India's Constitution. Had that project not been frustrated by premature death, the result would have been a volume of unique value enriched by his reflections and comments.

In the course of a career of great distinction, he dealt with a variety of topics in his own masterly fashion—Hindu law reform, riparian rights, Kashmir, Hyderabad, control of atomic energy, I.N.A. trials, etc. His main achievement, however—and one for which he will be best remembered by future generations in India—was in his capacity as the main architect of India's Constitution. His vast knowledge of constitutional law and practice in several countries and his gift for lucid and precise exposition enabled the Indian Constituent Assembly to complete the immense task of framing the permanent constitution in a period of less than three years. He assisted to a considerable extent Burma's Constituent Assembly to frame her post-war constitution ahead of schedule. His paper on the Constitution of Burma, first written for the *India Quarterly*, the journal of the Indian Council of World Affairs, is reproduced as the last chapter in this volume, with the permission of the Council.

My original intention was to make this volume a comprehensive one, the first part dealing with India's constitutional problems and the second covering other problems with many of which Sri B. N. Rau was concerned as India's permanent representative at the United Nations, either in the General Assembly or in the Security Council or in one of its committees. It was, however, found impracticable to bring them within the compass of a single volume. His statements before the United Nations and other papers, such as those dealing with Hindu law reform, riparian rights etc., have, therefore, been excluded for subsequent publication in a separate volume.

A delay of some years in the publication of this volume, regrettable as it is, was due to circumstances beyond my control. Nevertheless, the memoranda and notes written at different stages of the framing of India's Constitution will, it is hoped, prove to be of permanent value and interest. A few papers, like the draft of an Indo-British treaty, were prepared in anticipation of the main outlines of Britain's post-war policy in regard to India. The draft treaty, whose provisions were subjected to a detailed analysis by experts, both in New Delhi and in London, was ultimately considered unnecessary. Nevertheless, it has been included in this volume as a document of historical interest.

The different chapters in this volume follow, in their sequence, the broad pattern set by the Constituent Assembly. The adoption of the resolution on the Assembly's objectives, at the commencement of its proceedings, was followed by a consideration of the rules of procedure, the adoption of a provisional time-table for the Assembly and a discussion of different parts of the author's first draft constitution by committees created for the purpose; such as the Union and Provincial Constitution Committees, the Union Powers Committee, the *ad hoc* committee on the Union Judiciary, etc.

These committees made considerable alterations in the original draft of the constitution as a preliminary to a clause-by-clause discussion by the Constituent Assembly, under the general guidance of a drafting committee. At this stage the author prepared a number of papers on important aspects of the constitution for the benefit of the members of the Constituent Assembly. These papers (on fundamental rights, second chambers, head of the State, Union executive, linguistic provinces and regional arrangements, etc.) appear as later chapters in the volume.

The author was sent on deputation in October 1947 to the U.S.A., Canada, Eire (Ireland) and the U.K. to discuss with the leading constitutional authorities in those countries some of the basic provisions of the Indian Constitution. A report embodying the results of such discussions is included as a separate chapter.

It should be noted that in the chapter (20) on " Panchayats as Electoral Colleges ", the references to articles and clauses relate to the original draft of the Indian Constitution.

Some of the later chapters were written by the author, either on important questions arising out of the constitution after its final adoption (such as the position of India as a republic in the Commonwealth and common citizenship rights) or on specific matters, like the powers of the President under the constitution and the duties of the Finance Commission.

To Dr. Rajendra Prasad, our President, I owe a deep debt of gratitude for his encouragement and the keen interest he displayed at every stage of the preparation of this volume. I had free access to all the records of the Constituent Assembly in his possession and his permission to include some of the documents in this collection. Several friends gave their whole-hearted co-operation and greatly simplified my task; I must mention, in particular, Sri P. N. Krishna Mani, Under Secretary of the Rajya Sabha, whose close collaboration I found indispensable; also Sri M. P. Sarangapani, who took great pains to revise the manuscript and correct the proofs. To the editor of *The Hindu* I am grateful for his permission to reproduce two papers which originally appeared in that paper.

B. SHIVA RAO

New Delhi
1st February 1960

CONTENTS

Facsimile

A BIOGRAPHICAL SKETCH

SRI BENEGAL NARSINGA RAU—B. N. Rau, as he was known in his later years—had a career of singular brilliance from his early boyhood, obtaining a first class in every examination in the Madras University and standing first among the successful candidates on every occasion. He graduated in 1905 with a triple first in English, Physics and Sanskrit (adding a first in Mathematics in the following year) and won all the academic prizes and medals that were open to him. With a Government of India scholarship he proceeded to England and joined Trinity College, Cambridge, where he won a "major" scholarship, again being first in the competitive test in his first year. At the end of his career at Cambridge, the choice lay before him of either accepting a Fellowship at Trinity or entering the I.C.S. He chose the latter and returned to India in 1910.

As an I.C.S. officer, he was posted to (undivided) Bengal, where he spent about fourteen years. For a brief period he had his training as an executive officer; but by temperament he felt a preference for a judicial post and served as a judge in several districts, mostly in East Bengal, acquiring an intimate knowledge of the civil and criminal laws of the land.

The quality of his work as a district judge in Bengal attracted official notice, and the Assam Government offered him in 1925 the dual post of Secretary to the provincial Legislative Council and Legal Remembrancer to the government. It meant a different type of work; but even more attractive was the change from the humid, malarial districts of East Bengal to the bracing hill-station of Shillong. For a period of about eight years he served the Assam Government, but his duties were not strictly limited to the posts that he officially occupied. The provincial government was quick to see that his knowledge and talents could be used with great advantage in other spheres. When the Simon Commission toured India in 1928-29, he drafted the Assam Government's memorandum pleading for a generous financial deal for the province from the proceeds of the duty on tea. So favourable was the impression created by the memorandum on the Commission that the Assam Government decided to depute him to London, after the third Round Table Conference in 1933, to present its case before the Joint Select Committee of Parliament.

Sri B. N. Rau's wide knowledge of constitutional affairs was also utilised for a more general purpose. Sir John Kerr (at that time Governor of Assam) wrote to him about the proposal then under the consideration of the Joint Select Committee that seats in the new Council of States should be filled by election, on the basis of the single transferable vote, by the members of the provincial legislatures. The Joint Select Committee had asked Sir John Kerr to prepare a note on the manner in which the system could be worked. He passed on the request to Sri B. N. Rau as being more competent to deal with the problem than himself.

On his return to India in 1935 he could have gone to the Calcutta High Court as a judge; but the Government of India was eager to borrow his services, if he was willing to make the sacrifice, for work in New Delhi in connection with the new constitution.* This appointment (which he accepted)

---

* The Chief Secretary to the Bengal Government wrote to him:

"The appointment (with the Government of India) is likely to last for one year and might continue until the introduction of provincial autonomy. Your name has been suggested for this appointment, but before proceeding further, I should be glad to know your own views in the matter. Acceptance of the appointment would mean that you would have to forego any chance of acting in the High Court which might occur between now and the introduction of provincial autonomy, say, at the beginning of 1937."

proved to be the beginning of a new career; and in many ways it marked a period of intense activity in spheres for which he was well qualified by his earlier experience and talents.

The introduction of the constitution of 1935 had pushed to the forefront the intricate problem of revising all the existing Central and provincial statutes to bring them into accord with its provisions. The task involved enormous industry, a meticulous knowledge of the laws of the land and a high standard of draftsmanship. He accomplished it in less than eighteen months, thus enabling the constitution to be brought into operation without any delay.

On the completion of this assignment he could have continued to function in the Reforms Office of the Government of India. But Sir Maurice Gwyer, the first Chief Justice of India's Federal Court, was anxious to have him as a colleague; and one of the qualifications for appointment as a judge of the Federal Court was a minimum of five years' experience on the bench of a High Court. He, therefore, went to the Calcutta High Court, intending thus to qualify himself for a place on the Federal Court. His term as a judge was, however, not destined to run a smooth course. First came a dispute about wages and working conditions on the old G.I.P. Railway which had to be referred to a court of enquiry presided over by a High Court judge, and Sri B. N. Rau was invited to be its chairman.

Shortly after the completion of the enquiry a second interruption occurred, when the Government of India felt that Hindu Law reform, however desirable or acceptable to progressive opinion, could not be undertaken piecemeal. A committee, it was suggested, should first survey the entire field and make a report, as the ground-work for a series of planned reforms of different parts of Hindu Law. The choice for the chairmanship again fell on Sri B. N. Rau.

Even while this enquiry was in progress, came a difficult, complex and, for India at any rate, a new problem—that of

B

the equitable distribution of the waters of the Indus and some of her tributaries among several regions of undivided India. The main disputants were Sind and the Panjab; but there were others almost equally interested in an equitable solution, Bikaner, Bahawalpur and some other Princely States. His work as the chairman of the Indus waters Commission provides an illustration of the untiring industry, thoroughness and impartiality with which he tackled every problem. He familiarised himself with all aspects of the problems of irrigation, and the report that his committee submitted in 1942 on the dispute has been regarded, not only in India but outside, as a classic on riparian rights, covering the subject with great legal knowledge and technical accuracy.

After formal retirement from the Indian Civil Service early in 1944, he was persuaded by Sir Tej Bahadur Sapru (who enjoyed the confidence of the Maharaja of Kashmir) to accept the post of Prime Minister of that State. He served the State, in a sphere that was new to him, for about eighteen months. Differences with the Maharaja complicated his task and he offered his resignation in December 1944; but by June 1945 he felt that he could no longer carry on the administration of the State without a free hand and resigned the post. In a letter to the Maharaja he wrote:

"Briefly, Your Highness, I have been conscious for some time that we do not see eye to eye on certain fundamental matters of external and internal policy. And that leads, as it must lead, to disagreement in many a detail. I have never questioned, and I do not now question, the position that in all these matters Your Highness's decision must be final. The Prime Minister must either accept it or resign. To accept it without conviction would not be fair either to Your Highness or to the State, and I am grateful to Your Highness for letting me resign. . . . I need not repeat to Your Highness that if in the days to come I can be of any service to the State, wherever I may be, that service will be rendered gladly and freely."

At that time, the Second World War was in its final stages, and preliminary moves had already been initiated by the Viceroy, Lord Wavell, for breaking the political deadlock in India on the cessation of hostilities. Sri B. N. Rau had served for broken periods before and during the war in the Reforms Office of the Government of India, sometimes officiating as Reforms Commissioner. He had acquired an intimate knowledge of various facets of the constitutional problem, to which was now added the somewhat brief experience of administering as Prime Minister the State of Jammu and Kashmir.

On relinquishing this post, he was asked by the Government of India if he would consider the offer of a permanent judgeship of the Calcutta High Court. He replied in a brief letter to the Viceroy's Private Secretary, expressing gratitude for the consideration shown; but the offer was declined on the ground best stated in his own words:

"If personal prospects were all, a decision would have been easy; but I have now reached a stage in my official life when they ought to cease to count, and I have therefore to look at the matter from another point of view. The big thing before India is now Federation. I have spent, off and on, over a dozen years in the study of constitutional law in general and the Indian Constitution in particular; and within the limits permitted to me, I have had some share in the working out of the details of the federal scheme now taking shape. If, therefore, I have any choice, I should like to stay on here until Federation, in whatever form it ultimately comes, is an accomplished fact. This will mean the abandonment of any prospects in the High Court, or anywhere else *via* the High Court, but such things are inevitable."

The Viceroy, appreciating his point of view, placed him on special duty, with the status of a Secretary, on the Governor-General's Secretariat on the Reforms side. For nearly a year he occupied this post, until he became Constitutional Adviser to the Constituent Assembly on its establishment in July 1946.

During the two following years, he was kept busy with a number of other important assignments, very different in character, in addition to the main one of assisting the Constituent Assembly. Sir Jeremy Raisman, who was Finance Member during the greater part of the Second World War, was interested in introducing legislation for an estate (or death) duty. Taking advantage of his deep knowledge of Hindu Law in all its branches and his legal acumen, Sir Raisman asked him for the draft of a measure, with the main details worked out. The draft was later revised and modified, again by its author, under instructions from Sir Jeremy Raisman's successor, Sir Archibald Rowlands. The present law on the subject is largely modelled on this revised draft.

Another assignment, however interesting it might have been from the legal standpoint, was altogether unrelated to his official position and duties. Considerable interest had been roused in India, shortly after the end of the Second World War, in what have since come to be known as the Indian National Army trials. The first of these, involving three officers of the Indian army who had joined Netaji Subhash Chandra Bose's liberation forces in Malaya, had attracted a great deal of attention. The trial took place in Delhi's historic Red Fort and chief among the lawyers engaged for the defence was Sri Bhulabhai Desai, who argued the case with remarkable ability. The line of defence was suggested in a carefully drafted memorandum by Sri B. N. Rau.

An accidental meeting in New Delhi in December 1946 with U Aung San, Burma's young and brilliant Prime Minister, led to a quick decision by the latter to have Burma's Constitution framed on the principles and by the methods India had adopted. Burma's Constitutional Adviser was deputed to New Delhi where he spent some weeks in the early part of 1947 for daily and detailed consultations with Sri B. N. Rau. Later, in August of that year, he was invited to Rangoon to witness the passage of the final draft of Burma's Constitution. The first draft had been framed with such care and precision that the subsequent task of her Constituent Assembly was greatly simplified and the constitution was adopted far ahead of schedule.

All these were in reality side-occupations, however important in themselves. How he could find time for tackling the great problems placed before him was a matter of astonishment even for those who were aware of his capacity for hard, unremitting work and his brilliant versatility. None of these problems interfered with his main task of dealing with the post-war constitution of India. Almost immediately on joining the Governor-General's Secretariat, early in September 1945, he worked on the draft of an Indo-British treaty, assuming that the main principles of the Cripps offer of 1942 would be the starting point for fresh negotiations. The draft was ready for preliminary discussions with the relevant authorities in India by the end of November of that year.

In 1946, despite the Cabinet Mission's historic statement, little positive progress was made with the preparation of the constitution. The first session of the Constituent Assembly could not meet until December 9, 1946 though the Cabinet Mission's statement had been published on May 16 and the office of the Constituent Assembly came into existence early in July. All through the intervening months (between July and December) there were inconclusive discussions between the leaders of the Congress and the Muslim League about the interpretation of the Cabinet Mission's statement and the composition of the interim government. Sri B. N. Rau was frequently consulted by both sides on specific issues. Indeed, on one occasion (in September 1946) Mr. Jinnah had a discussion with him which covered almost every point. Pakistan and its viability were one of the main subjects to be discussed, judging from pencil notes recorded at the time.* Mr. Jinnah seemed more or less satisfied, at any rate temporarily, both as regards the procedure that the Constituent Assembly was

---

* For Mr. Jinnah's note and the reply, see the Introduction.

likely to adopt and the functions of the interim government.
When the negotiations took a more difficult turn later (in
November 1946), Lord Wavell suggested to Mr. Jinnah the
desirability of another such discussion. That, even if one
took place, seemed to have had no effect on the subsequent
developments.

Only in 1947, after Mr. (now Earl) Attlee's declaration on
20th February in the House of Commons foreshadowing the
inevitability of Pakistan, did the Indian Constituent Assembly
get down to serious business. The preliminaries were quickly
settled, mainly because of Sri B. N. Rau's skilful and competent handling of the several issues, and the Constituent
Assembly was able to commence the detailed consideration of
the draft constitution, section by section, in the late summer
of that year.

The declaration of Independence on 15th August, partition,
the numerous and difficult problems to which it gave rise
and the extremely heavy strain of dealing with the influx of
refugees reckoned by the million had little effect on the course
of the Constituent Assembly. By October of the year, Sri
B. N. Rau was able to leave for the U.S.A., Canada, Eire
and the United Kingdom for personal discussions with leading
constitutional authorities in those countries.

The study tour, apart from proving valuable in reaching
tentative decisions on certain provisions of the Indian Constitution, led to fruitful contacts. An interesting personality
whom he met in New York in November 1947 was Dr. Chaim
Weizmann, the distinguished founder of the State of Israel.
They discussed then, and again in an exchange of letters
later, the possibilities of Israel assisting India in her economic
development.

Justice Felix Frankfurter of the Supreme Court of the
U.S.A. was another with whom he came into intimate contact. The impression on the former must have been profound;
later, he stated to Sir Girja Shankar Bajpai, at that time

Secretary-General to the External Affairs Ministry: "If the President of the U.S.A. were to ask me to recommend a judge for our Supreme Court on the strength of his knowledge of the history and working of the American Constitution, B. N. Rau would be the first on my list".

Before the commencement of the Constituent Asssembly session in July 1948 for a detailed discussion of the draft constitution, the President (Dr. Rajendra Prasad) suggested in a letter to Sri B. N. Rau a preliminary personal discussion 'point by point' at Simla. The President also referred to other points in his letter: in particular, to India's position in the Commonwealth. Observing that Sri B. N. Rau's paper on the subject of India and the Commonwealth was "a useful and thought-provoking paper, intended to stimulate discussion rather than to offer advice," he added, "the question needs to be discussed on a plane higher than that ordinarily allotted to other questions of policy and you have raised it to that plane. It will, of course, be for the government and the members of the Assembly to take the decision in the matter, but it is useful and as well that people generally give thought to it".

The President also referred to the possibility of his being offered a new assignment by the Prime Minister and sought his reactions. In reply Sri B. N. Rau wrote:

"The Prime Minister has not mentioned anything to me; but I should like you to know what I feel generally. It is now nearly two years since I first took on my present job as Constitutional Adviser; and when I took it, I made it a condition that it should be on an honorary basis. It has largely been a labour of love all through, and I have been doing it in spite of various difficulties. Indeed, there were moments when, but for the fact that *you* were the President and perhaps needed me, I should have liked to retire from the scene. We are now nearing the end of our labours in the Constituent Assembly and I hope you will be able to spare me as soon as any work which is congenial to me offers itself."

With the Constituent Assembly busy over the detailed considerations of the provisions of the constitution, guided by the drafting committee, the main task of the Constitutional Adviser, as he had pointed out in his letter to the President, had virtually come to an end. But other problems were emerging, complex from a constitutional lawyer's point of view. For instance, the Nizam's advisers were claiming the right for Hyderabad to appeal to the U.N. Security Council against India's intervention in the State in 1948. Could an Indian State exercise such a right; in other words, did the Security Council have jurisdiction over relations between India and a Princely State?

The brief on this subject was prepared by Sri B. N. Rau in close consultation with the Prime Minister and the Minister who administered the portfolio of the States, Sardar Vallabh-bhai Patel. Sri A. Ramaswami Mudaliar argued the case before the Security Council in Paris in October 1948 on the lines of the brief. Sri B. N. Rau was sent on the Indian delegation to the U. N. General Assembly that year, mainly to assist India's spokesman on the Hyderabad issue. But he made his mark as an outstanding delegate, especially in the committee of the General Assembly which considered, for the first time, the peaceful uses of atomic energy.

Encouraged by the general support promised by a number of delegations, Sri B. N. Rau's name was proposed at that session for one of the vacancies in the International Court of Justice at the Hague. His prospects seemed good in the initial stages of the complicated ballot. But later a deadlock ensued, with India and Greece tying for the last place, followed by Yugoslavia in the vote. For reasons which had nothing to do with the merits of the candidates concerned in the contest, several Powers, which had earlier promised to support India and had voted accordingly in the preliminary ballots, suddenly switched over to Yugoslavia's candidate. Sri B. N. Rau was, however, elected at the same session of the General

Assembly to the International Law Commission, and continued to be a member until he was elected to the International Court of Justice at the end of 1951.*

The Hyderabad issue threatened to come up again before the Security Council in the spring of 1949, and Sri B. N. Rau was deputed by the Government of India to argue the case for India on this occasion. His reputation as a skilful and brilliant advocate had already been established in U. N. circles. There was little for him to do of any substance in the Constituent Assembly, though he utilised his visits to London for personal discussions with the Lord Chancellor and Sir Stafford Cripps

---

* A Brazilian colleague (also elected by the U. N. General Assembly in 1948) described him in the following terms in an article in a Brazilian journal towards the end of his term of office:

"In 1947, the Assembly 'in acknowledging the utility of creating a Commission composed of persons of acknowledged international legal competency and who jointly represent the first forms of civilisation and the principal systems of law', elected the 15 members of the Commission.

"I shall never forget that first meeting (in 1949), that first contact with men so different, coming from such different latitudes, representing juridical systems and forms of civilisations so diversified, some even opposed to each other.

"The meeting had been called in order to establish the activity programme of the Commission. After a long discussion during which all the members had talked with the exception of one member of the Commission, the second Vice-President, Sir Benegal Rau, who had been taking notes, started to speak; and with a very clear voice and melodious accent he read what he had written from the notes he had taken. His language was almost precious due to its perfection. The way of talking was elegant and somewhat remote—as if the speaker were not there. . . . But he was there. . . . And the solution he proposed was practical and under the circumstances the only one capable of satisfying everybody. Agreement was immediately reached. The Commission was able to start in the following session on its work, knowing what it was doing.

"A man of angelic appearance, extremely sweet in manners, a full idealist, but capable of dealing with reality and coldness from the right angle and not in a dreamy way, Sir Benegal is a man possessing the gift to surprise us when we least expect it. I do not wish to imply that Sir Benegal will solve a conflict which presents itself to many historical fates. It is not my purpose to give Brazil the hope that Sir Benegal may be able to bring peace and free us from the threats which are accumulating in Korea and China. But it is, indeed, a privilege to be able to put before the eyes of my countrymen such a beautiful expression of humanity, representing the highest and noblest human expression, indeed extremely human, the mirror of a culture many thousands of years old, which employs the language of the West in a better way than Occidentals do, because they do not possess the sense of eternity, of the everlasting. And it pleases me, in addition, to acquaint the Brazilian people with the fact that I work abroad in their name alongside Sir Benegal."

on the question of India retaining, as a republic, her membership of the Commonwealth. He drew up in April 1949, at
the Lord Chancellor's request, a formula briefly stating the
Indian and the British points of view.

It should not be assumed that this formula was easily
acceptable to the British Government. In February of that
year, Lord Jowitt, the Lord Chancellor, referring to a broadcast given by Sri B. N. Rau from Lake Success on " India and
the Commonwealth ", had commented in the course of a letter:

. . . . .

" It is true that it is of the essence of our Commonwealth
that all its members are equal in status. It is, of course, a
club from which any member can resign, if he is so minded.

" The only doubt I have is with regard to the first question
you formulate: ' Is there room within the Commonwealth for
a State with a republican constitution? ' I think you deal
with this in much too cavalier a fashion.

. . . . .

" Yet we can help each other and we shall each need the
other's help in the difficult days that confront us, and I believe
this help could be better given if we both belong to the club." *

The Constituent Assembly was drawing to a close towards
the end of 1949, and Sri B. N. Rau had already proved his
worthiness to represent India at the U.N. on such issues as
Hyderabad and Kashmir. Sir G. S. Bajpai was aware of the
great respect in which he was held and the influence he wield-
ed on his colleagues. As he wrote later, " though he came late
into the profession of diplomacy, in the three years that he represented India at the U.N. he made a deep impression,
both on the Security Council and the General Assembly by
his fairness, sincerity and the crystal-clarity of his mind ".

When India was elected a member of the Security Council,
Sri B. N. Rau was the natural choice of the Government of
India, with the rank of an Ambassador. During this period,

---

* The text of Lord Jowitt's letter is to be found on *p.* 353 of this volume.

in rapidly failing health, he worked hard as India's spokesman on such diverse topics as Kashmir, atomic energy, the future of the Italian colonies in Africa, Korea and China. Such was his sense of duty that within four weeks of undergoing an operation for cancer, he was in his seat in the Security Council, arguing the case on Kashmir from India's standpoint. He had also the satisfaction of having laid the enduring foundations of an Afro-Asian group in the U.N.

The work, especially in the Security Council, was hard and exacting. The preparation of his speeches on delicate issues like Kashmir involved a great deal of labour. Outside the U.N. he was much in demand, both as India's spokesman and as an earnest seeker after world peace.

By the end of 1951, he had reasons to fear a recurrence of cancer. He yearned for a position in which he could give some attention to his health. Moreover, India's term as a member of the Security Council was coming to an end, and he could hand over the responsibilities as India's permanent delegate to the U.N. to a successor, happy in the thought that he had done his best to maintain his country's reputation high.

It was in such circumstances that the invitation came to him from the External Affairs Ministry to stand for election to the International Court of Justice for one of the vacancies due to occur at the end of that year. The election came without much effort at canvassing by the Indian Delegation. When he was leaving New York early in 1952 to take his seat in the court at the Hague, his successor asked him for advice on the policy to be pursued by him. He replied: " Whatever be the theme, let your language be soft, but make your facts deadly ".

He was not destined to serve on the International Court for much more than a year. By the summer of 1953 it was clear that his old trouble had returned in an aggravated form, beyond the resources of his medical advisers. As he lay ill in a Zurich hospital, in October of that year, beyond hope of recovery, there was a moving incident. An unexpected visitor called on him, the late Mr. Ghulam Mahomed (at that time Governor-General of Pakistan). Leaning heavily on crutches, with his own health shattered by a paralytic stroke, he said in a voice that was hardly audible, " Come and be my guest at Karachi. We will look after you. We have no one like you in Pakistan ".

*   *   *   *

Anyone reading this narrative might imagine that life for Sri B. N. Rau was an unbroken series of successes. As a record of achievements in a world of events such an inference would probably be right. He had, however, his full share of sorrows and disappointments about which even those near him knew very little.

What sustained him through such a life no one can really tell. But there are glimpses of the influences which seemed to have guided him. One of the frequently-quoted passages in his speeches in the U.N. and outside was the following from a biography of Gladstone:

"We believe in no man's infallibility, but it is restful to be sure of one man's integrity."

In a memorable speech on Gandhiji that he delivered in Philadelphia in October 1950 he said:

"The atomic bomb is the greatest explosive force that we know in the physical world today. Yet, what starts this tremendous explosion is one single neutron—an infinitesimal, invisible particle which, acting as a kind of gun, first sets off two other guns and then each of these two sets off two others and so on, until there is a terrific force of almost earth-shaking dimensions. What is true of the physical world is also true of the moral: there also we may have vast chain-reactions radiating from a single individual. One of the lessons which we may learn from modern science, therefore, is the importance of the infinitesimally small and, by analogy, the tremendous potential worth of the individual human person and the immense value of individual freedom. If a single individual, organisation, or country can set in motion the right kind of idea, it may ultimately move the whole world."

Late in life, he had come into contact with Einstein and Gandhiji; and the influence of these two eminent personalities was great. He had a vision of the future which he placed before his audiences in the U.S.A. in words of superb quality:

"Let us consider for a moment man, not as an individual, but Man in the sum, Man with a capital M. The earth which he inhabits is a small planet revolving round an insignificant star (for that is what the Sun is)—so insignificant that if by any cosmic cataclysm it were to disappear, the event would not even be noticed from the remoter parts of our own galaxy, let alone the innumerable other galaxies in the Universe. On this planet, which is many millions of years old, Man is a very recent arrival, compared with other forms of life. His normal expectation of life is about 70 years. Thus on the purely physical plane, he is a mere speck in space and time. Most of his life is a struggle for existence, leaving little time for higher thought. And yet look at his achievements in the few thousands of years since civilisation began. 'Perched precariously on this rotating speck of mud and water' that we call the earth, Man, in the brief intervals of struggling to live, has by mere force of thought penetrated into the deepest mysteries of the Universe; has discovered the laws of the infinitely vast spaces around us as well as of the infinitely small world within the atom, and is now in the process of creating a miniature Sun that we call the hydrogen bomb. When we contemplate these truly wonderful conquests of external Nature, have we no reason for hoping that he will—before very long—discover the laws of his own well-being and learn to conquer himself rather than destroy himself? Surely, the end of all his labours could not merely be the destruction of the race."

These passages reflect, in language of which he alone was capable, the sentiments which moved him in all his actions and moulded his outlook on life. Some months after his election to the International Court in 1952, Justice Frankfurter of the Supreme Court of the U.S.A. said to him in the course of a letter:

> "Remembrance of you will, I am confident, be among the very last to fade. My talks with you (in October 1947) were among the pleasantest and most satisfying of all my experiences in Washington. On more than one occasion I said behind your back—and so I shall dare offend your modesty and say it to your face—that you are one of the few people I ever encountered who had a deep, instinctive sense of justice. I begrudged the years you gave, I am sure conscientiously, to diplomacy and rejoiced when you took your rightful place on the court."

Such was the measure of the man who represented India for a time in the United Nations and the International Court of Justice. He went somewhat before his time, but with the satisfaction of having won many friends for India in the United Nations and maintained her reputation high in the world.

INTRODUCTION

BRITISH policy towards India, in the two crowded years between the end of the Second World War and the grant of complete freedom in August 1947, appears in retrospect to fall into some well-defined, broad phases.

The first was a preliminary one, marked by Lord Wavell's efforts to bring into existence a coalition government representing the major communities and groups to function within the limitations of the Government of India Act, 1935. In the absence, however, of any intelligible principle to guide the Viceroy in his moves, failure was inevitable, leaving behind a trail of disappointment and frustration.

A touch of realism was imparted to the situation when, as a result of the British general elections in the late summer of 1945, a Labour Government under Mr. (now Earl) Attlee was installed in office. One of its first decisions, within a few weeks of its taking up office, was to summon Lord Wavell to London for consultations. From the beginning it seemed clear that the Labour Government's intention was to resume negotiations with Indian leaders from the point of their breakdown after the Cripps Mission of 1942.

Informal consultations were initiated in India under the Viceroy's instructions with leaders like Mr. Jawaharlal Nehru to ascertain their views on some of the problems that were bound to arise in the course of the negotiations. Sri B. N. Rau, who was at that time on special duty in the Governor-General's Secretariat, had a general discussion with Mr. Nehru on November 21, 1945. From a note prepared immediately after the discussion, it would appear that on the reconstitution of the Central Government for the transitional period, while the permanent constitution was being framed, Mr. Nehru expressed his preference for such reconstitution to await the results of all the elections, Central and provincial—announced for the end of the year—as "otherwise there would be confusion of issues and no satisfactory reconstitution would be possible".

On the procedure for the reconstitution of the Centre, Mr. Nehru was apprehensive that the provincial represent-atives, if consulted, would only complicate the situation;* but he had no objection to the Central legislature being asked for a panel of names for a final choice by the Governor-General.

In regard to the strength of the Constituent Assembly, the original Cripps' plan (of 1942) had visualised a membership of 200. Mr. Nehru did not consider it adequate. On the other hand, he thought that "it might with advantage consist of 300 or even 400 members," adding: "The actual drafting would be done by a committee appointed by the constitution-making body, which would probably lay down certain general principles, leaving the details to the committee. Having laid down the general principles and appointed the drafting committee, the constitution-making body would disperse for the time being and meet again to discuss the draft after it has been prepared by the committee. I do not think that this would lead to any delay. The disadvantage of a small body would be that the same members must necessarily participate in the discussion of all matters; and if there should be a deadlock, no fresh light would be forth-coming. A large body necessarily means more ideas thrown into the common pool and extreme views are not likely to prevail".

Another point in the discussion related to the decisions of the Constituent Assembly being considered as binding on all

---

* Mr. Nehru had obviously in mind Lord Wavell's unsuccessful efforts earlier, in the summer of 1945, to reconstitute the Central Government in consultation with Central and provincial legislators.

the provinces taking part in its deliberations. The questions
and answers on this point are reproduced below:

" *Question:* Will this (the binding character of the decisions)
not deter some of the provinces from joining in the deliberations?
For example, if you tell the Panjab or Sind that by coming into
the constitution-making body, they would be bound by its
decisions even when they themselves dissent from those decisions,
are they not likely to stand out from the very beginning? If, on
the other hand, you tell every province that it is free to come
in, contribute to the discussion and accept or reject the resulting
constitution as it thinks fit, is there not a greater chance of its
coming into the constitution-making body and of accepting the
constitution framed, either immediately or possibly at a later
date? Of course, if this plan is adopted, the decisions of the
constitution-making body must not be held to bind even the
dissentient units; these must be given a chance of accepting or
rejecting the constitution as they think fit. The Congress has
accepted the position that no unit can be coerced into a constitution of which it does not itself approve.

" *Sri Nehru:* Yes; I think it would be better to give an option
of adherence or accession to every unit, after the deliberations
of the constitution-making body are over. Undoubtedly, there
can be no coercion in the matter. I recognise that the psychological effect of telling a province that even if it comes into the
discussions, the door will still be open for it to go out, may be
that it will elect to stay in.

" *Question:* From another point of view also, would it not be
unreasonable to ask a province to join the constitution-making
body and compel it to accept a constitution which has not yet
been framed and is only to be framed by that body? The
province may very well say that without knowing what safeguards for minorities the proposed constitution is to contain, it
cannot be expected to take a leap in the dark.

" *Sri Nehru:* That is so. At the same time, I cannot help
thinking that the question of safeguards has not hitherto been
discussed in the context of existing conditions. For example,
take the question of recruitment to the Services: it is quite
possible that under a national government there will be such
an expansion of governmental activities in planning, industrial
development, etc., that there will be room in the Services for

C

everybody with certain minimum qualifications and the question of communal ratios will not arise at all. Everybody capable of making a contribution will have a job. Similarly, in the defence forces our plan may be to have a standing force of small dimensions, but extremely efficient and well-equipped, with a large reserve consisting of all able-bodied citizens, with perhaps compulsory military training for a certain period. On this plan, again, all communal questions would recede into the background. I should also like the new constitution to lay the greatest emphasis on State activities such as planning, industrial development, relief of unemployment, nationalisation of key industries, etc., which will cut across communal divisions. Another safeguard that I have in mind would be to give the Upper House of the Central legislature specific functions for the protection of minorities, the Upper House being constituted on a province-basis or otherwise, so as to produce a balance of the various interests concerned.

" *Question:* Even assuming that some or all of these safeguards are to be put into the constitution, don't you think that a province might very well say: ' Let us see exactly what safeguards go into the constitution before you ask us to accept it? '

" *Sri Nehru:* I agree that it should have the option of accepting or rejecting the constitution after it has been made."

Two other matters were discussed, more briefly. Should the proceedings of the Constituent Assembly be public or private? It was pointed out to Mr. Nehru that in Canada the Constitutional Convention sat behind closed doors; in Australia, the sittings were public; in South Africa they met in secret, following the Canadian rather than the Australian precedent. The results were that the Canadian Convention took 18 days to arrive at a draft of the constitution and South Africa took about three months, while Australia took nearly a year. The great advantage of private sittings (it was suggested) was that there would be no playing to the gallery and members could, therefore, without any embarrassment, abandon a position as soon as discussion showed it to be untenable; whereas if the proceedings were public, there were likely to be long speeches, with the press joining in on one side or the other, with the result that members would find it difficult to retreat from extreme positions, and agreed solutions would be retarded, if not prevented. Mr. Nehru tentatively favoured the proceedings being in secret, at any rate initially.

On the subject of representation of the Indian States in the Constituent Assembly, Mr. Nehru appeared to be non-committal, observing: " In the course of my discussions on this subject, the suggestion was made to me that the States' representatives might be on a fifty-fifty basis, that is to say, half the number to be elected by the elected members of the State legislatures and the other half nominated by the Ruler ".

The question was also raised, at this discussion, of adopting the Swiss idea of half-cantons, as a possible solution for the problem of partition of the country raised by Mr. Jinnah and the Muslim League. Mr. Nehru was asked, " Would it be possible to have ' half-provinces ' in what is now the Panjab or Bengal, with a certain degree of autonomy in cultural and other matters for each half? I [Sri B. N. Rau being the questioner] have not worked out the idea in detail, but would like to know your reactions ". Mr. Nehru seemed attracted by the suggestion, " as it would go a great way towards safeguarding territorial minorities ".

Such discussions with India's political leaders—informal and tentative—enabled the Labour Government to formulate its line of action with some knowledge of its likely repercussions. The second phase of British policy opened with Prime Minister Attlee making a carefully-prepared statement on March 15, 1946, with the approval of the Opposition, in the House of Commons. His main points were: (1) a Cabinet Mission (consisting of Lord Pethick-Lawrence, Sir Stafford Cripps and Lord Alexander) would make " the utmost endeavours to help India to attain her freedom as speedily and fully as possible "; and (2) India must decide for herself whether to remain in the Commonwealth or not. He added: " But if she does so elect, it must be by her own free will. The

British Commonwealth and Empire is not bound together by chains of external compulsion. It is a free association of free peoples. If, on the other hand, she elects for independence, in our view she has a right to do so. It will be for us to help to make the transition as smooth and easy as possible ".

After spending some weeks in India, during which detailed negotiations were held with different parties and groups, the Cabinet Mission announced on May 16, 1946 that while a new constitution was being framed on the procedure elaborated in the statement, an interim government would be set up to carry on the administration of the country. On the vital problem of partition, the Mission was convinced that there was " an almost universal desire, outside the supporters of the Muslim League, for the unity of India ". Nevertheless, the proposal was examined with great care and from every aspect. The Muslim League's claim for " a separate and fully independent sovereign State of Pakistan "—comprising two areas, (a) the Panjab, the North-Western Frontier and Baluchistan in the North-West; and (b) Bengal and Assam in the North-East—was rejected as administratively and economically unworkable. Alternatively, could a smaller sovereign Pakistan be set up, excluding from these areas regions in which the Muslims did not form a majority ? The Mission declared even in regard to a smaller-sized Pakistan: " We ourselves are also convinced that any solution which involves a radical partition of the Panjab and Bengal, as this would do, would be contrary to the wishes and interests of a very large proportion of the inhabitants of these provinces, the Panjab and Bengal; each has its own common language and a long history and tradition. Moreover, any division of the Panjab would of necessity divide the Sikhs, leaving substantial bodies of Sikhs on both sides of the boundary. We have, therefore, been forced to the conclusion that neither a larger nor a smaller sovereign State of Pakistan would provide an acceptable solution for the communal problem ".

In addition, said the Cabinet Mission, there were " weighty administrative, economic and military considerations ". Further, against any sort of partition there was " the geographical fact that the two halves of the proposed Pakistan State are separated by some seven hundred miles ". The Mission concluded this part of the statement with the categorical observation: " We are, therefore, unable to advise the British Government that the power which at present resides in British hands should be handed over to two entirely separate sovereign States ".

The Congress had suggested a scheme under which the provinces would have full autonomy, subject only to a minimum of Central subjects, such as foreign affairs, defence and communications. Under this scheme, the provinces, if they wished to take part in economic and administrative planning on a large scale, could cede to the Centre optional subjects in addition to the compulsory ones mentioned. That, again, seemed to the Cabinet Mission to present considerable constitutional disadvantages and anomalies.

Turning to the problem of the Indian States, the view was expressed that with the attainment of independence by (what was at the time) ' British ' India, whether inside or outside the British Commonwealth, the relationship which had hitherto existed between the Rulers of the States and the British Crown would no longer be possible: " Paramountcy can neither be retained by the British Crown nor transferred to the new government. This fact has been fully recognised by those whom we interviewed from the States. They have at the same time assured us that the States are ready and willing to co-operate in the new development of India. The precise form which their co-operation will take must be a matter for negotiation during the building up of the new constitutional structure, and it by no means follows that it will be identical for all the States."

A problem demanding separate attention, because of its exceptional character, was that of Bhutan, described from

1924 as "a State under British suzerainty, but not an Indian State". Her future was a matter of natural concern and interest, both to Bhutan and to India, in the light of the Cabinet Mission's statement. Certain questions arose regarding the precise relationship between independent India and Bhutan and her position *vis-a-vis* the Constituent Assembly. Sri B. N. Rau, to whom these questions were referred, argued in a note (see Chapter 25 of this volume) that Bhutan's representatives were not called upon by the relationship existing at that time to participate in the labours of the Constituent Assembly; but that it would be open to the two countries to enter into a fresh treaty at any time in the future.

The Cabinet Mission, after a comprehensive review of the situation, recommended that India's Constitution should take the following basic form:

(1) A Union of India, both British India and the States, which should deal with foreign affairs, defence and communications and have the powers necessary to raise the finances required for the above subjects; (2) the Union to have an executive and a legislature constituted from British Indian and States' representatives. Any question raising a major communal issue in the legislature should require for its decision a majority of the representatives present and voting of each of the two major communities, as well as a majority of all the members present and voting; (3) all subjects other than the Union subjects and all residuary powers to vest in the provinces; (4) the States to retain all subjects and powers other than those ceded to the Union; (5) the provinces to be free to form groups with executives and legislatures, and each group could determine the provincial subjects to be taken in common; (6) the constitutions of the Union and of the groups to contain a provision whereby any province could, by a majority vote of its legislative assembly, call for a reconsideration of the terms of the constitution after an

initial period of ten years and at ten-yearly intervals thereafter.

The Cabinet Mission explained, " It is not our object to lay out the details of a constitution on the above programme, but to set in motion machinery whereby a constitution can be settled by Indians for Indians. It has been necessary, however, for us to make this recommendation as to the broad basis of the future constitution, because it became clear to us in the course of our negotiations that not until that had been done was there any hope of getting the two major communities to join in the setting up of the constitution-making machinery ".

Dealing with the constitution-making machinery to be set up in India, the Cabinet Mission observed that the fairest and most practicable plan would be—

(a) to allot to each province a total number of seats proportional to its population, roughly in the ratio of one to a million, as the nearest substitute for representation by adult suffrage;

(b) to divide this provincial allocation of seats between the main communities in each province in proportion to their population; and

(c) to provide that the representatives allocated to each community in a province should be elected by members of that community in its legislative assembly.

With this end in view, the provinces were classified into three groups: A, comprising Madras, Bombay, United Provinces, Bihar, Central Provinces and Orissa; B, comprising the Panjab, the North-Western Frontier Province and Sind; and C, comprising Bengal and Assam. (The Chief Commissioners' Provinces of Delhi, Ajmer-Merwara and Coorg were included in group A.)

After a preliminary general meeting of representatives of all the groups to decide the general order of business, the election of a chairman and other office-bearers and of an

Advisory Committee on the rights of citizens, minorities, tribal and excluded areas, it was proposed that the provincial representatives should meet in three sections representing respectively groups A, B and C. These sections would then settle the provincial constitutions for the provinces and also decide whether any group constitution should be set up for those provinces and what should be the subjects to be dealt with by such a group constitution. It was further suggested that a province should have the power to opt out of a group in accordance with a provision to the effect that, as soon as the new constitutional arrangements came into operation, it should be open to any province to elect to come out of any group in which it had been placed; and such a decision should be taken by the legislature of the province after the first general election under the new constitution.

Regarding the Advisory Committee's functions, it was laid down that it would contain due representation of the interests affected and their function would be to report to the Union Constituent Assembly upon the list of fundamental rights, the clauses for protecting minorities and a scheme for the administration of tribal and excluded areas; and to advise whether these rights should be incorporated in the provincial, the group, or the Union constitutions.

On the subject of the Indian States, it was held that they would be given in the final Constituent Assembly appropriate representation which would not, on the basis of the calculation of population adopted for the rest of India, exceed 93; but the method of selection would have to be determined by consultation. The States would, in the preliminary stage, be represented by a negotiating committee.

A treaty would be necessary, said the Cabinet Mission, " between the Union Constituent Assembly and the United Kingdom to provide for certain matters arising out of the transfer of power ".

No one could predict with any assurance at that stage (*a*) whether India would remain in the Commonwealth or choose the path of independence without such membership; (*b*) whether India would retain her unity or have to accept partition as the price of her liberty; and (*c*) whether the Princely States would agree to integration with a united India, or have the option to accede to one of the two independent, sovereign States in the event of partition.

These were the main imponderables of the situation which influenced the draft of an Indo-British treaty. Sri B. N. Rau had already completed a memorandum on the subject which he finalised in November 1945.*

The Cabinet Mission's statement concluded with an earnest appeal to India:

"We hope that the new independent India may choose to be a member of the British Commonwealth. We hope, in any event, that you will remain in close and friendly association with our people. But these are matters for your own free choice. Whatever that choice may be, we look forward with you to your ever-increasing prosperity among the greatest nations of the world and to a future even more glorious than your past".

The general position that emerged out of this historic statement of the Cabinet Mission was that India could decide for herself whether to remain in the Commonwealth, or become completely independent; that an elected Constituent Assembly would be set up to frame a constitution; that the partition of India being from every point of view undesirable, power could not be transferred by Britain to two entirely separate sovereign States; and that efforts should, therefore, be made to preserve, if at all possible, the unity of the country (*a*) by restricting federal authority (as the Congress was willing to do) to three or four subjects, leaving all other subjects (including residuary powers) to the provinces; (*b*) by providing for a group of provinces to combine (if they so decided) for

---

* *Vide* Chapter 28.

certain common subjects; and (c) by giving a province the option to reconsider its position in relation to the group after a period of ten years. Meanwhile, the administration of the country during the period of transition would be in the hands of the leaders of the major political parties and groups to be run with the maximum of freedom on the basis of Dominion status.

The situation was thus uncertain and fluid, with some vital problems unsolved and the lines of development unpredictable. It was not clear whether Mr. Jinnah would advise the Muslim League to participate in the work of the Constituent Assembly under the conditions and with the stipulations prescribed by the Cabinet Mission. Further ahead loomed the issue of complete independence or retention of membership of the Commonwealth.

It seemed likely for some time, especially in the early stages of the negotiations, that the Muslim League would co-operate with the Constituent Assembly. It had declared: " The goal of a complete sovereign Pakistan still remains the unalterable objective of the Muslims in India "; but since " the basis and the foundation of Pakistan (were) inherent in the (Cabinet) Mission's plan (because) of the compulsory grouping of the six Muslim provinces in sections B and C ", the League's representatives were authorised by this resolution to participate in the work of the Constituent Assembly " in the hope that it would ultimately result in the establishment of a complete sovereign Pakistan ". The League attached importance to the provision in the Cabinet Mission's statement for the secession of provinces and groups from the Union reserving to itself the right of ultimate decision (on Pakistan) being contingent on the deliberations of the Constituent Assembly.*

The Constituent Assembly's office was set up on 1st July 1946, with Sri B. N. Rau in charge as Constitutional Adviser.

---

* See the resolution of the Council of the All-India Muslim League of 6th June 1946.

But the first session of the Assembly could not be summoned until the 9th December of that year, the intervening months having been taken up with such necessary preliminaries as the election of the provincial representatives in accordance with the Cabinet Mission's plan, but even more with difficult points of procedure raised by the Muslim League awaiting settlement.

In particular, the precise interpretation of the various proposals contained in the Cabinet Mission's statement gave rise to sharp controversy. Early in July 1946 the All-India Congress Committee endorsed the view of the Working Committee that the Cabinet Mission's offer might be accepted, without prejudice to the objectives of the Congress.*

This was immediately interpreted by the Muslim League as evidence that " all efforts to find a peaceful solution of the Indian problem by compromise and constitutional means

---

* The objectives of the Congress were thus defined in the resolution:

" The kind of independence Congress has aimed at is the establishment of a united democratic Indian Federation, with a Central authority, which would command respect from the nations of the world, maximum provincial autonomy and equal rights for all men and women in the country. Taking the proposals as a whole, there was sufficient scope for enlarging and strengthening the Central authority and for fully ensuring the right of a province to act according to its choice in regard to grouping, and to give protection to such minorities as might otherwise be placed at a disadvantage. . .

" The provisional government must have power and authority and responsibility and should function in fact, if not in law, as a *defacto* independent government leading to the full Independence to come. The members of such a government can only hold themselves responsible to the people and not to any external authority. In the formation of a provisional or other government the Congress can never give up the national character of the Congress, or accept an artificial and unjust parity, or agree to the veto of a communal group.

" The Congress should join the proposed Constituent Assembly, with a view to framing the constitution of a free, united and democratic India. . .

" While the committee have agreed to the Congress participation in the Constituent Assembly, it is in their opinion essential that a representative and responsible provisional national government be formed at the earliest possible date. The continuation of an authoritarian and unrepresentative government can only add to the suffering of the famishing masses and increase discontent. It will also put in jeopardy the work of the Constituent Assembly, which can only function in a free environment."

(had been) exhausted"; and it gave expression to its determination " to resist (by direct action) any attempt to impose any constitution-making machinery or any constitution, long-term or short-term, or the setting up of any interim government at the Centre without the approval and consent of the Muslim League ".

Efforts were renewed to persuade the Muslim League to adopt a conciliatory and constructive policy.

The Viceroy in a broadcast on 24th August (1946) said:

"It is desirable that the work of the Constituent Assembly should begin as early as possible. I can assure the Muslim League that the procedure laid down in the statement of May 16th regarding the framing of provincial and group constitutions will be faithfully adhered to; that there can be no question of any change in the fundamental principles proposed for the Constituent Assembly in paragraph 15 of the Cabinet Mission's statement, or of a decision on any main communal issue without a majority of both major communities; and that the Congress are ready to agree that any dispute of interpretation may be referred to the Federal Court. I sincerely trust that the Muslim League will reconsider their decision not to take part in a plan which promises to give them so wide a field in which to protect the interests and to decide the future of the Muslims of India."

He was followed by Sri Jawaharlal Nehru (also in a broadcast), a few days later, with an earnest appeal:

"An urgent and vital task for us is to conquer the spirit of discord that is abroad in India. Out of mutual conflict we shall never build the house of India's freedom of which we have dreamt so long. All of us in this land have to live and work together, whatever political developments might take place. Hatred and violence will not alter this basic fact, nor will they stop the changes that are taking place in India.

"There has been much heated argument about sections and groupings in the Constituent Assembly. We are perfectly prepared to, and have accepted, the position of sitting in sections which will consider the question of formation of groups.

I should like to make it clear, on behalf of my colleagues and myself, that we do not look upon the Constituent Assembly as an arena for conflict, or for the forcible imposition of one viewpoint over another. That would not be the way to build up a contented and united India. We seek agreed and integrated solutions with the largest measure of goodwill behind them.

" We shall go to the Constituent Assembly with the fixed determination of finding a common basis for agreement on all controversial issues. And so, in spite of all that has happened and the hard words that have been said, we have kept the path of co-operation open, and we invite even those who differ from us to enter the Constituent Assembly as equals and partners with us with no binding commitments. It may well be that when we meet and face common tasks our present difficulties will fade away."

Presumably, these two broadcasts by the Viceroy and Sri Nehru had some effect, at any rate temporarily, on Mr. Jinnah and the Muslim League. There was a visible shift in their basic position. Despite a strongly-worded resolution passed by the Council of the League (27th to 29th July 1946) Mr. Jinnah seemed to be in a mood to discuss several procedural points with Sri B. N. Rau in connection with the functioning of the Constituent Assembly. From the questions that he raised it is a fair inference that his mind had not been finally made up against the League's participation in the Constituent Assembly. In a document (hitherto unpublished) a report is recorded of a discussion on 18th September 1946, in the course of which Mr. Jinnah asked (in writing) for a clarification of the following points:

1. What will be the subjects for discussion at the preliminary meeting of the Constituent Assembly? The Cabinet Mission's statement mentions " the general order of business " among the subjects; but what exactly does the phrase include?

2. If there is to be a committee to draft rules of procedure, what will be its composition and how will such a committee be chosen?

3.   What will be the composition of the Advisory Committee mentioned in para 20 of the Cabinet Mission's statement and how will this committee be chosen?

4.   How will the chairman be elected? Would it be possible to have a "rotational chairman", *e.g.*, a Hindu chairman for a certain period, then a Muslim chairman, and so on?

5.   Will the sections frame their own "general order of business" and elect their own chairmen?

6.   In view of the confusion that has arisen about the "grouping clause", would it not be possible to set out its meaning in clear and unmistakable terms?

7.   Is it open to the Union Constituent Assembly to modify in any way the group or provincial constitutions as settled by the sections?

8.   If the Union Constituent Assembly claims a particular matter as falling within the Union subjects and a section claims it as falling outside those subjects, what is the machinery for deciding the dispute?

9.   Is the opinion of the Federal Court on a reference under paragraph 19 (vii) of the Cabinet Mission's statement binding on the chairman of the Constituent Assembly?

10.   In the event of any resolution passed, or decision taken by a majority in the Union Constituent Assembly, which varies the provisions of paragraph 15 of the Cabinet Mission's statement, who will decide the question whether it amounts to a variation or not?

Mr. Jinnah said that these were some of the points that had occurred to him and that there might be others. A list of these additional points would be sent in due course; and he would like to have all of them examined carefully. He would also like, he said, to have a copy of any draft rules of procedure which might have been framed.

Although he had raised a good many points, he felt that if an interim government representing all parties could be formed, most of the difficulties could be left to them to resolve. Sri B. N. Rau readily agreed that, in that event, the work of the Constituent Assembly would be greatly simplified.

A reply* was sent to Mr. Jinnah four days later (on 22nd September 1946) in the following terms:

" *Question* 1.—

The subjects for discussion at the preliminary meeting, so far as they can be foreseen at present, will be—

(1) the election of a chairman and a vice-chairman or vice-chairmen;

---

* With the reply to the specific questions raised by Mr. Jinnah was this covering letter:

Dear Mr. Jinnah,

I send you herewith answers to the questions which you put to me at our recent discussions. Needless to say, they embody only my own personal views and cannot bind anyone else.

As regards rules of procedure, my office has prepared a tentative draft; but it needs continuous revision in the light of new material and is not yet in a form which can be regarded as satisfactory. If you are content with this imperfect draft, I shall be glad to send you a copy. In any event, it is meant to be no more than a working basis for the committee on procedure; and it will not be placed before the committee unless the committee themselves ask for it.

Here my function as Constitutional Adviser ends. But you were good enough to mention to me, in some detail, more pressing problems connected with the interim government and to say, at one stage, that you valued my opinion. I shall, therefore, take the liberty of saying a few words on the subject.

Let me begin on a personal note. Almost the whole of my official life in the districts of Bengal and Assam was spent in predominantly Muslim areas at a time when the communal problem was hardly known. Chandpur, which figured in the papers recently as the scene of loot and arson and communal frenzy, was my first sub-division in Bengal nearly 35 years ago; Sylhet, another recent storm-centre, was my last district in Assam. I have the pleasantest recollections of both places, where I spent nearly nine years of my early official life. My views on present-day politics are inevitably coloured by these memories of happier days and by the hope that some way may be found of bringing them back.

The problems which confront us today are problems which concern Hindus and Muslims alike. In foreign affairs—whether in Indonesia, or in South Africa, or in the Middle East, or on the North-West Frontier—there is no cleavage between Sri Nehru's views and those of the Muslim League. In the domestic sphere, our main problems are, first, putting an end to the fratricidal strife which is now going on in Bengal, Bombay and elsewhere and in which the principal sufferers are Muslims no less than Hindus; secondly, procuring adequate supplies of food to stave off famine which, again, would affect both communities; and thirdly—and ultimately, perhaps, the most important of all—planning in all its vast ramifications, including large power and irrigation projects, for the purpose of raising the standard of living of " the common and forgotten man ". In none of these matters is there likely to be any divergence of interest or policy between Hindu and Muslim; and between them they would provide a fruitful field for co-operation now and for at least a decade to come. My own view—

(2) the election of a committee to draft rules of procedure (such a committee was set up by the Philadelphia Convention);

(3) the election of a ' Steering Committee ' to prepare the resolutions to be brought before the Constituent Assembly (such a committee was set up by the Quebec Convention);

(4) the election of a Finance and Establishment Committee;

(5) the appointment of an Advisory Committee on the rights of citizens, minorities and tribal and excluded areas under para 20 of the Cabinet Mission's statement of May 16, 1946;

(6) the appointment of a ' Corresponding Committee ' to negotiate with the Negotiating Committee of the Indian States; and

(7) discussion of such of the reports of the above committees as are ready. (The report of the Advisory Committee on the rights of citizens, etc., will not be ready for discussion during the preliminary session.)

The phrase ' general order of business ' is indefinite, but will cover the subjects mentioned above. There may, of course, be other subjects which this phrase would include but which are not enumerated in the above list.

---

for what it is worth—is that the League should come into the government to work as a united team with the Congress and the minorities for the accomplishment of these common tasks.

How team-work is to be secured is best settled by direct contact between the two organisations. To suggest this in the present atmosphere of suspicion and bitterness may seem a counsel of perfection; but I recall certain words of a great English statesman addressing his Unionist colleagues on the eve of the Irish settlement twenty-five years ago:

" *Now and again in the affairs of men, there comes a moment when courage is safer than prudence, when some great act of faith touching the hearts of men and stirring their emotions achieves a miracle that no art of statesmanship can compass. Such a moment may be passing before our eyes now as we meet.*"

To come back to the Constituent Assembly: a constitution is only a means to an end; when by working together as a team, the various parties realise that the ends are common, there will be little difficulty in agreeing upon the means.

Yours sincerely,

(Sd). B. N. RAU

" *Question* 2.—

Whether there should be a committee on rules of procedure and, if so, what should be its composition and how its members should be chosen are all matters for the decision of the Constituent Assembly. At the Philadelphia Convention, which framed the Constitution of the U.S.A., there was a committee of three, consisting of a delegate from Virginia, a delegate from New York and a delegate from South Carolina. The committee was appointed on the 25th May 1787, and its report was considered on the 28th May. At the Quebec Conference, there does not appear to have been any special committee on rules of procedure. Certain rules of procedure were proposed and accepted at a meeting of the conference itself on the first and second days of the session. At the Adelaide session of the Australian Convention also, there does not seem to have been any such special committee; the standing orders and the practice of the South Australian House of Assembly were proposed for adoption at a meeting of the whole Convention and accepted on the second day of the session. At the South African Convention also, there does not appear to have been any special committee for rules of procedure.

Whatever may be the composition of this or any other committee that may be appointed by the Constituent Assembly, there is no reason to think that minorities will not be given fair representation.

" *Question* 3.—

The Advisory Commitee will have multifarious functions to discharge and will very probably have to split up into sub-committees, one on the rights of citizens, one on the protection of minorities, one on the administration of excluded and partially excluded areas and one on tribal areas. The committee will, therefore, have to be a comparatively large one and may consist of about 40 members (including co-opted

D

members), who need not all be members of the Constituent Assembly. They will, doubtless, include (*a*) a certain number of Hindus from the provinces in British India where the Muslims are in a majority; (*b*) a certain number of Muslims from provinces in British India where the Hindus are in a majority; (*c*) a certain number of Sikhs from the Panjab and the N.W.F.P.; (*d*) a certain number of members of the scheduled castes; (*e*) a certain number of Indian Christians; (*f*) at least one Anglo-Indian; and (*g*) at least one Parsi. The committee will probably have to be given power to co-opt additional members, particularly for the tribal areas. It need hardly be repeated that the precise composition and mode of election of the committee will be matters for the Constituent Assembly to determine.

" *Question 4.*—

The mode of election of the chairman will have to be decided by the Constituent Assembly itself, with the provisional chairman presiding. If the Constituent Assembly so decides, there can be a rotational chairman. In the Constitutional Conventions of the U.S.A., Canada, Australia and South Africa, there was no rotational chairman: the same person was chairman throughout the Convention. At international conferences, there has been a practice of making the office rotate, *e.g.*, at the San Francisco Conference and, more recently, at the Peace Conference in Paris. Which plan is to be adopted for the chairmanship of the Constituent Assembly will be for the Assembly itself to decide.

" *Question 5.*—

The sections will elect their own chairmen and, broadly speaking, it will be open to them to frame their own general order of business. But it is possible that the Union Constituent Assembly may, by agreement between the major communities, prescribe certain rules of procedure not only for itself but also for the sections. For example, the Muslims

being in a minority in the Union Constituent Assembly and
the non-Muslims being in a minority in sections B and C,
it is conceivable that by agreement in the Union Constituent
Assembly a particular mode of voting or a particular mode
of electing the chairman may be prescribed, both for the
Union and for the sections. If this happens, the rules so
prescribed will be binding on the sections as well.

" *Question 6.*—

The confusion regarding the grouping clause has been
removed by paragraph 3 of the Viceroy's letter to Maulana
Azad dated June 15, 1946, and that position has now been
accepted by the Congress and the acceptance has been emphasised by Sri Jawaharlal Nehru in his broadcast of September 7, 1946. Any further explanation might start a fresh
dispute as to the meaning of the explanation.

" *Question 7.*—

Broadly speaking, the answer is in the negative, provided
the group and provincial constitutions confine themselves to
their legitimate spheres.

" *Question 8.*—

The dispute mentioned in this question relates to the
interpretation of that part of paragraph 15 of the Cabinet
Mission's statement of May 16, 1946, which defines the Union
subjects. It will be one of the duties of the Constituent
Assembly, when framing the rules of procedure, to provide
machinery for the decision of disputes regarding the interpretation of any part of this document. Several alternatives
are possible; these have been mentioned in Part VII of the
paper on *Points of Procedure.*

" *Question 9.*—

The opinion of the Federal Court has not, in express terms,
been made binding on the chairman of the Constituent
Assembly. In practice, however, the chairman will find it

impossible to depart from the court's advice, just as, in practice, the Governor-General does not depart from the court's advisory opinions given under section 213 of the Government of India Act, 1935.

" *Question* 10.—

The same machinery that has been suggested in the answer to question 8 above may be utilised for deciding disputes of the kind mentioned in the present question also. If the alleged conflict (with paragraph 15 of the Cabinet Mission's statement) is discovered after the resolution has been passed or the decision has been taken, the matter will have to be brought back before the Constituent Assembly for reconsideration. The rules of procedure will have to provide for such a contingency. From this point of view, the suggestion made in Part I of the paper on *Points of Procedure*, namely, that the constitution should be framed in two or more stages with a sufficient interval for criticism of the first draft, acquires additional importance."

*   *   *   *   *

The formation of an interim government for the transitional period, which was of vital importance, could no longer be delayed. The Congress Working Committee, with the approval of the All-India Congress Committee, decided to accept the Viceroy's invitation to assist him in the formation of such a government. What the Governor-General's position would be in a set-up of that kind was a matter of considerable interest to the Congress party. On a reference being made to Sri B. N. Rau, on 24th September 1946, he wrote, drawing on the experience of Canada:

"India is now in much the same position as Canada was in 1849 when Lord Elgin was Governor-General. Federation had not yet come in and Canada was still a Union under the Act of 1840. There were two provinces in the Union, differing in race and religion and bitterly hostile to each other. There was a Governor-General (sometimes referred to as the Governor) for the Union, with an Executive Council appointed by His Majesty. Demands had been made for responsible government and, in reply to one of them, Metcalfe, who was Governor-General between 1843 and 1845, had said: ' If you mean that the Governor is to have no exercise of his own judgment in the administration of the government and is to be a mere tool in the hands of the Council, I totally disagree with you. That is a condition to which I can never submit and which His Majesty's Government, in my opinion, can never sanction '.

" Metcalfe's immediate successor was Elgin who found it possible to practise Cabinet government, although the Act of 1840 remained unaltered. There is an interesting account of Elgin's administration in Kennedy's *Constitution of Canada*, 1922 (*pp.* 255-56):

Elgin remained long enough in Canada to show that Cabinet government had few of the terrors which its opponents feared. He gave full support to his executive independent of, and often against, his personal feeling and convictions. He taught the Canadians the true meaning of the constitutional convention. La Fontaine and Baldwin, ' the rebel and disloyal leaders ', found in the Governor an undisguised willingness to support them to the full constitutional limit.

When their party passed from power, he turned to his bitterest personal opponent, Sir Allan MacNab, and accepted a Ministry formed by him with equally full constitutional recognition.

The establishment of responsible government decided a principle, and in doing so certain corollaries followed. The office of Governor-General took on a new aspect. The Governor was lifted ' above the strife of parties ' and ceased to be a machine for registering ' rescripts from Downing Street '. His influence became ' wholly moral—an influence of persuasion, sympathy and moderation which (softened) the temper, while it (elevated) the aims of local politics '. Elgin found his position transfigured and transformed. Instead of being an object of suspicion to reformers and the peculiar private preserve of ' loyalists ' with all the undignified consequences of such a place, he acquired a remarkable influence. His opinion was respected, his advice sought. . . The most remarkable answer to Metcalfe's passionate cry of " What is to become of the Governor ? " is Elgin's: " In Jamaica there was no responsible government, but I had not half the power I have [in Canada] with my constitutional and changing Cabinet."

[It may be mentioned that both Metcalfe and Elgin had been Governors of Jamaica before coming to Canada.]

Elgin had a good deal of trouble during his tenure of office (1847-54). " In these seven years—years of political turmoil— he did more than any Governor-General before or after him to create a political civilisation for Canada . . . Elgin's fame will survive as long as the history of Great Britain's overseas Dominions is read." [Porritt's *Evolution of the Dominion of Canada,* 1918, *p.* 146.]

" These extracts show that the Cabinet form of government has the effect of exalting the Governor-General's moral position and influence, although reducing his legal powers."

After further negotiations, the interim government was finally formed on 25th October 1946. Unfortunately, in the interval Mr. Jinnah and the Muslim League had slipped back into a mood of deep suspicion regarding the functioning of the Constituent Assembly. On 5th November 1946, the Viceroy suggested to Mr. Jinnah that another discussion with Sri B. N. Rau on the interpretation of the Cabinet Mission's statement of 16th May might prove fruitful. Whether such a discussion took place or not, it is not possible to say. But lack of agreement as regards interpretation continued to worry Mr. Jinnah who quoted, in one of his letters to the Viceroy, a passage from a statement made by Gandhiji on October 23, 1946:

" The Constituent Assembly is based on the State Paper. That paper has put in cold storage the idea of Pakistan. It has recommended the device of ' grouping ' which the Congress interprets in one way, the League in another and the Cabinet Mission in a third way. No law-giver can give an authoritative interpretation of his own law. If, then, there is a dispute as to its interpretation, a duly constituted court of law must decide it."

Arrangements were, meanwhile, being finalised for the summoning of the Constituent Assembly early in December. In a final attempt to resolve, if possible, the deadlock before its inaugural session, the British Government invited to London the leaders of the Congress party, of the Muslim League and of the Sikhs in the first week of December for a personal discussion of the differences in the interpretation of the Cabinet Mission's plan.

Sri Nehru, in a letter to the Viceroy on 26th November, pointed out that it seemed to suggest " a re-opening and a reconsideration of the various decisions arrived at since the visit of the British Cabinet Mission to India ". He complained that the Muslim League had accepted places in the government " on the very clear understanding that they also accepted the long-term proposals contained in the Cabinet Mission's statement of May 16. Indeed, they could not join the government otherwise. But now the League has announced very definitely that they will not participate in the Constituent Assembly. We attach, as you are aware, great importance to the holding of the meeting of the Constituent Assembly on the date fixed, namely, December 9. Even this date, it must be remembered, is five months after the election of the members. Any further postponement in the present context would, in all probability, result in the abandonment of the plan and create a feeling of uncertainty all round which is not only undesirable, but actually, at the present juncture, would encourage various forms of violent propaganda ".

Mr. (now Earl) Attlee, the British Prime Minister, earnestly pleaded that a visit to London, was intended, in fact, to ensure a successful meeting of the Constituent Assembly; and he gave an unqualified assurance that there was no intention of abandoning either the decisions of the Constituent Assembly, which was shortly to meet, or the plan put forward by the Cabinet Mission. After further parleys, both Sri Nehru and Mr. Jinnah agreed to pay a brief visit to London (accompanied by Mr. Liaquat Ali Khan and Sardar Baldev Singh).

The visit proved a complete failure. On its termination, the British Government issued an official statement on 6th December, giving its interpretation of the Cabinet Mission's plan in regard to the grouping of provinces and the functioning of sections. Dealing with the general question of interpretation, the statement declared:

> "It is, however, clear that other questions of interpretation of the statement of May 16th may arise and the British Government hope that if the Council of the Muslim League are able to agree to participate in the Constituent Assembly, they will also agree, as have the Congress, that the Federal Court should be asked to decide matters of interpretation that may be referred to them by either side and will accept such decisions, so that the procedure, both in the Union Constituent Assembly and the sections, may accord with the Cabinet Mission's plan. On the matter immediately in dispute the British Government urge the Congress to accept the view of the Cabinet Mission in order that the way may be open for the Muslim League to reconsider their attitude. If, in spite of this reaffirming of the intention of the Cabinet Mission, the Constituent Assembly desires that this fundamental point should be made clear at a very early date, it will then be reasonable that meetings of sections of the Constituent Assembly should be postponed until the decision of the Federal Court is known.

> "There has never been any prospect of success for the Constituent Assembly, except upon the basis of an agreed procedure. Should a constitution come to be framed by a Constituent Assembly in which a large section of the Indian population had not been represented, the British Government could not, of course, contemplate—as the Congress have stated they would not contemplate—forcing such a constitution upon any unwilling parts of the country."

The Congress reaction to this statement was immediate and sharply critical. It drew attention to the fact that " the statement of May 16, 1946, laid down in paragraph 15, as the basic principles of the constitution, that "there should be a Union of India embracing both British India and the States", that "all subjects other than Union subjects and all residuary powers should vest in the provinces", and that the "provinces should be free to form groups". The provinces were thus intended to be autonomous, subject to the Union controlling certain specified subjects. Paragraph 19 laid down, *inter alia*, the procedure for sections to meet, for decisions to be taken as to whether groups should be formed or not, and for any province to elect to come out of the group in which it might have been placed.

"The Congress made it clear later that its objection was not to provinces entering sections, but to compulsory grouping and the possibility of a dominating province framing a constitution for another province entirely against the wishes of the latter. This might result in the framing of rules and the regulation of franchise, electorates, constituencies for elections and the composition of the legislature which might seriously prejudice or even nullify the provision for a province subsequently to opt out of a group.

"The Congress had expressed its willingness to refer, if necessity arose, the point of interpretation to the Federal Court, whose decision should be accepted by the parties concerned. In the course of his letter dated June 28, 1946, addressed to Mr. Jinnah, the Viceroy had stated that ' the Congress had accepted the statement of May 16 '. In the course of a broadcast on August 24, 1946, the Viceroy, in appealing to the Muslim League to co-operate, had pointed out that the Congress was ready to agree that any dispute of interpretation might be referred to the Federal Court.

"The Muslim League reversed its former decision and rejected the British Cabinet Mission's scheme by a formal resolution and even decided to resort to direct action. Its spokesmen have since repeatedly challenged the very basis of that scheme—that is, the constitution of a Union of India—and have reverted to their demand for a partition of India. Even after the British Government's statement of December 6, 1946, the leaders of the Muslim League have reiterated this demand for partition and the establishment of two separate independent governments in India."

After expressing "deep regret" that the British Government should have gone back on its own assurances, the resolution reiterated the Congress position in the following terms:

"The Congress seeks to frame, through the Constituent Assembly, a constitution of a free and independent India with the willing co-operation of all elements of the Indian people. The Working Committee regrets that Muslim League members of the Constituent Assembly have refrained from attending its opening session.

"The Committee, however, appreciates and expresses its gratification at the presence in the Constituent Assembly of representatives of all other interests and sections of the people of India, and notes with pleasure the spirit of co-operation in a common task and a high endeavour which has been in evidence during the sessions of the Assembly.

"The Committee will continue its efforts to make the Constituent Assembly fully representative of all the people of India and trusts that members of the Muslim League will give their co-operation in this great task. In order to achieve this, the Committee has advised Congress representatives in the Assembly to postpone consideration of important issues to a subsequent meeting.

"In their statement of December 6, 1946, the British Government, in giving their interpretation of a doubtful point of procedure, have referred to it as a 'fundamental point' and suggested that the Constituent Assembly may refer it to the Federal Court at a very early date. Subsequent statements made on behalf of the British Government have made it clear that they are not prepared to accept the decision of the court should it go against their own interpretation. On behalf of the Muslim League also it has been stated that they will not be bound by the decision of the Federal Court and a demand for the partition of India, which is a negation of the Cabinet Mission's scheme, continues to be put forward.

"While the Congress has always been willing to agree to a reference to the Federal Court, any reference now, when none of the other parties are prepared to join in it or to accept it, and one of them does not even accept the basis of the scheme, becomes totally uncalled for and unbecoming and unsuited to the dignity of either the Congress or the Federal Court. By their repeated statements, British statesmen have ruled this out.

"The Working Committee is still of the opinion that the interpretation put by the British Government in regard to the method of voting in the sections is not in conformity with provincial autonomy, which is one of the fundamental bases of the scheme proposed in the statement of May 16. The Committee is anxious to avoid anything that may come in the way of the successful working of the Constituent Assembly, and is prepared to do everything in its power to seek and obtain the largest measure of co-operation, provided that no fundamental principle is violated."

Undeterred by these conflicts as regards interpretation, which were further accentuated by the absence of Muslim League members from the opening meeting of the Constituent Assembly on 9th December 1946, the Assembly went ahead with its programme of business. On 15th December, Sri Jawaharlal Nehru moved an important resolution defining the Assembly's aims and objects in the following terms:

" (1) This Constituent Assembly declares its firm and solemn resolve to proclaim India as an independent sovereign republic and to draw up for her future governance a constitution;

" (2) wherein the territories that now comprise British India, the territories that now form the Indian States, and such other parts of India as are outside British India and the States, as well as such other territories as are willing to be constituted into the independent sovereign India, shall be a Union of them all; and

" (3) wherein the said territories, whether with their present boundaries or with such others as may be determined by the Constituent Assembly and thereafter according to the law of the constitution, shall possess and retain the status of autonomous units, together with residuary powers, and exercise all powers and functions of government and administration, save and except such powers and functions as are vested in or assigned to the Union, or as are inherent or implied in the Union or resulting therefrom; and

" (4) wherein all power and authority of the independent sovereign India, its constituent parts and organs of government, are derived from the people; and

" (5) wherein shall be guaranteed and secured to all the people of India justice, social, economic and political; equality of status, of opportunity and before the law; freedom of thought, expression, belief, faith, worship, vocation, association and action, subject to law and public morality; and

" (6) wherein adequate safeguards shall be provided for minorities, backward and tribal areas and depressed and other backward classes; and

" (7) whereby shall be maintained the integrity of the territory of the republic and its sovereign rights on land, sea and air, according to justice and the law of civilised nations, and

" (8) this ancient land attains its rightful and honoured place in the world and makes its full and willing contribution to the promotion of world peace and the welfare of mankind."

In the debate on the 'Objectives' resolution there were detailed and sometimes critical references to the problem of the future relations between India and the U. K. Before the Prime Minister replied to the debate, Sri B. N. Rau sent him the following note for his consideration:

May I take the liberty of suggesting that in your reply on the "Objectives Resolution" you might slightly amplify what you said in your opening speech about the future relations between India and England? Something on the following lines occurs to me, but you would know best what to say.

" *The question has sometimes been asked, what will be the relations between the new Indian Republic and the British*

Commonwealth? The answer is not difficult: in the world of to-day, the relations between States are not governed by labels. The U.S.A. has been a Republic for over 150 years; nevertheless, in two successive World Wars it fought on the same side as England to ward off a common peril. Ireland is treated by England as a Dominion and a member of the British Commonwealth; yet, in the last World War, Ireland remained neutral. And so these names have ceased to have much significance as regards mutual relations. The world has entered upon a new era and we have to think in new terms. We are now, all of us, part of a new World Organisation—the United Nations, units of a World Federation in the making. A vast ' multicellular ' Republic is being formed, of which the United Kingdom, the Dominions, India and all the other States of the world are, or will in due course be, members. India's relations with the other members will necessarily be of the friendliest and closest collaboration and co-operation in the pursuit of our common ideals."

An examination was undertaken at this stage of the apprehensions expressed by the Muslim League and also by the Sikhs regarding their respective positions. Two questions were referred by the President, Dr. Rajendra Prasad, to Sri B. N. Rau early in January 1947:

(1) Can the Union Assembly direct that the sections shall not meet until the Advisory Committee has submitted its report?

(2) What can be done to meet the Sikh demand for safeguards?

He sent a reply to the President in the following terms:

" As to (1), there is nothing to prevent such a direction, on the footing that until the Advisory Committee has reported, the sections cannot complete their business of settling the provincial constitutions. But we must be prepared for the possibility that the sections—or some of them—may hold their *preliminary* meeting in spite of the direction—on the footing that they will not be settling the provincial constitutions at such a preliminary meeting. They may contend that while they are prepared to wait for the Advisory Committee's report before finally settling the provincial constitutions, they cannot be prevented from holding at least their preliminary meeting immediately after the Union Assembly has finished its preliminary meeting. In support of this contention, they may point to the language of paragraph 19 (iv) which states that after the Union Assembly has held its preliminary meeting and set up the Advisory Committee, the provincial representatives will divide up into sections. Of course, if the Union Assembly has not completed the business prescribed for its preliminary meeting, the sections cannot meet; but, in that event, no direction from the Union Assembly is required.

" As to (2), the best course would be for us to get into touch with the Sikh members and ascertain what exactly they have in mind. It is just possible that we may be able to agree upon some formula, which, while giving them the substance of what they want, will not cause too much inconvenience."

In the open session of the Constituent Assembly, Dr. M. R. Jayakar sought by an amendment a postponement of the final decision on Sri Nehru's resolution with a view to securing the co-operation of the Muslim League and the Indian States in the deliberations of the Constituent Assembly. After a lengthy debate lasting several days, the amendment was rejected and the Assembly adopted the resolution, as the foundation of its labours, in January 1947.

The Council of the Muslim League interpreted this step as another indication that the Constituent Assembly had decided that the co-operation of the League's representatives was not essential. The Council passed a lengthy resolution, describing the Assembly's decision as a very vital one, because it had laid down the essentials of the new constitution and several features of fundamental importance to the constitution. It had spoken of a republic or " Union ", of functions and powers vested in the " Union or those inherent or implied in the Union; of present boundaries of States and present authorities, of residuary powers, of powers being derived from the people, of minority rights and fundamental rights ". All these, according to the League, were undoubtedly fundamentals of the constitution; but they were regarded by the League as beyond the limit of the powers and the terms of the Cabinet Mission's scheme of May 16. The resolution was, therefore, described as " illegal, *ultra vires* and not competent to the Constituent Assembly to adopt ".

Further, the League complained, the Assembly had appointed several committees and proceeded to elect an Advisory Committee (referred to in paragraph 20 of the statement of the Cabinet Mission and the Viceroy) on the rights of citizens, minorities, tribal and excluded areas; and it had appointed a Steering Committee and various other committees which had taken some decisions *in camera*. It had also passed the " rules of procedure " and assumed control of sections by means of these rules for which (the League asserted) there was no warrant or justification.

The League Council described the Constituent Assembly as " a packed committee of individuals chosen by the Congress ", which " had destroyed all fundamentals of the Cabinet Mission's statement ". It denounced further meetings of the Constituent Assembly as " void, invalid and illegal ".

The uncompromising tone and the contents of this lengthy resolution made it abundantly clear that there was no meeting ground whatsoever between the Congress and the Muslim League and further efforts at conciliation would be a waste of time and effort. It was, therefore, not surprising that the British Prime Minister made a policy statement in the House of Commons on 20th February 1947. Noting that the differences between the major parties had continued unresolved, and the Constituent Assembly could not function as it had been intended to do in the original plan, the Prime Minister declared:

"His Majesty's Government desire to hand over their responsibility to authorities established by a constitution approved by all parties in India in accordance with the Cabinet Mission's plan. But, unfortunately, there is at present no clear prospect that such a constitution and such authorities will emerge. The present state of uncertainty is fraught with danger and cannot be indefinitely prolonged. His Majesty's Government wish to make it clear that it is their definite intention to take necessary steps to effect the transference of power to responsible Indian hands by a date not later than June, 1948.

" His Majesty's Government are anxious to hand over their responsibilities to a government which, resting on the sure foundation of the support of the people, is capable of maintaining peace and administering India with justice and efficiency. It is, therefore, essential that all parties should sink their differences in order that they may be ready to shoulder the great responsibilities which will come upon them next year.

" His Majesty's Government, therefore, agree to recommend to Parliament a constitution worked out in accordance with the proposals made therein by a fully representative Constituent Assembly. But if it should appear that such a constitution will not have been worked out by a fully representative Assembly before the time mentioned in paragraph 7, His Majesty's Government will have to consider to whom the powers of the Central Government in British India should be handed over on the due date, whether as a whole or some form of Central government of British India, or in some areas to the existing provincial governments, or in such other way as may seem most reasonable and in the best interests of the Indian people."

It was a turning point in Indo-British relations. The Prime Minister, starting initially from the conviction that the desire for India's unity was " almost universal outside the ranks of the Muslim League " * felt compelled to take up the final position nine months later that partition was the inevitable solution for a deadlock which had baffled the best brains in Britain and India. His statement left the British Government uncommitted to the ultimate decisions of the Constituent Assembly, but the assurance of transfer of power to Indian hands by June 1948 was couched in firm and unqualified terms.

---

* See the Cabinet Mission's statement of 16th May 1946.

The effect of this declaration was immediate and profound. Sri Nehru welcomed it as " a wise and courageous decision " and proceeded to observe:

" The clear and definite declaration that the final transference of power will take place by a date not later than June 1948 not only removes all misconception and suspicion, but also brings reality and a certain dynamic quality to the present situation in India. That decision will undoubtedly have far-reaching consequences and puts a burden and responsibility on all concerned.

" The work of the Constituent Assembly must now be carried on with greater speed, so that the new and independent India may take shape and be clothed with a constitution worthy of her, bringing relief and opportunity to all her children. In this great work we invite afresh all those who have kept aloof and we ask all to be partners in this joint and historic undertaking casting aside fear and suspicion, which will become a great people on the eve of freedom.

" The Constituent Assembly, however constituted, can only proceed with its work on a voluntary basis. There can be no compulsion, except the compulsion of events, which none can ignore. The moment British rule goes, the responsibility for the governance of India must inevitably rest on her people and their representatives alone. They will have to shoulder that responsibility. Why then should we not accept this responsibility now and work together to find integrated solutions of our problems? No external authority is going to help or hinder us in future.

" The British Government on behalf of their people have expressed their goodwill and good wishes to the people of India. We have had a long past of conflict and illwill. But we earnestly hope that this past is over. We look forward to a peaceful and co-operative transition and to the establishment of close and friendly relations with the British people for the mutual advantage of both countries and for the advancement of the cause of peace and freedom all over the world."

By this time the Constituent Assembly had got down to the serious business of settling the general principles of a constitution. The initiative was thus beginning to pass from

E

the British Government to India's leaders. It was for them to reach a settlement or a compromise on the vital issue of partition before the final transfer of power in June 1948 and to frame a constitution in accordance with its terms.

The Working Committee of the Congress, meeting some days later (8th March 1947), made a last attempt to bring back the Muslim League's representatives into the Constituent Assembly. It declared:

"The work of the Constituent Assembly is essentially voluntary. The Working Committee has frequently stated that there can or should be no compulsion in the making of a constitution for India. It is the fear of compulsion or coercion that has given rise to distrust and suspicion and conflict. If this fear goes, as it must, it will be easy to determine India's future so as to safeguard the rights of all communities and give equal opportunities to all. It has been made clear that the constitution framed by the Constituent Assembly will apply only to those areas which accept it. It must also be understood that any province or part of a province which accepts the constitution and desires to join the Union cannot be prevented from doing so. Thus, there must be no compulsion either way, and the people will themselves decide their future. This peaceful and co-operative method is the only way to make democratic decisions with the maximum of consent.

" In this hour when final decisions have to be taken, and the future of India has to be shaped by Indian minds and hands, the Working Committee earnestly calls upon all parties and groups, and all Indians generally, to discard violent and coercive methods and co-operate peacefully and democratically in the making of a constitution. The time for decision has come and no one can stop it or stand by and remain unaffected. The end of an era is at hand and a new age will soon begin. Let this dawn of the new age be ushered in bravely, leaving hates and discords in the dead past."

Inviting the Muslim League to meet representatives of the Congress, the resolution said:

" In view of new developments which are leading to a swift transfer of power in India, it has become incumbent on the people of India to prepare themselves jointly and co-operatively for this change, so that this may be effected peacefully and to the advantage of all. The Working Committee, therefore, invites the All India Muslim League to nominate representatives to meet representatives of the Congress in order to consider the situation that has arisen and to devise means to meet it.

"The Working Committee will keep in close touch with the representatives of the Sikhs and other groups concerned with a view to co-operating with them in the steps that may have to be taken and in safeguarding their interest."

Some futile correspondence followed, for a fresh move towards an agreement, between the General Secretaries of the Congress and of the Muslim League; but the League was in no mood to meet the Congress to seek a solution, with the Constituent Assembly already in progress on the basis of its 'Aims and Objects' resolution. The deadlock was complete.

A further statement by the British Government accordingly followed on June 3, 1947. Since the previous statement on 20th February had not brought about any appreciable change in the relations between the major parties, the position was reviewed with an air of finality in the following terms:

"The majority of the representatives of the provinces of Madras, Bombay, the United Provinces, Bihar, Central Provinces and Berar, Assam, Orissa and the North-West Frontier Province, and the representatives of Delhi, Ajmer-Merwara and Coorg have already made progress in the task of evolving a new constitution. On the other hand, the Muslim League party, including in it a majority of the representatives of Bengal, the Panjab and Sind, as also the representative of British Baluchistan, has decided not to participate in the Constituent Assembly.

"It has always been the desire of His Majesty's Government that power should be transferred in accordance with the wishes of the Indian people themselves. This task would have been greatly facilitated if there had been agreement among the Indian political parties. In the absence of such agreement, the task of devising a method by which the wishes of the Indian people can be ascertained has devolved upon His Majesty's

Government. After full consultation with political leaders in India, His Majesty's Government have decided to adopt for this purpose the plan set out below. His Majesty's Government wish to make it clear that they have no intention of attempting to frame any ultimate constitution for India: this is a matter for the Indians themselves. Nor is there anything in this plan to preclude negotiations between communities for a united India."

The issue to be decided was whether the constitution for provinces with Muslim majorities was to be framed in the existing Constituent Assembly, or in a new and separate Constituent Assembly consisting of the representatives of those areas which had decided not to participate in the existing Constituent Assembly.

A detailed procedure was presented for a new Constituent Assembly for Bengal, the Panjab, Sind, the North-Western Frontier Province, (British) Baluchistan and Sylhet district in Assam. The plan urged the existing Constituent Assembly and the new one (if formed) to frame their respective constitutions.

Finally, in advancing the date of the final transfer of power from June 1948 (which was originally stipulated), the British statement said:

"The major political parties have repeatedly emphasised their desire that there should be the earliest possible transfer of power in India. With this desire His Majesty's Government are in full sympathy and they are willing to anticipate the date of June 1948, for the handing over of power, by the setting up of an independent Indian Government or governments at an even earlier date. Accordingly, as the most expeditious and indeed the only practicable way of meeting this desire, His Majesty's Government propose to introduce legislation during the current session for the transfer of power this year on a Dominion status basis to one or two successor authorities, according to the decisions taken as a result of this announcement. This will be without prejudice to the right of the Indian Constituent Assemblies to decide in due course whether or not the part of

India in respect of which they have authority will remain within the British Commonwealth."

The new Viceroy, Lord Mountbatten, explained the latest British plan in a broadcast:

"When the Muslim League demanded the partition of India, the Congress used the same arguments for demanding, in that event, the partition of certain provinces. To my mind this argument is unassailable. In fact, neither side proved willing to leave a substantial area in which their community have a majority under the government of the other. I am, of course, just as much opposed to the partition of provinces as I am to the partition of India herself, and for the same basic reasons.

"Once it was decided in what way to transfer power, the transfer should take place at the earliest possible moment ; but the dilemma was that if we waited until a constitutional set-up for all India was agreed, we should have to wait a long time, particularly if partition were decided on. Whereas if we handed over power before the Constituent Assemblies had finished their work, we should leave the country without a constitution. The solution to this dilemma, which I put forward, is that His Majesty's Government should transfer power now to one or two governments of British India, each having Dominion status as soon as the necessary arrangements can be made. This, I hope, will be within the next few months.

"Thus, the way is now open to an arrangement by which power can be transferred many months earlier than the most optimistic of us thought possible and at the same time leave it to the people of British India to decide for themselves on their future, which is the declared policy of His Majesty's Government."

Sri Nehru, following Lord Mountbatten, accepted the plan without any qualification. He said:

"I am speaking to you on another historic occasion when a vital change affecting the future of India is proposed. You have just heard an announcement on behalf of the British Government. This announcement lays down a procedure for self-determination in certain areas of India. It envisages on the one hand the possibility of these areas seceding from India; on the other, it promises a big advance towards complete independence. Such a big change must have the full concurrence of the people before effect can be given to it, for it must always be remembered that the future of India can only be decided by the people of India and not by any outside authority, however friendly. These proposals will be placed soon before representative assemblies of the people for consideration."

Partition, which the Congress leaders sought to avoid by every conceivable expedient or compromise, had, thus, become inevitable. In Sri Nehru's statement there was a note of regret:

" It is with no joy in my heart that I commend these proposals to you, though I have no doubt in my mind that this is the right course. For generations we have dreamt and struggled for a free and independent united India. The proposal to allow certain parts to secede, if they so will, is painful for any of us to contemplate. Nevertheless, I am convinced that our present decision is the right one even from the larger viewpoint. The united India that we have laboured for was not one of compulsion and coercion but a free and willing association of a free people. It may be that in this way we shall reach that united India sooner than otherwise and that she will have a stronger and more secure foundation."

This was the final stage, so far as Britain was concerned, in her long association with India. For India—divided but free—it meant that the Constituent Assembly could proceed, without further negotiations or interference from outside, with the task of framing her constitution.

INDIA'S CONSTITUTION IN THE MAKING

1

THE FIRST STEP

[In this note, Sri B. N. Rau discussed the steps to be taken pursuant to the British Prime Minister's statement of February 20, 1947, regarding the transfer of power to Indian hands by June 1948.]

THE BRITISH PRIME MINISTER's statement of February 20, 1947 in the House of Commons made it clear that power in India was to be transferred to responsible Indian hands not later than June 1948.*

Transference of power implies the existence of regular organs of government to exercise the transferred power. In other words, there must be a government of some kind, if

---

* [The statement, the full text of which is published as an Appendix to this volume, contains the following passage:

" It is with great regret that His Majesty's Government find that there are still differences among Indian parties which are preventing the Constituent Assembly from functioning as it was intended that it should. It is of the essence of the plan that the Assembly should be fully representative.

" His Majesty's Government desire to hand over their responsibility to authorities established by a constitution approved by all parties in India in accordance with the Cabinet Mission's plan. But unfortunately there is at present no clear prospect that such a constitution and such authorities will emerge. The present state of uncertainty is fraught with danger and cannot be indefinitely prolonged. His Majesty's Government wish to make it clear that it is their definite intention to take necessary steps to effect the transference of power to responsible Indian hands by a date not later than June 1948.

*   *   *   *   *   *

" After months of hard work by the Cabinet Mission, a great measure of agreement was obtained as to the method by which a constitution should be worked out. This was embodied in their statements of May last. His Majesty's Government there agreed to recommend to Parliament a constitution worked out in accordance with the proposals made therein by a fully representative Constituent Assembly. But if it should appear that such a constitution will not have been worked out by a fully representative Assembly before the time mentioned in paragraph 7 (June 1948), His Majesty's Government will have to consider to whom the powers of the Central Government in British India should

only a provisional government, to receive the power and there must be a constitution, if only a provisional constitution, to regulate the exercise of the power. It follows that if the final constitutional structure is not ready before the due date, we must have a provisional government functioning under a provisional constitution. It is pertinent to observe that we are still governed by the " transitional provisions " in Part XIII of the Government of India Act, 1935—twelve years after the passing of the Act—which is a warning that a provisional constitution may last longer than we now think.

What are the prospects of the final constitution being ready before June 30, 1948? There are two possibilities: either the Muslim League comes into the Constituent Assembly or it does not. If it comes in—which means that it accepts the Cabinet Mission's plan—the procedure prescribed in the plan can be followed and, with goodwill on all sides, enough of the final constitutional structure may be got ready to permit of the transfer of power by the date fixed. Something may still have to be left over, e.g., the precise relationship with Indian States or some of them; but this need not prevent the transfer of power as contemplated.

There is, however, the other possibility, which at the moment seems far the more likely of the two; namely, that the Muslim League does not come into the Constituent Assembly. If so, under the statement of December 6, 1946, any constitution that may be framed by that Assembly will not be binding upon the " unwilling parts of the country ". How these unwilling parts will be determined and what constitution they will have is at present unknown. One thing, however, seems to be reasonably certain, namely, that there will be some kind of division of India. If this happens, the task of framing a new constitution, even for the willing parts,

be handed over, on the due date, whether as a whole to some form of Central Government for British India, or in some areas to the existing provincial governments, or in such other way as may seem most reasonable and in the best interests of the Indian people."]

with all its immense mass of details will become formidable. The defence forces will have to be divided, the all-India Civil Services will have to be redistributed, property and liabilities of all kinds will have to be apportioned. We cannot yet tell how many new sovereignties there will be: at least two, possibly more. Agreements now subsisting between the Crown and the Indian States will have to be revised and renewed between the States and some or all of the new sovereignties. There will also have to be agreements between the new parts of India *inter se* relating to defence, external affairs, communications, customs and other matters of common concern. Boundaries between the new parts will have to be determined, perhaps by a Boundary Commission. If there is to be adult franchise under the new constitution, machinery for the new legislatures will have to be got ready and a multitude of other details will have to be settled. It is doubtful, to say the least, whether all this can be completed before June, 1948.

The separation of Burma was a simpler affair, but took several years of preliminary work. A great simplifying factor in the Burma problem was that His Majesty could make readjustments from time to time by Order-in-Council even after separation. No such expedient will be available to readjust relations between the different sovereignties in India, once the Crown ceases to exercise any functions.

If, for these reasons, the final constitutional structure is not ready before the due date, what then? We shall obviously have to have a provisional constitution ready. Certain features of such a provisional constitution are inevitable:

(1) Since, *ex hypothesi*, a constitution for a divided India is not ready, the provisional constitution will have to be for an undivided India during the transitional period, until all the details have been completed for the ultimate division, including the framing of the constitutions for the different parts, after which the final constitution will be brought into force.

(2) Since the "unwilling parts" have not yet declared whether they would like to have independence inside or outside the Commonwealth, the provisional constitution, which, as already pointed out, has to apply to these parts, as well as others, will necessarily have to be for an independent India within the British Commonwealth: in other words, for an India with full Dominion status.

(3) The provisional constitution must have the backing of the main elements in the country, if there is to be a peaceful transfer of power even to a provisional government. Of course, once it is made clear that the ultimate constitutional structure will proceed on the basis of a divided India and will be such as to involve no coercion of unwilling areas, agreement on the provisional structure may be easier to obtain.

These seem to be the inescapable conditions of the problem.

Assuming then that the Muslim League does not change its decision not to participate in the Constituent Assembly, we have to take steps not only for framing a final constitution, but also for framing a provisional constitution satisfying the above conditions, in the event of the final constitution not being ready.

These conditions do not make the problem more difficult. On the contrary, they might make it easier in many respects. It is obviously easier to frame a constitution for an undivided India than for a divided India. Again, if the interim constitution provides for an India within the Commonwealth, the sovereignty of the Crown will remain for the time being, and the treaties (including engagements, sanads and other instruments) now subsisting between the Crown and the Indian States will not lapse (except perhaps as to paramountcy); the functions of the Crown arising out of them will continue, the only difference being that instead of being discharged as at present on the advice of a Political Adviser outside the Central Government, they may have to be discharged on the advice of a responsible minister of the Central Government. We shall thus be spared the necessity for an immediate detailed revision of existing treaties or the immediate negotiation of new ones. It is possible that the Rulers may ask for certain safeguards if these functions are to be discharged on the advice of a responsible minister. It should not be difficult to arrive at a reasonable arrangement in this matter by discussion with those concerned.

The most important of the three conditions is the third one, namely, that the provisional constitution must have the backing of the main elements in the country. From this point of view, the arrangements under the existing constitution have proved to be defective. Recent events have shown that minorities in various provinces require better protection than they can get at present; and at the Centre, Muslims have often expressed their fear of being dominated by the Hindus. If the provisional constitution is to have the support of the main elements in the country, it must be such as to reduce these fears on opposite sides to a minimum. The Cabinet Mission's plan of May 16, 1946 took note of the fears of domination at the Centre (see para 12 of the statement of May 16, 1946 *); and the obvious way to reduce similar fears in the provinces is to extend the same idea to the provincial sphere.

It will be remembered that the essence of the Cabinet Mission's plan is to maintain a single Centre for the administration of a minimum number of subjects on an all-India basis, while the remaining subjects are to be dealt with on a regional basis. If we follow the same plan in the provinces, we must provide that where a province contains distinct regions (whether racial or religious or linguistic), most of the

* *vide* Appendix A.

provincial subjects may be dealt with on a regional basis and only the remaining few on a provincial or joint basis.

It may be mentioned here that in certain matters a regional basis of administration obtains even in the United Kingdom, although there is a single Cabinet. All the ministers there do not exercise their functions uniformly in the different parts of the Kingdom. For what may be called national purposes (army, navy, air force, foreign relations, treasury, etc.), there are common ministers for all parts; but for other purposes there are special ministers for special regions. For example, the departments of health, agriculture, police, prisons and education for Scotland are administered by the Secretary of State for Scotland and the separation has gone so far that the main departments and an Under Secretary have their headquarters in Edinburgh, although the Secretary of State is in London. The separation is even more far-reaching in the case of the judiciary, Scotland being completely independent, except for a common Supreme Court of Appeal in the House of Lords. Even in the sphere of legislation, there is some measure of regionalism in the United Kingdom. Thus all Bills relating exclusively to Scotland are referred, after second reading, to a Grand Committee consisting of the whole body of Scottish members, with the addition of 15 others specially responsible for each Bill.

It is interesting to note that a rather similar plan appears to obtain in the Russian Constitution. The Central departments (called the People's Commissariats) are in two classes, the all-Union departments (called the all-Union People's Commissariats) and the regional departments (called the Union-Republican People's Commissariats); the subjects requiring to be dealt with on an all-Union basis are administered by the former and subjects requiring regional administration by the latter. [See articles 74-78 of the Constitution of the U.S.S.R.]

There is, therefore, nothing novel in this idea; it only needs to be adapted to Indian conditions. If we examine the matter, we shall find that the idea can be carried out to a surprising extent, both at the Centre and in the provinces, even under the existing constitution.

Let us first consider the provincial sphere. Under section 50 of the Government of India Act of 1935, the Governor of each province has a Council of Ministers to aid and advise him in most provincial matters. Under section 59, he is required to make rules for the more convenient transaction of the business of the provincial government and for its allocation among the ministers. The rules at present in force make a subject-wise allocation on a provincial basis: that is to say, there is a minister for education for the whole province, there is another for public works, and so on. Where a province is homogeneous in character, this distribution may well be the best; but not if the province contains two or more sharply-contrasted regions. For simplicity, suppose there are only two such regions: a predominantly Muslim region A and a predominantly non-Muslim region B. For many provincial subjects, such as education, agriculture, local self-government, the two regions may have divergent interests and needs; let us call these " regional subjects ". There may, however, be a few subjects as to which their interests or needs cannot be divided, *e.g.*, finance or irrigation from common rivers or the High Court; we may refer to these as " joint subjects ". In these circumstances, the Governor may find it possible and more convenient to make a regional allocation of the business relating to regional subjects: that is to say, he may within one and the same Cabinet have one set of ministers exclusively to advise him on the regional subjects of A; another set of ministers exclusively to advise him on the regional subjects of B; and both sets of ministers together, in other words, the entire Cabinet, to advise him on joint subjects. Which are to be joint subjects and which regional in a given province will depend upon local circumstances and how exactly joint subjects marked for the entire Cabinet are to be dealt with is a matter for local discussion. If the number of joint subjects is small, they may all be dealt with by a single sub-committee of the Cabinet consisting, let us say, of the Prime Minister and the Deputy Prime Minister, cases going to the entire Cabinet only where these two differ. If the Prime Minister is of region A, the Deputy Prime Minister should be of region B and *vice versa*. There are variants of this plan possible; the Governor can frame his rules to suit the requirements of his particular province so as to secure the maximum of regional autonomy. If there is any area in the province which is neither markedly Muslim nor markedly non-Muslim, it can be treated as " joint territory " and any business relating thereto as a " joint subject ". As already indicated, there will be a single Cabinet with a Prime Minister and a Deputy Prime Minister, subject to a convention that if the Prime Minister is a Muslim, the Deputy Prime Minister will be non-Muslim and *vice versa*. There will also be a single legislature for the whole province; but a convention should be established that when legislation relating exclusively to a regional subject of one of the regions A or B is under consideration, the members representing territorial constituencies of the other region should abstain from voting.

Let us next consider the Central Government. Here, the plan that has come nearest to acceptance by all parties is the Cabinet Mission's plan of May 16, 1946, and the question, therefore, is how far that plan can be carried out under the existing constitution. Like the Governors in the provinces, the Governor-General at the Centre has power to make rules for the more convenient transaction of business in his Council (see section 40 of the Government of India Act in the ninth schedule to the Act of 1935). He may, in framing these rules, treat the groups referred to in the Cabinet Mission's plan, or any other groups that may be more acceptable, as distinct regions. The essence of the plan, as already stated, is that certain subjects, broadly categorised as defence, foreign affairs and communications together with incidental finance

—for the present we may include all finance under this head —should be treated on an all-India basis and the rest on a regional basis. At present, the Centre deals with these other subjects also on an all-India basis: *e.g.*, there is a single member for education for the whole of India, a single member for labour for the whole of India and so on. There are doubtless advantages in this kind of centralisation; but the Cabinet Mission's plan has recommended a different course in order to secure regional autonomy to the largest possible extent, and we are now trying to see how far this plan can be carried out under the existing constitution. To carry it out, we shall have to divide the existing Central departments into two classes:

(1) All-India departments, comprising the subjects connected with defence, foreign affairs and communications and, provisionally, including all finance.

(2) Regional departments comprising the rest.

Certain members of the Cabinet will be in charge of (1) for the whole of British India; the rest will form what we may call the Ministry of the Interior, of which there will be a branch for each region. Each branch of the Ministry of the Interior will deal with the regional departments for that particular region. Thus, there will be a single minister for defence for the whole of British India as at present; but instead of there being a single minister for education and one for agriculture and one for public health—for the whole of British India in each case—there may be one minister in charge of all the three subjects for the territories of Group A, another minister in charge of all the three subjects for Group B, and another minister in charge of all the three subjects for Group C. The total number of ministers need not be increased, if this is considered undesirable; only their duties will be allocated differently. A redistribution of work on these lines can be made under the existing constitution; it would correspond roughly to the division of work in the U.K. Cabinet with respect to England and Scotland and to the division of work under the Russian Constitution between the All-Union People's Commissariats and the Union-Republican People's Commissariats. There will, of course, as in the provinces, be a single Cabinet with a single Prime Minister and a Deputy Prime Minister; when the Prime Minister is a non-Muslim, the Deputy Prime Minister will be a Muslim and *vice versa*. As in the provincial sphere, a convention should be established that when legislation in respect of a regional subject appertaining exclusively to one of the regions is under consideration, members representing territorial constituencies of the other regions should not vote.

If the Central and provincial departments are so arranged as to secure the maximum of regional autonomy, the fear of domination of one region by another would be reduced to a minimum. And since this can be done even under the existing constitution, the provisional constitution that we have envisaged need not, in this respect, contain much that is new.

Indeed, a redistribution of departments, both at the Centre and in the provinces on the lines suggested above, may be immediately advisable. As already pointed out, this can be done under the existing constitution and it will have the following advantages:

(1) It may succeed in healing the existing differences, whether at the Centre or in the provinces.

(2) It will reveal the difficulties, if any, in more far-reaching schemes of partition or separation, including the Cabinet Mission's plan.

(3) If the redistribution proves inconvenient in any particular, it can be immediately amended by amending the rules of business; if necessary it can be entirely scrapped and the *status quo ante* restored.

The redistribution will not require the immediate splitting up of the Secretariat or of the subordinate administrative machinery.

2

THE CONSTITUENT ASSEMBLY: PROCEDURE

[Sri B. N. Rau saw Dr. Rajendra Prasad on March 9, 1947, as the President was anxious to discuss what should be done in view of the British Prime Minister's statement of February 20, 1947, and the subsequent developments. He recorded the following note after the discussion.]

ASSUMING that the Muslim League does not change its decision not to participate in the Constituent Assembly, the position will be that any constitution that may be framed by the Assembly will not be binding upon the " unwilling parts " of the country. How these unwilling parts will be determined and what constitution they will have is at present unknown. One thing, however, seems to be reasonably certain in view of the statements of December 6, 1946* and February 20, 1947, the debates in the Houses of Parliament and the Congress

---

* The relevant passages from the British Government's statement of December 6, 1946 are reproduced below:

" The main difficulty that has arisen has been over the interpretation of paragraph 19 (v) and (viii) of the Cabinet Mission's statement of May 16th relating to the meetings in sections which run as follows:

" Paragraph 19 (v).—' These sections shall proceed to settle provincial constitutions for the provinces included in each section and shall also decide whether any group constitution shall be set up for those provinces and if so with what provincial subjects the group should deal. Provinces shall have power to opt out of groups in accordance with provisions of sub-clause (viii) below.'

" Paragraph 19 (viii).—' As soon as new constitutional arrangements have come into operation, it shall be open to any province to elect to come out of any group in which it has been placed. Such a decision shall be taken by the new legislature of the province after the first general election under the new constitution.'

" The Cabinet Mission have throughout maintained the view that decisions of sections should, in the absence of agreement to the contrary, be taken by simple majority vote of representatives in the sections. This view has been

Working Committee's resolution; namely, that there will be some kind of division of India. If so, the task of framing a new constitution, with all its immense mass of details, will be a formidable one, as already stated.

The separation of Burma was a simpler affair, but I remember working unofficially on some of the details as early as 1934, although the actual separation did not take effect until 1937. A great simplifying factor in the Burma problem was (as mentioned in my earlier note), that His Majesty could make re-adjustments from time to time by Order-in-Council if any unforeseen difficulties arose after separation (see sections 158-160 of the Government of India Act, 1935, and sections 134-137 of the Burma Act). No such expedient will be possible now.

If the final constitutional structure is not ready before the due date, we shall have to have a provisional constitution and a provisional government. We may, if we choose, have a chapter headed " Transitional Provisions " in the new constitution and put the provisional constitution into the chapter. In fact, we are still governed by the " Transitional Provisions " in Part XIII of the Government of India Act, 1935, which is a warning that a provisional constitution may last longer than we think.

Let us now consider the nature of this provisional constitution. *Ex hypothesi*, the ultimate constitution providing for all the parts of a divided India may not be ready on the due date; if it is ready, there is of course no difficulty. But we are

---

accepted by the Muslim League but the Congress have put forward a different view. They have asserted that the true meaning of the statement read as a whole is that provinces have a right to decide both as to grouping and as to their own constitution.

" His Majesty's Government have had legal advice which confirms that the statement of May 16th means what the Cabinet Mission have always stated was their intention. This part of the statement as so interpreted must therefore be considered an essential part of the scheme of May 16th for enabling the Indian people to formulate a new constitution which His Majesty's Government would be prepared to submit to Parliament. It should therefore be accepted by all parties in the Constituent Assembly."

proceeding on the assumption that it may not be ready in the time prescribed. What then? Obviously, if a constitution for a divided India is not ready, we shall have to have a provisional constitution for an undivided India. In other words, the provisional constitution will have to be that of a single federation embracing the whole of what is now British India. This is the first point.

Another point also seems inevitable. Since the " unwilling parts " have not yet declared whether they would like to have independence within or without the British Commonwealth, the provisional constitution, which, as already pointed out, has to apply to these parts as well as others, will necessarily have to be that of a Federation enjoying independence within the British Commonwealth—in other words, enjoying full Dominion status.

The third point that emerges from the debates in Parliament is that even for the transfer of power to a provisional government, His Majesty's Government will require a fair measure of agreement between the different parties in India. Presumably, that agreement will be easier to obtain, so far as the Muslim League is concerned, if an ultimate division of India is provided for and if it is made clear that the provisional government is only for the interim period, during which the ultimate constitution is being hammered out. Be that as it may, His Majesty's Government obviously expect some degree of agreement, judging from Sir Stafford Cripps's remark in the House of Commons:

"In our statement of December 6, we stressed the fact that if a large section of the Indian population had not been fully represented in the Constituent Assembly, we could not accept the forcing of *unwilling provinces* into a united Indian Government if they have not been represented in the making of the constitution. To that principle, which has the assent of the Congress, we understand, we adhere and if it should eventuate that a large group of provinces—but not all—

agree upon the form of constitution, then it may be necessary to hand over power separately in areas which have not been fully represented.

" We shall have to consider in what way this can best be done to meet the best interests of the Indian people. The position is, however, sufficiently uncertain at this stage to make it impossible now to forecast what will be the wisest action to take when the time comes to make a decision. The only way to remove this uncertainty is to get agreement of the Indian communities as to what it is they wish us to do. We can hardly be accused of vagueness or uncertainty when the Indian communities themselves cannot come to any common agreement."

In other words, the uncertainty as to the transfer of power in the absence of an agreed final constitution is to be removed by agreement, which can only mean that there must be at least an agreed provisional constitution.

We shall, therefore, have to face the difficulty of framing an agreed provisional constitution as for a single Federation with Dominion status. The Muslims fear Hindu domination at the Centre, while the Hindus and the Sikhs fear Muslim domination in some of the existing provinces. Whatever provisional constitution may be devised will, therefore, have to be such as to reduce these fears on opposite sides to a minimum.

And such a provisional constitution will have to be got ready before June 1948. It follows, therefore, that side by side with the framing of the ultimate constitutional structure, we shall have to take even more urgent steps towards framing a satisfactory provisional constitution.

For the purpose of facilitating the framing of the final constitution, it may be of assistance if a questionnaire bearing on the salient features of the constitution were sent round to all the members of the various legislatures. They would be requested to send in their answers before April 10, 1947, so that we might be in a position to tabulate the answers before the next session of the Constituent Assembly. I have already taken in hand the preparation of such a questionnaire and hope to issue it in the course of the next few days. As most of the legislatures would be in session, we should be able to get into touch with the members quickly and they would have about a fortnight in which to send in their answers. It is, of course, possible that a good many members will not be able, or will not care, to answer the questions; even so, the answers of the others may supply us with sufficient material in the light of which to prepare a draft of the new constitution. A draft so prepared is more likely to find acceptance when it is subsequently circulated to the provinces and we may thus save valuable time.

I am also trying to prepare the outlines of a provisional constitution fulfilling as far as possible the various conditions mentioned above.

The President's idea is that at the end of the next session of the Constituent Assembly, it should divide up into sections and the sections should frame the provincial constitutions for each of the provinces included therein before, say, the end of June. Assam may take a little longer because of the preliminary touring in the tribal and excluded areas that will be required. Sections B and C will be functioning under obvious difficulties and the constitutions they frame for some of their provinces may not be regarded as valid. But, in any case, it may help the sections in their task to have before them the answers to the questionnaire. Assuming that the sections will be ready with their drafts of the provincial constitutions before the end of June or the middle of July, it may be possible to have the complete constitution, including the Union portion, before the end of September. It may also be possible to have a draft of the provisional constitution ready before the same date. These are all rough forecasts which have emerged from this morning's discussion with the President.

3

THE QUESTIONNAIRE

[A week after Sri B. N. Rau had seen the President to discuss the procedure to be adopted by the Constituent Assembly and the provisional time-table for the carrying on of the administration of the country in the interim period, a questionnaire was circulated to all members of the Central and provincial legislatures on 17th March 1947 with a covering letter. The text of the letter as well as the questionnaire are reproduced here.]

From

    Sri B. N. Rau,

        Constitutional Adviser,

           Constituent Assembly of India.

To

    All Members of the Central and Provincial Legislatures.

                New Delhi, the 17th March, 1947.

Sir,

    In order to facilitate the work of framing a new constitution before June 1948, it is considered desirable to issue a questionnaire, bearing on the salient features of the constitution, to all the members of the various provincial legislatures and of the Central legislature and to invite their individual views thereon.

    Such a questionnaire is annexed to this letter. The questionnaire is divided into five parts, and in each part are set out a certain number of questions bearing on its subject-matter. Brief explanatory notes have been inserted under each question.

The questionnaire, as will be noticed, deals only with the constitution of the Centre. But most of the questions will apply, *mutatis mutandis*, to the provincial sphere also. You are therefore requested to give your answers, both in regard to the Union constitution and in regard to the provincial constitutions.

Your answers may kindly be sent so as to reach this office as early as possible, and in any case before April 10, 1947, as the matter is very urgent.

It is considered unnecessary to frame any questionnaire regarding group constitutions until the sections have decided to set up such constitutions.

Yours faithfully,
B. N. Rau

THE QUESTIONNAIRE

A—HEAD OF THE INDIAN UNION

1. *What should be the designation of the head of the Indian Union?*

[*Note:* In this and the following notes reference has been made to the constitutions of various countries. But it must be remembered that the United Kingdom and Ireland are not Federations and even South Africa is not a true Federation.

U.S.A.
Switzerland } President.
Ireland

Canada } The local executive head is the Governor-
Australia } General on behalf of His Majesty.

South Africa— The local executive head is the Governor-General.]

2

2. *How should he be chosen?*

[*Note:* The answer will probably turn on whether the head of the Indian Union is to be a real head as in the U.S.A., or merely a nominal head as in Switzerland. If he is to be a real head, independent of the legislature, he may have to be elected otherwise than by the legislature as in the U.S.A. If he is to be a nominal head, not independent of the legislature, he may be elected by the legislature as in Switzerland. The case of Ireland is peculiar, because the President is elected by the direct vote of the people and yet is to a large extent a nominal head acting on the advice of ministers responsible to the legislature.

U.S.A.—The President is elected by an electoral college in which each State has as many electors as it has members in Congress (*i.e.*, the Federal Legislature, including both Houses), the electors being elected in each State by adult franchise. This mode of election is presumably due to the theory of the American Constitution that the executive power must be completely separated from the legislative power. An absolute majority is required for the election of the President. Where no candidate secures an absolute majority, the House of Representatives elects the President from among the highest three, each State having one vote.

Switzerland—The President is elected annually by the Federal Assembly (*i.e.*, the Federal Legislature, including both Houses) from amongst the members of the Federal Council (Executive), who are also elected by the Federal Legislature.

Ireland—The President is elected by the direct vote of the people (secret voting, on the system of proportional representation by means of the single transferable vote).]

3. *What should be his term of office?*
  [*Note:*

U.S.A.	4 years (elected every leap year).
Switzerland	1 year (annual election).

Ireland	7 years.
Canada	⎫
Australia	⎬ Customary term of 5 years.
South Africa	⎭

4. *Should he be eligible for re-election?*

[*Note:*

U.S.A.—Eligible for re-election: previous to Franklin Roosevelt, convention of not more than two terms. Franklin Roosevelt held office for four consecutive terms, the last one interrupted by death.

Switzerland—Re-election of the President who is in office is prohibited by the constitution. By usage, the office rotates among the members of the Federal Council.

Ireland—Eligible for re-election to the office once, but only once.]

5. *Should the office rotate among the different communities in turn? If so, how?*

[*Note:*

U.S.A.—No provision.

Switzerland—By usage, the offices of the President and the Vice-President rotate amongst the members of the Federal Council in which the main communities are represented.

Ireland—No statutory provision; but the first President was a Protestant (Dr. Hyde, elected in 1938); the present President is a Roman Catholic.]

6. *Assuming that the Indian Union is to have a President as its head, should there be a Vice-President or Vice-Presidents?*

[*Note:*

U.S.A.—There is a Vice-President who also presides over the Senate. The method of election is the same as that of the President, except that when he fails to secure an absolute majority of the votes of the electors, he is elected by the Senate from among the highest two.

Switzerland—There is one Vice-President elected by the Federal Assembly from amongst the members of the Federal Council.

Ireland—No provision for Vice-President.

U.S.S.R.—The Presidium has a President and 16 Vice-Presidents, corresponding to the number of Republics.]

7. *What should be the term of office of a Vice-President?*

[*Note:*

U.S.A.	4 years (election every leap year).
Switzerland	1 year.
Ireland	No Vice-President.]

8. *What should be the functions of the President?*

[*Note:*

U.S.A.—The President is the Commander-in-Chief of the army, navy and air force, receives ambassadors, etc., and makes treaties subject to the consent of two-thirds majority of the Senate. He appoints ambassadors and consuls, judges of the Supreme Court and such inferior officers as provided for by law. He recommends measures for the consideration of the Congress. He has an absolute veto over legislation which can only be overcome by a measure being passed by two-thirds majority of each of the two Houses. He has, also, what is called, the " pocket veto ", *i.e.*, a measure passed within ten days of the adjournment of Congress and not assented to by the President is deemed to have lapsed. He may grant reprieves and pardons (except in cases of impeachment) for offences against the State, commute sentences, etc. He is liable to impeachment.

Switzerland—The President has only formal or ceremonial functions, the principal one being that of presiding over the

Federal Council. He is in charge of one of the administrative departments.

Ireland—The President, on the nomination of Dail Eireann, appoints the Prime Minister (Taoiseach) or the head of the Government, who, in turn, recommends the appointment of other members of the Cabinet. He summons and dissolves Dail Eireann on the advice of the Prime Minister and in case the Prime Minister has lost the support of the majority in the Dail, the President may, in his absolute discretion, refuse to dissolve the Dail. The President may at any time after consultation with the Council of State convene a meeting of either or both of the Houses, communicate with them by message or address—which has received the approval of Government—on any matter of national or public importance or address a message approved by the Government to the nation at any time on any such matter. He is the Supreme Commander of all defence forces and all Commissions are held from him. He has a right of pardon and a power to commute or remit punishment. He is liable to impeachment.]

9. *What should be the functions of the Vice-President?*

[*Note:*

U.S.A.—Presides over the Senate; becomes President if President dies during term of office.

Switzerland—Member of the Federal Council, in charge of an administrative department, and presides over the Council in the absence of the President.]

10. *Should the President be liable to removal? If so, in what manner?*

[*Note:*

U.S.A.—The President is removable from office only by impeachment. The Lower Chamber initiates proceedings and the Senate sits as a court of trial. The President is removed on the majority vote of the Senate sitting as the court of impeachment.

Switzerland—No specific provision.

Ireland—Removable by impeachment. The President may be impeached for stated misbehaviour. A proposal against the President is entertained when moved in writing by at least 30 members of that House and is adopted when, at least, two-thirds of the total members support it. The other House investigates the charges or causes the charges to be investigated. If it sustains the charge by two-thirds majority of the total members, the President is removed.]

11. *How is a temporary vacancy in the office of the President to be filled?*

[*Note:*

U.S.A.—The Vice-President acts as President for the rest of the term.

Switzerland—Apparently the Vice-President acts as President.

Ireland—A Commission consisting of the Chief Justice, the Chairman of the Dail and the Chairman of the Senate acts for the President. The Commission may act by any two of their number.]

B—EXECUTIVE

12. *What should be the nature and type of the Union Executive? Should it be of the British type (parliamentary) or the American type (non-parliamentary) or the Swiss type (mixed) or any other type?*

[*Note:* From the point of view of practical administration this is perhaps the most important question in the framing of the new constitution. There are, as indicated in the questionnaire, three main types of executives. In the British type, the executive is responsible to the legislature and has to resign on loss of confidence of the legislature. In the American type, the executive is not responsible to the legislature; each derives its authority from the people direct and is not responsible to the other. In the Swiss type, the executive is elected by the legislature for a term of four years (which is also the life of the legislature) and no question of resignation during the term arises. In the Irish Free State Constitution of 1922, we find a fourth type: there was a Ministry of the British type *plus* certain additional ministers appointed rather on the Swiss plan—that is to say, they were nominated by the Dail on the recommendation of a special committee, they held office for the term of the Dail, and were responsible only to the Dail. The British type is the one with which we are most familiar in India and its features are well known. The main features of the Swiss type are: (1) it gives all sections a chance of being represented in the executive, the election being by proportional representation; (2) it enables the Ministry to concentrate on the real problems of the country for a fixed term of four years without being distracted by motions of no-confidence; (3) it ensures a substantial degree of responsibility to the legislature, inasmuch as the executive is not only elected by the legislature but is also subject to its directions. The Irish Free State type had a short life and has been abandoned in the new Irish Constitution, which has adopted the British type.

U.K. and the Dominions—By convention the executive (Cabinet) is responsible to the legislature and retains office so long as it enjoys the confidence of the legislature.

U.S.A.—The President is the head of the Federal Executive with a Cabinet of ten heads of departments called Secretaries, appointed by him, subject to the nominal approval of the Senate and answerable only to him. Executive not responsible to the legislature. Non-parliamentary.

Switzerland—The Federal Council consists of seven members elected by the legislature (by proportional representation) once in four years. They are eligible for re-election. Not more than one is elected from the same canton. A mixture of parliamentary and non-parliamentary.

Ireland—Ireland has put into statutory form what in U.K. is based on convention. The government consists of seven to 15 members appointed by the President. One of them acts as Prime Minister, and another as Deputy Prime Minister. Responsible to Dail Eireann, though the ministers may be chosen from both the Houses, at most two from the Senate. Parliamentary.]

13. *If parliamentary, should there be any special provision to secure a stable executive?*

[*Note:* The following observations in the Simon-Attlee Report are worth notice. Although they relate to the provincial sphere they are of general application:

" We think that under the conditions which have developed in the Indian provinces, ministers are too much at the mercy of hostile combinations against them for good work to be done. Ministers need to feel that they are assured of a reasonable period within which their policy may mature and its results may be judged; at present some of them are so much occupied in maintaining their position by securing the temporary support of this or that group of critics or malcontents that it must be very difficult to carry on the main work of ministerial government at all."

Ireland—In the Irish Constitution of 1922 an attempt was made to secure stable administration by providing for ministers, outside the Cabinet, who retained office even after the Cabinet had resigned. This experiment was carried out in the first two Dails, but apparently was found unworkable. See note under question No. 12 above.

China—In case there is disagreement on any matter between the legislature on the one hand and the Cabinet supported by the President on the other, the legislature can make its views prevail over those of the executive only by passing a measure or proposition by a two-thirds majority of members present.]

14. *What should be the composition of the executive? What should be the maximum, if any, of the number of ministers?*

[*Note:*

U.K.—No statutory maximum. The number at present in the Cabinet is 20 members including the Prime Minister.

Canada—No statutory maximum; the number at present is 20 members including the Prime Minister.

Australia—There is a statutory maximum of seven until Parliament otherwise provides. The number at present is 19 members including the Prime Minister. Ministers cannot remain in office more than three months without being members of one of the Houses of the legislature.

South Africa—There is a statutory maximum of 11. Ministers cannot remain in office more than three months without being members of one of the Houses of the legislature.

U.S.A.—President with ten heads of departments called Secretaries who are answerable only to him. None of these can be a member of either House of the legislature.

Switzerland—The Federal Council consists of seven members elected by the two Houses of the legislature at a joint sitting. None of them can be a member of either House, but all may sit and speak without voting.

Ireland—Consists of 7 to 15 ministers, selected from among the members of both the Houses, not more than two being selected from the Upper House. All continue to be members of the House from which they were selected.]

15. *Should provision be made to secure representation of different communities on the executive? If so, how?*

[*Note:*

U.S.A.—No provision.

Switzerland—Not more than one member of the Federal Council can be chosen from the same canton.

Canada—No statutory provision. In considering the claims of various candidates for ministerial office the Premier has to take into account race, religion and geographical factors. When the total number was 23, three were usually assigned to French Canada and three to Ontario; at least one was assigned to each of the provinces of Nova Scotia, New Brunswick, Manitoba, Saskatchewan, Alberta and British Columbia, and a politician of Irish extraction usually represented the English speaking Roman Catholic Church.]

16. *How should joint responsibility or co-ordination be secured?*

[*Note:*

U.K. and the Dominions—By convention all the ministers are jointly responsible to the legislature. They are chosen by the Prime Minister. The Government must be one which can work together and can secure the support of the Lower House. The first mark of the Cabinet is united and indivisible responsibility.

U.S.A.—No responsibility to the legislature. Co-ordination secured, because all the Secretaries hold office during the pleasure of the President and are answerable to him.

Switzerland—The Federal Council is bound by the decisions of the Federal Legislature. The Council arrives at a decision by majority vote. When the Council is not unanimous on any matter, it is open to ministers to speak against each other in the legislature and this sometimes happens; but when once the legislature decides the matter, all ministers loyally carry out the decision. The legislature may therefore be regarded as the co-ordinating factor in the last resort.

Ireland—The Cabinet is collectively responsible to Dail Eireann and holds office during its command of majority in the Dail. The statutory provisions follow the British convention.]

17. *How should the members of the executive be chosen?*

[*Note:*

U.K. and the Dominions—The choice of the Prime Minister is made by the King, or the Governor-General, as the case may be, and the nature of the choice depends upon the state of parties in the Lower House. The Prime Minister chooses his colleagues in the Cabinet.

U.S.A.—President (elected by an electoral college) selects his Secretaries subject to the formal approval of the Senate.

Switzerland—The members of the Federal Council chosen by the Federal Legislature at a joint sitting.

Ireland—The President appoints the Prime Minister on the recommendation of the Dail and other ministers on the recommendation of the Prime Minister.]

18. *What provisions should be made for the removal of the executive?*

[*Note:*

U.K. and the Dominions—The Cabinet holds office so long as it has the confidence of the Lower House. It can be removed by a vote of no-confidence by the Lower House.

U.S.A.—President may be removed by impeachment; Secretaries are removable by the President.

Switzerland—No specific provision.

Ireland—The Prime Minister and ministers hold office so long as they have the support of the majority in the Lower House. Individual ministers can be removed from office on the advice of the Prime Minister.]

19. *What should be the nature of relations between the head of the Union and the executive?*

[*Note:*

U.K.—The King is merely a formal head. In all political matters he acts on the advice of the Cabinet. He has certain prerogative powers, namely, (1) the right to dissolve Parliament, (2) the right to refuse a dissolution of Parliament and (3) the right to select the Prime Minister. These rights are circumscribed by many considerations and are very often of theoretical interest only. There are also certain personal prerogatives which he exercises on his own responsibility.

Dominions—The Cabinet is the *de facto* executive. In all political matters the Governor-General acts only on the advice of the Cabinet. He does not preside over the business meetings of the Cabinet, which are summoned in the name of the Prime Minister. The Governor-General acts merely as the constitutional head of the Government advised by the ministers.

U.S.A.—The President is the head of the Union, as well as the chief executive.

Switzerland—The President is the head of the Union and also a minister in charge of an administrative department like other ministers. No special powers, except those of a formal or ceremonial character, are vested in him.

Ireland—The President is the titular head and all laws are promulgated in his name. The President acts with the consent of the Prime Minister and his Cabinet except when the Cabinet loses the confidence of the Dail. In that case the President may, in his discretion, dissolve the Dail and call for fresh elections. The President is also advised by the Council of State which has the Prime Minister and Deputy Prime Minister among its members.]

C—LEGISLATURE

20. *Should the Union Legislature have a single Chamber or two Chambers?*

[*Note:* Second Chambers are set up for various reasons: *e.g.*, to represent special interests or classes as in Ireland; as a check on hasty and ill-conceived legislation of the Lower House as in France; to provide equal representation to the different constituent units of a federation as in the U.S.A. It may provide for a continuous term of office, only a portion of the members retiring at regular intervals as in the U.S.A., and the old French Constitution. This secures the representation of past as well as current opinion and helps in maintaining continuity in public policy.

There is a growing opposition to the Second Chamber for various reasons, *viz.*, (1) it may tend to be reactionary, over-conservative and check urgently-needed but radical reforms, (2) it may be instrumental in delaying legislation, (3) it tends to be undemocratic since it is very difficult to constitute a truly democratic Second Chamber on a different basis from the Lower Chamber, (4) it is expensive to the country, and politically-backward countries also lack able statesmen to man a Second Chamber properly.

U.K. and the
Dominions—All bicameral (two Chambers).

U.K.— House of Lords (Upper House).
House of Commons (Lower House).

Canada— Senate (Upper House).
House of Commons (Lower House).

Australia— Senate (Upper House).
House of Representatives (Lower House).

South Africa—Senate (Upper House).
House of Assembly (Lower House).

U.S.A.— Bicameral: Senate (Upper House).
House of Representatives (Lower House).

Switzerland— Bicameral: Council of States (Upper House).
National Council (Lower House).

Ireland— Bicameral: Seanad Eireann (Upper House).
Dail Eireann (Lower House).]

21. *If bicameral, how should the two Houses be constituted?*

[*Note:*
U.K.—The British House of Lords is of the traditional type. Most of the members are hereditary peers. In addition to these, 16 are elected by the Scottish peers for the duration of each Parliament. There are also some who are members of the House by virtue of office: the Archbishops and Bishops and the Law Lords.

House of Commons: Entirely elected.

Canada—Senate (Upper House). Senators nominated for life. There are 24 Senators from each of four territorial divisions: Ontario, Quebec, the Maritime Provinces (including Prince Edward Island) and the Western Provinces.

House of Commons (Lower House). Entirely elected, Quebec returning 65 members and other provinces in proportion to population relatively to Quebec.

Australia—Senate (Upper House). Entirely elected directly through territorial constituencies, six Senators from each State, until Parliament otherwise provides.

House of Representatives (Lower House). Entirely elected; total number of members is as nearly as possible double the number of Senators and is distributed among the States according to population, with a minimum of five for any State.

South Africa—Senate (Upper House). Partly elected—each province electing eight—and partly nominated, (eight) by the Governor-General-in-Council.

House of Assembly (Lower House). Entirely elected, the quota for each province depending upon the number of its European adult Union Nationals.

U.S.A.—Senate (Upper House). Constituted on the basis of direct election, each State forming a constituency and electing two Senators.

House of Representatives (Lower House). Entirely elected. Under the constitution, the total number of representatives must not exceed one for every 30,000 of the population but each State shall have at least one representative. The actual average representation at present is only one for every 300,000.

Switzerland—Council of States (Upper House). Each of the cantonal or half-cantonal units is free to determine the mode of election of its representatives. Direct election in 21 units and election by cantonal legislatures in the other four. Each canton elects two Senators and each half-canton one.

National Council (Lower House). Constituted on the basis of direct election. Entirely elected. One member for every 22,000 of the population.

Ireland—Seanad Eireann (Upper House). Out of a total of 60 members, 11 are nominated by the Taoiseach (Prime Minister) and the rest elected through electoral colleges to represent specified functional interests.

Dail Eireann (Lower House). Entirely elected on the basis of direct election. Not less than one member for every 30,000 of the population nor more than one member for every 20,000.]

22. *What provisions should be made for the adequate representation of different communities and interests?*

[*Note:*

U.K.—Universities are given special representation.*

South Africa—Four elected and four nominated to represent Native interests in the Upper House. Three seats allotted in the Lower House for Natives of Cape Colony.

U.S.A.—No provision.

Switzerland—No specific provision. The system of proportional representation helps to secure the adequate representation of different communities.

Ireland—Provision made for the representation of functional interests such as " agricultural and allied interests and fisheries ", " labour ", " industry and commerce " in the Upper House; system of proportional representation for the Lower House.]

23. *What should be* (a) *composition,* (b) *franchise,* (c) *electorate,* (d) *constituencies,* (e) *methods of election and* (f) *allocation of seats in respect of the Union legislature?*

(a) *COMPOSITION:*

[*Note:*

U.S.A.—House of Representatives. 435 members at present; under the Constitution the total number must not exceed one

---

* These seats have now been abolished.

for every 30,000 of the population, but each State shall have at least one representative. The actual average representation at present is only one for every 300,000.

Senate: 96 members (two from each of the 48 States).

Switzerland—National Council (Lower House). Varies according to population (one member for every 22,000 of the population); present strength—194 members.

Council of States (Upper House): 44 members (two members each from 19 full cantons, one each from the remaining six half-cantons).

Ireland—Dail Eireann (Lower House). Varies according to population (not less than one member for every 30,000 of the population nor more than one member for every 20,000); present strength—138.

Seanad Eireann (Upper House): 60 members.]

(*b*) *FRANCHISE:*

[*Note:*

U.S.A.—For both the Houses, the franchise is the same as for the State legislature if unicameral, or for the Lower House of the State legislature if bicameral. Disqualifications on the ground of race, colour or sex forbidden. Universal adult franchise in practice, subject to certain minimum literacy qualification.

Switzerland—Universal adult male franchise for the Lower House. Cantons and half-cantons free to fix the franchise qualifications for the Upper House.

Ireland—Adult franchise for the Lower House and indirect election for the Upper House.]

(*c*) *ELECTORATES:*

[*Note:* No separate or special electorates in the U.S.A. and Switzerland. For Ireland, see " Methods of Election ".]

(*d*) *CONSTITUENCIES:*

[*Note:* Single-member constituencies in the U.S.A. Multi-member constituencies for the Lower House in Switzerland

and Ireland where election is by the method of proportional representation.]

(e) METHODS OF ELECTION:

[*Note:*

U.S.A.—Single-member constituencies for both the Houses, the person getting the largest number of votes being declared elected.

Switzerland—Proportional representation for the Lower House. Each of the cantons or half-cantons free to determine the mode of election for the Upper House. Direct election in 21 cantonal or half-cantonal units and election by the legislatures of the units in the other four.

Ireland—Proportional representation for the Lower House. For the Upper House election is indirect. Nominations to elected seats are made by recognised functional associations, members of the Lower House, the Prime Minister, and persons who have held the office of the Prime Minister or the President. Election is by an electoral college composed of the members of the Dail Eireann and seven persons elected by each one of the councils of the counties or county boroughs. Voting is by the method of proportional representation by means of the single transferable vote.]

(f) ALLOCATION OF SEATS:

[*Note:*

U.S.A.—Lower House. 435 seats distributed on the basis of population, not exceeding one per 30,000 inhabitants, but with a minimum representation of one for each State.

Upper House: 96 seats, two Senators per State.

Switzerland—Lower House. One member for every 22,000 inhabitants, but at least one member for each canton or half-canton.

Ireland—Lower House. Allocation of seats as between constituencies on the basis of population.

Upper House: Of the 60 members, 11 are nominated by the Prime Minister, six are elected by the universities, and the remaining 43 are elected from five panels of candidates consituated on a vocational basis.]

24. *What should be the term of the Union legislature?*

[*Note:*

U.K.—Upper House. Largely hereditary.

Lower House: Five years, unless sooner dissolved.

Canada—Upper House. Senators are nominated for life.

Lower House: Five years.

Australia—Upper House. Continuous, half retiring every three years, term of membership being six years.

Lower House: Three years.

South Africa—Upper House. Normal term ten years.

Lower House: Five years.

U.S.A.—Lower House: Two years.

Upper House: Continuous, one-third retiring every two years, term of membership being six years.

Switzerland—Lower House. Four years.

Upper House: Each canton or half-canton free to fix the term of office of its representatives. Varies from one to four years.

Ireland—Lower House. Seven years, unless sooner dissolved. A shorter period may be fixed by law.

Upper House: Same as for Lower House.]

25. *If bicameral, what should be the relative powers of the two Houses? What provision should be made to resolve deadlocks?*

[*Note:*

U.K.—Until 1911 the powers of the House of Lords were largely co-extensive with those of the House of Commons. This led to occasional conflicts between the two Houses and finally the powers of the Upper House were curtailed by the enactment of the Parliament Act of 1911. At present, all money Bills, so certified by the Speaker of the House of

Commons, if not passed by the House of Lords without amendment, become law without their concurrence, on the royal assent being signified. Public Bills, other than money Bills or a Bill extending the maximum duration of Parliament, if passed by the House of Commons in three successive sessions, whether of the same Parliament or not and rejected each time, or not passed by the House of Lords, may become law without their concurrence, on the royal assent being signified, provided that two years have elapsed between the second reading in the first session of the House of Commons and the third reading in the third session. All Bills coming under this Act should reach the House of Lords at least one month before the end of the session.

Canada—The powers of the Canadian Senate are, in law, equal to those of the Lower House, excepting that money Bills must originate in the House of Commons and convention requires that they may be rejected but not amended. There are no adequate means to adjust differences between the two Houses: all that the framers of the constitution have done for this purpose is to provide for the appointment of additional members to the Senate, but since the total strength of the House cannot exceed 104, the maximum number that can be nominated at any time to resolve differences is eight.

Australia—The Senate has equal powers with the House of Representatives in respect of proposed laws except that money Bills must originate only in the Lower House and cannot be amended by the Senate. The Senate may, however, at any stage return to the House of Representatives any proposed law which the Senate may not amend, requesting by message, the omission or amendment of any items or provisions therein. But if there is a deadlock between the two Houses, the Senate can force the dissolution of both the Houses even in regard to money Bills. But such dissolution shall not take place within six months before the date of the expiry of the House of Representatives by efflux of time. If the deadlock continues even after the reconstituted Houses meet, it is resolved by a joint sitting of the two Houses. A majority of the total number of the members of the Senate and the House of Representatives is required for the measure to be passed into law.

South Africa—The South African Senate has only limited powers and is essentially a " House of review". Money Bills must originate in the House of Assembly only. The Senate may not amend any Bill which imposes taxation or appropriates revenue or moneys for the services of the government, nor can it amend any Bill so as to increase any proposed charges or burdens on the people. If there is a difference of opinion between the two Houses, the constitution provides for a joint sitting at which a majority of the members present—and not, as in Australia, a majority of the total number of members—is required for the Bill to be passed into law. In the case of a money Bill, the joint session is convened during the same session; in the case of other Bills, during the second session of the legislature.

U.S.A.—The Upper House has all the powers of the Lower House and a few more. Its consent is required for the appointment of ambassadors, judges and other high officials and it has the sole power to try all impeachments. Its consent by two-thirds majority is required for the conclusion of all treaties. A Joint Conference Committee tries to iron out differences, but no provision is made in the constitution for resolving deadlocks.

Switzerland—The two Houses have co-ordinate powers. In cases of difference of opinion, the respective committees of the two Houses try to arrive at a compromise, but no provision is made in the constitution for resolving deadlocks.

Ireland—The Upper House has a suspensory veto for a period of only 90 days in respect of Bills other than money Bills or urgent Bills. If it has the support of one-third of the members of the Lower House, it can ask the President for a referendum to ascertain the will of the people and the

President, in consultation with the Council of State, may grant the request. This procedure does not apply to Bills proposing to amend the constitution.]

D—JUDICIARY

26. *Should there be a separate chain of courts to administer Union laws?*

[*Note*: In the U.S.A., there is a separate chain of Federal Courts, but not in Canada, Australia or Switzerland.

U.S.A.—Under the constitution the judicial power of the United States is vested in a Supreme Court, and in such inferior courts as Congress may from time to time ordain and establish. There are, at present, two sets of inferior federal courts, namely, the Federal District Courts and the Circuit Courts of Appeal. The country is divided into 83 districts, each State constituting at least one district. From the Federal Courts of these districts there is an appeal to Circuit Courts, which are ten in number. There are also two special courts, namely, the Court of Claims and the Court of Customs Appeals. In certain cases, however, the State Courts may be, and are, permitted, in the exercise of the jurisdiction vested in them by the constitution or laws of their respective States, to deal with cases which are within the federal judicial power. But their jurisdiction in such cases may be qualified by the right of the defendant to have the case removed before trial into a Federal Court, or after trial the case may be taken by appeal to the Federal Supreme Court.

Australia—The judicial power of the Commonwealth is vested in a Federal Supreme Court, called the High Court of Australia and " in such other federal courts as the Parliament creates and in such other courts as it invests with federal jurisdiction ". The Parliament is also empowered to make laws investing any court of a State with federal jurisdiction. Thus, the constitution has left to the discretion of the Parliament the determination of the degree to which the agency of the State courts is to be utilised for the administration of federal laws.

Under the Judiciary Act of 1903, as amended from time to time, the several courts of the States are vested with federal jurisdiction in matters not within the exclusive jurisdiction of the High Court, and there is a right of appeal from these courts to the High Court.

Canada—Under the constitution the Canadian Parliament is empowered to establish a General Court of Appeal for Canada and other courts for the better administration of the laws of Canada. In the exercise of these powers, the Canadian Parliament has set up a Supreme Court of Appeal and an Exchequer Court. In other respects, the administration of justice, including the constitution, maintenance and organisation of civil and criminal courts and civil procedure is a provincial subject, while criminal law and procedure are assigned to the Federation. It may be noted that the constitution vests the Governor-General with power to appoint the judges of the superior, district and county courts of each province, subject to certain exceptions.]

E—AMENDMENTS TO THE CONSTITUTION

27. *What provisions should be made regarding amendments to the constitution?*

[*Note:*

U.K.—The British Constitution can be altered by an Act of Parliament.

Canada—The Constitution of the Dominion of Canada can only be amended by the Parliament of Great Britain. The Constitution Act itself does not contain any provision regarding such amendments and the Statute of Westminster clearly lays down that it should not be deemed to apply to the repeal, amendment or alteration of the British North America Acts of 1867 to 1930, or any order, rule or regulation made thereunder. As a matter of form, changes in the constitution have been carried out on addresses from the two Houses of the Dominion Parliament; but this would be difficult if a measure were opposed by one or more of the provincial legislatures. It may be noted that the last of the amendments to the constitution, passed in 1907, was based on the assent of all the provinces: British Columbia demanded better terms but finally agreed to the passing of the measure.

Australia—A proposal to amend the constitution must be passed by an absolute majority in each of the two Houses and, not less than two nor more than six months after its passage through both Houses, must be submitted in each State to the electors of the House of Representatives (Lower House). But if an amendment proposed by an absolute majority of one House is not agreed to by the other House and, if after an interval of three months, the amendment is again proposed by the first-mentioned House and again not agreed to by the other House, the Governor-General may submit the proposed amendment to the electors in each State. The proposed amendment cannot become law unless it is approved by a majority of electors voting and by a majority of the States. No amendment (1) diminishing the proportionate representation of any State in either House of Parliament, (2) diminishing the minimum number of representatives of a State in the House of Representatives, (3) increasing, diminishing, or otherwise altering the limits of a State and (4) affecting the provisions of the constitution in relation to the foregoing matters may be carried unless the majority of the electors voting in the State interested approve of the proposed law.

Union of South Africa—Except in regard to certain " entrenched " provisions, the Union Parliament may by law repeal or alter any of the provisions of the Constitution Act. As regards the excepted provisions, *viz.*, section 35 (protection of the Cape Native franchise), section 137 (equality of English, Dutch and Afrikaans languages), section 152 (amendment of the Constitution Act), proposals to amend them should be passed at a joint session of both Houses of Parliament, and at the third reading receive the assent of not less than two-thirds of the total number of members of both Houses.

U.S.A.—In the Constitution of the U.S.A. two methods of originating amendments are provided, and there are also two methods of enacting amendments, when so originated. In the first place, Congress itself may, by two-thirds majority in each House, draft and propose amendments; in the second place the legislatures of two-thirds of the several States may apply to Congress to call a convention for the purpose of proposing amendments. When amendments are proposed by Congress, or by a constitutional convention, they have to be submitted to the States and ratified in three-fourths of the States, either by the State legislatures or by State conventions specially elected in each State for the purpose.

Switzerland—There are several methods by which revisions of the constitution may be originated and ratified. A total revision of the constitution may be brought about in three ways: (1) The National Council and the Council of States may agree to an amendment, as in the case of an ordinary federal law. The constitution, as drawn up by the two Houses, must then be submitted to the popular vote and if it is approved by a majority of the people and by a majority of the cantons, it becomes law. (2) If one House votes for a total revision and the other refuses its assent, the question is then submitted to the electors in each canton or half-canton, " Do you wish the constitution to be revised—Yes or No? " If the majority of electors vote " Yes " in support of a revision, the two Houses are then dissolved, and a new Federal Assembly is elected, charged with the work of revising and drafting a new constitution. When this has been prepared, it is submitted to the popular vote and if it is approved by a majority of the people and by a majority of the cantons it becomes law. (3) If 50,000 citizens sign a petition in favour of a total revision of the constitution, it is the duty of the executive to submit the question to the electors, " Do you wish the constitution to be revised—Yes or No?" If a majority of the electors decide in favour of revision, the Federal Legislature has to carry out the popular wish and revise the constitution for submission to the people. If on such submission it is approved by the required double majority it becomes law.

There are two methods by which a partial revision or a partial amendment of the Swiss Constitution may be brought about. An amendment may be proposed by the two Federal Houses, as in the ordinary process of legislation. It must then be submitted to and accepted by a majority of the people and by a majority of the cantons. A demand for the adoption of a new article, or the alteration of an old one, may be made in writing by 50,000 Swiss citizens in the same way as a demand for a total revision. If the Federal Legislature agrees with the demand of the petitioners, it proceeds to formulate the required amendment and prepare it for submission to the people. If on the other hand it disagrees with the demand, the question is submitted to the people, " Are you in favour of a revision of the constitution—Yes or No?" If a majority of the people decide in favour of a revision, it becomes the duty of the Federal Legislature, acting as a Drafting Committee, to prepare the required amendment for submission to the people. It is then submitted to the popular vote and if it receives the support of the required statutory majority of people and of cantons, it becomes law. The final referendum is obligatory in every proposal to amend the constitution.

In reckoning a majority of the constituent units, the vote of a half-canton is counted as half a vote.

Ireland—Every proposal for amending the constitution must be initiated in the Lower House as a Bill and, after it is passed by both the Houses of the legislature, submitted to the people for their decision. The Bill is held to have been approved by the people if the majority of the votes cast is in favour of its enactment and it becomes law after it is signed and promulgated by the President in due form.]

4

POINTS OF PROCEDURE

I. Provincial Co-operation

ACCORDING to the scheme outlined in the Cabinet Delegation's statement of May 16, 1946, the provinces will, to a large extent, be autonomous units exercising all powers except those reserved to the Union. It will, therefore, be necessary to frame the constitution in such a way as to make it acceptable to the provinces to the largest possible extent; otherwise, it may not work smoothly. For example, the Union services, such as railways, or posts and telegraphs, or broadcasting may occasionally be dislocated by strikes and the Union Government may require the assistance of the law and order authorities of the provinces. Unless the constitution is such as to commend itself to the provinces, this assistance may not be readily forthcoming and may even be completely withheld. Again, as under section 124 of the Government of India Act, 1935, so under the new constitution, the Union may find it necessary, either by agreement or by law, to confer powers and impose duties on provincial authorities: e.g., to require provincial courts to try and punish offences against Union laws. Or, again, the Union may have to invoke provincial assistance to acquire land for Union purposes. What applies to the Union portion of the constitution applies with even greater force to the provincial. Hence the need for enlisting provincial co-operation as far as possible in the framing of every part of the constitution. Procedure in the Constituent Assembly and its sections has an important part to play in this connection. Let us see what was done in other countries to secure provincial co-operation.

MODE OF VOTING

U.S.A.—In the Philadelphia Convention of 1787, which framed the Constitution of the U.S.A., the representatives of 12 States were present. The strength of the delegation varied from State to State: thus Pennsylvania sent eight delegates, any four of them being competent to represent the State; while Connecticut sent three, any one or more of them being competent to act. The final draft was signed by 39 representatives in all. Early in the proceedings, the Convention appointed a committee to draw up rules of procedure. The first of these rules, adopted as a standing order of the Convention, was as follows:

" A House, to do business, shall consist of the Deputies of not less than seven States; *and all questions shall be decided by the greater number of these which shall be fully represented*; but a less number than seven may adjourn from day to day." (*Documentary History of the Constitution of the United States of America*, Vol. I, *p.* 51.)

It will thus be seen that each State, large or small, had one vote, decisions being by a majority of those that were fully represented. The question as to the mode of voting had been discussed among the members present while the Convention was waiting for a quorum and it had been urged by some that the large States should firmly refuse parity in this matter as unreasonable and as enabling the small States " to negative every good system of government ". Ultimately, however, it was felt that such an attempt might lead to fatal altercations and that it would be easier to persuade the smaller States to give in on particular issues than to disarm them on all.

How this worked out in practice may be seen from an actual instance. On June 29, 1787, the Convention debated a proposed provision of the new constitution that each State should have an equal vote in the Upper House of the Federal Legislature. The delegates from Connecticut and the other small States supported the proposal with great ability and vehemence; the large States opposed it bitterly. When the question was put to the vote on July 2, 1787, there was a tie, the votes of five States being in the affirmative, five in the negative and one divided. The divided vote was due to the fact that Georgia, though small at the moment, was a growing State, so that one of its delegates voted " Aye " and the other " No ". As the result of the tie, the Convention appointed a Compromise Committee consisting of one member from each State. The Committee recommended representation according to population for the Lower House of the Federal Legislature and an equal vote for every State in the Upper House. After several days of acrimonious discussion and the appointment of further committees, this recommendation, slightly modified as regards its first half, was adopted by the Convention by a narrow majority. It may be mentioned that at an early stage of the debate it had been proposed that one of the smaller States which happened to be absent should be specially requested to attend; but this was regarded as sharp practice and was promptly voted down. The procedure adopted and the whole course of the debate showed how every State, large or small, was given its due voice, how anything savouring of unfairness was avoided and how deadlocks were resolved by a pervading spirit of compromise.

CANADA—On the very first day of the Quebec Conference which framed the basis of the Canadian Constitution, it was proposed " that in taking the votes on all questions to be decided by the Conference, except questions of order, each province or colony, by whatever number of delegates represented, shall have one vote and that in voting Canada be

considered as two provinces". It should be remembered
that at that time Canada was a single province consisting of
Ontario or Upper Canada and Quebec or Lower Canada.
Under the new constitution, these two halves of old Canada
became separate provinces. This explains why in the matter
of voting upon the new constitution Canada was considered
as two provinces. In other words, what the Conference did
was to give one vote to each unit of the new Union. It may
further be mentioned that at the Conference, Canada (Ontario
and Quebec) was represented by 12 delegates, New Brunswick by seven, Nova Scotia by five, Prince Edward Island
by seven and Newfoundland by two. In spite of this
unequal representation, the units were given equal voting
power.

Next day (on October 11, 1864), the Conference adopted
the following rules of procedure:

1. That free individual discussion and suggestion be allowed.
2. That all motions and the discussions and votes thereon
   be in the first place as if in committee of the whole.
3. That after question put, no discussion be allowed.
4. That each province retire for consultation after question put.
5. That after the scheme is settled in committee of the
   whole, all the resolutions be reconsidered as if with
   Speaker in the chair.
6. That just before the breaking up of the Conference, the
   minutes be carefully gone over and settled, with a view
   to determining what is to be submitted to the Imperial
   and provincial governments and what is to be published
   for general information.

Let us see how the proceedings were actually conducted by
taking a concrete case. On October 19, 1864, the Conference
debated a proposal that representation to the House of
Commons, that is to say, the Lower House of the Federal
Legislature, should be on the basis of population. Prince

Edward Island, which would have been entitled only to five members out of nearly 200 on this basis, objected; but the motion was carried, all the others voting for it. Thereupon, Haviland (for Prince Edward Island) observed: " Prince Edward Island would rather be out of the Confederation than consent to this motion. We should have no status. Only five members out of 194 would give the Island no position." Tilley (for New Brunswick) pointed out that it had been fully understood at a previous Convention at Charlottetown that representation would be on a population basis. Palmer (for Prince Edward Island) protested that there had been no such understanding at Charlottetown and that representation by population is not applicable when a certain number of provinces— some with no public debt and low taxation, others with a heavy debt and high taxation—are throwing their resources into one Confederation and giving up their own self-government and individuality. Shea (for Newfoundland) supported Tilley. Coles (for Prince Edward Island) also supported Tilley and regretted his own colleague Palmer's attitude. Gray (for Prince Edward Island) also thought that the population basis had been fully accepted at Charlottetown. Galt (for Canada) requested the Prince Edward Island delegates to reconsider their decision, observing that " it would be a matter of reproach to us that the smallest colony should leave us ". Whelan (for Prince Edward Island), who had come prepared to vote with Haviland and Palmer, also suggested reconsideration. " I do not think, however, I could say that I was satisfied with the representation of five in the Federal House of Commons. We are in an isolated position. Our resources are large and our people would not be content to give up their present benefits for the representation of five members. It may be said that the Confederation will go on without Prince Edward Island and that we shall eventually be forced in. Better, however, *that* than that we should willingly go into the Confederation with that representation. But if the government who form the delegation will take the responsibility on them, I may support them." Next day, Palmer said that he had been under a misapprehension the previous evening and that he had since been told by his colleagues from Prince Edward Island that the financial settlement would follow the discussion about representation and that the matter of representation would depend on the financial resolutions. He conceded that that might alter his position. The matter was not, however, put to the vote again and the decision already taken remained.

[The subsequent history of this affair can be briefly told. Ultimately, Prince Edward Island refused to enter the Union, and hence section 146 was inserted in the British North America Act, providing that " it shall be lawful for the Queen, by and with the advice of Her Majesty's Most Honourable Privy Council, on addresses from the Houses of the Parliament of Canada and from the Houses of the respective legislatures of the colonies or provinces of Newfoundland, Prince Edward Island and British Columbia, to admit those colonies or provinces or any of them into the Union etc. on such terms and conditions in each case as are in the addresses expressed and as the Queen thinks fit to approve, subject to the provisions of this Act etc." In 1873, forced by financial circumstances, Prince Edward Island sought and obtained admission into the Dominion with a representation of six members in the House of Commons on the ground that its population had increased since the census of 1861.]

Two points are clear from this brief account:

(1) There was complete freedom of discussion at the Conference, the delegates from the same province often taking opposite sides.

(2) The Conference was most anxious to obtain the concurrence of every unit, however small.

AUSTRALIA—At the Australian Convention, which framed the Commonwealth Act, the voting was not by States; but, as against this, it must be noted that each of the States, large or small, had the same number of delegates, ten. There were in all five States at the Convention, two of them (New South Wales and Victoria) large, and the other three small in point of population. Thus, on the whole, the representatives of the smaller States were in a majority. The following extract from *The Annotated Constitution of the Australian Commonwealth* by Quick & Garran (*p.* 172) will serve to show that although at first the majority were inclined to rely merely on their numbers, ultimately a more accommodating spirit prevailed:

" Then, on the 13th April (1897), commenced the last great debate on the money Bill clauses—a debate which, though it occupied but two days, was certainly the most momentous in the Convention's whole history.   It established the recognition by the Convention of the fact that it was a negotiating, and not a legislative, body;   that the decision of a majority of representatives within that Chamber went for nothing unless it were a decision which was acceptable to the people of all the colonies.   Had that fact and its consequences not been recognised, the present prospects of federation must have been wrecked, and at the outset there seemed some danger that this might happen.   Sir John Forrest, for the small States, announced cheerfully and often that ' we have a majority '; and it seemed for a time that the equal representation of the colonies in the Convention—a necessary principle in an assemblage of contracting States—would exercise an undue influence on the form of the constitution.   The recognition of the fact that they must defer to the wishes of majorities outside marked the turning point of the Convention, and the entry of the really federal spirit of compromise—a spirit which thenceforward grew, slowly and steadily, through all the sittings of the Convention, and spread from the Convention to the people."

SOUTH AFRICA—In the South African Convention, the provinces were not equally represented, nor did they vote as single units; it must, however, be remembered that the Union of South Africa is not a federation, but a legislative

Union in which the provinces can hardly be said to be autonomous.

Can we adopt this mode of voting (according to which each province votes as a single unit) in our Constituent Assembly, whether at the Union level or in the sections? There will be certain difficulties: first of all, what about the Indian States? Will each of them, large or small, also vote as a single unit? If so, they will swamp the British Indian vote. There will be a similar difficulty, though not of the same order, in respect of the Chief Commissioners' provinces. These difficulties are not insuperable. For example, some such modified rule as the following may be adopted:

" (1) On all questions relating to the provisions of the new constitution on which a division is challenged, the votes of the representatives of the provinces shall be recorded province-wise in the division lists and of the Indian States in a separate group; and the Chairman in announcing the result of the division shall announce separately—

(a) the total number of Ayes and Noes in the ordinary way, and

(b) the total number of Ayes and Noes among the Governors' provinces, each such province being counted as a single unit—affirmative, negative, or neutral—according to the result of the division within the province.

(2) No such question shall be decided without a majority both of (a) and (b)."

This is to be without prejudice to paragraph 19 (vii) of the Cabinet Delegation's statement.

The reason for special treatment of Governors' provinces is—

(1) that unlike Indian States they have no option but to be in the Federal Union, and

(2) that unlike the Chief Commissioners' provinces they are for the most part to be autonomous.

There are other solutions possible which it is unnecessary to detail here.

4

FRAMING OF THE CONSTITUTION

(In two or more stages with an interval for criticism)

CANADA—The Canadian Constitution was in effect framed in two stages with an interval for provincial criticism. The resolutions of the Quebec Conference, 72 in number, were passed between October 10 and October 29, 1864. They were then submitted to the several provincial governments with a view to their being brought before the respective legislatures for acceptance. The result proved a great disappointment to the advocates of Federation. Only the legislature of one of the provinces, Canada, accepted the resolutions. The Prince Edward Island legislature openly repudiated its own delegates. All that the legislatures of Nova Scotia and New Brunswick could be induced to do was to agree to appoint new delegates " to arrange with the Imperial Government a scheme of Union which would effectually ensure just provision for the rights and interests of the provinces, each province to have an equal voice in such delegation, Upper and Lower Canada being for this purpose considered as separate provinces ". The New Brunswick legislature asked in addition for a provision for the immediate construction of the inter-colonial railway. Newfoundland definitely refused to come into the Union and is still outside. In December 1866, the new delegates of Canada, Nova Scotia and New Brunswick met at the Westminster Palace Hotel in London and reconsidered the Quebec resolutions. Certain modifications were found necessary to make them more acceptable to the several provinces. The 69 modified resolutions formed the basis of the British North America Act. In effect, therefore, the draft was prepared in two stages, first at the Quebec Conference in 1864 and then at the Westminster Palace Hotel Conference in 1866, with an interval for criticism by the provincial legislatures.

AUSTRALIA AND SOUTH AFRICA—In Australia and South Africa, the same plan was deliberately adopted from the very start. The Australian Convention first met at Adelaide on March 23, 1897. The proceedings lasted a little more than a month and at the end a Bill was settled, which, though it did not represent the unanimous voice of the delegates, at least bore witness to a gradual rapprochement among them which promised well for the future. The next session was held at Sydney in September 1897. During the interval the Bill was considered in the various State Parliaments. The last session was held at Melbourne between January 20, 1898 and March 17, 1898 from which the Bill emerged in its final shape. Thus, ample time was given to the several States to criticise the first draft before the final form of the Bill was settled.

Similarly, in South Africa the Convention held its first session at Durban in October 1908 and then adjourned to Cape Town where it completed the first draft by the end of the first week of February 1909. The Bill was then submitted to the parliaments of the four colonies for approval. The final session was held at Bloemfontein which considered the various amendments proposed by the several parliaments; by June 1909, the new constitution had been accepted by all the four colonies.

––––––––––

These precedents show another way in which provincial co-operation can be secured: the drafting of the constitution must be done in two or more stages with an interval for criticism in the various provinces.

FIRST DRAFT OF PROVINCIAL CONSTITUTIONS

(By provincial committees)

So far as India is concerned, yet another way which suggests itself is that the initial drafting of the provincial constitutions should, where possible, be entrusted to committees of the sections consisting only of representatives of the particular province concerned. The draft can then be considered by the section as a whole. Thus, the provincial constitution for Assam may first be drafted by the Assam representatives in section ' C ' and, after an interval for criticism by the Assam legislature, the section as a whole may consider the draft and settle the final form of the Bill.

II. Choice of the Chairman

The Convention that framed the Constitution of the United States met in Philadelphia on May 25, 1787. Its first duty was to choose a presiding officer.

" As President of the State in whose capital the Convention was meeting, as well as by virtue of his age and reputation, Franklin might have considered himself entitled to that honour. But when the session opened on the morning of the twenty-fifth with a majority of the States in attendance, Robert Morris on behalf of the Pennsylvania delegation formally proposed George Washington for President. Franklin himself was to have made the nomination, but as the weather was stormy he had not dared to venture out. No other names were offered, and the Convention proceeded at once, but formally, to ballot upon the nomination. Washington was declared to be unanimously elected, and was formally conducted to the chair by Robert Morris and John Rutledge." (*The Framing of the Constitution* by Farrand, *p.* 55.)

It must be remembered that Benjamin Franklin was at that time a very old man, 81 years of age, so feeble that all his speeches had to be read for him by his colleague, Wilson. Though highly respected, he does not appear to have taken a very prominent part in the proceedings except for a memorable observation which he made at the end while the last members were signing the completed constitution.

" Dr. Franklin, looking towards the President's chair, at the back of which a rising sun happened to be painted, observed to a few members near him that the painters had found it difficult to distinguish in their art a rising from a setting sun. I have, said he, often and often in the course of the session, and the vicissitudes of my hopes and fears as to its issue, looked at that behind the President without being able to tell whether it was rising or setting. But now at length I have the happiness to know that it is a rising and not a setting sun." (Farrand, *op. cit., p.* 194.)

George Washington, who was chosen President, was 55 years of age at the time and at the height of his popularity. The successful outcome of the Revolution had silenced all criticism of his conduct of the war and his retirement to Mount Vernon had appealed to the popular imagination. The feeling towards him was one of devotion, almost of awe and reverence. Of his part in the making of the constitution Farrand writes:

" The parts which were taken by various men in the debates of the Convention will be partially brought out in describing the proceedings, but it seems worth while to notice one man who took no part in the discussions but whose influence is believed to have been important. That man was George Washington, the presiding officer of the Convention. His commanding presence and the respect amounting almost to awe which he inspired must have carried weight, especially in so small a gathering in the ' long-room ' with the President sitting on a raised platform." (Farrand, *op. cit., p.* 64.)

A striking instance of Washington's personal influence may be found in an incident which occurred towards the close of the Convention. Just before the question was to be put, upon the adoption of the completed constitution, one of the delegates said that if it was not too late, he would like to see the ratio of representation in the Lower House of the Congress changed from one for every 40,000 inhabitants to one for every 30,000 inhabitants. This suggestion had been made at an earlier stage in the Convention and had been rejected. Nevertheless, when Washington rose to put the question, he said that although he recognised the impropriety of his speaking from the chair, he felt this amendment to be of such consequence that " he could not forbear expressing his wish that the alteration proposed might take place ". Not a single objection was made and the change was then unanimously agreed to.

CANADA—The Quebec Conference met in what was then a part of the province of Canada. The Prime Minister of Canada, Sir Etienne Pascal Taché, aged 69, was elected Chairman, being proposed by Gray (Prince Edward Island) and seconded by Tilley (New Brunswick).

AUSTRALIA—Unlike the Philadelphia Convention and the Quebec Conference, the Australian Convention held its sessions in public and we have therefore a full record of what took place. The first session was held in Parliament House, Adelaide, South Australia, on Monday, March 22, 1897. The delegates met in the House of Assembly Chamber at Parliament House, Adelaide. The Clerk of the Legislative Council of Adelaide read out the various proclamations relating to the meeting of the Convention and the certificates of appointment of the representatives to the Convention for the various States. He then requested the delegates to attend at the table and sign the roll. Thereafter, Sir Joseph Abbot, a delegate from New South Wales, proposed Mr. Kingston, Premier of South Australia, for the office of President in the following terms: " It is a very pleasing duty to me to follow what has been the established precedent in reference to these Conventions. For many years past in the colonies in which they have been held, invariably the Premiers of the colonies have been chosen to preside over the meetings of the Conventions, and that is a rule there is no justification in departing from on the present occasion." Sir Graham Berry, a delegate from Victoria, seconded the nomination: " Following the precedents which have always prevailed in the Australian colonies, that the Premier of the colony in which the Convention is being held shall preside, I think the motion will be unanimously carried and that Mr. Kingston's election will meet with the approval of the delegates." There was no other nomination and accordingly Mr. Kingston was elected President.

SOUTH AFRICA—The South African Convention held its first session in Durban (Natal) on October 12, 1908. Lord (then Sir Henry) de Villiers, Chief Justice of the Cape Colony, was chosen President and ex-President Steyn of the Orange River Colony was elected Vice-President. The Chairman had the right of speaking and voting and in the event of an equality of votes he had a casting vote. In acknowledging the honour conferred upon him, he said, among other things: " Failure is certain if we start with a feeling of distrust and suspicion of each other and with the sole desire to secure as many advantages as we can for our respective political parties or our respective colonies. Success is certain if we give each other our fullest confidence and act upon the principle that, while not neglectful of the interests of those who have sent us here, we are for the time being representatives of the whole of British South Africa." (*The Inner History of the National Convention of South Africa* by Walton, *p.* 40).

III. Language to be used

The question of language arose in an acute form in the South African Convention. It was found that though all the members could follow speeches in the English language, some found a difficulty in expressing themselves in any tongue but Dutch. It was therefore arranged that Dr. Bok, the Secretary to the Prime Minister, should attend the meetings and act as interpreter. General Botha spoke almost invariably in Dutch and so did several other delegates, while some of the bilingual speakers used either the one language or the other. Whenever Dr. Bok's services were requisitioned, the speech took twice as long to deliver as when spoken in English. However, there was the best possible understanding among the members on this subject throughout the whole of the sittings and no difficulty whatever was experienced. (Walton, *op. cit.,* *pp.* 37, 38).

IV. Whether Sessions should be open or in camera

U.S.A.—The sessions of the Philadelphia Convention of 1787, which framed the Constitution of the U.S.A., were strictly secret and sentries were planted without and within the building to prevent any person from coming near. The Convention also adopted a rule that " nothing spoken in the House be printed or otherwise published or communicated without leave ". There were of course many rumours current as to what was being done in the Convention and at one stage, when serious differences of opinion threatened to disrupt the Assembly, the following inspired item of news appeared in the press: " So great is the unanimity, we hear, that prevails in the Convention upon all great federal subjects that it has been proposed to call the room in which they assemble— ' Unanimity Hall '." It is related that on one occasion quite early in the proceedings one of the members dropped his copy of the agenda on the floor and it was picked up by another delegate and handed to the President, General Washington. After the day's debate, the President rose from his seat and reprimanded the member for his carelessness: " I must entreat gentlemen to be more careful, lest our transactions get into the newspapers and disturb the public repose by premature speculations. I know not whose paper it is, but there it is (throwing it down on the table), let him who owns it take it." He then bowed and quitted the room. None dared to own the paper.

The reason for adopting this rule of secrecy was that any publication of the opinions of members " would be an obstacle to a change of them on conviction and might furnish handles to the adversaries of the result of the meeting ".

CANADA—At the Quebec Conference which framed the basis of the Canadian Constitution, correspondents representing Canadian, British and American newspapers submitted a memorial asking for facilities to report the proceedings. The Secretary to the Conference told them in reply:

" Whilst the members of the Conference fully appreciate the motives by which you are actuated in your communication, and are equally sensible of the deep interest naturally felt by the people of the several British North American provinces in the objects of the Conference, they cannot but feel that it is inexpedient, at the present stage of the proceedings, to furnish information which must, of necessity, be incomplete; and that no communication of their proceedings can properly be made until they are enabled definitely to report the issue of their deliberations to the governments of the respective provinces." (Pope's *Confederation Documents, p.* 11).

AUSTRALIA—On the first day of the Adelaide session, one of the members gave notice of a motion that the proceedings of the Convention be open to the public except when otherwise ordered. The motion was taken up the next day and the speeches made are reproduced below:

" Mr. Holder: I move:

That the proceedings of the Convention be open to the public except when otherwise ordered.

I submit this motion, feeling assured that every member of the Convention will wish the proceedings to be as public as possible. We should take the public into our confidence at the earliest possible moment, and, while availing ourselves of the other powers in this Convention, the educative influences that will be exercised by admitting the public to this Convention will be largely promoted.

Sir Richard Baker: I second the motion.

Sir George Turner: I desire to ask whether the proceedings of the Convention will include the Convention in Committee.

Mr. Barton: Select Committee?

Sir George Turner: No; I understand that in Select Committee it would be desirable that we should discuss matters in private; but what I desire to make clear is whether, when the Convention goes into Committee, the proceedings of the Committee as a whole should be open to the public. I think that should be so; and I wish to know if the words are sufficiently wide. If they are I shall be perfectly satisfied.

The President: I take it that the words are sufficiently wide for the Committee of the whole, but not for Select Committees.

Question resolved in the affirmative." (Official Report of the National Australian Convention Debates, Adelaide, 1897, *p.* 8).

[Of an earlier Convention at Sydney in 1891, which also decided to hold its meetings in public, Egerton remarks:

" Rightly or wrongly—rightly from the point of view of future edification, perhaps wrongly in the interests of the swift dispatch of business—it was decided that the Convention should sit with open doors, though the actual work of drafting was done informally by sub-committees."]

SOUTH AFRICA—The South African Convention copied the U.S.A. and Canadian precedents rather than the Australian.

" Unlike its Australian predecessors, the (South African) Convention sat in secret, and therefore no reference to its proceedings can be made without a breach of confidence. It is impossible to doubt the wisdom of this procedure. The questions handled were so delicate, and the feeling upon them throughout the country so divided and so acute, that it is not conceivable that an agreement could have been reached in public. It is well known that, on more occasions than one, feeling in the Convention itself ran high. Its work was only brought to a successful issue because no appeal to the gallery was possible. The public was brought to recognise that the result must in any case be a delicately balanced equipoise and, instead of being daily inflamed, was content to wait and pass a final judgment on the completed work. Thus the men who represented it were emboldened to act calmly and with courage, and with a due sense, not only of the immediate present, but of their responsibility towards future generations. As it was, and as must no doubt always be the case in such matters, much was settled outside the Convention itself. Compromises that seemed impossible in the formal atmosphere of the Convention room settled themselves sooner or later through the medium of personal influences. This process of gradual solution, which was incessant throughout the Convention, would have been impossible in the glare of publicity." (*The Union of South Africa* by Brand, *pp.* 39-40).

V. Resignation of members, controverted elections and filling of casual vacancies

There is no provision in the Cabinet Delegation's statement of May 16, 1946 as to the manner in which a member of the Constituent Assembly may resign his seat or the circumstances or manner in which an election may be challenged or the manner in which a vacancy arising from death, resignation or other cause is to be filled. It cannot be assumed that members have an inherent right of resignation: for example, a member of the House of Commons in England has no such right, although in certain circumstances, prescribed by law, his seat is vacated. It may well be that until there is some rule providing for resignation or vacation of seat, a member once elected to the Constituent Assembly continues as such. Moreover, as the Constituent Assembly is an extra-legal body and its resolutions do not immediately affect any legal rights, it is not certain that the ordinary courts of law will have jurisdiction to entertain election disputes. It may be mentioned that the House of Commons provides for its own proper constitution, whether in the matter of filling vacancies, or determining election disputes outside the jurisdiction of the courts, or determining the right of its members to sit and vote in cases of doubt. In all these matters, therefore, the Constituent Assembly will have to make its own rules to fill any gaps.

VI. Grouping

It has sometimes been contended that freedom to opt out of a group already formed is not the same thing as freedom to

form a group and that there is therefore a conflict between
what is recommended in paragraph 15 (v) of the Cabinet
Delegation's statement of May 16, 1946 and what is granted
in paragraph 19 (v) and (viii). The conflict, if any, is of a
kind that can be reduced or removed, *inter alia*, by suitable
drafting technique. For example, the new constitution, like
the Government of India Act of 1935, may be framed in
parts: one part, say Part I, setting out the provincial con-.
stitutions, another part, say Part II, setting out the group
constitutions, and so on. As under the Government of India
Act of 1935, the several parts need not come into force
on the same date; it may be provided that Part I shall
come into force first and that Part II shall not come into force
as regards any particular province, until the legislative
assembly of that province formed after the first general election held under Part I has by resolution accepted Part II.
An affirmative resolution would mean that the province agrees
to form the proposed group; a negative resolution would be
equivalent to opting out of the proposed group. On this plan,
therefore, freedom to form a group as well as freedom to opt
out according to the Cabinet Delegation's statement is, in
effect, secured to each province. There may be other plans
possible, *e.g.*, those suggested under the heading "provincial
co-operation" above; all these are matters of procedure to
be discussed in due course.

VII. Interpretation

The Cabinet Delegation's statement of May 16, 1946 was
not drafted with the fulness or precision of a statute. But it
has come to be looked upon as a kind of fundamental law and
questions of interpretation of various words or phrases used in
the document are bound to arise from time to time in the
Constituent Assembly. In the House of Commons, there is an
officer known as the Speaker's Counsel to assist the Speaker

and the House generally in legal and quasi-judicial matters. On this analogy, the Constituent Assembly may have a special officer or tribunal of its own to assist in questions of interpretation or, if it thinks fit and if the judges of the Federal Court agree, may refer any such questions to the judges for an advisory opinion.

VIII. General Procedure

As regards general procedure, the Australian Convention adopted the standing orders and practice of the South Australian Assembly. Following this precedent, the Constituent Assembly may adopt, with suitable modifications, the rules and standing orders of the Indian Legislative Assembly.

5

MEMORANDUM
ON THE UNION CONSTITUTION

[*This memorandum was prepared by Sri B. N. Rau for the consideration of the Committee set up pursuant to a resolution passed by the Constituent Assembly on April 30, 1947, to report on the main principles of the Union constitution. Copies of the questionnaire, which had been earlier circulated to members of the Central and provincial legislatures, were circulated to members of this Committee. Only one member of the Committee (out of 15) sent replies to the questionnaire. Another member sent in a memorandum embodying general directives as well as a draft constitution. It was not, therefore, found possible to prepare a memorandum embodying what may be called the greatest common measure of the views of the several members. In these circumstances, Sri B. N. Rau prepared an independent memorandum together with a detailed draft of as many of the proposed provisions of the Union constitution as could usefully be drafted at that stage and submitted it on May 30, 1947.*]

WE, the people of India, seeking to promote the common good, do hereby, through our chosen representatives, enact, adopt and give to ourselves this constitution.

Preamble

PART I

UNION TERRITORY AND JURISDICTION

1. The Union hereby established shall be a sovereign independent State known as the Union of India

Name and territory of Union

and shall embrace all the territories included in India under the Government of India Act, 1935; but save as otherwise provided by or under treaty or agreement, only the territories included for the time being in schedule I shall be subject to the jurisdiction of the Union.

[*Note:* The first part of this clause proceeds on the basis of the Cabinet Mission's plan of May 16, 1946, according to which there should be a Union of India embracing both British India and the States. The second part is necessitated by the subsequent modification of that plan, according to which the constitution is not to be forced upon " unwilling parts of the country ". Schedule I, in its initial form, is intended to specify the " willing parts " at the date of the coming into operation of the constitution. If any other territories elect to come within Union jurisdiction later, the schedule is to be modified accordingly (see the next clause). The clause may be compared with articles 2 and 3 of the Constitution of Ireland. The parts of India not specified in the schedule are *in* the Union, but not *of* it.]

2. The Parliament of the Union may from time to time by

Admission of new territories

Act include new territories in schedule I upon such terms as it thinks fit.

3. The Parliament of the Union may by Act, with the consent of the legislature of every province

Creation of new provinces and alteration of provincial boundaries

affected thereby—

    (*a*) create a new province;

    (*b*) increase the area of any province;

    (*c*) diminish the area of any province;

    (*d*) alter the boundaries of any province;

and may with the like consent make such incidental and consequential provisions as it may deem necessary or proper.

4. The authorities established by or under this constitution

Jurisdiction in the scheduled territories shall succeed to the jurisdiction and powers of His Majesty in the scheduled provinces; and to the powers and jurisdiction of the Ruler in each scheduled State to the extent to which he has ceded them.

SCHEDULE I

TERRITORIES SUBJECT TO THE JURISDICTION OF THE UNION

I. *Governors' Provinces*
    Madras
    Bombay
    Bengal or West Bengal (?)
    The United Provinces
    Bihar
    The Panjab or East Panjab (?)
    The Central Provinces (and Berar?)
    Assam (*minus* Sylhet?)
    N.W.F. Province (?)
    Orissa
    Sind (?)

II. *Chief Commissioners' Provinces*
    Delhi
    British Baluchistan (?)
    Ajmer-Merwara
    Coorg
    The Andaman & Nicobar Islands
    Panth Piploda

III. *Indian States*
    [Here enumerate the acceding Indian States:
      (1) Single States (2) Groups of States]

PART II

CITIZENSHIP

1. At the date of commencement of this constitution—

Citizenship   every person domiciled in the territories included within the Union and subject to its jurisdiction—

   (*a*) who has been ordinarily resident in those territories for not less than five years immediately preceding that date, or

   (*b*) who, or whose parents, or either of whose parents, was or were born in India—

shall be a citizen of the Union:

Provided that any such person being a citizen of any other State may, in accordance with Union law, elect not to accept the citizenship hereby conferred.

2. After the commencement of this constitution—

   (*a*) every person who is born in the territories included within the Union and subject to its jurisdiction,

   (*b*) every person who is naturalised in accordance with Union law, and

   (*c*) every person, either of whose parents was, at the time of such person's birth, a citizen of the Union,

shall be a citizen of the Union.

3. Further provisions governing the acquisition and termination of Union citizenship may be made by Union law.

[*Note: Cf.* art. 3 of the Constitution of the Irish Free State (1922) which runs—

   " *Every person, without distinction of sex, domiciled in the area of the jurisdiction of the Irish Free State at the time of the coming into operation of this constitution, who was born in Ireland or either of whose parents was born in Ireland, or who has been ordinarily resident in the area of the jurisdiction of the Irish Free State for not less than seven years, is a citizen of the Irish Free State and shall, within the limits of the jurisdiction of the Irish*

5

Free State, enjoy the privileges and be subject to the obligations of such citizenship: Provided that any such person being a citizen of another State may elect not to accept the citizenship hereby conferred; and the conditions governing the future acquisition and termination of citizenship in the Irish Free State shall be determined by law."

Sub-clause (1) is on the lines of the above provision, except that a period of five years has been substituted for seven years in accordance with s. 3 (1) (c) of the Indian Naturalisation Act VII of 1926.

The sub-clause has had to be drafted with due regard to the possibility that, initially at least, the Union may not exercise jurisdiction over the whole of India.

A person born in India and domiciled in Bombay, who happens to be resident in London at the commencement of the new constitution, will be a citizen of the Union under this sub-clause; but not one domiciled in Baluchistan, if the Union does not initially exercise jurisdiction there.

Sub-clause (2) follows the provision suggested by the *ad hoc* Committee; it is not absolutely necessary, if we are content to leave the matter to Union law under sub-clause (3)].

PART III

FUNDAMENTAL RIGHTS INCLUDING DIRECTIVE PRINCIPLES OF STATE POLICY

Fundamental Rights

[Here enumerate fundamental rights and principles of State policy as passed by the Constituent Assembly.]

PART IV

CHAPTER I

THE UNION EXECUTIVE

Head of the Union

1. The head of the Union shall be the President, to be elected by the two Houses of the Union Parliament at a joint session by secret ballot, according to the system of proportional representation by the single transferable vote.

[*Note*: Since the President, under the proposed constitution, is intended merely to be a constitutional head, it seems unnecessary to provide for his election by direct vote of the people of the Union. Such an elaborate process might be appropriate for an all-powerful head like the President of the U.S.A. For a responsible head, we may content ourselves with the Swiss or French plan of election by the two Houses of the legislature.]

2. (1) The President shall hold office for five years, except in the event of death, resignation or removal.

Term of office

(2) The President may be removed from office for misbehaviour or infirmity of mind or body by a resolution of each of the two Houses of the Union Parliament supported by not less than two-thirds of the total membership of each House.

Removal from office

(3) The President shall be eligible for re-election once, but only once.

[*Note*: Since under this constitution it is proposed that the maximum term of the House of Representatives is to be five years and the President is to be elected by both Houses, the President's term of office has also been fixed at five years.

In the U.S.A., the President is removable from office on impeachment for, and conviction of, treason, bribery or other high crimes and misdemeanours. The House of Representatives has the sole power of impeachment and the Senate has the sole power to try all impeachments. There can be no conviction without the concurrence of at least two-thirds of the members of the Senate present. In Ireland, the President may be impeached for stated misbehaviour; the charge can be preferred by either House of Parliament, but requires the support of not less than two-thirds of the total membership of the House concerned. The other House investigates the charge; a conviction requires the support of not less than two-thirds of the total membership of the investigating House. The resolution embodying the conviction operates to remove the President from his office. Sub-clauses (1) and (2) are based on the U.S.A. and Irish precedents (omitting the impeachment procedure); subclause (3) is taken from the Irish Constitution.]

3. Every citizen of the Union who has reached his 35th *Age qualification* year of age shall be eligible for election as President.

[*Note*: This is taken from the Irish Constitution.]

4. The President shall not be a member of either House of *President not to be a member of either House* the Union Parliament and if a member of either House be elected President, he shall be deemed to have vacated his seat in that House.

5. Appropriate provision should be made for bye-elections *Provision for bye-elections* in the event of a casual vacancy, the detailed procedure for elections and bye-elections being left to be regulated by Act of the Union Parliament.

6. (1) In the event of the absence of the President or of *Commission to discharge President's functions in certain events* his death, resignation, removal from office or incapacity or failure to discharge his functions, his functions shall be discharged by a Commission consisting of—

> (i) the Chief Justice of the Supreme Court;
>
> (ii) the Chairman of the Senate; and
>
> (iii) the Speaker of the House of Representatives.

(2) The Council of State may, by a majority of its members, make such provision as they think fit for the discharge of the functions of the President in any unforeseen contingency.

[*Note*: In the U.S.A., there is a Vice-President who is elected in the same way as the President. The Vice-President automatically becomes the President upon the President's death or resignation or removal from office and, meanwhile, he functions *ex-officio* as the President of the Senate. If we were to adopt a similar plan under this constitution, we should have to say that the two Houses of the Union Parliament sitting together must elect a President and a Vice-President, the Vice-President then becoming the *ex-officio* Chairman of the Senate. This would mean that the Chairman of the Senate is to be elected by the two Houses in joint session, which seems inappropriate. Nor would it be appropriate to adopt the reverse plan and to make the Chairman of the Senate *ex-officio* Vice-President, considering that the President is the choice of both Houses sitting together. Moreover, in an executive of the parliamentary type, there is hardly any room for a Vice-President between the President and the Prime Minister. In these circumstances, the best course would appear to be to copy the Irish plan of having a Commission instead of a Vice-President to discharge the President's functions during a casual vacancy. This is what has been done in the draft.

It will be noticed that there is a reference to the " Council of State " in sub-clause (2). This institution also has been borrowed from the Irish Constitution. It is a kind of Privy Council to aid and advise the President on matters of national importance in the decision of which any party bias has to be avoided. The Council of State consists of the Prime Minister, the Deputy Prime Minister, the Chief Justice of the Union, the Speaker of the House of Representatives, the Chairman of the Senate, the Advocate-General, every ex-President, every ex-Prime Minister, every ex-Chief Justice and a limited number of other persons to be appointed by the President in his absolute discretion. It is a non-party Council of elder statesmen including judges. Such a Council may be found useful in India in such matters as the protection of minorities, the supervision, direction and control of elections and the appointment of judges of the Supreme Court and the High Courts.]

7. Subject to the provisions of this constitution, the execu-
Functions of President tive authority of the Union shall be exercised by the President; but this shall not prevent the Union Parliament from conferring functions upon any court, judge or officer or any local or other authority.

8. Subject to the provisions of this constitution, the execu-
Extent of executive authority of the Union tive authority of the Union shall extend to the matters with respect to which the Union Parliament has power to make laws and to any other matters with respect to which authority has been conferred on the Union by any treaty or agreement.

9. The executive authority of the Ruler of a scheduled State shall continue to be exercisable in that State even with

respect to Union subjects, save as taken away by Union law.

[*Note*: Like the corresponding provision in section 8(2) of the Government of India Act of 1935, this clause gives the Rulers of Indian States, who have acceded to the Union, concurrent executive power even in Union subjects, save as taken away by Union law. In this respect, the position of the provincial units is rather different: they have no executive power in respect of Union subjects save as given by Union law. Such a provision is necessary; for, otherwise, all statutory powers in respect of Union subjects will come to an end in the acceding States upon the commencement of this constitution.]

10. There shall be a Council of Ministers, with the Prime Minister at the head, to aid and advise the President in the exercise of his functions, except in so far as he is required by this constitution to act in his discretion.

Administration of Union affairs

[*Note*: Although under responsible government the head of the State acts for the most part on the advice of ministers responsible to the legislature, nevertheless there are certain matters in which he is entitled to exercise his own discretion: *e.g.*, (in certain events) in the choice of a Prime Minister and in the dissolution of Parliament. In India, such matters as the appointment of judges, the protection of minorities and the suppression of widespread disorder may properly be added to the list. Of course, it may not be always possible for the President to use his " discretionary " powers. Thus a Ministry may threaten to resign if in the exercise of " discretionary " power, he overrules them; in that case, the President can do so only if he has the support of the legislature and can get an alternative Ministry enjoying its confidence. Failing this, he can dissolve the legislature and appeal to the electorate in an extreme case. Thus the " discretionary " powers will at least give the President a chance of appealing to the legislature and, in the last resort, to the people.]

11. There shall be a Council of State whose advice shall be available to the President in all matters in which he is required to act in his discretion.

[See note under clause 6(2).]

12. The relations between the President and the Council of Ministers shall, as far as possible, be the same as between the King and his ministers in England.

Conventions of responsible government to be observed

13. (1) In the exercise of his functions, the President shall have the following special responsibilities: that is to say,

Special responsibilities of President

(a) the prevention of any grave menace to the peace or tranquillity of the Union or any part thereof;

(b) the safeguarding of the financial stability and credit of the Union Government;

(c) the safeguarding of the legitimate interests of minorities.

(2) Where any special responsibility of the President is involved, he shall exercise his discretion as to the action to be taken.

[*Note*: The matters referred to in this clause may be regarded as matters of national importance in the decision of which any party bias has to be avoided. The President is therefore enjoined in these matters to act in his discretion and will have available to him the advice of the Council of State.]

14. The President shall appoint a person, being one qualified to be appointed a judge of the Supreme Court, to be Advocate-General for the Union, to give advice to the Union Government upon legal matters that may be referred to him.

Advocate-General for the Union

15. (1) The executive action of the Union Government shall be expressed to be taken in the name of the President.

Conduct of business of the Union Government

(2) The President shall make rules of business providing, amongst other things, for the allocation of duties among his ministers.

CHAPTER II

THE COUNCIL OF STATE

16. There shall be a Council of State whom the President

Council of State   may consult on all matters in which he is
required by this constitution to act in his
discretion.

17. The Council of State shall consist of the following

Composition   members:

(1) *Ex-officio* members: the Prime Minister, the Deputy
Prime Minister, if any, the Chief Justice of the
Supreme Court, the Speaker of the House of Repre-
sentatives, the Chairman of the Senate and the
Advocate-General.

(2) Every person able and willing to act as a member,
who shall have held the office of President, or the
office of Prime Minister, or the office of Chief
Justice of the Supreme Court.

(3) Such other persons, if any, as may be appointed by
the President to be members.

18. The President may at any time, by warrant under his

hand and seal, appoint such other persons as
Appointment by President   in his discretion he may think fit to be
members of the Council of State, but not
more than seven persons so appointed shall be members of
the Council of State at the same time.

19. Every member of the Council of State appointed by the

President, unless he previously dies, resigns,
Term of office   becomes permanently incapacitated or is
removed from office, shall hold office until the successor of the
President by whom he was appointed shall have entered upon
his office.

20. Any member of the Council of State appointed by the

President may resign from office by writing
Resignation   under his hand addressed to the President.

21. The President may, for reasons which to him seem sufficient, by an order under his hand and seal, terminate the appointment of any member of the Council of State appointed by him.

Termination by President of appointments made by him

22. Meetings of the Council of State may be convened by the President at such times and places as he shall determine.

Meetings

[*Note*: These provisions have been adapted from the Irish Constitution. As already pointed out, the Council of State is a sort of Privy Council whose advice shall be available to the President whenever he chooses to obtain it in all matters of national importance in which he is required to act in his discretion. An institution of this kind may be useful in India in such matters as the appointment of judges, the protection of minorities and the superintendence, direction and control of elections. It may be pointed out that the impartial delimitation of constituencies and the readjustment of representation after every census are regarded as so important that in South Africa it is entrusted to a Commission consisting of three judges of the Supreme Court. In Canada, the members of the Opposition are associated with the members of the government in this matter so as to prevent gerrymandering. Clearly, therefore, an agency free from party bias is required for this purpose. Dr. Ambedkar was very particular that the superintendence, direction and control of all elections should be vested in a non-party Commission.]

CHAPTER III

THE UNION PARLIAMENT

23. The legislative power of the Union shall be vested in the Parliament of the Union which shall consist of the President and two Houses, the Senate and the House of Representatives.

Constitution of the Union Parliament

24. (1) (*a*) The Senate * shall consist of not more than 168 representatives of the provinces and not more than 112 representatives of the Indian States;

---

* For detailed allocation of seats in the Senate, see Table of Seats at the end of this chapter.

(*b*) The House of Representatives shall consist of representatives of the provinces and of the Indian States or groups of States (as the case may be) included in schedule I in the proportion of not less than one representative for every million of the population and not more than one representative for every 750 thousands of the population.

The ratio between the number of members to be elected at any time for each constituency and the population of that constituency, as ascertained at the last preceding census shall, so far as it is practicable, be the same throughout the territories subject to the jurisdiction of the Union.

(2) The said representatives shall be chosen in accordance with the provisions in that behalf contained in schedule—.

(3) Upon the completion of each decennial census, the representation of the several provinces and Indian States or groups of Indian States in the House of Representatives shall be readjusted by such authority, in such manner and from such time as the Union Parliament may by Act determine:

Provided that such readjustment shall not take effect until the dissolution of the then existing House of Representatives.

(4) The Senate shall be a permanent body not subject to dissolution, but as near as may be one-third of the members thereof shall retire in every third year in accordance with the provisions in that behalf contained in schedule—.

(5) Every House of Representatives, unless sooner dissolved, shall continue for five years from the date appointed for its first meeting and no longer, and the expiration of the said period of five years shall operate as a dissolution of the House of Representatives.

[*Note*: In all the principal federations of the world, the Lower House is elected on a population basis, the precise proportion of the number of representatives to the population varying from federation to federation. The composition of the House of Representatives proposed above follows that of the Constituent

Assembly. The composition of the Senate follows, as far as possible, that of the Council of State in the Government of India Act of 1935. The Council of State under that Act consists of 156 representatives of British India *plus* not more than 104 representatives of the Indian States. These figures are in the proportion of 3 : 2. Retaining the quantum of representation given to the several States or groups of States in the Act, with slight readjustments (so as to fit the new groups adopted for the Constituent Assembly), we find that the maximum number of representatives for the Indian States is 112; proportionately, the maximum number of representatives for the provinces should be 168. Under this plan, therefore, the maximum strength of the Senate is 280 and that of the House of Representatives (on the census of 1941) is 389. The corresponding figures under the Government of India Act of 1935 are 260 and 375, which are roughly in the same proportion.

Whether there should be an Upper House at all and, if so, on what principles it should be constructed, are fundamental questions which always arouse keen controversy. The above draft merely follows the Government of India Act of 1935 as being perhaps the line of least resistance. I have not attempted to give all the units equal representation in the Senate, because under present conditions this might mean that the provincial representatives, or to use a convenient term, the British Indian representatives, would be swamped by the representatives of the States. It should be remembered that there are 35 potential Indian States units in the Union and at present there are only 11 British Indian units excluding Chief Commissioners' provinces. It might be possible to differentiate between the units by providing that a unit without responsible government should have, say, three representatives in the Senate, while a unit with responsible government should be represented, say, by 15 representatives. It is doubtful whether such a scheme would be acceptable. An alternative which might be worth considering is a Senate with functional representation as in Ireland.]

25. The provisions for the summoning, prorogation and dissolution of Parliament, the relations between the two Houses, the mode of voting, the privileges of members, disqualifications for membership, parliamentary procedure, including procedure

Summoning, prorogation and dissolution of Parliament, etc.

in financial matters, etc., shall be on the lines of the corresponding provisions in the Government of India Act of 1935.

26. In the Union Parliament, business shall be transacted in *Language* Hindustani (Hindi or Urdu) or English, provided that the Chairman or the Speaker, as the case may be, may permit any member who cannot adequately express himself in either language to address the House in his mother tongue. The Chairman or the Speaker, as the case may be, shall make arrangements for giving the House, whenever he thinks fit, a summary of the speech in a language other than that used by the member and such summary shall be included in the record of the proceedings of the House.

[This follows the corresponding provision in the Constituent Assembly Rules.]

TABLE OF SEATS

THE SENATE

ALLOCATION OF SEATS

(i) *Representatives of British India*

Province	No. of Seats		
Madras	24		
Bombay	19		
Bengal	24	{East Bengal	17
		{West Bengal	7
United Provinces	24		
Panjab	19	{West Panjab	11
		{East Panjab	8
Bihar	19		
Central Provinces	9	{Berar	2
		{Rest	7
Assam	6	{North Assam	4
		{Sylhet	2
N.W.F. Province	6		
Orissa	6		
Sind	6		
British Baluchistan	2		
Delhi	2		
Ajmer-Merwara	1		
Coorg	1		
Total	168		

(ii) *Representatives of Indian States*

A—Single States

Division as shown in the Table of Seats appended to Part II of the First Schedule to the Govt. of India Act, 1935	Name of State	No. of Seats
I	Hyderabad	5
II	Mysore	3
III	Kashmir	3
IV	Gwalior	3
V	Baroda	3
IX	Travancore	2
IX	Cochin	2
X	Udaipur	2
X	Jaipur	2
X	Jodhpur	2
X	Bikaner	2
X	Alwar	1
X	Kotah	1
XI	Indore	2
XI	Bhopal	2
XI	Rewa	2
XIII	Kolhapur	2
XIV	Patiala	2
XIV	Bahawalpur	2
XVI	Mayurbhanj	1
	Total	44

B—Frontier Groups

Division	Names of the States in the Group	No. of Seats
VI	Kalat	
	Las Bela	
	Kharan	4
XIV	Khairpur	
VII	Sikkim	2
XV	Cooch Behar	
XV	Tripura	
XV	Manipur	2
XVII	Khasi States	
XVII	Amb	
XVII	Chitral	
XVII	Dir	1
XVII	Swat	
XVII	Phulra	
		Total 9

C—Interior Groups

VIII	Rampur	2
	Benares	
X	Bharatpur	
	Tonk	
	Dholpur	
	Karauli	
	Bundi	

DIVISION	NAMES OF THE STATES IN THE GROUP	NO. OF SEATS
(13 States)	Sirohi	11
	Dungarpur	
	Banswara	
	Partabgarh	
	Jhalawar	
	Jaisalmer	
	Kishengarh	
XI	Shahpura	
XI	Datia	
	Orchha	
	Dhar	
	Dewas (Senior)	
	Dewas (Junior)	
	Jaora	
	Ratlam	
	Panna	
	Samthar	
	Ajaigarh	
	Bijawar	
	Charkhari	
(26 States)	Chhatarpur	11
	Baoni	
	Nagod	
	Maihar	
	Baraundha	
	Barwani	
	Ali Rajpur	
	Jhabua	
	Sailana	
	Sitamau	
	Rajgarh	
	Narsingarh	
	Khilchipur	
XVII	Kurwai	

Division	Names of the States in the Group	No. of Seats
XII	Cutch	
	Idar	
	Nawanagar	
	Bhavnagar	
	Junagadh	
	Dhrangadhra	
	Gondal	
	Porbandar	
(16 States)	Morvi	9
	Radhanpur	
	Wankaner	
	Palitana	
	Dhrol	
	Limbdi	
	Wadhwan	
	Rajkot	
XII-A	Rajpipla	
	Palanpur	
	Cambay	
	Dharampur	
	Balasinor	
	Baria	
	Chhota Udepur	
(15 States)	Sant	
	Lunawada	
	Bansda	
	Sachin	
	Jawahar	
	Danta	
XIII	Janjira	
	Jafrabad	

6

Division	Names of the States in the Group	No. of Seats
XIII (17 States)	Sangli Savantvadi Mudhol Bhor Jamkhandi Miraj (Senior) Miraj (Junior) Kurundwad (Senior) Kurundwad (Junior) Akalkot Phaltan Jath Aundh Ramdurg	5
IX	Pudukottai Banganapalle Sandur	
XIV (14 States)	Kapurthala Jind Nabha Mandi Bilaspur Suket Tehri-Garhwal Sirmur Chamba Faridkot Malerkotla Loharu	7
XVII	Kalsia Bashahr	

Division	Names of the States in the Group	No. of Seats
XVI	Sonepur	
	Patna	
	Kalahandi	
	Keonjhar	
	Dhenkanal	
	Nayagarh	
	Talcher	
(25 States)	Nilgiri	
	Gangpur	
	Bamra	
	Seraikela	
	Baud	
	Bonai	
		4
XVII	Athgarh	
	Pal Lahara	
	Athmalik	
	Hindol	
	Narsingpur	
	Baramba	
	Tigiria	
	Khanpara	
	Ranpur	
	Daspalla	
	Rairakhol	
	Kharsawan	

Division	Names of the States in the Group	No. of Seats
XVI-A	Bastar	
	Surguja	
	Raigarh	
	Nandgaon	
	Khairagarh	
(14 States)	Jashpur	
	Kanker	3
	Korea	
	Sarangarh	
XVII	Changbhakar	
	Chhuikhadan	
	Kawardha	
	Sakti	
	Udaipur	
XVII	All other States	2
		59
	Total for Indian States	112
	Grand total for India	**280**

CHAPTER IV

LEGISLATIVE POWERS OF THE PRESIDENT

27. (1) If at any time, when the Union Parliament is not in session, the President is satisfied that circumstances exist which render it necessary for him to take immediate action, he may promulgate such ordinances as the circumstances appear to him to require.

Power of President to promulgate ordinances during recess of Parliament

(2) An ordinance promulgated under this section shall have the same force and effect as an Act of the Union Parliament assented to by the President, but every such ordinance

(a) shall be laid before the Union Parliament and shall cease to operate at the expiration of six weeks from the reassembly of the Union Parliament, or, if before the expiration of that period resolutions disapproving it are passed by both Houses, upon the passing of the second of those resolutions; and

(b) may be withdrawn at any time by the President.

(3) If and so far as an ordinance under this section makes any provision which the Union Parliament would not under this constitution be competent to enact, it shall be void.

[Note: The ordinance-making power has been the subject of great criticism under the present constitution. It must, however, be pointed out that circumstances may exist where the immediate promulgation of a law is absolutely necessary and there is no time in which to summon the Union Parliament. I recall that Lord Reading found it necessary to make an ordinance abolishing the cotton excise duty when such action was immediately and imperatively required in the interests of the country. The President who is elected by the two Houses of Parliament and who has normally to act on the advice of ministers responsible to Parliament is not at all likely to abuse any ordinance-making power with which he may be invested. Hence the proposed provision.]

CHAPTER V

THE UNION JUDICATURE

28. There shall be a Supreme Court in the Union with
Supreme Court powers and jurisdiction as recommended by the *ad hoc* Committee on the Union Judiciary.

[*Note*: The *ad hoc* Committee on the Supreme Court has observed that it will not be expedient to leave the power of appointing judges of the Supreme Court to the unfettered discretion of the President of the Union. They have suggested two alternatives, both of which involve the setting up of a special panel of eleven members. According to one alternative, the President, in consultation with the Chief Justice, is to nominate a person for appointment as puisne judge and the nomination has to be confirmed by at least seven members of the panel. According to the other alternative, the panel should recommend three names, out of which the President, in consultation with the Chief Justice, is to select one for the appointment. The relevant section in the draft clauses adopts substantially the first alternative, utilising at the same time the Council of State for this purpose. It will be noticed that the Council of State includes the Chief Justice among its members and its composition is such as to secure freedom from party bias. It should, therefore, be a satisfactory substitute for the panel recommended by the *ad hoc* Committee.]

CHAPTER VI

AUDITOR-GENERAL OF THE UNION

29. There shall be an Auditor-General of the Union who
Auditor-General   shall be appointed by the President and shall
only be removed from office in like manner, and on the like grounds, as a judge of the Supreme Court.

30. The duties and powers of the Auditor-General shall
Functions of Auditor-General   follow the lines of the corresponding provisions in the Government of India Act
of 1935.

CHAPTER VII

PUBLIC SERVICE COMMISSION

31. There shall be a Public Service Commission for the
Public Service Commission   Union whose composition and functions
shall follow the lines of the corresponding provisions in the Government of India Act of 1935.

CHAPTER VIII

UNION RAILWAY AUTHORITY

32. In the Government of India Act of 1935, there is a Part providing for the establishment of a Federal Railway Authority. This Part of the Act has never come into force, and the question is whether we should make provision for a Union Railway Authority on the lines of the Federal Railway Authority. Until a decision is arrived at on this point, it has not been considered necessary to draft any specific provisions.

Union Railway Authority

CHAPTER IX

UNION DEFENCE COUNCIL

33. In most of the Dominions, there is no Commander-in-Chief, but instead there is a Defence Council. In Canada, there is a Defence Council consisting of the Minister (President), the Deputy Minister (Vice-President), the Chiefs of the General and Naval Staffs, the Quarter Master-General, the Director of the Royal Canadian Air Force and certain other members. In Australia, there is a Council of Defence with the Prime Minister as President, for co-ordinating defence policy on sea, on land and in the air. In South Africa, there is a Council of Defence presided over by the Minister for Defence, with the Chief of the General Staff, the Quarter Master-General, the Adjutant-General and others as members. The question, therefore, arises whether we should take steps to have a Defence Council for the Union.

Union Defence Council

Incidentally, this might make it possible for countries like Burma and Ceylon to collaborate with the Union in defence matters. Until a decision has been arrived at on this question, it is not possible to draft specific provisions.

CHAPTER X

UNION ECONOMIC COUNCIL

Union Economic Council

34. Professor K. T. Shah has suggested that there should be an Economic Council for the Union consisting of 150 members, who are to be economic and scientific experts. The functions of the Council are to be to examine any questions referred to it and to make recommendations on various economic and fiscal matters, such as internal and external trade, fiscal policy, currency and coinage, railway rates and fares and so on. There was provision for a similar body in the German Reich under the Weimar Constitution. It has been considered unnecessary to draft specific provisions until a decision has been reached whether such a Council should be established in India.

CHAPTER XI

FRANCHISE FOR THE UNION PARLIAMENT

Franchise

35. The Union Parliament may, from time to time, make provision with respect to all or any of the following matters: that is to say,

   (*a*) the delimitation of territorial constituencies;

   (*b*) the qualifications for the franchise and the preparation of electoral rolls;

   (*c*) the qualifications for being elected as a member of either House;

   (*d*) the filling of casual vacancies in either House;

   (*e*) the conduct of elections under this constitution and the methods of voting thereat;

   (*f*) the expenses of candidates at such elections;

   (*g*) corrupt practices and other offences at or in connection with such elections;

(*h*) the decision of doubts and disputes arising out of or in connection with such elections; and

(*i*) matters ancillary to any such matter as aforesaid:

Provided that the superintendence, direction and control of elections, including the appointment of election tribunals, shall be vested in the President acting in his discretion.

[*Note*: The effect of vesting these powers in the President acting in his discretion will be to make available to him the advice of the Council of State.]

PART V

INTERNATIONAL RELATIONS

1. The Union affirms its adherence to the Charter of the United Nations and to the purposes and principles enunciated therein.

[*Note*: The purposes and principles of the Charter are enunciated in articles 1 and 2. For convenience of reference, the main purposes and principles are set out below:

The purposes of the United Nations are:

(1) To maintain international peace and security and to bring about by peaceful means, and in conformity with the principles of justice and international law, the adjustment or settlement of international disputes;

(2) to develop friendly relations among nations based on respect for the principle of equal rights and self-determination of peoples and to take other appropriate measures to strengthen universal peace;

(3) to achieve international co-operation in solving international problems, and in promoting and encouraging respect for human rights and for fundamental freedoms for all, without distinction as to race, sex, language or religion.

The Organisation and its members in pursuit of the above purposes shall act in accordance with the following principles:

(1) The Organisation is based on the principle of the sovereign equality of all its members.

(2) All members shall fulfil in good faith the obligations assumed by them in accordance with the Charter.

(3) All members shall settle their international disputes by peaceful means in such a manner that international peace and security and justice are not endangered.

(4) All members shall refrain in their international relations from the threat or use of force against the territorial integrity or political independence of any State, or in any other manner inconsistent with the purposes of the United Nations.

(5) All members shall give the United Nations every assistance in any action it takes in accordance with the Charter and shall refrain from giving assistance to any State against which the United Nations is taking preventive or enforcement action.]

2. For the purpose of the exercise of any executive function of the Union in or in connection with its defence or its external affairs, the government may, subject to the provisions of the Charter of the United Nations, avail itself of or adopt any organ, instrument or method of procedure used or adopted for the like purpose by any other State or by the members of any group or organisation of nations with which the Union is or becomes associated for the purpose of international co-operation in matters of common concern.

3. (1) Every international agreement to which the Union becomes a party shall be laid before the House of Representatives.

(2) The Union shall not be bound by any international agreement involving a charge upon the revenues of the Union, unless the terms of the agreement shall have been approved by the House of Representatives.

Explanation: This section shall not apply to inter-governmental agreements of a technical or administrative character.

4. No international agreement shall be part of the municipal law of the Union, save as may be determined by the Parliament of the Union.

[These clauses correspond to art. 29 of the Constitution of Ireland.]

5. The Union shall honour all legitimate obligations arising out of any treaties or agreements which, immediately before the commencement of this constitution, were in force between India and any other State, provided that such other State recognises the Union as a sovereign State and honours all reciprocal obligations towards the Union.

[*Note*: The legal position as regards treaties and agreements now subsisting between British India and other States will require careful consideration, particularly in the event of British India being divided into two or more sovereignties.

Different views seem to have been held by different countries, and even by the same country at different times, on questions of State succession. For example:

(1) When Columbia was split up into three new States (New Granada, Venezuela and Ecuador) in 1829-31, the question arose whether a treaty of 1825 between Columbia and the United Kingdom continued to be binding on the three new States. The King's Advocate advised in 1834 that the treaty of 1825 was still binding upon each of the three new States until they respectively gave due notice that they considered themselves no longer bound by it. He qualified the opinion by stating that it would be more regular and formal to enter into new and separate treaties with each of the three new States.

(2) When, in 1905, the Real Union of Sweden and Norway was dissolved, His Majesty's Government's view as to the effect upon previous treaties was: " Although the dissolution of the Union between Sweden and Norway undoubtedly affords His Majesty's Government the right to examine, *de novo*, the treaty engagements by which Great Britain was bound to the dual monarchy, they gladly take note of the desire of the Swedish Government that these engagements should remain in force pending a further study of the subject."

(3) When the Republic of Finland was formed at the end of the Great War and was recognised by Great Britain and other countries, His Majesty's Government defined their attitude towards Finland in the matter of treaties in the following terms:

" In the case of a new State being formed out of part of an old State there is no succession by the new State to the treaties of the old one, though the obligations of the old State in relation to such matters as the navigation of rivers, which are in the nature of servitude, would normally pass to the new State. Consequently there are no treaties in existence between Finland and this country."

(See McNair's *Law of Treaties*, 1938, *pp.* 412-427. The French Government's view as to the effect of the dissolution of the Union of Sweden and Norway in 1905 upon a treaty of 1855 was apparently that the treaty continued to be binding as between England and France on the one hand and each of the two separate Kingdoms of Sweden and Norway on the other. *Op. cit., p.* 422.)

Thus three different views have been taken as to the effect of the splitting up of a State into two or more new States upon the treaties of the old:

(1) that the old treaties continue to be binding on the new States;

(2) that the dissolution or dismemberment gives the other party to any treaty the right to re-examine the position;

(3) that there is no succession by the new States to the treaties of the old.]

PART VI

DISTRIBUTION OF LEGISLATIVE POWERS BETWEEN UNION AND UNITS

The provisions to be inserted under this head will depend upon the decisions that may be taken upon the report of the Union Powers Committee. It may be mentioned in this connection that Sardar Panikkar has advanced powerful arguments in support of the view that the constitution of the Union should be of the unitary type. If it is decided to abandon the Cabinet Mission's plan of May 16, 1946, the whole matter may have to be considered afresh. In that event, we may either have a unitary type of constitution, as before the Government of India Act of 1935, or we may have a federation with the present distribution of powers between the

Centre and the units. The former, however desirable, may no longer be practical politics. Until a decision is arrived at on this point, it is hardly possible to draft specific provisions. If a federal type of constitution is decided upon, a provision on the following lines should find place therein:

" Upon being authorised in this behalf by resolutions of the legislatures of two or more units, the Union Parliament may by Act provide for the administration of any region extending over the units concerned or any parts thereof in respect of all or any of the subjects that may be specified in the resolutions, and may for this purpose establish appropriate legislative, executive, judicial, or other authorities."

Such a provision would enable the units to form groups for regional administration of selected subjects, to set up joint universities, joint High Courts, or joint authorities like the TVA.

PART VII

ADMINISTRATIVE RELATIONS BETWEEN UNION AND UNITS AND BETWEEN UNITS INTER SE

The provisions of this Part will depend upon the distribution of legislative powers between the Union and the units in Part VI and specific provisions cannot be drafted until the provisions of Part VI have been decided upon. [See Part VI of the Government of India Act, 1935.]

PART VIII

AMENDMENT OF THE CONSTITUTION

An amendment to the constitution may be initiated in either House of the Union Parliament and when the proposed amendment is passed in each House by a majority of not less than two-thirds of the total number of members of that House and is ratified by the legislatures of not less than two-thirds of the units of the Union, excluding the Chief Commissioners' provinces, it shall be presented to the President for his assent; and upon such assent being given, the amendment shall come into operation.

Explanation I: For the purposes of this clause, only the legislatures of the units specified in schedule — shall be recognised.

Explanation II: The Union Parliament may, from time to time, make such additions or alterations in the aforesaid schedule — as it thinks fit and such additions or alterations shall have effect as if enacted in this constitution.

[*Note*: The explanations are necessary, because some of the units, particularly where they consist of groups of Indian States, may not possess proper legislatures. If care is taken not to admit a unit to the Union, unless it possesses a proper legislature, the explanations may not be necessary.]

PART IX

TRANSITIONAL PROVISIONS

1. The Government of the Union shall be the successor to the Government of India established under the Government of India Act, 1935, as regards all property, assets, rights and liabilities.

2. (1) Subject to this constitution, the laws in force in the territories included in schedule I immediately before the commencement of the constitution shall continue in force therein until altered, or repealed, or amended by a competent legislature or other competent authority.

(2) The President may by Order provide that, as from a specified date, any law in force in the aforesaid territories shall, until repealed or amended by competent authority, have effect subject to such adaptations and modifications as

appear to him to be necessary or expedient for bringing the provisions of that law into accord with the provisions of this constitution.

3. All courts, including the Judicial Committee of the Privy Council, existing at the commencement of this constitution shall continue to exercise their jurisdiction until new courts are established by law in accordance with this constitution: Provided that all cases pending in the said courts shall be disposed of by them as if this constitution had not come into operation.

4. Excepting holders of the offices specified in schedule— every person who immediately before the date of the commencement of this constitution, was in the service of the Crown in India, shall, on that date, at his option, be transferred to the appropriate service of the Union, or the unit concerned and shall hold office by a tenure corresponding to his previous tenure.

[*Note*: It is obvious that under the new constitution the Governor-General and the present Governors of the several provinces cannot continue in office. The same may be true of the holders of certain other offices. All such offices may be enumerated in a schedule. The proposed provision applies to persons holding offices other than those mentioned in the schedule.]

5. (1) Until both the Houses of the Union Parliament have been duly constituted and summoned under this constitution, the Constituent Assembly shall itself exercise all the powers and discharge all the duties of both the Houses.

(2) X, who has been elected in this behalf by the Constituent Assembly, shall be the President of the Union until a President has been duly elected as provided in Part IV of this constitution.

(3) A, B, C, etc., etc., who have been appointed in this behalf by X, shall be the President's Council of Ministers until

ministers are duly appointed as provided in Part IV of this
constitution.

[*Note*: It is essential that on the date of commencement of
this constitution there should be a legislature and an executive
ready to take over power. The existing Indian legislature is not
sufficiently democratic to be given power even provisionally.
Hence the above proposal that the Constituent Assembly should
itself be the provisional legislature. The clause regarding the
provisional executive is consequential.]

6. Whereas difficulties may arise in relation to the transition
from the provisions of the Government of India Act, 1935,
to the provisions of this constitution, and

Whereas the nature of these difficulties and of the provision
which should be made for meeting them cannot at the date
of the commencement of this constitution be fully foreseen,

Now, therefore, for the purpose of facilitating the said
transition, the Union Parliament may, notwithstanding anything contained in Part VIII, by Act—

    (*a*) direct that this constitution, except the provisions of
        the said Part and of this clause, shall, during such
        period as may be specified in the Act, have effect
        subject to such adaptations and modifications as may
        be so specified;

    (*b*) make such other temporary provisions for the pur-
        pose of removing any such difficulties as aforesaid as
        may be specified in the Act.

No Act shall be made under this clause after the expiration
of three years from the commencement of this constitution.

[*Note*: The-removal-of-difficulties-clause is now quite usual:
see, for example, section 310 of the Government of India Act,
1935. The period of three years has been borrowed from article
51 of the Irish Constitution.]

6

DRAFT CLAUSES OF THE UNION CONSTITUTION

WE, the people of India, seeking to promote the common
good, do hereby, through our chosen re-
Preamble   presentatives, enact, adopt and give to ourselves this constitution.

PART I

UNION TERRITORY AND JURISDICTION

1. The Union hereby established shall be a sovereign inde-
Name and terri-   pendent State known as the Union of India
tory of Union   and shall embrace all the territories included
in India under the Government of India Act, 1935; but save
as otherwise provided by or under treaty or agreement, only
the territories included for the time being in schedule I shall
be subject to the jurisdiction of the Union.

[The first part of this clause proceeds on the basis of the
Cabinet Mission's plan of May 16, 1946, according to which
there should be a Union of India embracing both British India
and the States. The second part is necessitated by the subsequent modification of that plan, according to which the constitution is not to be forced upon "unwilling parts of the
country". Schedule I in its initial form is intended to specify
the "willing parts" at the date of the coming into operation of
the constitution. If any other territories elect to come within
Union jurisdiction later, the schedule is to be modified accordingly (see the next clause). The clause may be compared

7

with articles 2 and 3 of the Constitution of Ireland. The parts of India not specified in the schedule are *in* the Union, but not *of* it.]

2. The Parliament of the Union may from time to time by *Admission of new territories* Act include new territories in schedule I upon such terms as it thinks fit.

3. The Parliament of the Union may by Act, with the *Creation of new provinces and alteration of provincial boundaries* consent of the legislature of every province affected thereby—

(*a*) create a new province;

(*b*) increase the area of any province;

(*c*) diminish the area of any province;

(*d*) alter the boundaries of any province;

and may with the like consent make such incidental and consequential provisions as it may deem necessary or proper.

4. The provisions of any such Act as is referred to in sections 2 and 3 shall have effect as if they were embodied in this constitution.

[Clauses 2-4 above correspond to art. IV, s. 3, of the U.S.A. Constitution; s. 146 of the British North America Act; ss. 121-124 of the Commonwealth of Australia Act; ss. 149-151 of the Union of South Africa Act; s. 290 of the Government of India Act, 1935.]

5. (1) All rights, authority and jurisdiction heretofore exercisable *Jurisdiction in the scheduled provinces* by or on behalf of His Majesty the King in or in relation to such of the territories included in schedule I as were parts of British India shall hereafter be exercised by the appropriate authorities provided by or under the constitution.

(2) The said rights, authority and jurisdiction shall include any rights, authority or jurisdiction heretofore exercisable in or in relation to the aforesaid territories by the Secretary of State, the Crown Representative, the Governor-General, the Governor-General-in-Council or any Governor whether by delegation from His Majesty or otherwise.

6. All rights, authority and jurisdiction heretofore exercisable by or on behalf of the Ruler of any
Jurisdiction in the Indian State included in schedule I in or
scheduled Indian
States in relation to the State shall hereafter, to
the extent to which they have been ceded by the Ruler to the
Union by the Instrument of Accession of the State and subject
to the terms of the Instrument, be exercised by the appropriate
authorities provided by or under this constitution.

Explanation: The Instrument of Accession referred to in this
section is an Instrument executed by the Ruler and approved
by the Constituent Assembly whereby the Ruler, on behalf of
the State —————,

(*a*) has declared that he accedes to the Union with the
intent that the authorities provided by or under this
constitution for the purposes of the Union shall, by
virtue of the Instrument of Accession, but subject to the
terms thereof, exercise in relation to the State such
functions as may be vested in them by or under this
constitution;

(*b*) has assumed the obligation of ensuring that due effect is
given within the State to the provisions of this constitution so far as they are applicable therein by virtue
of the Instrument of Accession.

The term " Ruler " includes any persons for the time being
exercising the powers of the Ruler whether by reason of the
Ruler's minority or for any other reason.

[*Note:* Clauses 5 and 6 are intended to define the jurisdiction
of the Union at the commencement of the new constitution.
If new territories are admitted later, the Union's jurisdiction in
relation to those territories will be defined by the Act admitting
them (see clause 2).

The legal position as regards treaties and agreements now
subsisting between the Crown and various Indian States will
require careful consideration, particularly in the event of
British India being divided into two or more new sovereignties.
As regards the Indian States in schedule I, presumably the
position will have to be clarified in the Instruments of Accession.
As regards Indian States outside schedule I, the position can

only be clarified after negotiations with the State authorities. The position may well be different for different States, *e.g.*, for States acceding to Pakistan (if there is one) and for States acceding neither to Pakistan nor to Hindustan, although both classes of States will be outside schedule I. See also note under Part IV of Memorandum.]

SCHEDULE I

TERRITORIES SUBJECT TO THE JURISDICTION OF THE UNION

I. *Governors' Provinces*

Madras

Bombay

Bengal or West Bengal (?)

The United Provinces

Bihar

The Panjab or East Panjab (?)

The Central Provinces (and Berar ?)

Assam (*minus* Sylhet ?)

N.W.F. Province (?)

Orissa

Sind (?)

II. *Chief Commissioners' Provinces*

Delhi

British Baluchistan (?)

Ajmer-Merwara

Coorg

The Andaman & Nicobar Islands

Panth Piploda

III. *Indian States*

[Here enumerate the acceding Indian States :

(1) Single States

(2) Groups of States.]

PART II

CITIZENSHIP

1. At the date of commencement of this constitution—

Citizenship every person domiciled in the territories included within the Union and subject to its jurisdiction—

(*a*) who has been ordinarily resident in those territories for not less than five years immediately preceding that date, or

(*b*) who, or whose parents, or either of whose parents, was or were born in India,

shall be a citizen of the Union:

Provided that any such person being a citizen of any other State may, in accordance with the Union law, elect not to accept the citizenship hereby conferred.

2. After the commencement of this constitution—

(*a*) every person who is born in the territories included within the Union and subject to its jurisdiction;

(*b*) every person who is naturalised in accordance with the Union law; and

(*c*) every person either of whose parents was, at the time of such person's birth, a citizen of the Union,

shall be a citizen of the Union.

3. Further provisions governing the acquisition and termination of the Union citizenship may be made by the Union law.

[See note under Part II of Memorandum.]

PART III

FUNDAMENTAL RIGHTS INCLUDING DIRECTIVE PRINCIPLES OF STATE POLICY

Fundamental Rights [Here enumerate Fundamental Rights and Principles of State Policy as passed by the Constituent Assembly.]

PART IV

CHAPTER I

THE UNION EXECUTIVE

THE PRESIDENT

1. (1) As soon as may be after the date of commencement *Election of Presi-* of this constitution, and thereafter, as often *dent* as a vacancy occurs, the two Houses of the Union Parliament shall, at a joint sitting, elect a suitable person to be the head of the Union, hereinafter referred to as " the President ".

(2) The voting shall be by secret ballot according to the system of proportional representation by the single transferable vote.

[See note under Part IV, clause 1 of Memorandum.]

2. (1) The President shall hold office for five years: *President's term* Provided that— *of office*

(*a*) a President may by resignation under his hand addressed to the Chairman of the Senate and the Speaker of the House of Representatives resign his office;

(*b*) a President may be removed from office for misbehaviour or infirmity of mind or body by a resolution of each of the two Houses of the Union Parliament supported by not less than two-thirds of the total membership of each House.

(2) A person who holds, or who has held, office as President shall be eligible for re-election to that office once, but only once.

[*Note:* Since under this constitution it is proposed that the maximum term of the House of Representatives is to be five years and the President is to be elected by both Houses, the President's term of office has also been fixed at five years.

In the U.S.A., the President is removable from office on impeachment for, and conviction of, treason, bribery or other

high crimes and misdemeanours. The House of Representatives
has the sole power of impeachment and the Senate has the sole
power to try all impeachments. There can be no conviction
without the concurrence of at least two-thirds of the members
of the Senate present. In Ireland, the President may be
impeached for stated misbehaviour; the charge can be preferred
by either House of Parliament but requires the support of not
less than two-thirds of the total membership of the House concerned. The other House investigates the charge; a conviction
requires the support of not less than two-thirds of the total
membership of the investigating House. The resolution embodying the conviction operates to remove the President from
his office. Sub-clause (1) of the present clause is an adaptation
of the U.S.A. and the Irish precedents (omitting the impeachment procedure). Sub-clause (2) is borrowed from the Irish
Constitution.]

3. (1) An election for the office of President shall be held
not later than, and not earlier than, the 30th
day before the date of the expiration of the
term of office of the outgoing President; but, upon the occurrence of a casual vacancy (from death, resignation, or removal
from office), an election to fill the vacancy shall be held
within 30 days after its occurrence.

By-elections

(2) An election to fill a casual vacancy shall be held in
the same manner as that for the permanent vacancy immediately preceding, and the person elected may serve only for the
remainder of his predecessor's term of office.

4. Every citizen of the Union who has reached his 35th year
of age is eligible for election to the office of
President.

Age limit

5. Subject to the provisions of this Part, election for the
office of President shall be regulated by
Act of the Union Parliament.

*Presidential elec-
tion to be regulated
by Union law subject
to this Part*

[*Note:* Assuming that this constitution comes into operation
on July 1, 1948, it is clear that the House of Representatives
and the Senate can be elected under the constitution only

after that date. If any elections are attempted to be held in advance of that date, they can only be on an informal basis not resting on any law. Moreover, if anything like adult suffrage is contemplated, it may not be possible to get all the machinery ready before the date fixed for the transfer of power.

On July 1, 1948, therefore, we shall have to have a " provisional government " and a " provisional legislature " that can function pending the election or the setting up of a properly constituted legislature and a properly constituted government under the new constitution. For this purpose, it may be necessary to insert appropriate transitional provisions. These will be found in Part VIII of this constitution.]

6. (1) The President shall not be a member of either House *Conditions of President's office* of the Union Parliament; and if a member of either House be elected President, he shall be deemed to have vacated his seat in that House.

(2) The President shall not hold any other office or position of emolument.

(3) The President shall have an official residence and shall receive such emoluments and allowances as may be determined by Act of the Union Parliament and, until then, such as are prescribed in schedule II.

(4) The emoluments and allowances of the President shall not be diminished during his term of office.

7. The first President shall enter upon his office as soon as *Commencement of term of office* may be after his election, and every subsequent President shall enter upon his office on the day following the expiration of the term of office of his predecessor or as soon as may be thereafter or, in the case of a President elected to fill a casual vacancy, as soon as may be after the election.

8. Every President shall enter upon his office by taking and *Oath of office* subscribing in the presence of the members of both Houses of the Union Parliament a declaration according to the form set out in that behalf in schedule — to this constitution.

9. The President shall not leave India during his term of
Absence from office save with the consent of his Council
India of Ministers.

10. (1) In the event of the absence of the President or of his
        death, resignation, removal from office, or
Provision for dis- incapacity or failure to exercise and perform
charge of President's
functions during ab- the powers and functions of his office or at
sence or vacancy any time at which the office of the President may be vacant, the powers and functions conferred upon
the President by this constitution shall be exercised and
performed by a Commission as hereinafter provided in this
section.

(2) (*a*) The Commission shall consist of the following
persons, namely,

  (i) the Chief Justice of the Supreme Court;

  (ii) the Chairman of the Senate; and

  (iii) the Speaker of the House of Representatives.

(*b*) On any occasion on which the office of the Chief
Justice of the Supreme Court is vacant or on which the Chief
Justice is unable to act, the senior judge of the Supreme Court
shall act in his place as a member of the Commission.

(*c*) The Deputy Chairman of the Senate shall act as
a member of the Commission in the place of the Chairman on
any occasion on which the office of Chairman is vacant or on
which the Chairman is unable to act.

(*d*) The Deputy Speaker of the House of Representatives shall act as a member of the Commission in the place
of the Speaker on any occasion on which the office of Speaker
is vacant or on which the Speaker is unable to act.

(3) The Commission may act by any two of their number
and may act notwithstanding a vacancy in their membership.

(4) In the event of the failure of the President to exercise
or perform any power or function, which he is by this constitution required to exercise or perform within a specified time,
the said power or function shall be exercised or performed

under this section, as soon as may be after the expiration of the time so specified.

(5) The Council of State may by a majority of its members make such provision as to them may seem fit for the exercise and performance of the powers and functions conferred on the President by this constitution in any contingency which is not provided for by this section.

(6) The provisions of this constitution which relate to the exercise and performance by the President of the powers and functions conferred upon him by this constitution shall apply to the exercise and performance of the said powers and functions by the Commission under this section.

[See note under Part IV, clause 6 of Memorandum.]

11. Subject to the provisions of this constitution, the executive authority of the Union shall be exercised by the President, either directly or through officers subordinate to him, but nothing in this section shall prevent the Union Parliament from conferring functions upon subordinate authorities, or be deemed to transfer to the President any functions conferred by any existing Indian law on any court, judge or officer, or on any local or other authority.

Functions of President

12. (1) Subject to the provisions of this constitution, the executive authority of the Union extends—

Extent of executive authority of the Union

(a) to the matters with respect to which the Union Parliament has power to make laws;

(b) to the governance, in accordance with the provisions of any treaty or agreement in this behalf, of any armed forces not raised in the Union that may, with the consent of the Government of the Union, be stationed in the Union or placed at the disposal of the Union; and

(c) to the exercise, in accordance with the provisions of any treaty or agreement in this behalf, of such rights, authority and jurisdiction in or in relation to any territories not included in schedule I as may be vested in the Government of the Union by such treaty or agreement:

Provided that—

(i) the said authority does not, save as expressly provided in this constitution, extend in any province to matters with respect to which the provincial legislature has power to make laws; and

(ii) the said authority does not, save as expressly provided in this constitution, extend in any Indian State included in schedule I, save in matters with respect to which the Union Parliament has power to make laws for that State and the exercise thereof in each State shall be subject to such limitations, if any, as may be specified in the Instrument of Accession of the State.

(2) The executive authority of the Ruler of a State included in schedule I shall, notwithstanding anything in this section, continue to be exercisable in that State with respect to matters with respect to which the Union Parliament has power to make laws for that State except in so far as the executive authority of the Union becomes exercisable in the State to the exclusion of the executive authority of the Ruler by virtue of a Union law.

[*Note:* Clause 12 (1) (*a*) above is consequential upon the legislative power of the Union. The matters specified in (*b*) and (*c*) are normally outside the legislative power of the Union, and the executive power of the Union with respect to such matters has therefore to be derived from some special treaty or agreement; (*c*) would apply to the tribal areas as well as to Indian States not included in schedule I.

Clause 12 (2), like the corresponding provision in section 8 (2) of the Government of India Act of 1935, gives the Rulers of Indian State units of the Union concurrent executive power even in Union subjects, save as taken away by Union law. In this respect, the position of the provincial units is rather different: they have no executive power in respect of Union subjects save as given by Union law.]

ADMINISTRATION OF UNION AFFAIRS

13. (1) There shall be a Council of Ministers not exceeding — in number, with the Prime Minister at the head, to aid and advise the President in the exercise of his functions, except in so far as he is, by or under this constitution, required to exercise his functions or any of them in his discretion.

(2) If any question arises whether any matter is or is not a matter as respects which the President is (by or under this constitution) required to act in his discretion, the decision of the President in his discretion shall be final, and the validity of anything done by the President shall not be called in question on the ground that he ought or ought not to have acted in his discretion.

[*Note:* Although under responsible government, the President will almost always act on the advice of ministers, there will be a few matters in respect of which he will have to act in his own discretion. Even in the English Constitution, there are certain matters in respect of which it is a moot question whether the King is bound to act on the advice of the Prime Minister, *e.g.*, in the matter of dissolving the House of Commons when the Prime Minister has lost its confidence. See also note under Part IV, clause 10 of Memorandum.]

14. (1) The President's ministers shall be chosen and summoned by him, shall be sworn as members *Other provisions* of the Council, and shall hold office during *as to ministers* his pleasure.

(2) A minister who for any period of six consecutive months is not a member of either House of the Union Parliament shall at the expiration of that period cease to be a minister.

(3) The salaries of ministers shall be such as the Union Parliament may, from time to time, by Act determine and, until the Union Parliament so determine, shall be determined by the President:

Provided that the salary of a minister shall not be varied during his term of office.

(4) The question whether any and, if so, what advice was tendered by ministers to the President shall not be inquired into in any court.

(5) The functions of the President, with respect to the choosing and summoning and the dismissal of ministers, and with respect to the determination of their salaries, shall be exercised by him in his discretion.

15. (1) In the exercise of his functions the President shall
Special responsi- have the following special responsibilities,
bilities of President that is to say,

(*a*) the prevention of any grave menace to the peace or tranquillity of the Union or any part thereof;

(*b*) the safeguarding of the financial stability and credit of the Union Government;

(*c*) the safeguarding of the legitimate interests of minorities.

(2) If and in so far as any special responsibility of the President is involved, he shall in the exercise of his functions exercise his discretion as to the action to be taken.

[See note under Part IV, clause 13 of Memorandum.]

16. (1) The President shall appoint a person, being a person
Advocate-General qualified to be appointed a judge of the
for the Union Supreme Court, to be Advocate-General for the Union.

(2) It shall be the duty of the Advocate-General to give advice to the Union Government upon such legal matters, and to perform such other duties of a legal character, as may be referred or assigned to him by the President, and, in the

performance of his duties, he shall have right of audience in all courts in the provinces and, in a case in which the Union interests are concerned, in all courts in any Indian State included in schedule I.

(3) The Advocate-General shall hold office during the pleasure of the President and shall receive such remuneration as the President may determine.

17. (1) All executive action of the Union Government shall *Conduct of business of Union Government* be expressed to be taken in the name of the President.

(2) Orders and other instruments made and executed in the name of the President shall be authenticated in such manner as may be specified in rules to be made by the President, and the validity of an order or instrument which is so authenticated shall not be called in question on the ground that it is not an order or instrument made or executed by the President.

(3) The President shall make rules for the more convenient transaction of the business of the Union Government, and for the allocation among ministers of the said business in so far as it is not business with respect to which the President is, by or under this constitution, required to act in his discretion.

CHAPTER II

THE COUNCIL OF STATE

18. There shall be a Council of State whom the President *Council of State* may consult on all matters in which he is required by this constitution to act in his discretion.

19. The Council of State shall consist of the following *Composition* members:

(1) *Ex-officio* members: the Prime Minister, the Deputy Prime Minister, if any, the Chief Justice of the

Supreme Court, the Speaker of the House of Representatives, the Chairman of the Senate and the Advocate-General.

(2) Every person able and willing to act as a member who shall have held the office of President, or the office of Prime Minister, or the office of Chief Justice of the Supreme Court.

(3) Such other persons, if any, as may be appointed by the President to be members.

20. The President may, at any time, by warrant under his hand and seal appoint such other persons as in his discretion he may think fit to be members of the Council of State, but not more than seven persons so appointed shall be members of the Council of State at the same time.

Appointments by President

21. Every member of the Council of State appointed by the President, unless he previously dies, resigns, becomes permanently incapacitated, or is removed from office, shall hold office until the successor of the President by whom he was appointed shall have entered upon his office.

Term of office

22. Any member of the Council of State appointed by the President may resign from office by writing under his hand addressed to the President.

Resignation

23. The President may for reasons which to him seem sufficient by an order under his hand and seal terminate the appointment of any member of the Council of State appointed by him.

Termination by President of appointments made by him

24. Meetings of the Council of State may be convened by the President at such times and places as he shall determine.

Meetings

[See note under Part IV, clause 22 of Memorandum.]

CHAPTER III

THE UNION PARLIAMENT

25. (1) The legislative power of the Union shall be vested in
Constitution of the the Parliament of the Union (hereinafter
Union Parliament referred to as the Union Parliament) which
shall consist of the President and two Houses, the Senate and
the House of Representatives.

(2) (*a*) The Senate * shall consist of not more than 168
representatives of the provinces and not more than 112 representatives of the Indian States.

(*b*) The House of Representatives shall consist of representatives of the provinces and of the Indian States or groups
of States (as the case may be) included in schedule I in the
proportion of not less than one representative for every million
of the population and not more than one representative for
every 750 thousands of the population.

The ratio between the number of members to be elected at
any time for each constituency and the population of that
constituency, as ascertained at the last preceding census shall,
so far as it is practicable, be the same throughout the territories
subject to the jurisdiction of the Union.

(*c*) The said representatives shall be chosen in
accordance with the provisions in that behalf contained in
schedule —.

(3) Upon the completion of each decennial census, the
representation of the several provinces and Indian States or
groups of Indian States in the House of Representatives shall
be readjusted by such authority, in such manner, and from
such time as the Union Parliament may by Act determine:

Provided that such readjustment shall not take effect until
the dissolution of the then existing House of Representatives.

---

* For detailed allocation of seats in the Senate see Table of Seats at the end
of Chapter III of Part IV of Memorandum.

(4) The Senate shall be a permanent body not subject to dissolution, but as near as may be one-third of the members thereof shall retire in every third year in accordance with the provisions in that behalf contained in schedule —.

(5) Every House of Representatives, unless sooner dissolved, shall continue for five years from the date appointed for their first meeting and no longer, and the expiration of the said period of five years shall operate as a dissolution of the House of Representatives.

[See note under Part IV, clause 24 of Memorandum.]

26. (1) The Houses of the Union Parliament shall be summoned to meet once at least in every year, and twelve months shall not intervene between their last sitting in one session and the date appointed for their first sitting in the next session.

Sessions of the Union Parliament, prorogation and dissolution

(2) Subject to the provisions of this section, the President may from time to time—

(*a*) summon the Houses or either House to meet at such time and place as he thinks fit;

(*b*) prorogue the Houses;

(*c*) dissolve the House of Representatives:

Provided that the President may in his discretion refuse to dissolve the House of Representatives on the advice of a Prime Minister who has ceased to retain the support of the majority in that House.

(3) The Houses shall be summoned to meet for their first session as early as possible after the commencement of this constitution.

27. (1) The President may in his discretion address either House of the Union Parliament or both Houses assembled together, and for that purpose require the attendance of members.

Right of President to address and send messages to Houses

(2) The President may in his discretion send messages to either House of the Union Parliament, whether with respect to

8

a Bill then pending in the Union Parliament or otherwise, and a House to whom any message is so sent shall with all convenient dispatch consider any matter which they are required by the message to take into consideration.

28. Every minister and the Advocate-General shall have the

Right of ministers and Advocate-General as respects Houses

right to speak in, and otherwise to take part in the proceedings of either House, any joint sitting of the Houses, and any committee of the Union Parliament of which he may be named a member, but shall not by virtue of this section be entitled to vote.

29. (1) The Senate shall, as soon as may be, choose two

Officers of Houses

members of the House to be respectively Chairman and Deputy Chairman thereof and so often as the office of Chairman or Deputy Chairman becomes vacant; the Senate shall choose another member to be Chairman or Deputy Chairman, as the case may be.

(2) A member holding office as Chairman or Deputy Chairman of the Senate shall vacate his office if he ceases to be a member of the Senate, may at any time resign his office by writing under his hand addressed to the President, and may be removed from his office by a resolution of the Senate passed by a majority of all the then members of the Senate; but no resolution for the purpose of this sub-section shall be moved unless at least 14 days' notice has been given of the intention to move the resolution.

(3) While the office of Chairman is vacant, the duties of the office shall be performed by the Deputy Chairman, or, if the office of Deputy Chairman is also vacant, by such member of the Senate as the President may in his discretion appoint for the purpose, and during any absence of the Chairman from any sitting of the Senate the Deputy Chairman, or, if he is also absent, such person as may be determined by the rules of procedure of the Senate, or, if no such person is present, such

other person as may be determined by the Senate, shall act as Chairman.

(4) There shall be paid to the Chairman and the Deputy Chairman of the Senate such salaries as may be respectively fixed by Act of the Union Parliament, and, until provision in that behalf is so made, such salaries as the President may determine.

(5) The foregoing provisions of this section shall apply in relation to the House of Representatives as they apply in relation to the Senate with the substitution of the titles ' Speaker ' and ' Deputy Speaker ' for the titles ' Chairman ' and ' Deputy Chairman ' respectively, and with the substitution of references to the House of Representatives for references to the Senate:

Provided that, without prejudice to the provisions of sub-section (2) of this section as applied by this sub-section, whenever the House of Representatives is dissolved, the Speaker shall not vacate his office until immediately before the first meeting of the House of Representatives after the dissolution.

30. (1) Save as provided in the last preceding section, all
Voting in Houses, power of Houses to act notwithstanding vacancies, and quorum
questions at any sitting or joint sitting of the Houses shall be determined by a majority of votes of the members present and voting, other than the Chairman or Speaker or person acting as such.

The Chairman or Speaker or person acting as such shall not vote in the first instance, but shall have and exercise a casting vote in the case of an equality of votes.

(2) A House of the Union Parliament shall have power to act notwithstanding any vacancy in the membership thereof, and any proceedings in the Union Parliament shall be valid notwithstanding that it is discovered subsequently that some person who was not entitled so to do sat or voted or otherwise took part in the proceedings.

(3) If at any time during a meeting of a House less than one-sixth of the total number of members of the House are present, it shall be the duty of the Chairman or Speaker, or person acting as such either to, adjourn the House, or to suspend the meeting until at least one-sixth of the members are present.

31. Every member of either House shall, before taking his *Oath of members* seat, make and subscribe before the President, or some person appointed by him, an oath according to that one of the forms set out in schedule —of this constitution which the member accepts as appropriate in his case.

32. (1) No person shall be a member of both Houses, and *Vacation of seats* rules made by the President shall provide for the vacation by a person who is chosen a member of both Houses of his seat in one House or the other.

. (2) If a member of either House—

(*a*) becomes, subject to any of the disqualifications mentioned in sub-section (1) of the next succeeding section; or

(*b*) by writing under his hand addressed to the President resigns his seat,

his seat shall thereupon become vacant.

(3) If for sixty days a member of either House is, without permission of the House, absent from all meetings thereof, the House may declare his seat vacant:

Provided that in computing the said period of sixty days no account shall be taken of any period during which the House is prorogued, or is adjourned for more than four consecutive days.

33. (1) A person shall be disqualified for being chosen *Disqualifications* as, and for being, a member of either *for membership* House—

(*a*) if he holds any office of profit under the Union or any unit other than an office declared by Act of the Union Parliament not to disqualify its holder;

(*b*) if he is of unsound mind and stands so declared by a competent court;

(*c*) if he is an undischarged insolvent;

(*d*) if, whether before or after the commencement of this constitution, he has been convicted, or has, in proceedings for questioning the validity or regularity of an election, been found to have been guilty of any offence or corrupt or illegal practice relating to elections which has been declared by an Act of the Union Parliament to be an offence or practice entailing disqualification for membership of the Union Parliament, unless such period has elapsed as may be specified in that behalf by the provisions of that Act;

(*e*) if, whether before or after the commencement of this constitution, he has been convicted of any other offence by a court within British India or within the territories subject to the jurisdiction of the Union (as the case may be) and sentenced to transportation or to imprisonment for not less than two years, unless a period of five years, or such less period as the President, acting in his discretion, may allow in any particular case, has elapsed since his release;

(*f*) if, having been nominated as a candidate for the Union Parliament or any provincial legislature, or having acted as an election agent of any person so nominated, he has failed to lodge a return of election expenses within the time and in the manner required by any Act of the Union Parliament or the provincial legislature, unless five years have elapsed from the date by which the return ought to have been lodged, or the President, acting in his discretion, has removed the disqualification:

Provided that a disqualification under paragraph (*f*) of this sub-section shall not take effect until the expiration of one month from the date by which the return ought to have been lodged or of such longer period as the President, acting in his discretion, may in any particular case allow.

(2) A person shall not be capable of being chosen a member of either House while he is serving a sentence of transportation or of imprisonment for a criminal offence.

(3) Where a person, who, by virtue of a conviction or a conviction and a sentence, becomes disqualified by virtue of paragraph (*d*) or paragraph (*e*) of sub-section (1) of this section, is at the date of the disqualification a member of the Union Parliament, his seat shall, notwithstanding anything in this or the last preceding section, not become vacant by reason of the disqualification until three months have elapsed from the date thereof, or, if within those three months an appeal or petition for revision is brought in respect of the conviction or the sentence, until that appeal or petition is disposed of, but during any period during which his membership is preserved by this sub-section he shall not sit or vote.

(4) For the purposes of this section a person shall not be deemed to hold an office of profit under the Union or any unit by reason only that—

(*a*) he is a minister either for the Union or for a province; or

(*b*) while serving an Indian State, he remains a member of one of the services of the Union or of any unit and retains all or any of his rights as such.

34. If a person sits or votes as a member of either House when he is not qualified or is disqualified *Penalty for sitting and voting when not qualified, or when disqualified* for membership thereof, or when he is prohibited from so doing by the provisions of sub-section (3) of the last preceding section, he shall be liable in respect of each day on which he so sits or votes, to a penalty of five hundred rupees to be recovered as a debt due to the Union.

35. (1) Subject to the provisions of this constitution and to *Privileges, etc., of members* the rules and standing orders regulating the procedure of the Union Parliament, there shall be freedom of speech in the Union Parliament, and

no member of the Union Parliament shall be liable to any proceedings in any court in respect of anything said or any vote given by him in the Union Parliament or any committee thereof, and no person shall be so liable in respect of the publication by or under the authority of either House of the Union Parliament of any report, paper, votes or proceedings.

(2) In other respects, the privileges of members of the Houses shall be such as may from time to time be defined by Act of the Union Parliament and, until so defined, shall be such as were immediately before the commencement of this constitution enjoyed by members of the Indian Legislature.

(3) The provisions of sub-sections (1) and (2) of this section shall apply in relation to persons who by virtue of this constitution have the right to speak in, and otherwise take part in the proceedings of, a House as they apply in relation to members of the Union Parliament.

36. Members of either House shall be entitled to receive such

Salaries and allowances of members

salaries and allowances as may from time to time be determined by Act of the Union Parliament and, until provision in that respect is so made, allowances at such rates and upon such conditions as were, immediately before the date of the commencement of this constitution, applicable in the case of members of the Legislative Assembly of the Indian Legislature.

LEGISLATIVE PROCEDURE

37. (1) Subject to the special provisions of this Part

Provisions as to introduction and passing of Bills

of this constitution with respect to financial Bills, a Bill may originate in either House.

(2) Subject to the provisions of the next succeeding section, a Bill shall not be deemed to have been passed by the Houses of the Union Parliament unless it has been agreed to by both Houses, either without amendment

or with such amendments only as are agreed to by both Houses.

(3) A Bill pending in the Union Parliament shall not lapse by reason of the prorogation of the Houses.

(4) A Bill pending in the Senate which has not been passed by the House of Representatives shall not lapse on a dissolution of the House of Representatives.

(5) A Bill which is pending in the House of Representatives or which, having been passed by the House of Representatives, is pending in the Senate shall, subject to the provisions of the next succeeding section, lapse on a dissolution of the House.

38. (1) If after a Bill has been passed by one House and transmitted to the other House—

Joint sittings of both Houses in certain cases

    (a) the Bill is rejected by the other House; or

    (b) the Houses have finally disagreed as to the amendments to be made in the Bill; or

    (c) more than six months elapse from the date of the reception of the Bill by the other House without the Bill being presented to the President for his assent;

the President may, unless the Bill has lapsed by reason of a dissolution of the House of Representatives, notify to the Houses, by message if they are sitting or by public notification if they are not sitting, his intention to summon them to meet in a joint sitting for the purpose of deliberating and voting on the Bill:

Provided that, if it appears to the President that the Bill relates to finance or to any matter which affects the discharge of his functions in so far as he is by or under this constitution required to act in his discretion, he may so notify the Houses, notwithstanding that there has been no rejection of or final disagreement as to the Bill and notwithstanding that the said period of six months has not elapsed, if he is satisfied that there is no reasonable prospect of the Bill being presented to him for his assent without undue delay.

In reckoning any such period of six months as is referred to in this sub-section, no account shall be taken of any time during which the Union Parliament is prorogued or during which both Houses are adjourned for more than four days.

(2) Where the President has notified his intention of summoning the Houses to meet in a joint sitting, neither House shall proceed further with the Bill, but the President may at any time in the next session after the expiration of six months from the date of his notification summon the Houses, to meet in a joint sitting for the purpose specified in his notification and, if he does so, the Houses shall meet accordingly:

Provided that, if it appears to the President that the Bill is such a Bill as is mentioned in the proviso to sub-section (1) of this section, he may summon the Houses to meet in a joint sitting for the purpose aforesaid at any date, whether in the same session or in the next session.

(3) The functions of the President under the provisos to the two last preceding sub-sections shall be exercised by him in his discretion.

(4) If at the joint sitting of the two Houses the Bill, with such amendments, if any, as are agreed to in joint sitting, is passed by a majority of the total number of members of both Houses present and voting, it shall be deemed for the purposes of this constitution to have been passed by both Houses:

Provided that at a joint sitting—

(a) if the Bill, having been passed by one House, has not been passed by the other House with amendments and returned to the House in which it originated, no amendment shall be proposed to the Bill other than such amendments (if any) as are made necessary by the delay in the passage of the Bill;

(b) if the Bill has been so passed and returned, only such amendments as aforesaid shall be proposed to the

Bill and such other amendments as are relevant to
the matters with respect to which the Houses have
not agreed;

and the decision of the person presiding as to the amendments
which are admissible under this sub-section shall be final.

(5) A joint sitting may be held under this section and a
Bill passed thereat, notwithstanding that a dissolution of the
House of Representatives has intervened since the President
notified his intention to summon the Houses to meet therein.

39. When a Bill has been passed by the Houses, it shall be
Assent to Bills presented to the President, and the President
shall in his discretion declare either that he
assents to the Bill, or that he withholds assent therefrom:

Provided that the President may in his discretion return the
Bill to the Houses with a request that they will reconsider the
Bill or any specified provisions thereof and, in particular, will
consider the desirability of introducing any such amendments
as he may recommend in his request, and the Houses shall
reconsider the Bill accordingly.

PROCEDURE IN FINANCIAL MATTERS

40. (1) The President shall in respect of every financial year
Annual financial cause to be laid before both Houses of the
statement Union Parliament a statement of the estimated receipts and expenditure of the Union for that year,
in this part of this constitution referred to as the " annual
financial statement ".

(2) The estimates of expenditure embodied in the annual
financial statement shall show separately—

(a) the sums required to meet expenditure described by
this constitution as expenditure charged upon the revenues
of the Union; and

(b) the sums required to meet other expenditure proposed to be made from the revenues of the Union, and

shall distinguish expenditure on revenue account from other expenditure, and indicate the sums, if any, which are included solely because the President has directed their inclusion as being necessary for the due discharge of any of his special responsibilities.

(3) The following expenditure shall be expenditure charged on the revenues of the Union:

(a) the salary and allowances of the President and other expenditure relating to his office;

(b) debt charges for which the Union is liable, including interest, sinking fund charges and redemption charges, and other expenditure relating to the raising of loans and the service and redemption of debt;

(c) the salaries, allowances and pensions payable to or in respect of judges of the Supreme Court;

(d) expenditure for the purpose of the discharge by the President of his functions in so far as he is by or under this constitution required in the exercise thereof to act in his discretion;

(e) any sums required to satisfy any judgment, decree or award of any court or arbitral tribunal; and

(f) any other expenditure declared by this constitution or any Act of Parliament to be so charged.

(4) Any question whether any proposed expenditure falls within a class of expenditure charged on the revenues of the Union shall be decided by the President in his discretion.

41. (1) So much of the estimates of expenditure as relates to

Procedure in Parliament with respect to estimates

expenditure charged upon the revenues of the Union shall not be submitted to the vote of the Union Parliament, but nothing in this sub-section shall be construed as preventing the discussion in either House of the Union Parliament of any of those estimates.

(2) So much of the said estimates as relates to other expenditure shall be submitted in the form of demands for

grants to the House of Representatives and thereafter to the Senate, and either House shall have power to assent, or to refuse to assent, to any demand, or to assent to any demand subject to a reduction of the amount specified therein:

Provided that, where the House of Representatives has refused to assent to any demand, that demand shall not be submitted to the Senate, unless the President so directs and, where the House of Representatives has assented to a demand subject to a reduction of the amount specified therein, a demand for the reduced amount only shall be submitted to the Senate, unless the President otherwise directs; and where, in either of the said cases, such a direction is given, the demand submitted to the Senate shall be for such amount, not being a greater amount than that originally demanded, as may be specified in the direction.

(3) If the Houses differ with respect to any demand, the President shall summon the two Houses to meet in a joint sitting for the purpose of deliberating and voting on the demand as to which they disagree, and the decision of the majority of the members of both Houses present and voting shall be deemed to be the decision of the two Houses.

(4) No demand for a grant shall be made except on the recommendation of the President.

42. (1) The President shall authenticate by his signature a schedule specifying—

Authentication of schedule of autho-rised expenditure

(a) the grants made by the Houses under the last preceding section;

(b) the several sums required to meet the expenditure charged on the revenues of the Union, but not exceeding, in the case of any sum, the sum shown in the statement previously laid before the Union Parliament:

Provided that, if the Houses have not assented to any demand for a grant or have assented subject to a reduction of the amount specified therein, the President may, if in his opinion the refusal or reduction would affect the due discharge of any of his special responsibilities, include in the schedule such additional amount, if any, not exceeding the amount of the rejected demand or the reduction, as the case may be, as appears to him necessary in order to enable him to discharge that responsibility.

(2) The schedule so authenticated shall be laid before both Houses, but shall not be open to discussion or vote therein.

(3) Subject to the provisions of the next succeeding section, no expenditure from the revenues of the Union shall be deemed to be duly authorised unless it is specified in the schedule so authenticated.

43. If in respect of any financial year further expenditure

Supplementary statements of expenditure

from the revenues of the Union becomes necessary over and above the expenditure theretofore authorised for that year, the President shall cause to be laid before both Houses of the Union Parliament a supplementary statement showing the estimated amount of that expenditure, and the provisions of the preceding sections shall have effect in relation to that statement and that expenditure as they have effect in relation to the annual financial statement and the expenditure mentioned therein.

44. (1) A Bill or amendment making provision—

Special provisions as to financial Bills

(a) for imposing or increasing any tax; or

(b) for regulating the borrowing of money or the giving of any guarantee by the Union Government, or for amending the law with respect to any financial obligations undertaken or to be undertaken by the Union Government; or

(c) for declaring any expenditure to be expenditure charged on the revenues of the Union, or for increasing the amount of any such expenditure;

shall not be introduced or moved except on the recommendation of the President, and a Bill making such provision shall not be introduced in the Senate.

(2) A Bill or amendment shall not be deemed to make provision for any of the purposes aforesaid by reason only that it provides for the imposition of fines or other pecuniary penalties, or for the demand or payment of fees for licences or fees for services rendered.

(3) A Bill which, if enacted and brought into operation, would involve expenditure from the revenues of the Union shall not be passed by either House unless the President has recommended to that House the consideration of the Bill.

GENERAL PROCEDURE

45. (1) Each House of the Union Parliament may make *Rules of procedure* rules for regulating, subject to the provisions of this constitution, their procedure and the conduct of their business.

(2) The President, after consultation with the Chairman of the Senate and the Speaker of the House of Representatives, may make rules as to the procedure with respect to joint sittings of, and communications between, the two Houses.

(3) Until rules are made under this section, the rules of procedure and standing orders in force immediately before the commencement of this constitution with respect to the Indian legislature shall have effect in relation to the Union Parliament subject to such modifications and adaptations as may be made therein by the President.

(4) At a joint sitting of the two Houses the Chairman of the Senate, or in his absence such person as may be determined by rules of procedure made under this section, shall preside.

46. In the Union Parliament, business shall be transacted in Hindustani (Hindi or Urdu) or English, pro- *Language in the Union Parliament* vided that the Chairman or the Speaker, as the case may be, may permit any member who cannot adequately express himself in either language to

address the House in his mother-tongue. The Chairman or the Speaker, as the case may be, shall make arrangements for giving the House, whenever he thinks fit, a summary of the speech in a language other than that used by the member and such summary shall be included in the record of the proceedings of the House.

47. No discussion shall take place in the Union Parliament with respect to the conduct of any judge of *Restrictions on discussion in Parliament* the Supreme Court or a High Court in the discharge of his duties, except upon a motion for presenting an address to the President praying for the removal of the judge as hereinafter provided.

In this section the reference to a High Court shall be construed as including a reference to any court in an Indian State which is included in schedule I and which is a High Court for the purposes of Part— of this constitution.

48. (1) The validity of any proceedings in the Union Parliament shall not be called in question *Courts not to inquire into proceedings of Parliament* on the ground of any alleged irregularity of procedure.

(2) No officer or other member of the Union Parliament in whom powers are vested by or under this constitution for regulating procedure or the conduct of business, or for maintaining order in the Union Parliament shall be subject to the jurisdiction of any court in respect of the exercise by him of those powers.

CHAPTER IV

LEGISLATIVE POWERS OF THE PRESIDENT

49. (1) If at any time when the Union Parliament is not in session the President is satisfied that circum- *Power of President to promulgate ordinances during recess of Parliament* stances exist which render it necessary for him to take immediate action, he may promulgate such ordinances as the circumstances appear to him to require.

(2) An ordinance promulgated under this section shall have the same force and effect as an Act of the Union Parliament assented to by the President, but every such ordinance—

(*a*) shall be laid before the Union Parliament and shall cease to operate at the expiration of six weeks from the reassembly of the Union Parliament, or, if before the expiration of that period resolutions disapproving it are passed by both Houses, upon the passing of the second of those resolutions; and

(*b*) may be withdrawn at any time by the President.

(3) If and so far as an ordinance under this section makes any provision which the Union Parliament would not under this constitution be competent to enact, it shall be void.

[*Note:* The ordinance-making power has been the subject of great criticism under the present constitution. It must, however, be pointed out that circumstances may exist where the immediate promulgation of a law is absolutely necessary and there is no time in which to summon the Union Parliament. I recall that Lord Reading found it necessary to make an ordinance abolishing the cotton excise duty, when such action was immediately and imperatively required in the interests of the country. The President who is elected by the two Houses of Parliament and who has normally to act on the advice of ministers responsible to Parliament is not at all likely to abuse any ordinance-making power with which he may be invested. Hence the proposed provision.]

CHAPTER V

THE UNION JUDICATURE

50. (1) There shall be a Supreme Court in the Union

Establishment and constitution of Supreme Court

consisting of a Chief Justice and such number of other judges not being less than ten as the Union Parliament may deem necessary.

(2) Every judge of the Supreme Court shall be appointed by the President by warrant under his hand and seal (with the approval of not less than two-thirds of the members of the Council of State) and shall hold office until he attains the age of sixty-five years:

Provided that—

(a) a judge may by resignation under his hand addressed to the President resign his office;

(b) a judge may be removed from his office by the President by Order under his hand and seal on an address from both Houses of the Union Parliament praying for his removal on the ground of misbehaviour or incapacity.

[*Note:* The *ad hoc* Committee on the Supreme Court has observed that it will not be expedient to leave the power of appointing judges of the Supreme Court to the unfettered discretion of the President of the Union. They have suggested two alternatives, both of which involve the setting up of a special panel of 11 members. According to one alternative, the President, in consultation with the Chief Justice, is to nominate a person for appointment as puisne judge and the nomination has to be confirmed by at least seven members of the panel. According to the other alternative, the panel should recommend three names, out of which the President, in consultation with the Chief Justice, is to select one for the appointment. The above draft adopts substantially the first alternative, utilising at the same time the Council of State for this purpose. It will be noticed that the Council of State includes the Chief Justice among its members and its composition is such as to secure freedom from party bias. It should, therefore, be a satisfactory substitute for the panel recommended by the *ad hoc* Committee.]

(4) A person shall not be qualified for appointment as a judge of the Supreme Court unless he—

(a) has been for at least five years a judge of a High Court; or

(b) is a barrister of England or Northern Ireland of at least ten years' standing or a member of the Faculty

9

of Advocates in Scotland of at least ten years' standing; or

(c) has been for at least ten years a pleader of a High Court or of two or more of such courts in succession.

Explanation I: In this sub-section " High Court " means a High Court which exercises or which, before the commencement of this constitution, exercised jurisdiction in any territory included in schedule I.

Explanation II: In computing for the purposes of this sub-section the standing of a barrister or a member of the Faculty of Advocates, or the period during which a person has been a pleader, any period during which a person has held judicial office after he became a barrister, a member of the Faculty of Advocates or a pleader, as the case may be, shall be included.

(5) Every person appointed to be a judge of the Supreme Court shall, before he enters upon his office, make and subscribe before the President or some person appointed by him an oath according to the form set out in that behalf in the schedule— to this constitution.

51. The judges of the Supreme Court shall be entitled to *Salaries, etc., of judges* such salaries and allowances, including allowances for expenses in respect of equipment and travelling, upon appointment, and to such rights in respect of leave and pensions, as may from time to time be fixed by or under the Union law and until they are so fixed, to such salaries, etc. as may be fixed by the President:

Provided that neither the salary of a judge nor his rights in respect of leave of absence or pension shall be varied to his disadvantage after his appointment.

52. If the office of Chief Justice of the Supreme Court *Temporary Appointment of acting Chief Justice* becomes vacant, or if the Chief Justice is, by reason of absence or for any other reason, unable to perform the duties of his office, those duties shall, until some person appointed by the

President to the vacant office has entered on the duties thereof, or until the Chief Justice has resumed his duties, as the case may be, be performed by such one of the other judges of the court as the President may appoint for the purpose.

53. (1) If at any time there should not be a quorum of the judges of the Supreme Court available to hold *Appointment of ad hoc judges* or continue any session of the court, owing to a vacancy or vacancies, or to the absence through illness or on leave or in the discharge of other duties assigned by statute or otherwise, or to the disqualification of a judge or judges, or if by reason of any temporary increase in the business of the court, the strength of the court requires to be increased, the Chief Justice or, in his absence, the senior puisne judge, may in writing request the attendance at the sittings of the court, as an *ad hoc* judge, for such period as may be necessary, of a judge of a High Court, to be designated in writing by the Chief Justice or in his absence by any acting Chief Justice or the senior puisne judge of such High Court upon such request being made to him in writing.

(2) It shall be the duty of the judge whose attendance has been so requested or who has been so designated, in priority to the other duties of his office, to attend the sittings of the Supreme Court at the time and for the period for which his attendance shall be required, and while so attending he shall possess the powers and privileges and shall discharge the duties of a puisne judge of the Supreme Court.

[*Note:* This provision has been borrowed from section 30 of the Canadian Supreme Court Act. The words " or if by reason of any temporary increase in the business of the court, the strength of the court requires to be increased " do not occur in the Canadian Act and have been added for obvious reasons.]

54. The Supreme Court shall be a court of record and shall *Seat of Supreme Court* sit in Delhi and at such other place or places, if any, as the Chief Justice may, with the approval of the President, from time to time appoint.

55. Subject to the provisions of this constitution, the

Original jurisdiction of the Supreme Court

Supreme Court shall, to the exclusion of any other court, have an original jurisdiction in any dispute between any two or more of the following parties, that is to say, the Union and any of the units, if and in so far as the dispute involves any question (whether of law or fact) on which the existence or extent of a legal right depends:

Provided that the said jurisdiction shall not extend to a dispute to which an Indian State unit is a party, if the dispute arises out of any provision of a treaty agreement, engagement, sanad, or other similar instrument, which was entered into or executed before the commencement of this constitution, or which expressly provides that the said jurisdiction shall not extend to such a dispute.

56. (1) An appeal shall lie to the Supreme Court from any

Appellate jurisdiction of Supreme Court in appeals from High Courts in provinces in certain cases

judgment, decree or final order of a High Court of a province if the High Court certifies that the case involves a substantial question of law as to the interpretation of this constitution and it shall be the duty of every such High Court to consider in every case whether or not any such question is involved and of its own motion to give or to withhold a certificate accordingly.

(2) Where such a certificate is given, any party in the case may appeal to the Supreme Court on the ground that any such question as aforesaid has been wrongly decided and, with the leave of the Supreme Court, on any other ground as well.

57. Subject to such rules as the Supreme Court may make in

Appellate jurisdiction of Supreme Court in appeals from High Courts in provinces in other cases

this behalf, an appeal shall lie to the Supreme Court from a judgment, decree or final order of a High Court in a province without any such certificate as aforesaid, provided that—

(a) the amount or value of the subject matter of the dispute in the court of first instance and still in

dispute on appeal was and is not less than twenty
thousand rupees or the judgment, decree or final
order involves directly or indirectly some claim or
question respecting property of the like amount or
value and provided further that where the judgment, decree, or final order appealed from affirms
the decision of the court immediately below and
the appeal involves some substantial question of
law; or

(*b*) the Supreme Court gives special leave to appeal.

58. (1) An appeal shall lie to the Supreme Court from any

*Appellate jurisdic-
tion of Supreme
Court in appeals from
Indian States*

judgment, decree or final order of a High
Court in an Indian State included in
schedule I if the case involves a substantial
question of law as to the interpretation of
this constitution or of any law of the Union Parliament, or of
the legislature of any unit other than the State concerned.

(2) An appeal under this section shall be by way of
special case to be stated for the opinion of the Supreme Court
by the High Court, and the Supreme Court may require a
case to be so stated and may return any case so stated in
order that further facts may be stated therein.

59. (1) The Supreme Court shall have such further juris-

*Enlargement of
the jurisdiction of
the Supreme Court*

diction and powers with respect to any of the
matters in the Union legislative list as the
Union Parliament may by Act confer.

(2) The Supreme Court shall have such further jurisdiction and powers with respect to any matter as the Union
and any unit may by special agreement confer.

60. Without prejudice to the powers that may be vested in

*Power of Supreme
Court to issue cer-
tain writs*

this behalf in other courts, the Supreme
Court shall have power to issue directions
in the nature of the writs of *habeas corpus*,
mandamus, prohibition, *quo warranto* and *certiorari* appropriate
to any of the rights guaranteed in Part III of the constitution.

61. (1) All authorities, civil and judicial, in the territories subject to the jurisdiction of the Union shall act in aid of the Supreme Court.

Enforcement of decrees and orders of Supreme Court and orders as to discovery etc.

(2) The Supreme Court shall, as respects the said territories, have power to make any order for the purpose of securing the attendance of any person, the discovery or production of any documents, or the investigation or punishment of any contempt of court, which any High Court has power to make as respects the territory within its jurisdiction, and any such orders and any orders of the Supreme Court as to the costs of and incidental to any proceedings therein, shall be enforceable by all courts and authorities in every part of the territories subject to the jurisdiction of the Union, as if they were orders duly made by the highest court exercising civil or criminal jurisdiction, as the case may be, in that part.

62. Where in any case the Supreme Court requires a special case to be stated or restated by, or remit a case to, or order a stay of execution in a case from, a High Court in an Indian State included in schedule I, or require the aid of the civil or judicial authorities in such State, the Supreme Court shall cause letters of request in that behalf to be sent to the Ruler of the State, and the Ruler shall cause such communication to be made to the highest court or to any judicial or civil authority as the circumstances may require.

Letters of request to Indian States

63. The law declared by the Supreme Court shall, so far as applicable, be recognised as binding on, and shall be followed by, all courts within the territories subject to the jurisdiction of the Union.

Law declared by Supreme Court to be binding on all courts

64. (1) If at any time it appears to the President that a question of law has arisen, or is likely to arise, which is of such a nature and such public importance that it is expedient to obtain the opinion of the Supreme Court upon it, he may in his

Power of President to consult Supreme Court

discretion .refer the question to that court for consideration, and the court may, after such hearing as they think fit, report to the President thereon.

(2) No report shall be made under this section save in accordance with an opinion delivered in open court with the concurrence of a majority of the judges present at the hearing of the case, but nothing in this sub-section shall be deemed to prevent a judge who does not concur from delivering a dissenting opinion.

65. (1) The Supreme Court may from time to time, with *Rules of court, etc.* the approval of the President in his discretion, make rules of court for regulating generally the practice and procedure of the court, including rules as to the persons practising before the court, as to the time within which appeals to the court are to be entered, as to the costs of and incidental to any proceedings in the court, and as to the fees to be charged in respect of proceedings therein, and in particular may make rules providing for the summary determination of any appeal which appears to the court to be frivolous or vexatious or brought for the purpose of delay.

(2) Rules made under this section may fix the minimum number of judges who are to sit for any purpose, so that no case shall be decided by less than three judges:

Provided that all references under section 57 shall be heard by the full court.

(3) Subject to the provisions of any rules of court, the Chief Justice shall determine what judges are to constitute any division of the court and what judges are to sit for any purpose.

(4) No judgment shall be delivered by the Supreme Court save in open court and with the concurrence of a majority of the judges present at the hearing of the case, but nothing in this sub-section shall be deemed to prevent a judge who does not concur from delivering a dissenting judgment.

66. The Union Parliament may make provisions by Act for conferring upon the Supreme Court such supplemental powers, not inconsistent with any of the provisions of this constitution, as may appear to be necessary or desirable for the purpose of enabling the court more effectively to exercise the jurisdiction conferred upon it by or under this constitution.

Ancillary powers of Supreme Court

67. The administrative expenses of the Supreme Court, including all salaries, allowances and pensions payable to, or in respect of, the officers and servants of the court, shall be charged upon the revenues of the Union, and any fees or other moneys taken by the court shall form part of those revenues.

Expenses of the Supreme Court

68. References in any provision of this part of this constitution to a High Court in, or exercising jurisdiction in, an Indian State included in schedule I shall be construed as references to any court which the President may, after communication with the Ruler of the State, declare to be a High Court for the purposes of that provision.

Construction of references to High Courts in Indian States

CHAPTER VI
AUDITOR-GENERAL OF THE UNION

[Clauses to be drafted.]

CHAPTER VII
PUBLIC SERVICE COMMISSION

[Clauses to be drafted.]

CHAPTER VIII
UNION RAILWAY AUTHORITY

[Clauses to be drafted, if it is decided that provision should be made for a Union Railway Authority, on the lines of the Federal Railway Authority as in the Government of India Act of 1935.]

CHAPTER IX

UNION DEFENCE COUNCIL

[Clauses to be drafted, if it is decided to set up a Union Defence Council.]

CHAPTER X

UNION ECONOMIC COUNCIL

[Clauses to be drafted, if it is decided to set up a Union Economic Council.]

CHAPTER XI

FRANCHISE FOR THE UNION PARLIAMENT

The Union Parliament may from time to time make provision with respect to all or any of the following matters, that is to say,

    (a) the delimitation of territorial constituencies;

    (b) the qualifications for the franchise and the preparation of electoral rolls;

    (c) the qualifications for being elected as a member of either House;

    (d) the filling of casual vacancies in either House;

    (e) the conduct of elections under this constitution and the methods of voting thereat;

    (f) the expenses of candidates at such elections;

    (g) corrupt practices and other offences at or in connection with such elections;

    (h) the decision of doubts and disputes arising out of or in connection with such elections;

    (i) matters ancillary to any such matter as aforesaid:

Provided that the superintendence, direction and control of elections, including the appointment of election tribunals, shall be vested in the President acting in his discretion.

[*Note:* The effect of vesting these powers in the President acting in his discretion will be to make available to him the advice of the Council of State.]

PART V

INTERNATIONAL RELATIONS

1. The Union affirms its adherence to the Charter of the United Nations and to the purposes and principles enunciated therein.

[See note under Part V, clause 1 of Memorandum.]

2. For the purpose of the exercise of any executive function of the Union in or in connection with its defence or its external affairs, the Government may, subject to the provisions of the Charter of the United Nations, avail itself of or adopt any organ, instrument or method of procedure used or adopted for the like purpose by any other State or by the members of any group or organisation of nations with which the Union is or becomes associated for the purpose of international co-operation in matters of common concern.

3. (1) Every international agreement to which the Union becomes a party shall be laid before the House of Representatives.

(2) The Union shall not be bound by any international agreement involving a charge upon the revenues of the Union unless the terms of the agreement shall have been approved by the House of Representatives.

Explanation: This section shall not apply to inter-governmental agreements of a technical or administrative character.

4. No international agreement shall be part of the municipal law of the Union, save as may be determined by the Parliament of the Union.

[*Note:* These clauses correspond to art. 29 of the Constitution of Ireland.]

5. The Union shall honour all legitimate obligations arising out of any treaties or agreements which immediately before the commencement of this constitution were in force between His Majesty or the Government of India or any other competent authority and the head or the government of any other State, provided that such other State honours any reciprocal obligations towards the Union.

[See note under Part V, clause 5 of Memorandum.]

PART VI

DISTRIBUTION OF LEGISLATIVE POWERS BETWEEN UNION AND UNITS

[Clauses to be drafted.]

PART VII

ADMINISTRATIVE RELATIONS BETWEEN UNION AND UNITS AND BETWEEN UNITS INTER SE

[Clauses to be drafted.]

PART VIII

AMENDMENT OF THE CONSTITUTION

An amendment to the constitution may be initiated in either House of the Union Parliament and when the proposed amendment is passed in each House by a majority of not less than two-thirds of the total number of members of that House and is ratified by the legislatures of not less than two-thirds of the units of the Union, excluding the Chief Commissioners' provinces, it shall be presented to the President for his assent; and upon such assent being given, the amendment shall come into operation.

Explanation I: For the purposes of this section, only the legislatures of the units specified in schedule— shall be recognised.

Explanation II: The Union Parliament may, from time to time, make such additions or alterations in the aforesaid schedule— as it thinks fit and such additions or alterations shall have effect as if enacted in this constitution.

[*Note:* The explanations are necessary, because some of the units, particularly where they consist of groups of Indian States, may not possess proper legislatures. If care is taken not to admit a unit to the Union unless it possesses a proper legislature, the explanations may not be necessary.]

PART IX

TRANSITIONAL PROVISIONS

[See Part IX of Memorandum.]

A MODEL PROVINCIAL CONSTITUTION

[*At its sitting held on April* 30, 1947, *the Constituent Assembly of India set up two committees, one to report on the main principles of the Union constitution* (*see Chapter* 6) *and the other on the principles of a model provincial constitution. Of the* 25 *members of the Provincial Constitution Committee, seven sent replies. The following is an independent memorandum prepared by Sri B. N. Rau and submitted by him for the consideration of the committee.*]

PART I

GOVERNORS' PROVINCES

CHAPTER I

THE PROVINCIAL EXECUTIVE

1. For each province there shall be a Governor elected
Governor　by the provincial legislature by secret vote according to the system of proportional representation by the single transferable vote.

[*Note:* In a unitary constitution and even in a federal constitution approximating to the unitary type like that of Canada, provincial Governors may be appointed by the Central Government. Under the Cabinet Mission's plan of May 16, 1946, the Union Government will not have this power and some other method of selecting Governors has to be adopted. We can either have direct election by the people of the province or some system of indirect election. As the Governors are intended for the most part to be responsible heads acting on the advice of ministers, it is perhaps unnecessary to have direct election with all its complications. As at the Centre, we may have election by the legislature. This is what has been proposed in the above provision.]

2. (1) The Governor shall hold office for a term of five years, except in the event of death, resignation or removal.

(2) The Governor may be removed from office for misbehaviour or infirmity of mind or body by a resolution of the provincial legislature supported by not less than two-thirds of the total membership of the legislature.

(3) The Governor shall be eligible for re-election once, but only once.

[*Note:* I have not suggested any provision in this memo-randum as to how casual vacancies in the office of Governor are to be filled. The majority of the replies from the members of the committee propose that there should be a Deputy Governor, elected in the same manner as the Governor, who would take his place in the event of a casual vacancy. The proposal requires careful consideration. With a parliamentary type of executive, there is hardly room for a Deputy Governor in the sense that he can hardly be given any regular functions. Where the legislature is bicameral, he might perhaps be made *ex-officio* Chairman of the Upper Chamber in the same way as the Vice-President of the U.S.A. is the Chairman of the Senate. But most of the replies are against the creation of an Upper Chamber. The result will be that we shall have a Deputy Governor with no normal functions. There are obvious risks in the creation of such an office. I have accordingly, for the present, omitted any provision for a Deputy Governor.

The Commission device which has been adopted for casual vacancies at the Centre would hardly be appropriate in a province, because most of the provincial legislatures will be unicameral. A possible solution would be to utilise the Council of State; if this is acceptable, the provision would run thus:

" *The Council of State may by a majority of its members make such provision as they think fit for the discharge of the functions of the Governor in the event of any casual vacancy or other unforeseen contingency.*"]

3. The executive authority of the province shall be exercised by the Governor either directly or through officers subordinate to him, but this shall not prevent the Union Parliament or the provincial legislature from conferring functions upon subordinate authorities, nor shall it be deemed to transfer to the Governor any functions conferred by any existing Indian law on any court, judge or officer or local or other authority.

Executive authority of province

4. Subject to the provisions of this constitution and of any special agreement, the executive authority of each province shall extend to the matters with respect to which the legislature of the province has power to make laws.

Extent of the executive authority of province

[*Note:* The reference to special agreements in this provision requires a word of explanation. It is possible that in the future there may be Indian States or groups of Indian States desiring to have a common administration with a neighbouring province in certain specified matters of common interest. In such cases, the Rulers concerned may, by a special agreement, cede the necessary jurisdiction to the province. Needless to say, this will not interfere with the accession of the State or States concerned to the Union, because the accession to the Union will be in respect of Union subjects, whereas the cession of jurisdiction contemplated here is in respect of provincial subjects.]

5. There shall be a Council of Ministers to aid and advise the Governor in the exercise of his functions except in so far as he is, by or under this constitution, required to exercise his functions or any of them in his discretion.

Council of Ministers

[*Note:* For the most part, the Governor will act on advice, but there are certain functions which even a responsible head has to exercise in his discretion *e.g.*, the choice of the Prime Minister, the dissolution of the legislature (in certain events) and so on. In the present circumstances, similar discretion may have to be vested in the Governor in the matter of the protection of minorities and the maintenance of law and order. Of course, it is possible that if in any of these " discretionary "

matters, the Governor were to act against the advice of the
Ministry, the Ministry might resign and the Governor might
not be able to find an alternative Ministry. In such cases the
Governor would normally accept the advice of the Ministry in
preference to his own judgment, but in an extreme case he
might dissolve the legislature. If the new legislature endorses
his view of the situation and returns a different party to power,
his action will have justified itself. If, however, it returns the
same party to power, the Governor will then have no option
except to act in accordance with the advice of his former
ministers. The "discretionary" power will, in such cases,
have at least the effect of bringing the issue before the
electorate.]

6. If any question arises whether a matter is one for the
Governor's discretion or not, the decision of the Governor in
his discretion shall be final.

7. The question whether any and, if so, what advice was
tendered by the ministers to the Governor shall not be
enquired into in any court.

8. Subject to the provisions of the next succeeding clause,
Other provisions the Governor's ministers shall be chosen
as to ministers and summoned by him and shall hold office
during his pleasure.

9. (1) The Governor may, if he thinks fit, leave all his
ministers to be elected according to the system of proportional
representation, by means of the single transferable vote, by the
provincial legislature or, where the legislature is bicameral,
by the Lower Chamber of the provincial legislature.

(2) The normal term of office of the ministers so elected
shall expire with the term of the provincial legislature or,
where the legislature is bicameral, the term of the Lower
Chamber of the provincial legislature which elected them:

Provided that they shall continue in office until the election
or appointment of their successors.

(3) Any minister so elected shall not be removable
from office during his normal term except by a decision of

the provincial legislature or, where the legislature is bicameral,
by a decision of the Lower Chamber of the provincial legislature supported by not less than two-thirds of the total number of
members of the legislature or the Chamber, as the case may be.

(4) Vacancies among the ministers so elected arising within the normal term of office shall be filled at the next meeting
of the provincial legislature for the remainder of that term.

[*Note:* This provision is an attempt to introduce something
like the Swiss type of executive in those provinces where this
type is considered preferable. The choice is left to the Governor
whether he will have this type or the British type.]

10. (1) A minister who for any period of six consecutive
months is not a member of the provincial legislature shall
at the expiration of that period cease to be a minister.

(2) The salaries of ministers shall be such as the
provincial legislature may from time to time by Act determine and, until the provincial legislature so determine, shall
be determined by the Governor:

Provided that the salary of a minister shall not be varied
during his term of office.

11. The functions of the Governor with respect to the
choosing and summoning and the dismissal of ministers
(except where he leaves them to be elected by the legislature
under clause 9) and with respect to the determination of their
salaries shall be exercised by him in his discretion.

12. The relations between the Governor and his ministers
(except where he leaves them to be elected by the legislature
under clause 9) shall, as nearly as possible, be the same as
those between the King and his ministers in England.

13. (1) In the exercise of his functions, the Governor
Special responsi- shall have the following special responsi-
bilities of Governor bilities: that is to say,

    (*a*) the prevention of any grave menace to the peace
        and tranquillity of the province or any part
        thereof; and

10

(*b*) the safeguarding of the legitimate interests of minorities.

[*Note:* Until the advisory committee has proposed a scheme for the administration of the excluded and partially excluded areas, it will not be possible to say whether the Governor should be given any special responsibilities in connection with their administration.]

(2) If and in so far as any special responsibility of the Governor is involved, he shall, in the exercise of his functions, act in his discretion.

14. (1) The Governor shall appoint a person, being a *Advocate-General* person qualified to be a judge of a High *for province* Court, to be Advocate-General for the province to give advice to the provincial government upon legal matters.

(2) The Advocate-General shall hold office during the pleasure of the Governor and shall receive such remuneration as the Governor may determine.

15. All executive action of the government of a province *Conduct of busi-* shall be expressed to be taken in the name *ness of provincial government* of the Governor.

16. The Governor shall make rules for the more convenient transaction of the business of the *Rules of business* provincial government and for the allocation of duties among ministers.

CHAPTER II

THE PROVINCIAL LEGISLATURE

17. (1) There shall for every province be a provincial legislature which will consist of the Gover- *Constitution of provincial legisla-* nor and the Legislative Assembly; in the *tures* following provinces, there shall, in addition, be a Legislative Council (here enumerate those provinces, if any, which desire to have an Upper Chamber).

(2) The representation of the different territorial constituencies in the Legislative Assembly shall be on the basis of population and shall not be more than one representative for every lakh of the population.

(3) Every Legislative Assembly of every province, unless sooner dissolved, shall continue for five years from the date appointed for its first meeting.

[*Note:* Under the existing constitution, Madras, Bombay, Bengal, the United Provinces, Bihar and Assam have two Chambers and the rest one. Mr. Kher, Chief Minister of Bombay and Dr. P. Subbarayan, Minister in Madras, no longer desire an Upper Chamber in their respective provinces. The question whether there is to be an Upper Chamber or not in any province and, if there is to be one, how it is to be constituted will probably have to be left to the decision of the representatives of that province in the Constituent Assembly. So too the question whether there is to be special representation in the Legislative Assembly for universities, for labour, for women and so on.]

18. The provisions for the meeting, prorogation and dissolution of the provincial legislature, the *Composition of provincial legislatures, etc.* relations between the two Chambers (where there are two Chambers), the mode of voting, the privileges of members, disqualification for membership, parliamentary procedure, including procedure in financial matters, etc. shall be on the lines of the corresponding provisions in the Act of 1935.

19. In the provincial legislature, business shall be transacted in Hindustani (Hindi or Urdu) or *Language* English, provided that the Chairman (where there is an Upper Chamber) or the Speaker, as the case may be, may permit any member who cannot adequately express himself in either language to address the Chamber in his mother-tongue. The Chairman (where there is an Upper Chamber) or the Speaker, as the case may be, shall make arrangements for giving the Chamber, whenever he thinks

fit, a summary of the speech in a language other than that used by the member and such summary shall be included in the record of the proceedings of the Chamber.

[This follows the corresponding provision in the Constituent Assembly rules.]

20. The provincial legislature may from time to time make provisions with respect to all or any of the following matters; that is to say,

Franchise for provincial legislature

(a) the delimitation of territorial constituencies;

(b) the qualifications for the franchise and the preparation of electoral rolls;

(c) the qualifications for being elected as a member of either Chamber;

(d) the filling of casual vacancies in either Chamber;

(e) the conduct of elections under this constitution and the methods of voting thereat;

(f) the expenses of candidates at such elections;

(g) corrupt practices and other offences at or in connection with such elections;

(h) the decision of doubts and disputes arising out of or in connection with such elections;

(i) matters ancillary to any such matter as aforesaid:

Provided that the superintendence, direction and control of elections, including the appointment of election tribunals, shall be vested in the President acting in his discretion, but subject to the approval of the Council of State.

CHAPTER III

LEGISLATIVE POWERS OF GOVERNOR

21. (1) If at any time when the provincial legislature is not in session, the Governor is satisfied that circumstances exist which render it necessary for him to take immediate action, he may promulgate such ordinances as the circumstances appear to him to require.

(2) An ordinance promulgated under this clause shall have the same force and effect as an Act of the provincial legislature assented to by the Governor, but every such ordinance—

(a) shall be laid before the provincial legislature and shall cease to operate at the expiration of six weeks from the reassembly of the provincial legislature, or, if before the expiration of that period resolutions disapproving it are passed by the legislature, upon the passing of the second of those resolutions; and

(b) may be withdrawn at any time by the Governor.

(3) If and so far as an ordinance under this clause makes any provision which the provincial legislature would not under this constitution be competent to enact, it shall be void.

[*Note:* The ordinance-making power has been the subject of great criticism under the present constitution. It must, however, be pointed out that circumstances may exist where the immediate promulgation of a law is absolutely necessary and there is no time in which to summon the provincial legislature. As stated earlier, Lord Reading found it necessary to make an ordinance abolishing the cotton excise duty when such action was immediately and imperatively required in the interests of the country. The Governor who is elected by the provincial legislature and who has normally to act on the advice of ministers responsible to the legislature is not at all likely to abuse any ordinance-making power with which he may be invested. Hence the proposed provision.]

CHAPTER IV

DISTRIBUTION OF LEGISLATIVE POWERS

[This will have to await decisions on the report of the Union Powers Committee. But in any event there should be a clause on the following lines:

" *Provision may be made by provincial law in the interests of regional autonomy for delegation to representative bodies of defined regions legislative powers in respect of such matters as the law may prescribe. Any such law shall determine the rights, powers and duties of such bodies and their relation to the provincial legislature and to the provincial government."*]

CHAPTER V

EXCLUDED AND PARTIALLY EXCLUDED AREAS

[The provisions of this Chapter cannot be framed until the Advisory Committee has reported.]

PART II

CHIEF COMMISSIONERS' PROVINCES

1. Subject to the other provisions of this Part, a Chief Commissioner's province shall be administered by the President of the Union acting, to such extent as he thinks fit, through a Chief Commissioner, or the Governor of a neighbouring province, or the Ruler of a neighbouring Indian State.

2. (1) The President shall not act through the Governor of a neighbouring province or the Ruler of a neighbouring Indian State, save—

   (i) with the consent of the Governor or Ruler concerned; and

   (ii) in accordance with the wishes of the people of the Chief Commissioner's province concerned, ascertained in such manner as he considers most appropriate.

   (2) If the consent of the Governor or the Ruler or the people concerned is not forthcoming or is withdrawn, the President shall act through a Chief Commissioner.

[*Note:* These provisions have been suggested because some people from Coorg have expressed a desire that Coorg should be administered as if it were a part of the province of Madras; others, as if it were a part of the State of Mysore.]

3. The President may, by Order, create or continue for any province administered through a Chief Commissioner—

(1) a local legislature; and/or

(2) a council of advisers

with such constitution, powers and functions, in each case, as may be specified in the Order.

4. Until other provision is made in this behalf by the President, the constitution, powers and functions of the Coorg Legislative Council and the arrangements with respect to revenues collected in Coorg and expenses in respect of Coorg shall remain unchanged.

PART III

THE PROVINCIAL JUDICIARY

The provisions of the Government of India Act, 1935, relating to High Courts may be adopted *mutatis mutandis*. As regards the appointment of High Court judges, it should be provided that judges shall be appointed by the Governor with the approval of at least two-thirds of the members of the Council of State.

[*Note:* The Council of State is a kind of Privy Council mainly for advising the President of the Union in certain matters where he is required to act in his discretion. It has been proposed in the memorandum relating to the Union constitution that the appointment of judges of the Supreme Court should be made by the President with the approval of at least two-thirds of the members of the Council of State. It is a non-party body of elder statesmen and judges including the Chief Justice and every ex-Chief Justice of the Supreme Court. It will, therefore, be a suitable body for approving of the appointment of judges, whether of the Supreme Court or of the High Courts. It should be remembered that High Court judges may be potential judges of the Supreme Court; it is, therefore, not inappropriate that their appointment should be made subject to the approval of the Council of State.]

PART IV

P.P.S.C. AND PROVINCIAL AUDITORS-GENERAL

Provisions regarding Public Service Commissions and Auditors-General should be inserted on the lines of the provisions in the Act of 1935.

PART V

TRANSITIONAL PROVISIONS

1. Any person holding office as Governor in any province immediately before the commencement of this constitution shall continue as such and shall be deemed to be the Governor of the province under this constitution until a successor, duly elected under this constitution, assumes office.

2. There should be similar provisions, *mutatis mutandis*, in respect of the Council of Ministers, the Legislative Assembly and the Legislative Council (in provinces which decide to have an Upper Chamber).

[These provisions are necessary in order that there may be a legislature and a government ready to take over power in each province as soon as the transfer of power takes place in or before June 1948.]

3. The government of each Governor's province under this constitution shall be the successor of the government of the corresponding province under the Act of 1935 in respect of all property, assets, rights and liabilities.

8

OPTING IN AND OPTING OUT

[THE POSSIBILITY of a provision to enable provinces to opt in or to opt out of the Federal Union of India had been visualised in the original Cripps plan of 1942. In an informal discussion in November 1945 (some months before the Cabinet Mission's statement of 16th May 1946, Sri B. N. Rau had sought Sri Jawaharlal Nehru's view on the nature of the voting in the constitution-making body. When it was suggested that to make the vote binding on all the participants might deter some provinces from even coming into the constitution-making body, Sri Nehru agreed that an element of coercion might have that undesirable effect. The relevant questions and answers are reproduced below: *

> *Question:* If you tell the Panjab or Sind that, by coming into the constitution-making body, they would be bound by its decisions even when they themselves dissent from those decisions, are they not likely to stand out from the very beginning? If, on the other hand, you tell every province that it is free to come in, contribute to the discussion, and accept or reject the resulting constitution as it thinks fit, is there not a greater chance of its coming into the constitution-making body and of accepting the constitution framed, either immediately or possibly at a later date? Of course, if this plan is adopted, the decisions of the constitution-making body must not be held to bind even the dissentient units: these must be given a chance of accepting or rejecting the constitution as they think fit. The Congress has accepted the position that no unit can be coerced into a constitution of which it does not itself approve.

---

* For a full statement, see the Introduction.

J. N.: Yes; I think it would be better to give an option of adherence or accession to every unit, after the deliberations of the constitution-making body are over. Undoubtedly, there can be no coercion in the matter. I recognise that the psychological effect of telling a province that even if it comes into the discussions the door will still be open for it to go out, may be that it will elect to stay in.

Question: From another point of view also, would it not be unreasonable to ask a province to join the constitution-making body and compel it to accept a constitution which has not yet been framed and is only to be framed by that body? The province may very well say that without knowing what safeguards for minorities the proposed constitution is to contain, it cannot be expected to take a leap in the dark.

J. N.: That is so. At the same time, I cannot help thinking that the question of safeguards has not hitherto been discussed in the context of existing conditions.

Later, in a similar discussion with Mr. Jinnah (after the publication of the Cabinet Mission's statement), the question of Pakistan presumably figured somewhat prominently. At any rate, Sri B. N. Rau recorded in a note after the discussion:

" The assumption underlying Pakistan is that there are certain areas in India which are predominantly Muslim and whose affairs can be administered in complete isolation from the rest of the country. The Muslim League in demanding Pakistan and the Congress in conceding self-determination, both assumed this; and if the assumption were true there would be no question left except of demarcating areas to be separated. Unfortunately, the investigations heretofore made show that Pakistan, however its boundary may be drawn—whether provincewise, districtwise or in any other manner—cannot be self-supporting, as regards defence; nor will it be able, unaided, to solve the problem of raising the standard of life of its population. For this purpose at least, it cannot isolate itself from the rest of India.

" Either the Cripps plan or some alternative (the details of which have been tentatively worked out) will probably offer no difficulty except in the Panjab and Bengal. In these two provinces neither plan ensures self-determination for the Muslims, or for the Hindus and Sikhs; for it is possible that on either plan a province as a whole may be found to be voting ' in ', although the majority of the Muslims may vote ' out ', or voting ' out ', while the Hindus and Sikhs may vote ' in '.

" To give effect to the provincial vote as a whole and to put the entire province ' in ' or ' out ' in such cases is a matter requiring the most anxious consideration and the decision may turn to some extent on factors which cannot be known or even specified just now.

" For example, if Sind and the North-Western Frontier Province vote ' in ' and the Panjab as a whole votes 'in ', while a majority of the Muslims vote ' out ', it would hardly be practical politics to carve out a portion of the Panjab and put it out of the Union. We cannot tell now how Sind and the N.W.F.P. will vote as the draft constitution may contain other relevant but indisputable factors.

" Therefore, a third plan would be to leave out the controversial cases for future consideration in the light of all the circumstances then prevailing and to provide now merely for others. Thus we may, for the present, say that in the Panjab and in Bengal (a) if the majority of the Muslims and the majority communities of other than Muslims separately vote for, the province may be deemed to have accepted the plan; (b) if they have voted against, it may be deemed to have been rejected.

" The question is, which of these plans does the Congress propose ? "]

The following memorandum on " Opting in and Opting out " was circulated to the members of the Constituent Assembly:

QUEENSLAND

The following extracts from the *Historical Introduction to the Constitution of the Australian Commonwealth* by Quick and Garran are relevant. In order to understand the extracts it may be of assistance to remember that the Convention, which drafted the Australian Commonwealth Constitution, began its first session in 1897, the idea of such a Convention having been decided upon at a Conference of Premiers in 1895.

The Premiers' Conference: " The Conference of Premiers met at Hobart on 29th January 1895, the Premiers present being Mr. Reid (New South Wales), Mr. (afterwards Sir) George Turner (Victoria), Mr. (afterwards Sir) Hugh M. Nelson (Queensland), Mr. C. C. Kingston (South Australia), Sir Edward Braddon (Tasmania), and Sir John Forrest (Western Australia). The following resolutions, submitted by Mr. Reid, were carried:

(1) That this Conference regards Federation as the great and pressing question of Australasian politics.

(2) That a Convention, consisting of ten representatives from each colony, directly chosen by the electors, be charged with the duty of framing a federal constitution.

(3) That the constitution so framed be submitted to the electors for acceptance or rejection by a direct vote.

(4) That such a constitution, if accepted by the electors of three or more colonies, be transmitted to the Queen by an Address from the Parliaments of those colonies praying for the necessary legislative enactment.

(5) That a Bill be submitted to the Parliament of each colony for the purpose of giving effect to the foregoing resolutions.

(6) That Messrs. Turner and Kingston be requested to prepare a draft Bill for the consideration of this Conference. (*pp.* 158-159, *op. cit.*) . . . .

" On 6th February the draft Bill prepared by Mr. Turner and Mr. Kingston was ' considered, amended and agreed to as the draft of a type of Bill suitable for giving effect to the resolutions of the Conference'. Mr. Reid intimated that ' so soon as practicable after the reassembling of the New South Wales Parliament his Government would introduce a measure providing for the chief objects of the Bill as defined in the draft '. Messrs. Turner, Kingston and Nelson and Sir Edward Braddon intimated that as soon as New South Wales had passed the Bill they would follow suit—Mr. Nelson, however, reserving the right to dispense with the direct reference to the electors." (*p.* 159 *op. cit.*) . . . .

" New South Wales having redeemed her pledge and led the way, other colonies were not slow to follow." (*p.* 161 *op. cit.*) . . . .

" Queensland and Western Australia were now being waited for. But Sir Hugh Nelson, the Queensland Premier, had meanwhile discovered difficulties in the way of passing a Bill in the form agreed upon. Queensland was tripartite in interest, the North and the Centre being arrayed against the South in their demand to be erected into separate colonies. This question of separation became interwoven with the question of Federation. The North and the Centre looked forward to Federation, not only for its own sake, but also as a step towards sub-division; whilst Brisbane and the South feared that their trade would suffer from open competition with New South Wales and its metropolis. Each of the three divisions preferred to have separate representation in the Convention rather than to trust to the chances of a single electorate. Moreover, the government and a large section of the Parliament favoured parliamentary rather than direct election. Sir Hugh Nelson accordingly provided in his Bill that the Queensland representatives should be elected by the members of the Legislative Assembly, grouped according to the three great districts. The Premiers of the four colonies which had substantially adopted the model Bill joined in a remonstrance against this departure from the Hobart understanding, but without avail. Sir Hugh Nelson proceeded with the Bill, but somewhat half-heartedly, without committing himself to the whole of the process, and reserving to the Parliament the right to send the constitution to the people or not, as it pleased. He made no profession of being an ardent federalist, but argued that it could do no harm to have a voice in framing the constitution which they would afterwards be free to accept or reject. On the motion for the second reading, Mr. G. S. Curtis moved an amendment affirming that no enabling Bill would be acceptable which did not provide for the election of representatives by direct popular vote. This was negatived by 36 votes to 26 and the Bill passed the Assembly in July 1896. But in the Council (*i.e.*, the Upper House) it was not unnaturally claimed that if the election was to be parliamentary, both Houses should take part in it; and accordingly the Bill was returned to the Assembly amended to that effect. The Assembly, however, denied the representative character of a nominee House. The difference between the Houses proved irreconcilable; and in November—though Mr. Reid journeyed to Brisbane to assist a settlement—the Bill was laid aside." (*p.* 162 *op. cit.*)

Thus, Queensland opted out of the Convention, so to speak, at the beginning. But the sequel is interesting. The Convention, with representatives from the other States, proceeded with the constitution-making without Queensland. Then there was another Premiers' Conference in 1899, after the constitution had been drafted, for the purpose of considering certain suggestions made by New South Wales. At this Conference Queensland was represented by its new Premier. What happened when the amended draft of the constitution was sent round to the States for adoption is thus described: " The real interest now centred in Queensland. The Premier, Mr. Dickson, ably supported by his colleague, Mr. R Philp, took up the cause with enthusiasm. . . . One difficulty to be faced was that Queensland—though it had been ably represented at the 1891 Convention, whose work was the basis of the draft constitution now presented—had, through the fault of its politicians, taken no part (except through its Premier, Mr. Dickson, at the Premiers' Conference) in the actual framing of the constitution." Ultimately, however, in spite of this drawback the amended draft constitution was accepted by Queensland at a referendum by 38,488 votes against 30,996.

Thus, although Queensland opted out at the beginning and deprived itself of a voice in the making of the constitution, it opted in at the end with a sense of grievance against those who were responsible for the initial opting out.

PRINCE EDWARD ISLAND & NEWFOUNDLAND

" The task of framing the resolutions on which the British North America Act was based—the task so successfully performed at Quebec in October 1864—was achieved by the thirty-three men who in Canada today are always spoken of with veneration as the Fathers of Confederation." (Porritt's *Evolution of the Dominion of Canada*, p. 208.)

" At the Quebec Convention the United Provinces (Quebec and Ontario) were represented by twelve delegates; Nova Scotia by five; New Brunswick by seven: Prince Edward Island by seven; and Newfoundland by two." (*op. cit., p.* 209.)

" These resolutions (*i.e.*, the Quebec resolutions) having been adopted by the legislatures of the United Provinces (Quebec and Ontario), Nova Scotia* and New Brunswick, they were embodied in the British North America Act which was passed by the Imperial Parliament." And in a footnote, " Newfoundland and Prince Edward Island withdrew from the negotiations after the Quebec Conference, although Prince Edward Island came into Confederation in 1873." (*op. cit., p.* 200.)

Owing to the withdrawal of Prince Edward Island and Newfoundland, the British North America Act, 1867, contains two sections providing for their subsequent admission:

Section 146: " It shall be lawful for the Queen, by and with the advice of Her Majesty's Most Honourable Privy Council, on Addresses from the Houses of the Parliament of Canada, and from the Houses of the respective legislatures of the colonies or provinces of Newfoundland, Prince Edward Island and British Columbia, to admit those colonies or provinces, or any of them, into the Union, etc."

---

* Actually, the Quebec Resolutions were adopted only by the legislature of the United Provinces. They were subsequently adopted, with slight modifications, by the delegates of Nova Scotia and New Brunswick, as well as of the United Provinces to the Westminster Palace Hotel Conference in London and were then embodied in the British North America Act. (See Egerton's *Federations and Unions in the British Empire*, Introduction, *pp.* 31-33).

Section 147: "In case of the admission of Newfoundland and Prince Edward Island or either of them, each shall be entitled to a representation, in the Senate of Canada, of four members, etc."

"In 1873, the Dominion secured a new member by the entrance into it of Prince Edward Island under the terms of the same section of the British North America Act as that which applied to British Columbia. In this case financial exigencies effected what had hitherto proved impossible. . . . In 1895 Newfoundland, under the stress of financial failures, sought to join the Confederation; but the Dominion Ministry was not quick to seize the proffered hand and the opportunity, once missed, has never recurred." (Introduction to Egerton's *Federations and Unions in the British Empire*, *p*. 38.)

It is clear from these extracts that both Prince Edward Island and Newfoundland participated in the Quebec Convention which framed the basis of the Canadian Constitution; they subsequently "opted out" and remained outside the Federation; then, owing to financial difficulties, Prince Edward Island "opted in"; but Newfoundland*, although at one time desirous of opting in, lost the opportunity and still remains outside the Federation.

---

* Earlier also (on *p*. 50) it is stated that "Newfoundland definitely refused to come into the Union (Canada) and *is still outside*." That was so at the time Sri B. N. Rau wrote his exposition on "Points of Procedure" (Ch. 4). Subsequently, on March 31, 1949, Newfoundland joined Canada.

At a second referendum (1948), eighteen out of the twenty-five electoral districts of Newfoundland showed a clear majority in favour of confederation. A delegation from Newfoundland held negotiations with the Canadian Government. Finally in 1949 the British Government consented by an Act of Parliament to a union between Canada and Newfoundland on terms which were mutually acceptable.—Ed.

9

THE RIGHT OF SECESSION

[*The question arose early in the proceedings of the Constituent Assembly whether, in the context of the passage of the Indian Independence Act by the British Parliament on 18th July 1947, there was any difference as to the right of secession between one Dominion and another. Two independent Dominions were created by the Act, India and Pakistan. Section 6 of the Act, relating to legislation for the new Dominions, was in the following terms:*

6. (1) The legislature of each of the new Dominions shall have full power to make laws for that Dominion, including laws having extra-territorial operation.

(2) No law and no provision of any law made by the legislature of either of the new Dominions shall be void or inoperative on the ground that it is repugnant to the law of England, or to the provisions of this or any existing or future Act of Parliament of the United Kingdom or to any order, rule or regulation made under any such Act, and the powers of the legislature of each Dominion include the power to repeal or amend any such Act, order, rule or regulation in so far as it is part of the law of the Dominion.

(3) The Governor-General of each of the new Dominions shall have full power to assent, in His Majesty's name, to any law of the legislature of that Dominion and so much of any Act as relates to the disallowance of laws by His Majesty or the reservation of laws for the signification of His Majesty's pleasure thereon or the suspension of the operation of laws until the signification of His Majesty's pleasure thereon, shall not apply to laws of the legislature of either of the new Dominions.

(4) No Act of Parliament of the United Kingdom passed on or after the appointed day shall extend, or be deemed to extend, to either of the new Dominions as part of the law of that

11

Dominion unless it is extended thereto by a law of the legislature of the Dominion.

(5) No Order-in-Council made on or after the appointed day under any Act passed before the appointed day, and no order, rule or other instrument made on or after the appointed day under any such Act by any United Kingdom minister or other authority, shall extend, or be deemed to extend, to either of the new Dominions as part of the law of that Dominion.

(6) The power referred to in sub-section (1) of this section extends to the making of laws limiting for the future the powers of the legislature of the Dominion.

Sri B. N. Rau examined the question in this note on 1st August 1947.]

I SHOULD LIKE to mention at the outset that the subject is one on which there is still room for controversy. Prof. Keith's view as to the right of a Dominion under the Statute of Westminster to secede from the Commonwealth will be clear from the following extracts from his book *The Dominions as Sovereign States*, 1938. The date of this book is important, because it was written not only after the enactment of the Statute of Westminster, but also after the enactment of the Irish Constitution of 1937 in which Ireland is described as a sovereign, independent, democratic State:

" The United Kingdom and the Dominions recognise the same sovereign, and the fact is solemnly recorded in the preamble to the Statute of Westminster in accordance with the decision of the Imperial Conference of 1930: ' It is meet and proper to set out by way of preamble to this Act that, inasmuch as the Crown is the symbol of the free association of the members of the British Commonwealth of Nations, and as they are united by a common allegiance to the Crown, it would be in accord with the established constitutional position of all the members of the Commonwealth in relation to one another that any alteration in the law touching the succession to the throne or the royal style and titles shall hereafter require the assent of the Parliaments of all the Dominions as of the Parliament of the United Kingdom '. The declaration thus solemnly asserts that any change in the succession must be made by common action, and it is inevitable that the conclusion should thence be derived that the union of the parts of the Commonwealth is one which cannot be dissolved by unilateral action.

*   *   *   *

" What is obvious and is never denied is that, if any Dominion should really decide to sever itself from the Empire, it would not be held proper by the other parts of the Empire to seek to prevent it from doing so by the application of armed force. This is a doctrine which was recognised as early as 1920 by Mr. Bonar Law and has often been admitted since. More recently it was made clear in the discussions of the attitude of the Irish Free State in the matter of the oath and the withholding of the land annuities and other payments due to the British Government that, if the Free State should determine to declare itself a republic, the British Government would not make war to prevent such a result. But that view, of course, has nothing to do with the legal aspect of the case.

" From the legal point of view the matter is *prima facie* simple enough. The Dominions were created as organised governments under the British Crown, and there is no provision in their constitutions which contemplates that they have the right to eliminate the Crown or to sever their connection with it. The language of the British North America Act, 1867, is emphatic; the Act was passed to unite the provinces in a federal union under the Crown of the United Kingdom. The Commonwealth of Australia Constitution Act, 1900 is based, as the preamble states, on the agreement of the people of the colonies of Australia to unite in one indissoluble Federal Commonwealth under the Crown of the United Kingdom. The South Africa Act, 1909 was passed in order to unite the colonies in a legislative union under the Crown of the United Kingdom. The Irish Free State was created by an agreement which assigns to it the same place in the Empire as is enjoyed by Canada.

*   *   *   *

" It is not surprising that, in the face of these facts, General Smuts has consistently maintained in the past, and even now perhaps holds, that even the King himself could not with due regard to his duty assent to a measure of a Dominion Parliament purporting to destroy the connection with the Crown, and that still less could the Governor-General exercise the power. It is indeed now seriously open to argue that to effect separation, there would in law be necessary an Imperial as well as a Dominion measure, and that under the principle enunciated by the Statute of Westminster the concurrence of the other Dominions would also be requisite."

It is clear from these extracts that, according to Keith, neither Canada nor Australia nor South Africa nor Ireland nor any of the other Dominions under the Statute of Westminster can legally secede from the Commonwealth by unilateral action, and that in order to effect a valid separation, there would be required in addition to a Dominion Act, an Act of Parliament of the United Kingdom passed with the concurrence of the other Dominions.

On the other side, we have another authority, K. C. Wheare who in his book, *The Statute of Westminster and Dominion Status* (also published in 1938), after discussing the judgment of the Privy Council in *Moore v. Attorney-General for the Irish Free State* [1935] A.C. *p.* 484, goes on to say: "It would follow, too, that any enactment of the Oireachtas (the Irish Parliament) to abolish the monarchy, or to provide for secession from the Commonwealth, or to declare neutrality, would in strict law be valid."

The question was considered by the King's Bench Division in *Murray v. Parker* in 1942. The Chief Justice Lord Caldecote's view (in which the other judges concurred in effect) was:

" The removal by the Statute of Westminster in 1931 of any restriction upon the power of the legislature of the Irish Free State to pass legislation, whether repugnant or not to an Imperial Act, did not either expressly or by implication provide for any separation, described sometimes as the right to secede, from the British Commonwealth of Nations. Nor at any time, so far as I am aware after listening to the agreement of the appellant, has it ever been declared in terms by the Government of Eire that the so-called right to secede has in fact been exercised. . . . If I am wrong in the opinion I have thus expressed, it would still be a matter for consideration whether secession by Eire could be effective unless and until the other members of the British

Commonwealth of Nations had given recognition to Eire as a foreign State."

The balance of authority at present would thus seem to be in favour of Keith's view. On that view, there is no right of secession under the Statute of Westminster either for Canada, or Australia or South Africa or Ireland by any unilateral Act.

The terms of the Indian Independence Act are wider than those of the Statute of Westminster. In the first place, there is no restrictive preamble to the Act; secondly, section 6 (2) of the Act expressly permits repeal of the Act itself (so far as it is part of the law of the Dominion) by Dominion legislation; finally, the name of the Act is significant. For these reasons, the position of India in respect of the right of secession may be different from that of the Dominions under the Statute of Westminster.

10

LINGUISTIC PROVINCES AND REGIONAL ARRANGEMENTS

ONE of the most difficult problems in the framing of India's new Constitution will be to satisfy the demand for linguistic provinces and other demands of a like nature without creating a large number of new provinces. In the first place, it may be contended that the creation of new provinces is inconsistent with the Cabinet Delegation's statement of May 16; for, sub-clause (v) of paragraph 19 lays down that " provinces should have power to opt out of groups in accordance with the provisions of sub-clause (viii) ", and sub-clause (viii) goes on to say that " such a decision shall be taken by the legislature of the province after the first general election under the new constitution ". These statements may be held to imply that the integrity of the existing provinces is to be preserved at least until the first general election under the new constitution; for, otherwise, the new legislature will not be of the province and the right of opting out given to it will be defeated. It may, therefore, be urged that the existing boundaries of the several provinces are not to be disturbed under the new constitution, at least initially. But, whether permissible under the Cabinet Delegation's scheme or not, the creation of a number of new provinces with separate governmental heads etc., will mean an increase of expenditure as well as a fragmentation of financial resources. The problem will, therefore, arise how the desire for separation of distinct racial or linguistic areas can best be met without creating separate provinces. Similar problems have arisen elsewhere

and it is instructive to see how they were solved or sought
to be solved.

I. Hungary Before World War I

Between the Compact of 1867 and end of World War I,
Austria and Hungary were separate States under a common
monarch. In Indian terminology, we may describe them as
two provinces forming a loose Union. The head of the Union
was styled "Emperor of Austria etc., and Apostolic King
of Hungary"; the Union dealt with the three common
subjects of foreign affairs, defence and finance. The Union
executive consisted of three ministers—one for each of these
common subjects—appointed by the Emperor-King. The
Union legislature, if it may be so called, consisted of two
delegations, one from Austria and the other from Hungary,
each composed of 60 members, of whom 20 were chosen by
the Upper and 40 by the Lower Chamber of each of the two
provincial legislatures, the delegations being re-elected every
year. The delegations were summoned to meet by the
Emperor-King at least once a year. The two delegations sat
separately except when they disagreed about any measure,
in which case there had to be a joint session.

Turning now to Hungary as the "province", we find
that the provincial head was, as already stated, the same as
the head of the Union, being styled in that capacity as the
King of Hungary. As head of the province, he had power
to summon, adjourn and dissolve the provincial legislature
(that is to say, the Hungarian Parliament) and to appoint
the provincial ministers. The provincial legislature was
composed of two Chambers, the Upper, known as the Table
of Magnates and the Lower, known as the Table of Deputies.
The Upper Chamber contained a large number of hereditary
members as well as a certain number of others; the Table of
Deputies contained 453 elected members.

Now comes a particularly interesting feature. Within the "province" of Hungary was the sub-province of Croatia inhabited mainly by the Croats, a race distinct from the Magyars of Hungary. This sub-province had its own legislature, the Croatian Diet, consisting of a single Chamber of 125 members. Certain subjects, including provincial finance, were reserved to the "provincial legislature" (that is, the Hungarian Parliament) as being of common concern to all parts of the province, including Croatia. Other subjects were left to the Croatian Diet. The head of the sub-province was the same as that of the province, namely, the King of Hungary, who in that capacity was styled King of Croatia. As head of the sub-province, he summoned, adjourned and dissolved the Diet and also appointed the Croatian executive. The Croatian Diet had the right to elect 40 members to the Lower Chamber of the provincial legislature (that is, the Hungarian Parliament) and three of the non-hereditary members of the Upper Chamber. The Deputies from Croatia in both these Chambers were chosen for the term of the Hungarian Parliament; but in case the Croatian Diet was dissolved earlier, they were elected afresh. Further, the provincial Cabinet, that is to say, the Hungarian Cabinet, always contained a member specially designated to supervise relations with Croatia. What was more, the provincial delegation, that is to say, the Hungarian delegation to the Union legislature, which, as already mentioned, consisted of 60 members, had to contain five Croatians. Croatian was the official language in Croatia and the Croatian Deputies spoke in their native tongue in the Hungarian Parliament.

To summarise, if we may call Austria-Hungary of the pre-1914 era a Union, Hungary a province of the Union, and Croatia a sub-province of Hungary, the relations between the Union, the province and the sub-province were briefly these:

(1) The Union, the province and the sub-province had a common head, the Emperor-King.

(2) Each had its own legislature and executive dealing with its own subjects.

(3) The sub-province had a special minister in the provincial Cabinet.

(4) The sub-province had its own contingent of members, both in the provincial legislature and in the Union legislature.

(5) The sub-province had its own official language.

It is interesting to note that besides Austria and Hungary, the Union contained the territory of Bosnia and Herzegovina. It was found impracticable to divide this territory between Austria and Hungary and neither half of the monarchy would have consented to its annexation as a whole by the other. The administration of the territory was, therefore, made a joint affair—a Union subject under the Union Finance Minister.

II. IRELAND UNDER THE GOVERNMENT OF IRELAND ACT, 1920

The Government of Ireland Act, 1920, which divided Ireland into Northern Ireland and Southern Ireland, proved a dead letter in Southern Ireland (because the South objected to partition) and has survived in Northern Ireland only in a modified form. Nevertheless, the scheme of the Act is interesting and well worth examination, for it may work where there is a common desire for separation.

The Act divided Ireland into two parts, six counties in the north-east forming Northern Ireland and the remaining 26 counties forming Southern Ireland. The proportion of Protestants to Catholics in Northern Ireland was about 2 : 1 and in Southern Ireland about 1 : 19. Each part had its own legislature with certain limited powers. Speaking broadly, defence, foreign affairs, foreign trade, customs duties and currency were among the subjects not included therein. In addition, there was a Council of Ireland for the whole of

Ireland. It consisted of a nominated President and 40 elected members, 20 from the legislature of Northern Ireland and 20 from the legislature of Southern Ireland. This Council had legislative power in respect of certain subjects of common concern requiring uniform administration, such as railways, fisheries and contagious diseases of animals.

Both parts of the island had a common local executive head, the Lord Lieutenant, and he had a Privy Council of Ireland to aid and advise him in the exercise of his functions. But—and this was the most interesting feature of the scheme—there were separate Cabinets for Northern Ireland and Southern Ireland, each Cabinet being described as an Executive Committee of the Privy Council of Ireland. The Lord Lieutenant was to be advised by the Cabinet of Northern Ireland in regard to the affairs of Northern Ireland and by the Cabinet of Southern Ireland in regard to the affairs of the South. If we may translate this scheme into current Indian phraseology, the United Kingdom of Great Britain and Ireland formed a Union, of which Ireland was a province. Defence, foreign affairs, foreign trade, customs and currency were among the Union subjects. The province had two sub-provinces, Northern Ireland and Southern Ireland. The executive head of the Union was His Majesty the King, that of the province and of each of the sub-provinces was a Lord Lieutenant appointed by His Majesty. Each sub-province had its own legislature and its own Cabinet to deal with its own list of subjects, and the province had, in addition, a legislature to deal with provincial subjects of common concern to both the sub-provinces. The two Cabinets formed committees of a single Privy Council for the whole province. Further, each sub-province had its own contingent of members in the Union Parliament.

Which were the subjects of common concern? Three were enumerated in the Act itself, namely, railways, fisheries and the administration of the Diseases of Animals Act; others could be added by identical Acts of the two sub-provincial legislatures.

The imposition and collection of customs duties and certain other taxes was a function of the Union. The provincial share of the amount collected was to be calculated and, after certain deductions, to be apportioned between the sub-provinces by a joint Exchequer Board consisting of two members appointed by the Union Treasury and one member appointed by each of the sub-provincial treasuries and a chairman appointed by the head of the Union.

These, in brief outline, were the regional arrangements which prevailed at one time in Hungary and were at one time contemplated in Ireland. It may be possible to adapt them to Indian conditions so as to meet, to a considerable extent, the desire for linguistic provinces without the actual creation of new provinces. Briefly, where an existing province contains distinct racial or linguistic areas, they can be made sub-provinces within the province on the analogy of Croatia in Hungary before World War I or the two parts of Ireland under the Act of 1920. Taking, for example, the case of Madras, we may consider some such scheme as the following:

(1) Madras will continue as a single province with its existing boundaries.

(2) For the more convenient transaction of the business of the provincial government, the territories of the province will be divided into two sub-provinces, North Madras and South Madras, and the district of Madras (comprising the city and its neighbourhood)—the district of Madras being " joint territory " between the two sub-provinces.

(3) Each sub-province will have its own legislature and its own Cabinet to deal with its own affairs.

(4) Affairs of joint concern, such as the administration of the Madras district, will be dealt with by a joint legislature containing an equal number of members from

the sub-provincial legislatures *plus* an appropriate number from the district of Madras and by a joint Cabinet containing an equal number of members from the sub-provincial cabinets *plus* one minister from Madras district. All the legislatures, whether separate or joint, will be regarded merely as branches, for certain special purposes, of the provincial legislature, and similarly all the Cabinets, whether joint or separate, will be regarded as committees, for special purposes, of the provincial Council of Ministers. The Cabinets may be chosen on the Swiss plan, all the legislatures and Cabinets having the same fixed term.

(5) The executive head of the province will also be the executive head of the sub-province. For convenience we may continue to call him the Governor, although he may no longer be appointed by the Crown as at present.

(6) The Governor will be advised by the Cabinet of North Madras in affairs relating solely to North Madras; by the Cabinet of South Madras in the affairs of the South; and by the joint Cabinet in affairs of joint concern. But all executive action will be expressed to be taken in the name of the Governor of the province and be deemed to be the executive action of the Government of the province. How and by whom he is advised on a given matter is a domestic detail with which the public outside has no concern.

(7) Similarly all legislation, whether enacted by the legislature of a sub-province or by the joint legislature, will be described as and deemed to be legislation of the provincial legislature. Through which particular set of legislators the provincial legislature acts for a given purpose is again a domestic detail.

(8) Which subjects are to be regarded as matters of joint concern and which are to be regarded as the sole

concern of each sub-province will be prescribed by the rules of business to be made by the Governor on the advice of the joint Cabinet.

(9) Each sub-province may have its own official language or languages.

(10) Provincial representation in the Upper Chamber of the Union legislature will be apportioned between the sub-provinces and the district of Madras in the ratio, say, of 2 : 2 : 1. Thus, if the province of Madras should be entitled to send 20 members to the Union Council of State, eight will be from North Madras, eight from South Madras and four from the district of Madras. In the Lower Chamber, the representation will probably be based on population and no special rule of apportionment will be needed.

Such are the broad outlines of the plan. It has several advantages:

(a) It meets to a large extent the demand for separate linguistic provinces. By extending or reducing the list of joint subjects, the degree of separation can be varied in either direction to any desired extent, so that the scheme is flexible.

(b) It avoids unnecessary overhead expenditure.

(c) It can be extended to the administration of excluded or partially excluded areas within a province; of the predominantly Muslim and the predominantly non-Muslim areas in Bengal and the Panjab; of the two valleys and the hill districts in Assam; and, generally speaking, of distinct racial or other areas in any province.

(d) It does not create new provinces and is indeed no more than a particular way of administering existing provinces.

Among the defects of the plan is that it does not provide for a case where the linguistic or other area is spread over

two or more provinces. But even in such a case, the demarcation of the portions of the area in each province, which the
plan compels, would be a useful step towards their subsequent
integration when the creation of new provinces becomes
possible. Meanwhile, even if they are in different provinces
for the time being, they can act together by mutual agreement
in cultural and social matters, implementing the agreement,
if necessary, by identical Acts of their respective legislatures.

The plan suggested above, on this subject, may at first
sight seem cumbrous, although the actual provisions in the
constitution necessary to give effect to it are very few. The
detailed arrangements will, in fact, have to be secured, not
by provisions in the constitution itself, but by rules of
business framed under the constitution. If any particular
arrangement is found to be needlessly cumbrous, it can be
altered immediately by altering the relevant rule of business,
no amendment of the constitution being required.

An alternative plan is suggested by an analysis of the
governmental machinery in the United Kingdom. For this
purpose, it is useful to study the administrative arrangements
that obtained in that country, say, in 1912, when the whole
of Ireland was still a part of the United Kingdom. In the
United Kingdom Cabinet of 1912, there were 15 members
concerned with domestic administration. Of these, only four
dealt with subjects of common concern and exercised their
administrative powers uniformly in each of the three parts of
the United Kingdom, i.e., England (including Wales),
Scotland and Ireland. Of the rest, three were exclusively
English officials in the sense that their functions were confined
to England; one (the Secretary of State for Scotland) had
functions only in Scotland; one (the Chief Secretary to the
Lord Lieutenant) had functions only in Ireland; others had
some functions in one part and some in more than one. But
all fifteen were members of one Cabinet, responsible to one
Parliament. There was, besides, another member in a

peculiar position: the Secretary of State for India. His functions related to the administration of territory not included in the United Kingdom at all and not sending any representatives to Parliament. He was, therefore, provided with a Council designed to give him the necessary local knowledge, and although responsible to Parliament, he could not act, in certain matters, except with the concurrence of a majority of the Council.

On the legislative side also, although in theory there is but one Parliament, in practice there is some measure of regionalism. Thus all Bills relating exclusively to Scotland are referred, after second reading, to a Grand Committee consisting of the whole body of Scottish members, with the addition of 15 others specially appointed for each Bill. Moreover, although the legislature itself is unitary, the resulting legislation is not; for example, out of 458 public Acts passed during the decade 1901-1910, only 252 applied uniformly to the whole of the United Kingdom. [See Marriott's *Mechanism of the Modern State*, Vol. I, *pp.* 166, 167.]

Let us apply this plan to a province like Assam and consider the arrangements that would result. Assam comprises two sharply-contrasted valleys, the Assam Valley and the Surma Valley, besides certain tracts forming the "excluded areas" and certain other tracts forming the "partially excluded areas" of the Government of India Act of 1935. The "excluded areas" in Assam do not send any representatives to the provincial legislature and are, to that extent, in the same position as India with respect to the Parliament of the United Kingdom. Proceeding on the United Kingdom analogy, we should, therefore, have for Assam some such arrangements as the following :

(1) There would be a single Cabinet responsible to the provincial legislature.

(2) Some members of the Cabinet would deal with subjects of common concern to all parts of the province and

would, in respect of these subjects, exercise functions over the whole province, including the excluded and partially excluded areas as well as the two valleys.

(3) There would be a minister or group of ministers for the Assam Valley to deal with the other subjects for that valley; similarly there would be another minister or group of ministers to deal with the same subjects for the Surma Valley; so too, a minister for the partially excluded areas and a minister for the excluded areas. These last-mentioned areas are not likely to require more than a single minister each.

(4) As the excluded areas are not represented in the provincial legislature, the minister for those areas might be provided with a council of advisers with local knowledge, whose concurrence might be made obligatory in certain matters.

(5) Legislation relating exclusively to one or more of the four regions might, by convention, be committed exclusively to representatives of the affected region or regions, representatives of the other regions refraining from taking part in the proceedings at any stage.

These arrangements do not involve the creation of new provinces, but only constitute a particular mode of administering an existing province.

11

UNION SUBJECTS

I

PARAGRAPH 15 (1) of the Cabinet Delegation's statement, dated May 16, 1946, recommends that there should be a Union of India which should deal with the subjects of foreign affairs, defence and communications. The precise content of each of these categories has not been defined and questions will doubtless arise on this point in the course of the proceedings of the Constituent Assembly. The following references may be useful:

AMBIT OF "FOREIGN AFFAIRS"

The plain dictionary meaning of "foreign": "Dealing with matters concerning other countries." (*New Oxford English Dictionary*.)

The sense in which the term has been used in Empire constitutions:

(1) Section 51 (xxix) of the Australian Constitution, "External Affairs". See Dr. Wynes's *Legislative and Executive Powers in Australia*, 1936, *pp.* 205-222; also Quick and Garran's commentary on the section. These authors agree that "external affairs" as used in the section extends to—

   (i) the external representation of Australia by accredited agents;

   (ii) the conduct of the business and promotion of the interests of Australia in outside countries; and

12

(iii) extradition.

(2) Entry 3 of list I in the seventh schedule to the Government of India Act, 1935 runs:

> " External affairs; implementing of treaties and agreements with other countries; extradition, including the surrender of criminals and accused persons to parts of His Majesty's Dominions outside India."

The items following " external affairs " in this entry are, it may be contended, illustrative of what constitutes " external affairs ". But are they exhaustive? For example, take immigration and emigration or naturalisation. Both in the Australian Constitution and in the Government of India Act of 1935, these subjects are mentioned separately from " external affairs ". [Section 51 (xxvii) and (xix) of the Australian Constitution and entries 17 and 49 of list I in the seventh schedule to the Government of India Act, 1935.] Does this necessarily imply that these subjects are not included in " external affairs "? Note in this connection that " the relations of the Commonwealth with the islands of the Pacific " is also separately enumerated in the Australian Constitution [section 51 (xxx)], although this is obviously " external affairs ", which shows that the enumerations are not always mutually exclusive. Note further that the Foreign Office in England deals not only with treaties and extradition, but also, *inter alia*, with nationality, naturalisation, prize courts, territorial waters, deportations, passports and visas. [*The Foreign Office* by Sir John Tilley and Stephen Gaselee, 1933, *p.* 287]. In nationality cases, the Foreign Office works very closely with the Home Office (*op. cit.*, *p.* 291). As will be pointed out presently, administrative practice may be relevant in this matter.

To what extent can foreign trade and commerce be said to be comprised in " foreign affairs "? If we may be guided by English practice, it is relevant to observe that the English Foreign Office was always concerned with the promotion of trade (*op. cit.*, *p.* 228) and there has been a sort of rivalry between that Office and the Board of Trade as to who should be master of the Department of Overseas Trade. It is now partly under the Foreign Office and partly under the Board of Trade (*op. cit.*, *p.* 249). General commercial policy is the responsibility of the Board of Trade; the duty of the Overseas Trade Department is to give effect to that policy. In other words, general commercial policy is not included in " foreign affairs ", but giving effect to it in foreign countries is (*op. cit.*, *pp.* 249-250).

How far is administrative practice a legitimate criterion in these matters? In *Croft v. Dunphy* [1933] A. C. 156, 165, the Privy Council observed: " When a power is conferred to legislate on a particular topic, it is important, in determining the scope of the power, to have regard to what is ordinarily treated as embraced within that topic in legislative practice and particularly in the legislative practice of the State which has conferred the power." By analogy, a power to " deal with " a certain topic must be similarly construed in the light of administrative practice. And since the power in the present case may be said to be conferred by the Cabinet Delegation's statement, it is the administrative practice of the United Kingdom that is particularly relevant.

Can the Union utilise the treaty-making power given to it by the category " foreign affairs " for the purpose, say, of enforcing a forty-hour week in selected Indian industries, " conditions of labour " being assumed to be a provincial subject? Dr. Wynes answers a similar question under the Australian Constitution in the affirmative [" Legislative and Executive Powers in Australia ", 1936, *p.* 209]; but he wrote before the Privy Council decision in *Attorney-General for Canada v. Attorney-General for Ontario and Others* (1937 A. C. *p.* 326). In this case, the Privy Council ruled as invalid certain Acts of the Canadian Parliament regulating conditions of labour in various ways, as the legislation related to a provincial subject, although it was sought to be justified on the ground that it was required to give effect to certain international conventions which had been ratified by the Dominion of Canada.

> " The Dominion cannot, merely by making promises to foreign countries, clothe itself with legislative authority inconsistent with the constitution which gave it birth. . . . It must not be thought that the result of this decision is that Canada is incompetent to legislate in performance of treaty obligations. In totality of legislative powers, Dominion and provincial together, she is fully equipped. But the legislative powers remain distributed and if, in the exercise of her new functions derived from her new international status, Canada incurs obligations, they must, so far as legislation be concerned, when they deal with provincial classes of subjects, be dealt with by co-operation between the Dominion and the provinces."

It is interesting to note that the existing provision on this point in the Government of India Act, 1935, follows a similar view. See section 106 (1): " The Federal Legislature shall not, by reason only of the entry in the Federal legislative list relating to the implementing of treaties and agreements with other countries, have power to make any law for any province except with the previous consent of the Governor."

The American case, *The United States of America v. Curtiss-Wright Export Corporation*, reported in 299 U.S. 304-333, contains a useful discussion of the " foreign relations " power in the U.S.A. The point of interest is that in certain circumstances a penal tariff or even a total prohibition of the import of goods may come within its ambit. For example, if a foreign country discriminates against the nationals or the goods of the Indian Union, the Union may, in the discharge of its functions in relation to foreign affairs, retaliate either by prescribing a penal duty on the import of the goods of that country or by prohibiting their import altogether. [See foot-note at *p.* 324 of the above report.] In certain circumstances, therefore, the " foreign affairs " power may include powers in relation to the import of goods from a foreign country, although normally the powers may be distinct.

It may be useful to note the classes of external matters, whether described as foreign or external affairs or not, which are dealt with by the Centre in various constitutions:

THE UNITED STATES OF AMERICA

Article 1—

Section 8.—The Congress shall have power . . . to regulate commerce with foreign nations . . . ; to establish a uniform rule of naturalisation . . . ; to regulate the value of foreign coin . . . ; to define and punish piracies and felonies committed on the high seas; and offences against the law of nations; to declare war . . . ; and to make all laws, which shall be necessary and proper for carrying into execution the foregoing powers.

Section 9.—The migration or importation of such persons as any of the States now existing shall think proper to admit shall not be prohibited by Congress prior to the year 1808, but a tax or duty may be imposed on such importation not exceeding 10 dollars for each person.

CANADA

The Canadian Parliament has power to make laws for the peace, order and good government of Canada in relation to all matters not coming within the classes of subjects assigned exclusively to the legislatures of the provinces. No aspect of foreign affairs is assigned to the provincial legislatures. On the other hand, for greater certainty and without prejudice to the generality of the residuary powers of the Canadian Parliament, the following powers have been expressly conferred exclusively on the Parliament of Canada:

The regulation of trade and commerce; and naturalisation and aliens.

(*See* section 91, entries 2 and 25.)

AUSTRALIA

The Commonwealth Parliament has power to make laws with respect to—

Trade and commerce with other countries, naturalisation and aliens, foreign corporations, immigration and emigration, external affairs, the relations of the Commonwealth with the islands of the Pacific, and matters incidental to the execution of any of these powers.

[*See* section 51, items (*i*), (*xix*), (*xx*), (*xxvii*), (*xxix*), (*xxx*) and (*xxxix*).]

SOUTH AFRICA

The Union Parliament has full power to make laws for the peace, order and good government of the Union; in other words, it has plenary powers in respect of all subjects. (*See* section 59 of the Union Constitution.)

INDIA

Under the Act of 1935, the Federal legislative list comprises—

Preventive detention for reasons of State connected with external affairs.

External affairs; the implementing of treaties and agreements with other countries; extradition.

Admission into, and emigration and expulsion from, India; pilgrimages to places beyond India.

Import and export across customs frontiers.

Admiralty jurisdiction.

Naturalisation.

(*See* entries 1, 3, 17, 19, 21 and 49 in list I of the seventh schedule to the Act.)

Austria-Hungary

Under the Compact of 1867, the following subjects were declared to be common to the two halves of the dual monarchy:

> Foreign affairs, including diplomatic and commercial agencies *vis-a-vis* foreign countries; but the ratification of treaties, so far as it was constitutionally required, was reserved to the two separate Parliaments.

Among subjects which were not common, but were to be dealt with according to principles agreed upon from time to time, were:

> Commercial affairs and especially the tariff; indirect taxes affecting industrial production; money and coinage; and the military system.

These subjects, most of which, in other federations, fall within the province of the Central legislature, were regulated in the dual monarchy by concurrent statutes of the two Parliaments and thus nearly everything in the nature of positive law had to be enacted separately in Austria and Hungary.

(*See* Lowell's *Governments and Parties in Continental Europe*, 1917, Vol. II, *pp.* 162-179.)

Switzerland

Article 8—

The Confederation alone has the right to declare war and to make peace as well as to conclude alliances and treaties with foreign States, especially customs arrangements and commercial treaties.

Article 9—

In exceptional cases, the cantons retain the right to conclude treaties with foreign States on matters concerning public economy and neighbourhood and police relations;

however, such treaties shall contain nothing contrary to the Confederation and to the rights of other cantons.*

Article 10—

The official relations between the cantons and foreign governments or their representatives shall take place through the medium of the Federal Council.

However, the cantons may correspond directly with the subordinate authorities and agents of a foreign State when dealing with the matters mentioned in the preceding article.

Article 69 (a)—

The Confederation is responsible for the control of imports on the national frontier.

Article 69 (b)—

The Confederation has the right to legislate on foreigners entering and leaving the country and on their sojourn and establishment within it.

The cantons shall, in accordance with federal law, decide on the sojourn and establishment of foreigners. However, the Confederation has the right to decide in final appeal—

    (a) on cantonal authorisation of prolonged sojourn and establishment, as well as on favours granted in this connection,

    (b) on the violation of treaties of establishment,

    (c) on cantonal expulsions when they have repercussions on the territory of the Confederation,

    (d) on the refusal of the right of asylum.

Article 70—

The Confederation has the right to expel from its territory the foreigners who jeopardise the interior or exterior security of Switzerland.

---

* For instance, if the canton of Ticino concludes a treaty with Italy for furnishing salt this does not affect the Confederation. See *The Swiss Confederation* by Adams and Cunningham, 1889, *p.* 30, footnote.

U. S. S. R.

Article 14—

The jurisdiction of the Union of Soviet Socialist Republics, as represented by its highest organs of State authority and organs of government, extends to—

(*a*) representation of the Union in international relations, conclusion and ratification of treaties with other States; and the establishment of the general character of the relations between the Union Republic and foreign States.

(*b*) questions of war and peace;

.   .   .   .

(*h*) foreign trade on the basis of State monopoly;

.   .   .   .

(*v*) laws on the rights of foreigners.

AMBIT OF DEFENCE POWER

1. See the Report of the Joint Committee on Indian Constitutional Reforms, Vol. I, para. 238: "Apart from a considerable revision of the language of the first five entries of list I, as they appear in the White Paper, which collectively define the ambit of the reserved subject of defence, etc." From this it follows that in the opinion of the Joint Committee the first five entries of list I of the White Paper collectively define the ambit of " defence ". The White Paper in question is printed as Appendix VI to the Report and it will be seen that the first five entries of list I of that Paper are equivalent to entries 1 and 2 of list I in the seventh schedule to the Act of 1935 *plus* " the common defence of India in time of an emergency declared by the Governor-General " *plus* " the employment of the armed forces of His Majesty for the defence of the provinces against internal disturbance and for the execution and maintenance of the laws of the Federation and the provinces ". The defence of India in a declared emergency is now provided for in section 102 of the Act of 1935.

2. See the Australian Bread Case, 21 C.L.R. 433 (*Farey v. Burvett*), in which the validity of a war-time regulation fixing the maximum price of bread was impugned. The regulation was held valid by a majority of 5 to 2. Isaacs J. held that "defence" included *everything in relation to national defence that the Commonwealth Parliament might deem advisable to enact* (*p.* 455). Griffith C. J.—"The word 'defence' of itself includes all acts of such a kind as may be done in the United Kingdom either under the authority of Parliament or under the Royal Prerogative for the purpose of the defence of the realm . . . *It includes preparation for war in time of peace* and any such action in time of war as may conduce to the successful prosecution of the war and defeat of the enemy." (*Ibid.*, *p.* 440.)

3. Note that in Australia the entry in section 51 (*vi*) of the Commonwealth Constitution relates to the "naval and military defence" of the Commonwealth. Hence the dissentient judgment in the above case that price-fixing was outside Commonwealth powers.

4. See Dr. Wynes's *Legislative and Executive Powers in Australia*, *pp.* 178-190, where the author discusses a large number of reported cases bearing on the subject of defence.

5. It has been held in Australia—

(*a*) that it is not competent for the Commonwealth Parliament under its defence power to set up manufacturing or engineering businesses for general commercial purposes in peace-time, merely because such activities may conduce to the works of a department of the defence administration [*Commonwealth v. Australian Shipping Board* (1926) 39 C.L.R. 1];

(*b*) but that it is competent for a Commonwealth clothing factory, created essentially for defence purposes, to engage incidentally in commercial transactions. [*Attorney-General for Victoria v. The Commonwealth* (1934-5) 52 C.L.R. 533.]

The latter decision has distinguished the former on the ground that the Australian shipping board was not an organ of the Executive Government itself. The Commonwealth clothing factory, on the other hand, had been established by the Commonwealth Government itself in 1911 for the manufacture of naval and military equipment and uniforms. During the war of 1914-1918, there was a large increase in the output of the factory; at the end of the war, the demand for naval and military clothing was very greatly reduced; but, rather than reduce staff or plant, the factory accepted orders from other Government departments and from public bodies. The legality of this course was challenged at the instance of the Victorian chamber of manufacturers. The High Court held in effect that it was clearly " necessary for the efficient defence of the Commonwealth to maintain intact the trained complement of the factory so as to be prepared to meet the demands which would inevitably be made upon the factory in the event of war ".

" It is obvious that the maintenance of a factory to make naval and military equipment is within the field of legislative power. The method of its internal organisation in time of peace is largely a matter for determination by those to whom is entrusted the sole responsibility for the conduct of naval and military defence. In particular, the retention of all members of a specially trained and specially efficient staff might well be considered necessary and it might well be thought that the policy involved in such retention could not be effectively carried out unless that staff was fully engaged. Consequently, the sales of clothing to bodies outside the regular naval and military forces are not to be regarded as the main or essential purpose of this part of the business, but as incidents in the maintenance for war purposes of an essential part of the munitions branch of the defence arm. In such a matter, much must be left to the discretion of the Governor-General and the responsible ministers." (*p.* 558)

6. In the U.S.A., the " war power " of Congress extends to—

> the raising and supporting of armies, the provision
> and maintenance of a navy, the governance of the
> land and naval forces, and the organising and calling
> forth of the militia;

but the right of the people to keep and bear arms is not to
be infringed. In addition, Congress has of course the power
to make all laws necessary and proper for carrying into
execution the foregoing powers. (See article I, section 8, of
the Constitution of the U.S.A.)

Writing in 1942, Dodd, in *Cases on Constitutional Law* (Shorter
Selection), says:

> " The participation of the United States in the world war
> (1917-1919) was the occasion for a more extensive exercise of
> federal war powers than ever before in our history, both as
> regards strictly military matters and the incidental civil control
> of the energy and resources of the nation. No act of Congress
> was held invalid by the Federal Supreme Court, as outside the
> war power, and only part of one—the Lever Act—for exercising
> a war power in a forbidden way." (*p.* 338)

For the almost limitless activities which may be undertaken
in exercise of the war power, see *pp.* 59 to 184 of the United
States Government Manual, 1945, first edition, describing the
" Council of National Defence " (formed under an Act of
Congress in 1916, for the " co-ordination of industries and
resources for the national security and welfare " and " the
creation of relations which render possible in time of need
the immediate concentration and utilisation of the resources
of the nation ") and the various emergency war agencies set
up during the last two world wars.

7. The following accounts—

    (*a*) of the Austro-Hungarian defence system and

    (*b*) of the Swiss defence system,

taken respectively from Lowell's *Governments and Parties in
Continental Europe* (*pp.* 171-172) and *Governments of Continental
Europe*, 1940, edited by James T. Shotwell (*pp.* 1028-1030),
may be of interest:

THE AUSTRO-HUNGARIAN DEFENCE SYSTEM

" The next department of the joint administration is that of
war, and here again is found the strange mixture of federal
union and international alliance that is characteristic of the
relations of Austria and Hungary. The regular army and the
navy are institutions of the joint monarchy, although they are
governed by separate standing laws of the two States, which are,
of course, substantially identical. These laws determine, among
other things, the number of the troops, and provide that the
men shall be furnished by the two countries in proportion to
population; but the contingent of recruits required from each
country is voted annually by its own Parliament. It is useless to
inquire what would happen if either half of the Empire should
refuse to raise its quota of troops, for there is no possible means
of compulsion; and in this, as in most other cases, the smooth
working of the joint government depends ultimately on a constant harmony between the Cabinets of Vienna and Buda-Pesth.
After the recruits are enlisted they are under the control and in
the pay of the joint administration. The Emperor, as Commander-in-Chief, appoints the officers, and regulates the organisation of the army. The minister of war, curiously enough, is
not required to countersign acts of this nature,* but he is
responsible for all other matters, such as the commissariat,
equipment and military schools.

" Besides the regular army, which belongs to the joint government, there are military bodies, called in Austria the *Landwehr*,
and in Hungary the *Honveds*, which are special institutions of
the separate halves of the monarchy. These troops are composed
of the recruits that are not needed for the contingents to the
regular army and of the men who have already served their
time in it. They form a sort of reserve, but cannot be ordered
to march out of their own state without the permission of its
Parliament; except that in case of absolute necessity, when the
Parliament is not in session, the permission may be given by the
Cabinet of the country to which they belong. After such a
permission has been granted, however, they are subject to the
orders of the general commanding the regular army. The *Landwehr* and *Honveds* are organised under independent laws which
happen to be very much alike but are not necessarily so, and

---

* Law of Dec. 21, 1867, sec. 5.

their ordinary expenses are borne entirely by the country to which they belong, only the increase of cost arising from their actual use in war being defrayed out of the joint treasury."

THE SWISS DEFENCE SYSTEM

" *Unusual Features of the Army:* For the defence of their neutrality the Swiss rely not merely upon the pledges of other States but also upon their own army and auxiliary air service. The Swiss army differs quite remarkably from the prevailing Continental military systems. To be sure, like all her neighbours, Switzerland has adopted universal and compulsory military service. Except for those exempted for reasons of physical or mental incapacity who, incidentally, are required to pay a military exemption tax, every Swiss citizen must begin his initial period of army service during his ninteenth year. This initial period, however, is not the two or even one-year interval normally required of other Continental military recruits. The Swiss infantry recruit is called to the colours for a period of approximately three months, during which he is thoroughly grounded in military essentials. At the end of this period he is considered a full-fledged member of the army's first-line troops, known as the *Auszug* or *Elite*, and resumes his civilian activities. Recruits in other branches of the service have similar training periods, ranging from 60 days for the medical and supply corps to 102 days for the cavalry. During the next 12 years the infantry recruit is called to the colours annually for 13-day periods to repeat the courses of instruction he received as a recruit and to supplement that instruction. From the end of his thirty-second year until his forty-first, the Swiss soldier is enrolled in the *Landwehr* or first reserve and from his forty-first year until his forty-eighth, in the *Landsturm* or second reserve. During these 16 years the time actually spent with the colours in periods of peace is about two weeks. Altogether, therefore, the formal training of the Swiss soldier throughout his active affiliation with the army rarely exceeds seven or eight months. It must be added that both before and during his military career, the Swiss infantryman's formal training is usually supplemented by practice in drill and marksmanship in the various volunteer rifle clubs which dot the land and receive active support from the public authorities. Recently annual practice in musketry under the jurisdiction of a rifle club has been made compulsory for all first-line and *Landwehr* troops.

" Still another unusual feature of the Swiss military system is the absence of a permanent professional military staff. No person can be appointed to the rank of commander-in-chief except in time of national emergency when the Federal Assembly has decreed general mobilisation; the appointment, moreover, lapses as soon as the emergency has passed. A Commander-in-Chief has been appointed on four different occasions since 1848. The most recent appointment is that of Colonel Henri Guisan, who took charge of the forces which the Confederation mobilised at the outbreak of the European War in September, 1939. The only military officials in the permanent service of the federal government are those engaged in staff work in the military department of the Federal Council and those officers and non-commissioned officers who instruct army recruits. Of these there are at present about 300. The regular commissioned and non-commissioned officers of the army are recruited from the ranks and, like the private soldiers, are called upon only intermittently to serve with the colours after their initial period of training and study; at other times they are engaged in ordinary civilian pursuits.

" *Dual Political Control:* A third distinctive feature of the Swiss army system is the dual character of the political authority which has jurisdiction over it. Although the current of constitutional reform since 1874 has run strongly in the direction of centralising military jurisdiction in the government of the Confederation, the cantonal governments still exercise many military prerogatives. Within their respective territories they enforce most of the federal military regulations, keep the military registers, call the troops to the colours, and provide them with their personal equipment. They also form the principal infantry units and appoint their non-commissioned and commissioned officers, the latter up to the rank of captain. Military powers are exercised by the cantonal authorities under the supervision and with the approval of the Federal military department; and for at least a portion of the expenditure they incur, the cantons are reimbursed by the Federal Government.

" *New Defence Measures:* The Swiss military system provides an organised and disciplined force of approximately 425,000 first- and second-line troops subject to mobilisation during periods of national emergency. It is a system well adapted to the nation's democratic and federalistic political institutions; and despite the strictures of certain Swiss politicians, there is little evidence that the system inspires the militaristic influence commonly associated with professional armies. Whether this system can provide Switzerland with an adequate defence organisation at a time like the present is another question. With neighbouring belligerent Great Powers but poorly concealing irredentist and imperial ambitions which could quite logically include Switzerland, and with offensive military weapons developed to such a point that not even Switzerland's peculiar topography any longer affords a serious obstacle to invasion, this question has become a very grave one. The Swiss themselves appear to be pondering it at length and to have concluded that their defence needs strengthening. At any rate the Federal Council, with the concurrence of a popular majority in a referendum held in 1936, has taken steps to increase the period of active training with the army, to supplement military aviation and artillery service, to perfect anti-aircraft defence and defence against gas attacks, and to strengthen every variety of border fortification. Moreover, as long as the period of national emergency, decreed at the end of August 1939, continues, the Swiss army, at least partially mobilised, will maintain a continuous watch on the nation's frontiers."

AMBIT OF " COMMUNICATIONS "

1. " Communications " is a wide term and, interpreted in the widest possible sense, would include even village roads. Some such qualification as " inter-unit " may have to be imported, if " communications " not extending beyond the limits of a province or State and not connected with any inter-unit line of communications are not to be dealt with by the Union.

2. As to the detailed items which " communications " may include, see, in particular, entry 7 of list I and entry 18 of list II in the seventh schedule to the Government of India Act, 1935. It is clear from the former that posts and telegraphs, including telephones, wireless and broadcasting would be included under the existing constitution as " forms of communication ". The latter entry runs: " Communications, that is to say, roads, bridges, ferries and other means of

communication not specified in list I, etc." The " means of communication " included in list I are mainly railways, seaways and airways. Seaports, being related to sea communications in much the same way as railway stations are related to railways, would also probably be included in the term " communications ", and similarly lighthouses and other safety devices for shipping and aircraft; so too, the carriage of passengers and goods by rail or sea or air. Port quarantine can hardly be dissociated from seaports or airports. Practically, therefore, entries 7, 18, 20, 21, 22, 24, 25 and 26 of list I in the seventh schedule to the Act of 1935 would be largely included in the term " communications ", even if we limit it to inter-unit communications.

3. In Canada, besides the regulation of trade and commerce and the postal services, the following enumerated subjects fall within the authority of the Canadian Parliament:

> Navigation and shipping; quarantine; lighthouses; ferries between a province and any British or foreign country or between two provinces; lines of steam or other ships, railways, canals, telegraphs and other works and undertakings connecting a province with any other province or provinces or extending beyond the limits of a province; lines of steamships between a province and any British or foreign country; and such works as, although situate within a province, are declared by the Parliament of Canada to be for the general advantage of Canada or for the advantage of two or more provinces. (*See* section 91, entries 9, 10, 11 and 13, and section 92, entry 10.)

4. In Australia, the Commonwealth Parliament has power to make laws with respect to—

> (1) trade and commerce with other countries and among the States;
> (2) postal, telegraphic, telephonic and other like services;
> (3) lighthouses;
> (4) quarantine;
> (5) the control of railways with respect to transport for the naval and military purposes of the Commonwealth;

13

(6) the acquisition, with the consent of a State, of any railways
     of the State on terms arranged between the Common-
     wealth and the State; and

(7) railway construction and extension in any State with the
     consent of that State.

[*See* section 51, items (*i*), (*v*), (*vii*), (*ix*), (*xxxii*), (*xxxiii*) and
(*xxxiv*) of the Australian Constitution.]

It has also been made clear in a subsequent provision (section
98 of the constitution) that the power of the Parliament to
make laws with respect to trade and commerce extends to
navigation and shipping and to railways owned by any State.

Railways in Australia occupy, and occupied in 1900, a
special position in that they were and are owned and carried
on by the various State governments. Hence the power of
the Commonwealth Parliament in respect of railways is somewhat limited. [*See* Dr. Wynes's *Legislative and Executive Powers
in Australia*, *p*. 160.]

5. In the U. S. A., Congress has been granted express
power to establish post offices and post roads. See article I,
section 8, U. S. A. Constitution. In other respects, federal
power appears to have developed as incident to " inter-State
commerce ". It has been held that " commerce " includes
the telegraph, the telephone, the radio and communication by
correspondence through the mails, besides railways and navigation. (*See* Dodd's *Cases on Constitutional Law*, Shorter Selection, 1942, *pp*. 356 and 391.)

6. In Switzerland, the Confederation is responsible for legislation concerning navigation, as also legislation on the construction and working of rail roads and on aerial navigation.
The postal and telegraph services belong to the Confederation. The Confederation can order at its expense or encourage
by means of subsidies public works which interest the whole
or any considerable part of Switzerland. The Confederation
also exercises supreme control over the roads and bridges in
whose maintenance it is interested and can decree provisions

concerning motor traffic. (*See* articles 23, 24*b*, 26, 36, 37, 37*a* and 37*b*.)

7. In the U. S. S. R., the powers of the Union extend to the "administration of transport and means of communication". [*See* article 14 (*m*) of the Constitution of the U. S. S. R.]. There are separate departments ("People's Commissariats") for railways, communications and water transport.

II

Paragraph 15 (1) of the Cabinet Mission's statement of May 16, 1946 recommends that the Union of India should deal with foreign affairs, defence and communications and should have the powers necessary to raise the finances required for these subjects. Whether these powers should be powers of direct taxation in the right of the Union or merely powers to levy contributions from the provinces is a question of great importance on which the statement is silent. One view is that the finances should be raised only by contribution and not by taxation. The other is that the Union should have the power of taxation. The experience of other countries may be useful in this connection.

U.S.A.

Before the present Constitution of the U.S.A. was framed by the Philadelphia Convention, the States had been linked together in a loose confederacy by certain articles of Confederation. Under these articles, they had only one central organ, the Congress of States, in which all the States were on an equal footing. The purpose of the confederacy was to provide for the common defence of the States, the security of their liberties, and their general welfare. Article 8 provided that "all charges of war, and all other expenses that shall be incurred for the common defence or general welfare, and

allowed by the United States in Congress assembled, shall be
defrayed out of a common treasury, which shall be supplied
by the several States, in proportion to the value of all land
within each State, granted to or surveyed for any person
. . . . The taxes for paying that proportion shall be laid
and levied by the authority and direction of the legislatures of
the several States within the time agreed upon by the United
States in Congress assembled." In other words, Congress was
to determine the amount of money needed and to apportion
to each State its share.

" Congress did so, but the States honoured the requisitions
exactly to the extent that each saw fit, and Congress had no
power and no right to enforce payment. What was the result?
If one may judge by the complaints that were entered, it was
more profitable to disobey than to obey. In the dire straits for
funds to which it found itself reduced, Congress took advantage
of the lack of information on land values to juggle with the
estimates, so as to demand more of those States that had
previously shown a willingness to pay. The financial situation
was so serious that early in 1781 before the articles had been
finally ratified, Congress had already proposed to the States an
amendment authorising the levy of a five per cent duty upon
imports and upon goods condemned in prize cases. The amendment was agreed to by twelve States. But another weakness of
the Confederation was here revealed, in that the articles could
only be amended with the consent of all of the thirteen States.
The refusal of Rhode Island was sufficient to block a measure
that was approved of by the twelve others. In 1783 Congress
made another attempt to obtain a revenue by requesting authority for twenty-five years that the States should contribute in
proportion $1,500,000 annually, the basis of apportionment being
changed from land values to numbers of population, in which
three-fifths of the slaves should be counted. In three years only
nine of the States had given their consent and some of those had
consented in such a way as would have hampered the effective-
ness of the plan. It was, however, the only relief in sight and in
1786 Congress made a special appeal to the remaining States to
act. Before the end of the year, all of the States had responded
with the exception of New York. Again the inaction of a single

State effectually blocked the will of all the others." (*The Framing of the Constitution* by Farrand, *pp.* 4-5.)

It was to rectify these and other defects that the Philadelphia Convention was called. Under the constitution framed by that Convention—which is substantially the present Constitution of the U.S.A.—Congress has been given " power to lay and collect taxes, duties, imposts and excises to pay the debts and provide for the common defence and general welfare of the United States"; "to borrow money on the credit of the United States"; "to coin money, regulate the value thereof and of foreign coin". Thus, the right of direct taxation was substituted for the right of levying contributions.

CANADA

Under the British North America Act (section 91, item 2), the Centre has the power to raise money by any mode or system of taxation; to borrow money on the public credit; to regulate currency, coinage and legal tender as also the issue of paper money. The provinces are limited to direct taxation within their own borders in order to the raising of revenue for provincial purposes and the borrowing of money on their own credit.

AUSTRALIA

The Commonwealth, that is to say, the Centre, and the States have concurrent powers of taxation except that the imposition of duties of customs and excise belongs exclusively to the Commonwealth. Currency, coinage, legal tender and the issue of paper money are also Commonwealth subjects, the States being prohibited from coining money or making anything but gold and silver coin legal tender.* But even where the powers are concurrent, section 109 of the Constitution

---

* [See sections 51, 52, 69 and 115 of the Commonwealth of Australia Constitution Act, 1900.]

Act provides that when a law of a State is inconsistent with a law of the Commonwealth, the latter shall prevail and the former shall, to the extent of the inconsistency, be invalid.

SOUTH AFRICA

In South Africa the Union (Centre) has plenary powers of taxation, because under section 59 of the Constitution Act, the Union Parliament has full powers to make laws for the peace, order and good government of the Union. The power of the provinces is severely limited:

"Subject to the provisions of this Act and the assent of the Governor-General-in-Council as hereinafter provided, the Provincial Council may make ordinances in relation to matters coming within the following classes of subjects, that is to say,

(i) direct taxation within the province in order to raise a revenue for provincial purposes;

(ii) the borrowing of money on the sole credit of the province with the consent of the Governor-General-in-Council and in accordance with the regulations to be framed by Parliament (of the Union). . ."

(See section 85 of the Constitution Act.) But of course the Union of South Africa is not a federation and the provinces are almost completely subordinate to the Centre.

SWITZERLAND

According to article 42 of the constitution, the expenses of the Confederation have to be met—

(a) from the income of federal property;

(b) from the proceeds of the federal customs;

(c) from the proceeds of posts and telegraphs;

(d) from the proceeds of the powder monopoly;

(e) from half of the gross receipts from the tax on military exemptions levied by the cantons;

(f) from the contributions of the cantons which shall be
determined by federal legislation with due regard to
their wealth and resources; and

(g) from stamp duties.

" As stated in the constitution, this is a decidedly imposing
array of resources, but upon analysis it shrinks considerably.
Contributions by the cantons recall the old régime when the
small sums necessary for the support of the Diet were thus
procured. An ideal system for the apportionment of such contributions under the present federal government was worked out
in 1875, but the central authorities have never asked for assistance
on this basis. Posts, telegraphs and telephones yield moderate
returns. The purpose of the powder monopoly established in
1848 was not to secure revenue but to assure the government
adequate supplies for all purposes of this military necessity.
Blasting powder is not included. However, the monopoly has
been made to produce a small net profit annually. Receipts from
the military exemption tax law are not large. They amounted to
a little over a million francs a year in the beginning, increasing
to 2,143,062 francs in 1910. As to the income from federal
property, it must be remembered that the new Central government possessed very little property at the time of its creation in
1848. All in all, therefore, in spite of the number of different
sources of revenue enumerated in the constitution, the real
burden of providing for the expenditures of the Federation
devolved very largely upon one of them—namely, the federal
customs." (*Government and Politics of Switzerland* by Brooks,
pp. 180-181.)

The history of currency and coinage in Switzerland is
interesting. By the constitution of 1874, the Federation was
given the power to regulate by law the issue and redemption
of bank notes, but it was specifically prohibited from creating
a monopoly for the issue of such notes. This left the numerous
banks chartered by the cantons actually in control of the
field. In 1880, advocates of a national bank endeavoured to
amend the constitution by initiative, but were unsuccessful.
Eleven years later the movement succeeded. In its present

form article 39 of the constitution confers the right to issue bank notes and other similar paper money exclusively upon the Federation.

A national bank with headquarters in Berne and Zürich was opened in 1907. "As the agent of the government in its difficult tasks of war finance, particularly in floating the mobilisation loans, the new national bank has proved itself one of the strongest foundation-stones of the whole federal structure." (Brook, *op. cit., p.* 194.)

Under article 38, the Federation alone has the right to coin money.

"In Switzerland the original division of taxing powers in the constitution of 1848 allotted customs duties to the Central government [that is, the Federal Government] and practically no other taxing power. The remaining powers of indirect taxation and the whole power of direct taxation seem to have been left to the cantons. This distribution came to be modified when Switzerland felt the effect of an event which probably affected federal public finance more than any other single factor—the First World War. Switzerland was not a belligerent but she felt the effects of the war none the less. Her army was completely or partially mobilised for over fifty months; her customs revenue fell sharply with the decline of international trade; and the revenue from the federal railways declined. To meet these increases in expenditure and decreases in revenue constitutional amendments were passed to authorise the Federal Government to enter the field of direct taxation. Taxation of incomes, property and profits was imposed by amendments of 1915 and 1919 and a tax on securities, insurance premiums and the like, by an amendment of 1917. In all the three cases, as I have mentioned earlier, an arrangement was made that the cantons should obtain some share in the proceeds of the tax. In 1925 a tax on tobacco was authorised by constitutional amendment. In 1938, largely to meet increased defence expenditure, an amendment of the constitution authorised taxes on war profits, income and capital, a tax on beer, and repealed the arrangement of 1917 by which the cantons shared in the yield of the stamp taxes." (K. C. Wheare, *Federal Government, p.* 108.)

AUSTRIA-HUNGARY

(Between 1867 and World War I)

As already mentioned, during this period Austria and Hungary were separate States with a common monarch and a common administration in respect of foreign affairs, defence and finance. Except for a few insignificant matters, such as the lease of State property, the sale of old material and the profits of the powder monopoly, the only direct source of revenue belonging to the joint government was the customs tariff, which rested upon a treaty made between the two countries for ten years at a time in the form of identical Acts of the two Parliaments. Side by side with the budget of each State, there was a common budget which comprised the expenditure necessary for the common affairs. The revenues of the joint budget consisted mainly of the net proceeds of the customs and the quota or the proportional contributions of the two States. This quota was fixed for a period of ten years and generally coincided with the duration of the customs treaty. Until 1897, Austria contributed 70 per cent and Hungary 30 per cent of the joint expenditure remaining after deduction of the yield from customs and other common revenues. Subsequently, Hungary's quota was slightly increased and in 1907, it was a little over 36 per cent.

SIR BASIL BLACKETT'S VERDICT ON PROVINCIAL CONTRIBUTIONS
IN INDIA UNDER THE MESTON AWARD

"Ever since the reforms were inaugurated, the provincial contributions have been a millstone round the neck both of the Central Government and of the provincial governments, poisoning their mutual relations and hampering their every action. Their quality, even more than their amount, has strained the resources of the giver and the patience of the recipient. They have brought curses, not blessings, both to him who has given and to him who has taken."
[Budget Statement (1927-8)]

12

DEMOCRATIC EXECUTIVES

HERE are some particulars of the type, nature and functions of the executives in ten democratic States: the United Kingdom, Canada, Australia, South Africa, Ireland, the U.S.A., Switzerland, the U.S.S.R., Sweden and Austria-Hungary before its break-up at the end of the First World War.

For each of these countries, the composition of the executive, the manner of its formation, its relation to the head of the State and its relation to the legislature are given.

It will be seen that the executives in six of the ten States are of the British responsible type. Their chief characteristics are (1) that they are composed of leaders of a party or a coalition of parties; (2) the dominance of the Prime Minister; (3) dependence on the majority of the legislature; and (4) collective responsibility. In spite of different constitutional provisions, the head of the State in these cases acts upon the advice of the executive except when it has lost the support of the legislature, when he has to replace it by another which has that support. Even in such cases, he normally takes the advice of the outgoing Ministry.

The constitution of the executive in the U.S.A. is entirely different in all respects except that the President dominates over his colleagues even more than the Prime Minister. There is no collective responsibility and neither the President nor the other members of the executive can be removed from office by any adverse vote of the legislature.

The executive in Switzerland is midway between the two. It is elected by the legislature but holds office for a fixed period. It sits in the Parliament but is not responsible to it. There is no person who dominates it like the Prime Minister of Britain or the President of the U.S.A. There is no strict collective responsibility but the executive normally acts as a team.

In the U.S.S.R., the executive is elected by the Supreme Soviet and is responsible to it and, when it is not in session, to the President. Here collective responsibility seems to be enforced not so much by the constitution as by the dominating influence of the communist party.

A description of the executive of Austria-Hungary under the Compact of 1867 has been added, because it was a curious instance of an executive without a legislature.

THE UNITED KINGDOM

The conduct of general executive business as well as the superintendence and control of the executive branches of government and of the various departments of public administration is vested in the Cabinet. It is a body of party politicians selected from among the members of the party or group of parties which has a majority in the House of Commons. It is increasingly recognised, although there have been exceptions to the rule, that the Prime Minister must be in the House of Commons, as the government owes responsibility to that House alone. The composition of that House determines the nature of the government. Until recently, the office of Prime Minister was unknown to law and the holder of that office was always holding a ministerial position, normally that of the First Lord of the Treasury. In the Ministers of the Crown Act, 1937, statutory recognition has been given to this office. The choice of the Prime Minister is made by the King and the nature of the choice necessarily depends upon the state of parties in the House of Commons. The simplest case is that in which a party has a clear majority. The government must clearly be formed out of that majority and, if it has a recognised leader, he will be the Prime Minister. The other members of the government are not elected by the House of Commons. They are chosen by the Prime Minister. This does not mean that the Sovereign may not have considerable influence. Royal influence has even kept individuals out of office altogether. But as against the King the Prime Minister has the final word. He must have a government which can work together and which can secure the support of the House of Commons. If he says that for this reason he must have the assistance of a certain person, the King must either give way or find another Prime Minister. The King cannot commission another member of the same party; for that is to interfere with the internal affairs of the party and is contrary to precedent. He must, therefore, find another party which can secure the support of the House of Commons and it must be a strange House that is willing to support two alternative governments. Though the Prime Minister nominates or technically recommends, it is the King who appoints. Consequently, though a new Prime Minister may recommend that one minister be superseded by another, it is not necessary for him to recommend that the existing minister be reappointed. That minister remains in office until his appointment is terminated. Though the right of choice of colleagues rests with the Prime Minister, he has to secure a coherent Cabinet. For this purpose consultations with other members of his party are usually inevitable. Consequently, the Prime Minister's free choice applies generally only to the less important Cabinet posts and to minor offices. But here again he has to consider the views of the heads of departments. The practice is that the Prime Minister makes the appointment, but he consults the minister under whom the junior minister will work. The Prime Minister's free choice is further limited by the necessity of allocating offices between the House of Commons and the House of Lords. It is provided by law that not more than six

Secretaries of State nor more than seven Under Secretaries of State shall sit in the House of Commons. But the Chancellor of the Exchequer, the Financial Secretary to the Treasury, Parliamentary Secretary and junior Lords of the Treasury and the Financial Secretary to the War Office are usually in the House of Commons. The Lord Chancellor must be in the House of Lords, whether a peer or not. In practice he is always made a peer. If the head of a department is in the House of Lords, his Under Secretary or Secretary must be in the House of Commons. The few heads of departments in the House of Lords are supported by the Lord President of the Council, the Lord Privy Seal or the Paymaster-General (if any of these is a peer) and by the chief household officers. The responsibility of answering for the various unrepresented departments is divided among the holders of these offices.

The House of Commons is suspicious of a minister without portfolio. The institution is less necessary in the British than in most Cabinets. For the Lord Privy Seal has no administrative duties; the functions of the Lord President of the Council and the Chancellor of the Duchy of Lancaster are light; and the work of the First Commissioner of Works is not heavy. Thus the Prime Minister has at his disposal three or four offices which can be filled by statesmen whose advice in the Cabinet is desired but who are unwilling or unable to undertake heavy administrative work. Ministers without portfolio are, nevertheless, not unknown.

All the members of government are not members of the Cabinet. In filling the offices, the Prime Minister has to determine who shall be in the Cabinet. The Lord President of the Council, the Lord Privy Seal, the eight Secretaries of State, the Chancellor of the Exchequer, the Presidents of the Board of Trade and Education, the First Lord of Admiralty and the ministers of health, labour and agriculture and fisheries are always in the Cabinet. Twenty is now the minimum. Strictly, it is not necessary to take the King's pleasure as to the promotion of a minister to Cabinet rank. The Cabinet is not a local entity and Cabinet rank is not due to an office. He is invited to attend by a purely informal note from the Prime Minister. For the Cabinet is merely a private meeting of the more important ministers. It is, however, the rule that Cabinet ministers should be sworn of the Council so as to apply to them the Privy Councillor's oath. Since this involves an appointment the King's consent must be obtained. Whatever the number of the Cabinet, or of the Ministry as a whole, there is joint and undivided responsibility to Parliament. A minister can never plead that he was ignorant or unaware of what his colleagues were doing. The first mark of the Cabinet is united and indivisible responsibility. There is political homogeneity which is accompanied by the ascendancy of the Prime Minister. A minister who is not prepared to defend a Cabinet decision must resign. Questions are sometimes left as " open questions," so that any minister may vote or speak as he pleases. The Sovereign is excluded from the meetings of the Cabinet. When the retiring Prime Minister goes out of office the whole Cabinet is dissolved. The consequence is that all ministerial offices are placed at the Prime Minister's disposal. This is so even if the new Prime Minister is the " old " Prime Minister, that is when the Prime Minister is commissioned to form a new government. This, however, does not mean that all offices are immediately vacant. It means only that the King, on the Prime Minister's advice, can exercise his legal right to dismiss the holder of any office held at the pleasure of the Crown. All the members of the Cabinet continue to hold their offices for transaction of current business until their successors are appointed.

The government is responsible to the House of Commons. Responsibility does not mean that every government act has to be reported to and approved by the House of Commons. The government needs express parliamentary approval for its legislative proposals and most of its expenditure. It has to seek approval, too, of most of its proposals for taxation. It is called upon to explain and justify its administrative policy. If the House of Commons clearly shows that it does not propose to support the government—if, that is, the government has lost the " confidence of the House "—it must resign or dissolve Parliament, both because of constitutional conventions and because government without constant parliamentary support is legally impossible. It must not be thought, however, that a single defeat necessarily demands either resignation or dissolution. Such a result follows only where the defeat implies loss of confidence. What the government will treat as a matter of sufficient importance to demand resignation or dissolution is, primarily, a question for the government. The Opposition can always test the opinion of the House by a vote of no-confidence. Minority governments are more common than is commonly supposed. They are undoubtedly weaker than majority governments. But they are not so weak that they cannot govern. And a government without a majority is not entirely disarmed. It still possesses the weapon of dissolution.

British Governments are in fact expected to govern. If necessary they are expected to act even when they have no legal powers. They can rely on their majorities and on the commonsense of the House to ratify their acts. There is and can be no limitation to retroactive legislation.

An able monarch can have a considerable influence on the policy of the government. He is in close touch with the Prime Minister and he reads the Cabinet minutes. He may also have outside sources of information. He can criticise governmental proposals and governmental acts. Though he must in the last resort accept a Cabinet decision, he is not bound to accept anything less. He can, therefore, insist on the submission of any question raised by a department and he can raise any question which ought in his opinion to be submitted to the Cabinet. He receives and has a right to receive an account of every Cabinet meeting. There are, however, certain prerogative powers which he exercises on his own responsibility and which may fitly be called personal prerogatives. Exactly what they are is by no means clear, for there are differences of opinion in respect of several of them. There is no controversy that he need not accept advice from a retiring Prime Minister as to the appointment of his successor or that he need not accept advice as to the creation of peers so as to override the opposition of the House of Lords. There is controversy as to whether he can dismiss a government or dissolve Parliament when advised to do so. It has also been suggested that he could summon Parliament to meet where he pleased.

There has been no precedent for dismissal of ministers in modern conditions. On the question of dismissal of a government, the general opinion is that it is not for the King to intervene except by warnings and protests. It is inevitable that a Sovereign who dismisses ministers or compels them to resign would be regarded as the ally of the Opposition and as such be made the subject of attack. The King's function is to see that the constitution functions in the normal manner. It functions in the normal manner so long as the electors are asked to decide between parties at intervals of reasonable length. He would be justified in refusing to assent to a policy which subverted the democratic basis of the constitution by unnecessary and indefinite prolongation of the life of Parliament, by gerrymandering of the constituency in the interests of one party or by fundamental modification of the electoral system to the same end. He would not be justified in other circumstances.

The King cannot dissolve Parliament without advice. The dissolution involves the acquiescence of ministers. It necessitates an Order-in-Council and the Lord President accepts responsibility for summoning the Council. It necessitates a proclamation and writs of summons under the great seal for which the Lord Chancellor accepts responsibility. Consequently the King cannot secure a dissolution without "advice". If ministers refuse to give such advice he can do no more than dismiss them.

There has been no instance during the last 100 years of a refusal of a dissolution by the King when advised by the Cabinet. There has been nevertheless a persistent tradition that he could refuse if the circumstances arose, but this has been maintained only in theory. It can hardly be exercised in practice.

THE DOMINIONS IN GENERAL

The Dominions referred to in this chapter are the Dominion of Canada, the Commonwealth of Australia and the Union of South Africa. They belong to three different types. Canada is a Federation in which the units have certain enumerated powers exclusively to themselves, while the residuary powers, some of which are also enumerated for greater certainty, are vested exclusively in the Centre. Australia is also a Federation; but here the Centre has certain enumerated powers exclusively to itself; certain other powers, also enumerated, belong concurrently to the Centre and the units; while the residuary powers are vested exclusively in the units. South Africa is not a Federation at all; it is a Union. Although there is a Centre with four units, the units have no *exclusive* powers. They have powers in certain specified matters, but subject to the overriding powers of the Centre. Here we are concerned only with the form of the Central Government in each country. Nevertheless, one aspect of the provincial administrations in South Africa deserves mention. The provincial executive authority is vested in an executive committee consisting of an administrator appointed by the Governor-General-in-Council and four members *elected by the provincial legislature* after each general election.

14

There are certain features common to all the Dominion constitutions:

(1) The executive authority of the Dominion is vested in the King and exercisable on his behalf by the Governor-General, who in practice is appointed by the King primarily, if not solely, on the advice of the Dominion Ministry.

(2) The Governor-General is advised, or aided and advised, by a Council variously called " the Queen's Privy Council " (in Canada) or " the Federal Executive Council " (in Australia) or simply " the Executive Council " (in South Africa). Although the function of " aid and advice " is legally vested in the whole of the Council, in practice it is exercised by a smaller body, namely, the Cabinet of the day. Members of the Cabinet are, of course, also members of the Council. In addition, *ex*-ministers and sometimes persons who have never been ministers at all (for example, the Speakers of the legislature in Canada) are also members of the Council. Nevertheless, as already stated, it is only the Cabinet of the day that actually exercises the function of " aid and advice ".

(3) A third feature of the Dominion constitutions, stating broadly, is that though the written constitution distinguishes functions to be exercised by the Governor-General-in-Council from those to be exercised by him individually, in practice the distinction has ceased to exist. Thus, in the Canadian Constitution, section 12 makes a distinction in terms between the powers, authorities and functions exercisable by the Governor-General with the advice and consent of, or in conjunction with, the Council or any members thereof and those exercisable by the Governor-General individually; and the succeeding sections make it clear that certain functions, such as the summoning of the House

of Commons, filling up vacancies in the Senate, appointing judges of the superior courts in the provinces, assenting to Bills, etc., are to be exercised by the Governor-General individually. In the written Australian Constitution also there are certain functions vested in the Governor-General-in-Council and others vested in the Governor-General alone. So, too, in the written South African Constitution. In practice, however, these distinctions have disappeared and conventions have grown up whereby the Governor-General almost always acts on advice.

(4) The important point to note is that the constitution *in fact* is often very different from the constitution *in theory*. A great Canadian judge, lecturing on " The Canadian Constitution in Form and in Fact ", warned his audience at the outset that much of that constitution is unwritten and that much of what is written is or may be misleading.

CANADA

Section 11 of the British North America Act provides that " there shall be a Council to aid and advise in the Government of Canada, to be styled ' the Queen's Privy Council for Canada '; and the persons who are to be members of that Council shall be from time to time chosen and summoned by the Governor-General and sworn in as Privy Councillors, and members thereof may be from time to time removed by the Governor-General."

In practice, however, the function of " aid and advice " is exercised by a small group of Privy Councillors—the Cabinet. The constitution of the Cabinet is, as in England, based on convention. The main principles are that the Cabinet should be chosen only from the political party which commands a majority in the House of Commons and that only members of Parliament can hold Cabinet offices. There is no statutory or other written prohibition against a non-member being a minister, and instances have been known of a minister being for a short time without a seat in either House. But the unwritten rule is as stated above. Appointment to all Cabinet offices is made by the Governor-General on the recommendation of the Premier. It is the right and privilege of the Premier to choose his colleagues and to submit these names to the Governor-General for appointment. Every member of a Cabinet so chosen must, in the event of death or resignation of the Premier, at once resign his portfolio. It is open to a member of the Cabinet before a government Bill is submitted to Parliament to take issue with his colleagues as to the policy embodied in the measure or as to its principles or as to details. If his colleagues refuse to accept his view and he persists in his opposition, constitutional usage demands that he resign. A Bill submitted to Parliament as a government measure may—and often does—involve the fate of the government. Every member of the Cabinet must, therefore, support it in Parliament by voice and vote. There can be differences of opinion between members of the Cabinet on " open questions ". The difference of opinion should not be expressed on any motion which originated from the Cabinet.

It is usual for the Premier of the Dominion to summon to his Cabinet men who are Premiers of provincial governments or leaders of the Opposition in provincial legislatures. Men so summoned to Ottawa are, of course, initially without seats in the Dominion House of Commons. If they accept the Premier's offer, as they usually do, they have to resign their offices in the provincial governments and their seats in the provincial legislatures, and seats have to be found for them in the Dominion House of Commons without delay. These are usually secured by persuading sitting members to resign on the promise of a nomination to the Senate.

In considering the claims of various candidates for ministerial office, the Premier of the Dominion, unlike the Prime

Minister in England, has to take into account race, religion and geographical factors. When the total number was 23, three were usually assigned to French-Canada and three to Ontario; at least one was assigned to each of the provinces of Nova Scotia, New Brunswick, Manitoba, Saskatchewan, Alberta and British Columbia, and a politician of Irish extraction usually represented the English-speaking Roman Catholic Church. There is also a custom, though this is not invariably followed, to assign certain Cabinet offices to particular provinces. The freedom of choice of the Premier has in recent years been further restricted by the claims of the financial interests of Montreal and Toronto and the tariff interests centering in these cities that they must have a voice in the selection of the minister of finance.

All Cabinets contain two or even three ministers without portfolio. These ministers are sworn as members of the King's Privy Council of Canada. They attend Cabinet meetings and share in the collective responsibility of the Cabinet. The appointment of such ministers is often made—

(1) to secure for the Cabinet the aid and influence of strong men who are not free to devote themselves entirely to politics;

(2) to satisfy the claims of a province which otherwise might not be represented in the Cabinet;

(3) to honour a man who has claims on the party in power.

The Dominion legislature is composed of an Upper House, styled the Senate, and the House of Commons. Senators are, in fact, selected by the Cabinet, although under the Constitution Act, vacancies are to be filled by the Governor-General; the result is that when a political party is in power for a long time and is then defeated in the House of Commons, its majority in the Upper House may still persist for a time. By convention, a Ministry can remain in office only so long as it can command a majority in the House of Commons. A

Ministry must in the beginning have a working control of the House, though occasionally it can carry on with amazingly little foundation. The rule that any defeat on an issue of importance is fatal is not accepted in Canada; the government will not be discredited if it announces that it regards a matter as of consequence and yet overlooks a defeat. If the control of the legislature passes from the government, it can choose between resignation and dissolution.

The Cabinet is the *de facto* executive of the Dominion. The Governor-General, whenever there is a vacancy in the office, is appointed by the King primarily, if not solely, on the advice of the Canadian Cabinet. In all political matters the Governor-General acts only on the advice of the Cabinet. The Governor-General does not preside at meetings of the Cabinet. He can, however, discuss and advise; but if after discussion the Ministry declines to modify its proposed line of action, there is normally no option for the Governor-General but to assent, for the responsibility belongs to ministers and not to him. A Governor-General may reject advice if he can secure, in the event of the resignation of the Ministry in consequence of his action, a new Ministry which will accept responsibility *ex post facto* for rejection of that advice.

COMMONWEALTH OF AUSTRALIA

The Federal ministers are appointed by the Governor-General. The number of ministers is at present limited to ten and they hold such offices as the Parliament prescribes or, in the absence of such provision, as the Governor-General directs. No minister can hold office for a longer period than three months unless he becomes a Senator or a member of the House of Representatives. The power to advise the Governor-General is formally vested in the " Federal Executive Council " whose members are appointed by the Governor-General. The ministers are all members of the Executive Council and for all practical purposes they constitute the Council. There are in addition assistant ministers who correspond to honorary ministers.

In practice, appointments of ministers are made on the initiative of the Prime Minister. The number of ministers drawn from the Senate is usually two. The Premier has, of course, to secure the Governor-General's approval of his selection, but that is a formality, though the Governor-General has the right to object on personal grounds to any unfit person. In the Labour governments of Australia the selection of ministers is done by the parliamentary caucus and this extends even to the Premier. In these cases the Premier's right is reduced to the allocation of portfolios, even if so much is conceded.

As in the other Dominions and the United Kingdom, the unity of the Cabinet depends on the personality of the Prime Minister and it follows, therefore, that on his resignation the whole body of his ministers are held to have resigned and merely to be remaining in office until routine business is disposed of and new ministers take their place.

Ministers must possess the confidence of a majority of the House of Representatives (the Lower House of the legislature). On defeat in that House on a vital issue a Ministry must resign unless it is granted a dissolution. As in Canada, so too in Australia, the principle that defeat on any issue of importance is fatal to the Ministry is not rigidly accepted. The government will not be discredited if it announces that it regards a matter as of consequence and yet overlooks a defeat. If the control of the House passes from the government through internal dissension or coalition of Opposition elements or other grounds, it can choose between resignation and dissolution; normally the latter course is preferred, for the former is regarded as an admission of failure. Further, practice has shown that it is a distinct advantage to be in a party which dissolves and under whose auspices an election is held.

As in Canada, the Governor-General, whenever there is a vacancy in the office, is appointed by the Crown primarily, if not solely, on the advice of the Cabinet in the Commonwealth. The Governor-General does not preside over business meetings of the Cabinet, which are summoned in the name of the Premier. He acts as the constitutional head of the government advised by ministers.

That a Governor-General should act on ministerial advice is admitted in the Commonwealth; but, as in Canada, with an important proviso. A Governor-General may reject advice if he can secure, in the event of the resignation of the Ministry in consequence of his action, a new Ministry which will accept responsibility *ex post facto* for rejection of that advice.

UNION OF SOUTH AFRICA

The Governor-General appoints his ministers, not exceeding eleven in number, to administer such departments of State of the Union as the Governor-General-in-Council may establish: they hold office during the pleasure of the Governor-General. No minister can hold office for a longer period than three months unless he is or becomes a member of either House of Parliament. Whenever any minister is from any cause unable to perform any of the functions of his office, the Governor-General-in-Council may appoint any member of the Executive Council (whether he has or has not been appointed as a minister of State) to act for that minister, either generally or in the performance of any particular function.

In law the body in which the power to tender advice to the Governor-General is vested is the Executive Council of which the ministers are also members. The ministers of State act in an advisory capacity only in so far as they are members of the Executive Council. The Executive Council is the larger body—like the Privy Council in England—and consists of all those persons who at any time have been sworn in as

Executive Councillors, including not only the existing Cabinet Ministers but also those of the past. The members of the Executive Council are never dismissed, nor do they retire from the Council. The practice of constitutional government does not require the attendance of the whole Executive Council to advise the Governor-General: indeed such a course would be contrary to all ideas of government by a Cabinet responsible to an elected assembly. Only those Executive Councillors who are present ministers of State are summoned to advise the Governor-General. Practice has rendered the Executive Council a more or less dormant body kept alive only by the phraseology of proclamations and other documents of State. In the theory of law the executive power of the government of the Union is vested in the Governor-General acting with the advice of the Executive Council; but in practice the Cabinet functions as the Executive Council.

The Cabinet system in the Union of South Africa follows British precedents in every respect. The Governor-General summons the person whom he considers the most fitted for the purpose and requests him to undertake the task of forming the Ministry. The choice is in practice limited to one or other of the persons recognised by Parliament as the leader of the party which commands a majority in the House of Assembly. The Premier has unfettered discretion in choosing a Cabinet. Ministers are chosen from party leaders and those members of Parliament who are prominent in party councils. They are chosen for their administrative and political skill, or because the power and influence which they wield with the electors make them useful and necessary elements of a democratic government. The Premier is undoubtedly influenced by these considerations as well as by geographical factors such as endeavouring to give each province some representation in his Ministry. The most striking characteristic of South African politics is the remarkable stability of the Ministries. There is collective responsibility in the Cabinet.

Accordingly, on the resignation of the Premier the whole body of ministers are held to have resigned.

The Governor-General is appointed on a commission countersigned by the Prime Minister of the Union and not by a British Secretary of State. The Union Government is thus solely responsible for the appointment.

The relations between the Cabinet and the Governor-General are substantially the same as in Canada or Australia; so too those between the Cabinet and the legislature.

IRELAND

The government consists of not less than seven or more than fifteen members. The Prime Minister (Taoiseach) is the master in his government. He is nominated by the Dail (as the Lower House is called) and appoined by the President. The Prime Minister, with the approval of the Dail, nominates for appointment by the President the other members of the government. The Prime Minister appoints a deputy (Tanaiste) who acts for all purposes in his place if he dies or becomes permanently incapacitated or is temporarily absent. The Prime Minister, his deputy and the minister in charge of the finance department must be members of the Dail. The other ministers must be in one Chamber or another, but not more than two in the Senate (Seanad).

The government is declared by the constitution to be responsible to the Dail. It acts as a body and is collectively responsible for the departments of State administered by the members of the government. When the Prime Minister resigns from office the other members of the government are also deemed to have resigned from office, but the Prime Minister and other members of the government continue in office till the appointment of their successors. The Prime Minister can request any member of the government to resign. If he refuses to comply with the request, his appointment can be terminated by the President if the Prime Minister so advises. There cannot be any change of government during a period of dissolution.

The Prime Minister must resign if he ceases to retain the support of a majority in the Dail unless on his advice the President allows him a dissolution and on the reassembly of the Dail he secures the support of a majority in the Dail.

The President is elected by the people. The electorate is the same as that for the Dail. The election is by secret ballot on the system of proportional representation with the single transferable vote. He holds office for seven years from the date upon which he enters upon his office, unless before the expiration of that period he dies or resigns or is removed from office, or becomes permanently incapacitated, such incapacity being established to the satisfaction of the Supreme Court consisting of not less than five judges. A President is eligible for re-election to that office but only once. He shall not leave the State during his term of office save with the consent of the government. He may be impeached for stated misbehaviour. A proposal in either House of the legislature to prefer a charge against the President shall not be entertained unless upon a notice of motion in writing signed by not less than 30 members of that House. Any such proposal shall be adopted by a House only upon a resolution of that House supported by not less than two-thirds of the total membership thereof. When a charge is prepared by one House, the other House shall investigate the charge or cause the charge to be investigated. The President shall have the right to appear and to be represented at the investigation of the charge. If, as a result of the investigation, a resolution is passed supported by not less than two-thirds of the total membership of the House of the legislature by which the charge was investigated or caused to be investigated, declaring that the charge preferred against the President has been sustained and that the misbehaviour, the subject of the charge, was such as to render him unfit to continue in office, such resolution shall operate to remove the President from his office.

The powers and functions conferred on the President by the constitution shall be exercisable and performable by him only on the advice of the government, save where it is provided that he shall act in his absolute discretion or after consultation with or in relation to the Council of State, a purely advisory body composed of *ex-officio* the Taoiseach, the Tanaiste, the Chief Justice, the President of the High Court, the Chairmen of the Dail and the Senate, the Attorney-General, any ex-President or ex-Taoiseach or ex-Chief Justice or ex-President of the Free State, and such other persons not exceeding seven as may be appointed by the President, or on the advice or nomination of, or on receipt of any other communication from any other person or body. No power or function conferred on the President by any law shall be exercisable by him save only on the advice of the government. In the event of the absence of the President, or his temporary incapacity or failure to exercise and perform the powers and functions of his office or any of them, the powers and functions conferred on the President shall be exercised and performed by a Commission consisting of the Chief Justice (or in his absence the President of the High Court), the Chairman of the Dail (or in his absence the Deputy Chairman) and the Chairman of the Senate (or in his absence the Deputy Chairman).

As instances of functions which the President may exercise in his absolute discretion or must exercise after consultation with the Council of State, we may mention the following: The President may in his absolute discretion refuse to dissolve the Dail on the advice of a Prime Minister who has ceased to retain the support of a majority in the Dail. The President may at any time after consultation with the Council of State convene a meeting of either or both of the Houses of the legislature, communicate with the Houses by message or address—which has received the approval of the government—on any matter of national or public importance or address a message approved by the government to the nation at any time on any such matter. He may, after consulting the Council of State but in his discretion, ask the Supreme Court for an opinion on the question of the validity of any Bill which he is asked to sign. If the report is unfavourable he must refuse to sign. In the case of a Bill carried over the head of the Senate, if, within four days of its passage, a majority of the members of the Senate and not less than one-third of those of the Dail petition the President to decline signature, he may after consultation with the Council of State decide that the measure is of such national importance that the will of the people thereon should be obtained. Thereupon he can sign the measure only if approved at a referendum or by a resolution of the Dail passed within 18 months of his decision after a dissolution.

SWEDEN

In Sweden the executive power is vested in the King, who, however, acts only in Council. In theory, the King possesses an absolute veto; but in practice, the government is carried on in conformity with the views of the Cabinet which in turn derives its authority from the support it receives in the legislature. The constitution does not prevent the King from acting against the advice of his minister and while the King's decisions must always be countersigned by the minister's signature, it does not mean that responsibility has been assumed. If the decision is unconstitutional in the opinion of the minister he must refuse to countersign. Since 1914, the King has not even on a single occasion forced decisions not acceptable to his ministers. The procedure prescribed by the constitution has, therefore, become a mere formality.

The general principle that the Cabinet should have the positive support of the majority in Parliament is not observed, nor does the Cabinet secure a vote of confidence before it begins to function. The Cabinet continues in office so long as it is tolerated and makes room for a new Ministry only when the dissatisfaction of the legislature is manifest. When a Cabinet crisis occurs, the usual course is for the Opposition that has defeated the Cabinet to assume responsibility for the formation of a new Ministry; but occasionally, Parliament is dissolved in order that a new basis for the Ministry may be furnished. Sometimes resort has also been had to brief " Civil Servants " Ministries. The legislature, the Riksdag, has the power to examine the function and labours of the Cabinet and to impeach its members. The constitution provides for the appointment, in each regular session of the Riksdag, of two parliamentary officials whose special task is to supervise, on behalf of the legislature, the civil and military administration of the country. These officials receive complaints of citizens against government officials and are empowered to have recourse to the courts. This manner of safeguarding the rights of the citizen is said to be very effective in Sweden.

SWITZERLAND

The executive department of the Swiss Government is the Federal Council. It consists of seven members elected by the Federal Assembly acting as a unitary body, i.e., the Council of State and the National Council sitting together under the chairmanship of the President of the latter House. Constitutional usage prescribes that Zurich and Berne, being among the oldest of the cantons and having the largest population, shall always be represented. A similar right is guaranteed in the same manner to Vaud, the largest of the French speaking cantons. Usage further prescribes that another Romance canton besides Vaud shall always be represented. The legal term of service of the councillors is four years. There are seven separate administrative departments, each headed by one of the Federal Councillors. In theory, all important executive decisions are made by the Council as a body and the Council assumes corporate responsibility for them. In actual practice, however, many important executive decisions are made by the individual Councillors. Furthermore, many activities originally performed by the Council as a body have been passed on to specific Councillors and by them to their subordinates.

In theory, the executive is a servant of the Federal Assembly. This is implied in the Assembly's election of the Federal Council and the Assembly's use of the Council as a sort of Legislative Drafting Bureau. Executive servitude is made still more obvious by the Assembly's supervision over the executive. The executive must secure the Assembly's previous authorisation or subsequent ratification for all acts relating to foreign nations, armed forces or even the ordinary conduct of public administration. The Assembly frequently issues directions in the form of resolutions or motions indicating the way in which the Council's functions are to be discharged. Though the Councillors are not members of the Assembly, they have the privilege of attending all plenary legislative sessions or committee meetings of the Assembly and participating in the debate. Neither the constitution nor convention requires the resignation of Federal Councillors, should their policy conflict with the Assembly's. In such a case the Councillors change their policy in order to make it conform to the Assembly's expressed will.

Annually the Federal Assembly designates a member of the Federal Council to serve as President of the Confederation and a second member to serve as Vice-President. The constitution forbids the re-election of a serving President or Vice-President for a second consecutive term. Usually, the Vice-President succeeds the President and the two offices rotate among the members of the Federal Council. Although the Presidency of the Confederation is an office of some dignity, it has none but purely formal prerogatives, the principal one being that of presiding over the deliberations of the Federal Council.

In the opinion of two well-known English students, " the members of the Federal Council " yield to no other government in Europe in devotion to their country, in incessant hard work for a poor salary, and in thorough honesty and incorruptibility. A diplomatist, who knew them well and appreciated their good qualities, aptly remarked that they reminded him of a characteristic industry of their own country—that of watch-making. For, having to deal with very minute and intricate affairs, their attention is unremittingly engaged by the most delicate mechanism of government, by the wheels within wheels of Federal and cantonal attributes, by the most careful balancing of relations between contending sects and Churches and by endeavours to preserve the proper counterpoise between two (French and German), not to say three (the third being Italian) nationalities. [Adams and Cunningham, *The Swiss Confederation*, p. 38.]

U.S.A.

The executive power is vested in the President. He holds office for four years and is chosen directly by the people through an electoral college of about 530 members which is elected by the electors for Congress from the 48 States. He is the Commander-in-Chief of the Army and Navy of the United States and all the militia of the several States. He has power, by and with the advice and consent of the Senate, to make treaties, provided two-thirds of the Senators present concur. He has also power to nominate and to appoint with like consent ambassadors, members of the Cabinet, judges of the Supreme Court, and certain other high officers. Every Bill passed by the House of Representatives and the Senate before it becomes law must be presented to the President of the United States. If he approves, he signs it. If not, he returns it with his objections to the House in which it originated. If after such reconsideration two-thirds of that House agree to pass the Bill in its original form, it is sent together with the objections to the other House by which it is likewise to be considered. If it is approved by two-thirds of that House, it becomes law. The President does not take any initiative in the matter of legislation either directly or through his ministers. All he does is to inform Congress of the state of the nation and to recommend the measures which his experience in administration shows to be necessary. This function is discharged by a message which the President addresses to Congress, the most important being sent at the beginning of each session.

To assist him in the administration, the President has a Cabinet of ten appointed by him subject to the consent of the Senate. Any member of the Cabinet may be removed by the President. None of these ministers can sit or vote in Congress. The most important office in the Cabinet is that of the Secretary of State. He is in charge of the State Department, the chief duty of which is the conduct of foreign affairs. The other important posts are the Secretary of the Treasury, the Secretary of War and the Attorney-General (who is also the Minister of Justice). The ministers are not responsible to anybody except the President. The ministers' acts are legally the acts of the President. The Cabinet does not work as a whole. It is a group of persons, each individually dependent on and answerable to the President, but with no joint policy and no collective responsibility except such as results from their common subordination to the President.

The President is personally responsible for his acts not to Congress but to the people by whom he is chosen. He cannot avoid responsibility by alleging the advice of his ministers, for he need not follow it and they are bound to obey him or retire. The adverse vote of Congress does not affect his position. If he proposes to take a step which

15

requires money and Congress refuses the requisite appropriation, the step cannot be taken. Votes of censure will neither
compel the President nor his ministers to resign. The President,
unless, of course, he is convinced that the nation has changed
its mind since it elected him, is morally bound to follow up the
policy which he professed as a candidate and which the majority
of the nation must be held, in electing him, to have approved.
If that policy is opposed to the views of the majority of
Congress, it may check it as far as it can. He has got the right
to follow his own views and principles in spite of Congress
so far as the constitution and the funds at his disposal permit.

The President and his Cabinet have no recognised spokesmen in either House. The executive has no opportunity of
leading and guiding the legislature and of justifying in debates
its administrative acts. Either House of Congress or both
Houses jointly can pass resolutions calling on the President or
his ministers to take certain steps or disapproving steps they
have already taken. The President need not obey such resolutions, need not even notice them. They do not shorten
his term or limit his discretion. Either House of Congress
can direct a committee to summon and examine a minister.
The committee can do nothing more than question him. He
may evade their questions and with impunity tell them that
he means to take his own course. Congress may refuse to
the President the legislation he requires and by embarrassing
him seek to compel his compliance with its wishes. In the
conduct of foreign affairs the President is obliged to bring his
policy into harmony with the views of the majority of the
Senate whose consent by two-thirds majority is essential to
the making of treaties. Congress can control the President
to a certain extent by refusing supplies on special projects.
Ordinary supplies are, however, not withheld. In short, the
President cannot be turned out of the White House or deprived
of his title to the obedience of all federal officials except by a
successful impeachment.

U. S. S. R.

The U.S.S.R. (Union of Soviet Socialist Republics) is a federal State formed on the basis of voluntary union by 12 Soviet Socialist Republics. The Centre has wide powers: foreign relations; national defence and internal security (that is, police); admission of new republics to the Union; establishment of the economic plan for the Union; banking and industrial, agricultural and commercial enterprises of all Union significance; money, credit and insurance; determination of the fundamental principles of the use of land and the exploitation of natural resources; determination of the fundamental principles of education and public health; the organisation of the judiciary; and so on. Not only does the enumeration cover a wide field, but "the establishment of the economic plan," which is a Central function, comprises almost every aspect of the life of the community and offers unlimited opportunities for interference with the units, in spite of the fact that the residuary or unenumerated powers are vested in them. These have, indeed, "the right freely to secede from the U.S.S.R.," but any activities in this direction are apparently treated by the Soviet courts as treasonable, so that the practical value of the right is questionable.

The legislative power of the Union belongs to the Supreme Soviet, which is elected for four years and consists of two Chambers with equal powers. The Supreme Soviet, sitting as a body, elects its "Presidium" consisting of a Chairman, 11 Vice-Chairmen, a secretary and 24 members. The Presidium appears to be a Standing Committee of the Supreme Soviet, exercising the highest powers; it convenes the sessions of the Supreme Soviet; it dissolves the Supreme Soviet when the two Chambers fail to agree; it holds referendums; it revokes the decisions and orders of the Council of People's Commissars of the Union (the Federal Executive Council) and of the units, if they violate the law; in the intervals between the sessions of the Supreme Soviet, it removes from office and appoints People's Commissars of the Union (that is, members of the Federal Executive Council) subject to subsequent confirmation by the Supreme Soviet; it bestows honours and decorations; it exercises the right of pardon; it appoints and dismisses the high command of the armed forces; in the intervals between sessions of the Supreme Soviet, it has power to declare war, and at all times to order mobilisation, to ratify and denounce international treaties; and so on. The Presidium—a committee of the legislature—thus exercises many of the executive powers which in British India are exercised by the Governor-General and even more.

The main executive and administrative organ of State power in the U.S.S.R. is the Council of People's Commissars of the U.S.S.R. This Council is appointed by the federal legislature —the Supreme Soviet—at a joint session of the two Chambers and is composed of a Chairman, a Vice-Chairman, the People's Commissars of the U.S.S.R., the Chairman of the State Planning Commission and several other high officials. The composition has been somewhat altered since the adoption of the constitution of 1936. The People's Commissars of the U.S.S.R. are in charge of the federal departments (People's Commissariats of the U.S.S.R.). The People's Commissariats of the U.S.S.R. are of two kinds: (1) All-Union and (2) Union-republic. The distinction between the two groups is that the first is concerned with what are regarded as purely federal matters, while the second deals with questions of joint concern to the Centre and the units. The All-Union People's Commissariats direct the branch of State administration entrusted to them over the entire territory of the U.S.S.R., either directly or through organs appointed by them. The Union-republic People's Commissariats direct the branch of State administration entrusted to them through identically named People's Commissariats of the units, namely, the Union republics, and administer directly only a specific, limited number of enterprises as listed and sanctioned by the Presidium of the Supreme Soviet. The All-Union People's Commissariats are defence, foreign affairs, foreign trade, railways, communications, water transport, heavy industry and defence industry. The Union-republic People's Commissariats are food industry, light industry, timber industry, agriculture, State grain and livestock farms, finance, home trade, home affairs, justice and health. There have been alterations since the constitution was adopted; in particular, the republics of the U.S.S.R. have been given powers in the sphere of foreign relations and defence. The units have the right " to enter into direct relations with foreign States and conclude treaties with them " and also " to organise battle units of their own ".

This Council is responsible to the Supreme Soviet of the U.S.S.R. and accountable to it; and, between session of the Supreme Soviet, to the Presidium of the Supreme Soviet. The Council of People's Commissars issues decisions and orders on the basis of and in fulfilment of the laws in force and controls their execution. Decisions and orders of the Council of People's Commissars of the U.S.S.R. have obligatory force and must be carried out throughout the entire territory of the U.S.S.R. The Council has the right, in respect of those branches of administration and economy which fall within the jurisdiction of the U.S.S.R., to suspend decisions and orders of the Councils of People's Commissars of the Union republics and to annul orders and instructions of individual People's Commissars of the U.S.S.R.

AUSTRIA-HUNGARY

[*Under the Compact of* 1867 *and supplementary statutes*]

The Union was a political curiosity; it was not due to any ties of affection or loyalty to a common Fatherland, but rather to a fear of absorption by Germany or Italy in the case of Austria and by Russia in the case of Hungary.

There was a common monarch—Emperor of Austria and King of Hungary. He supervised the administration of matters common to both countries and appointed ministers for the purpose.

The two units had a common army, a common direction of foreign affairs and a terminable customs union. The ministers of the Union were not responsible to any Central legislature, for there was hardly any such legislature. Even the customs tariff was enacted in the form of identical Acts of the legislatures of the two units functioning separately. Besides the separate territories of the two units, there was joint territory; for this, apparently, there was no joint legislature.

For the administration of the common affairs, there were three joint ministers: the Minister of Foreign Affairs, the Minister of War and the Minister of Finance. It must be noted that the authority of the joint ministers was restricted to common affairs and that they were not allowed to direct or exercise any influence on affairs of government affecting separately one of the halves of the monarchy. The Minister of Foreign Affairs conducted the international relations of the dual monarchy and concluded international treaties, but commercial treaties and such State treaties as imposed burdens on the State or parts of the State or involved a change of territory required the preliminary assent of both units. The Minister of War was the head for the administration of military affairs, except those of the special armies of the two units. But the supreme command of the army was vested in the monarch who had the power to take all measures regarding the whole army. It followed, therefore, that the total armed power of the dual monarchy formed a whole under the supreme command of the Sovereign. The Minister of Finance had charge of the finances of common affairs, prepared the joint budget and administered the joint State debt.

The joint executive was in some measures "responsible" to a deliberative body whose function was practically confined to voting supplies and controlling the administration by examining the accounts, addressing interpellations, and the like. Even this body consisted of two halves sitting separately except in the single case of a difference of opinion. Each half or delegation contained 60 members and at a joint session, the number present from each had to be the same, any excess being excluded by lot. The ministers could be impeached by a concurrent vote of the two halves. As the Hungarian delegation was almost solidly Magyar while the Austrian delegation was split up into various groups (Germans, Poles, etc.), this system, in practice, gave an advantage to Hungary. Indeed, it used to be said that Hungary enjoyed 70 per cent of the power in the Empire for 30 per cent of the cost. (In regard to the expenses of the joint monarchy, the arrangement was that they should be defrayed, as far as possible, out of the joint revenue, and that any balance should be paid, 70 per cent by Austria and 30 per cent by Hungary, that being about the ratio of the sums raised in 1867 by taxation in the two countries. The original arrangement was valid for ten years, but continued, with slight modifications, for a much longer period.)

Hungary had in fact a privileged position: she paid 32 per cent of the expenses, furnished 44.1 per cent of the troops, was given 50 per cent of the power by law and had 70 per cent of the power in practice. Apart from this feature, the arrangement furnishes a curious instance of a joint executive without a joint legislature and of a supply-voting body distinct from the law-making body. Although owing to political necessity, the arrangement was made to work for nearly fifty years, the machinery was clumsy and required for its management an infinite amount of tact and skill. Government was, in fact, an endless series of compromises between legislative bodies belonging to different races jealous of each other.

13

FUNDAMENTAL RIGHTS

I

THIS is a subject with a long history going back to the Magna Carta and perhaps earlier, into the details of which it is unnecessary to enter here. It is sufficient for our present purpose to explain the nature of the problem and to indicate how it has been sought to be solved in other countries.

The constitutions of a great many countries contain an imposing array of such rights, sometimes described as " fundamental rights ". Reference is invited in this connection (1) to amendments 1-10, 13-15 and 19 to the Constitution of the U.S.A., (2) to articles 4, 31, 44, 45, 49, 50, 55-58, 60 and 65 of the Swiss Constitution, (3) to articles 109-160 of the German Constitution of 1919, (4) to articles 118-128 of the Constitution of the U.S.S.R., and (5) to articles 40-44 of the Constitution of Ireland (printed in the Second Series of *Constitutional Precedents*). England has no written constitution, but the great charters, the Magna Carta, the Petition of Rights and the Bill of Rights form part of the constitution.

Broadly speaking, the rights declared in these constitutions relate to equality before the law, freedom of speech, freedom of the press, freedom of religion, freedom of assembly, freedom of association, security of person and security of property. Within limits these are all well-recognised rights and it may be useful to draw attention to them by embodying them in the constitutional charter. The difficulty is in defining the precise limits in each case and in devising effective protection

for the rights so limited. Some of the constitutions have
attempted to define the limits of some of these rights and in
doing so have gone far towards destroying them. As an
example, we may take article 153 of the German Constitution of 1919, which runs:

> " Property is guaranteed by the constitution. Its extent and
> the restrictions placed upon it are defined by law.
> " Expropriation may be effected only for the benefit of the
> general community and upon the basis of law. It shall be accom-
> panied by due compensation save in so far as may be otherwise
> provided by a law of the Reich."

In other words, the rights of private property are said to
be inviolable except where the law otherwise provides, which
means that the rights are not inviolable. Similarly, article
115 provides, " the residence of every German is an inviolable sanctuary for him; exceptions are admissible only in
virtue of laws ". The fact of the matter is that while these
rights can be enunciated in broad terms, it is not possible
to enumerate in advance every possible exception; the framers
of the constitution, therefore, leave the exception to be put
in from time to time by the ordinary legislature. The result
is that there is no constitutional guarantee against an oppressive legislature.

The other difficulty, namely, that of devising effective protection for the rights defined, really arises out of the difficulty
of definition already pointed out. Where a right can only be
indicated in broad terms, there is an obvious risk in allowing
it to be enforced in the ordinary court, because there is no
knowing how broadly they might interpret it. There are at
least three alternatives possible in this connection:

(1) to take this risk and allow the rights, however imper-
    fectly defined, to be enforced in the ordinary courts;
(2) to set out the rights merely as moral precepts for the
    authorities concerned and to bar the jurisdiction of the
    ordinary courts either expressly or by implication;

(3) to allow the more easily definable rights to be enforced in the ordinary courts and keep the rest out of their purview.

The difficulties of the problem are best elucidated by a few concrete cases. Let us take one of the most frequently enumerated of these rights, that of equality before the law; and let us take a country where the rights are enforceable by the courts: the United States of America. The fourteenth amendment to the Constitution of the U.S.A., which came into operation in 1868, puts it in the form that no State shall " deny to any person within its jurisdiction the equal protection of the laws ". Obviously, these words are not to be taken too literally; otherwise, they would render invalid even a State law granting special protection to women or children, as distinguished from other inhabitants, *e.g.*, a law that exempted children under the age of seven from all criminal liability. And so it has been held by the Supreme Court that the mere fact that a law applies to a particular class of inhabitants and not to other classes is not sufficient to invalidate it. But even within the same main class, does the fourteenth amendment require absolute equality?

In *Radice v. New York*, a case decided in 1924 (264 U. S. 292) the Supreme Court was called upon to decide whether a New York law which prohibited the employment of certain classes of women in restaurants of certain classes of cities between 10 p.m. and 6 a.m. was valid or not. The law, it will be noticed, not only did not apply to male employees, but did not even apply equally to all classes of women employees; accordingly, it was attacked as a breach of the fourteenth amendment. Nevertheless, the court held that there was no breach. The legislature can select special classes or sub-classes for special treatment, provided that the classification is not arbitrary, oppressive, or capricious and, of course, the court is to decide whether it is so or not in any given case.

But the court has not found this task easy. In 1902, in *Connoly v. Union Sewer Pipe Company* (184 U. S. 540), an anti-trust statute of Illinois of 1893 came under scrutiny. The statute made trusts or combinations for certain specified purposes a criminal offence, but added that its provisions did not apply to agricultural products or livestock in the hands of the producer or raiser. It was argued against this statute that the exemption of agriculturists and stockmen was repugnant to the " equal protection " clause and, therefore, that the entire statute was invalid. The Supreme Court, in accepting both these contentions, observed:

" If combinations of capital, skill, or acts, in respect of the sale or purchase of goods, merchandise, or commodities, whereby such combinations may, for their benefit exclusively, control or establish prices, are hurtful to the public interests and should be suppressed, it is impossible to perceive why like-combinations in respect of agricultural products and livestock are not also hurtful. Two or more engaged in selling dry goods, or groceries, or meat, or fuel, or clothing, or medicines are, under the statute, criminals and subject to a fine, if they combine their capital, skill, or acts for the purpose of establishing, controlling, increasing, or reducing prices, or of preventing free and unre-strained competition amongst themselves or others in the sale of their goods or merchandise; but their neighbours, who happen to be agriculturists and livestock raisers, may make combinations of that character in reference to their grain or livestock without incurring the prescribed penalty. Under what rule of permissible classification can such legislation be sustained as consistent with the equal protection of the laws?

" We conclude this part of the discussion by saying that to declare that some of the class engaged in domestic trade or commerce shall be deemed criminals if they violate the regulations prescribed by the State for the purpose of protecting the public against illegal combinations formed to destroy competition and to control prices, and that others of the same class shall not be bound to regard those regulations, but may combine their capital, skill, or acts to destroy competition and to control prices for their special benefits, is so manifestly a denial of the equal protection of the laws that further or extended argument to establish that position would seem to be unnecessary." (184 U.S. 564).

Nearly forty years later, in 1940, in *Tigner v. Texas* (310 U. S. 141), an anti-trust law of Texas of a similar character and containing a similar exemption in favour of agricultural products and livestock again came before the Supreme Court. This time the court upheld the law, observing:

> " The equality at which the 'equal protection' clause aims is not a disembodied equality. The fourteenth amendment enjoins ' the equal protection of the laws ', and laws are not abstract propositions. They do not relate to abstract units A, B and C, but are expressions of policy arising out of specific difficulties, addressed to the attainment of specific ends by the use of specific remedies. The constitution does not require things which are different in fact or opinion to be treated in law as though they were the same. And so we conclude that to write into law the differences between agriculture and other economic pursuits was within the power of the Texas legislature. Connoly's case has been worn away by the erosion of time and we are of opinion that it is no longer controlling."

If the above qualification were incorporated in the fourteenth amendment, the "equal protection" clause would be diluted into the mild injunction that the State shall treat as equal in law only those persons within its jurisdiction who are equal in fact. It is, of course, for the courts to judge whether persons are equal in fact; but, we may add, the same classes of persons that appeared to the courts in 1902 to be manifestly equal in fact were found in 1940 to be in truth, unequal. The protection offered by the clause has thus worn very thin. Indeed, even a Nazi State might have accepted it on its present interpretation, for its courts could be trusted to rule " a Jew is not equal to an Aryan in fact and there is therefore no ground for treating him as equal in law ".

Needless to say, the Supreme Court of the United States has a higher conception of the dignity of man and the constitutional protection, though " worn away by the erosion of time " in certain other spheres, is still potent in the racial. In *Missouri v. Gaines*, a case decided in 1938 (305 U. S. 337), a Negro named Lloyd Gaines, who had been refused admission to the School of Law of the State University of Missouri, sought to compel the university authorities to admit him upon the strength of the " equal protection " clause in the constitution. The matter, after going through various courts in the States, ultimately came before the Supreme Court of the United States. The following extracts from the judgment give the full facts of the case and show the view taken by the majority:

" Petitioner is a citizen of Missouri. In August 1935, he was graduated with the degree of Bachelor of Arts at the Lincoln University, an institution maintained by the State of Missouri for the higher education of Negroes. That university has no law school. Upon the filling of his application for admission to the Law School of the University of Missouri, the Registrar advised him to communicate with the President of Lincoln University and the latter directed petitioner's attention to section 9622 of the Revised Statutes of Missouri (1929), Mo St. Ann *9622, *p.* 7328, providing as follows:

" *9622. May arrange for attendance at university of any adjacent State —tuition fees—*Pending the full development of the Lincoln University, the Board of Curators shall have the authority to arrange for the attendance of Negro residents of the State of Missouri at the university of any adjacent State to take any course or to study at subjects provided for at the State University of Missouri and which are not taught at the Lincoln University and to pay the reasonable tuition fees for such attendance; provided that whenever the Board of Curators deem it advisable they shall have the power to open any necessary school or depart-ment. (Laws 1921, *p.* 86*7).

" Petitioner was advised to apply to the State Superintendent of Schools for aid under that statute. It was admitted at the trial that petitioner's ' work and credits at the Lincoln Univer-sity would qualify him for admission to the School of Law of the University of Missouri if he were found otherwise eligible '. He was refused admission upon the ground that it was ' contrary to the constitution, laws and public policy of the State to admit a Negro as a student in the University of Missouri '. It appears that there are schools of law in connection with the State universities, of four adjacent States, Kansas, Nebraska, Iowa and Illinois where non-resident Negroes are admitted.

" In answering petitioner's contention that this discrimination constituted a denial of his constitutional right, the State Court has fully recognised the obligation of the State to provide Negroes with advantages for higher education substantially equal to the advantages afforded to white students. The State has sought to fulfil that obligation by furnishing equal facilities in separate schools, a method the validity of which has been sustained by our decisions.

" But the fact remains that instruction in law for Negroes is not now afforded by the State, either at Lincoln University or elsewhere within the State, and that the State excludes Negroes from the advantages of the Law School it has established at the University of Missouri.

" The State Court stresses the advantages that are afforded by the law schools of the adjacent States, Kansas, Nebraska, Iowa, and Illinois, which admit non-resident Negroes. The court considered that these were schools of high standing where one desiring to practise law in Missouri can get ' as sound, comprehensive, valuable legal education ' as in the University of Missouri; that the system of education in the former is the same as that in the latter and is designed to give the students a basis for the practice of law in any State where the Anglo-American system of law obtains; that the Law School of the University of Missouri does not specialise in Missouri law and that the course of study and the case books used in the five schools are substantially identical. Petitioner insists that for one intending to practise in Missouri there are special advantages in attending a law school there, both in relation to the opportunities for the particular study of Missouri law and for the observation of the local courts, and also in view of the prestige of the Missouri Law School among the citizens of the State, his prospective clients. Proceeding with its examination of relative advantages, the State Court found that the difference in distances to be travelled afforded no substantial ground of complaint and that there was an adequate appropriation to meet the full tuition fees which petitioner would have to pay.

" We think that these matters are beside the point. The basic consideration is not as to what sort of opportunities other States provide, or whether they are as good as those in Missouri, but as to what opportunities Missouri itself furnishes to white students and denies to Negroes solely upon the ground of colour. The admissibility of laws separating the races in the enjoyment of privileges afforded by the State rests wholly upon the equality of the privileges which the laws give to the separated groups within the State. The question here is not of a duty of the State to supply legal training, or of the quality of the training which it does supply, but of its duty when it provides such training to furnish it to the residents of the State upon the basis of an equality of right. By the operation of the laws of Missouri a privilege has been created for white law students which is denied to Negroes by reason of their race. The white resident is afforded legal education within the State: the Negro resident having the same qualifications is refused it there and must go outside the State to obtain it. That is a denial of the equality of legal right to the enjoyment of the privilege which the State has set up, and the provision for the payment of tuition fees in another State does not remove the discrimination.

" Nor can we regard the fact that there is but a limited demand in Missouri for the legal education of Negroes as excusing the discrimination in favour of whites. We had occasion to consider a cognate question in the case of *McCabe v. Atchison, Topeka and Santa Fe Railway Co., Supra*. There the argument was advanced, in relation to the provision by a carrier of sleeping cars, dining and chair cars, that the limited demand by Negroes justified the State in permitting the furnishing of such accommodation exclusively for white persons. We found that argument to be without merit. It made, we said, the constitutional right ' depend upon the number of persons who may be discriminated against, whereas the essence of the constitutional right is that it is a personal one. Whether or not particular facilities shall be provided may doubtless be conditioned upon there being a reasonable demand therefor; but, if facilities are provided, substantial equality of treatment of persons travelling under like conditions cannot be refused. It is the individual who is entitled to the equal protection of the laws, and if he is denied by a common carrier, acting in the matter under the authority of a State law, a facility or convenience in the course of his journey

which, under substantially the same circumstances, is furnished
to another traveller, he may properly complain that his constitutional privilege has been invaded.' Id., 235 U.S., *pp.* 161,
162, 35 S.Ct., *p.* 71.

" Here, petitioner's right was a personal one. It was as an
individual that he was entitled to the equal protection of the
laws, and the State was bound to furnish him within its borders
facilities for legal education substantially equal to those which
the State there afforded for persons of the white race, whether
or not other Negroes sought the same opportunity.

" It is urged, however, that the provision for tuition outside
the State is a temporary one—that it is intended to operate
merely pending the establishment of a law department for
Negroes at Lincoln University. While in that sense the discrimination may be termed temporary, it may nevertheless continue
for an indefinite period by reason of the discretion given to the
curators of Lincoln University and the alternative of arranging
for tuition in other States, as permitted by the State law as
construed by the State Court, so long as the curators find it
unnecessary and impracticable to provide facilities for the legal
instruction of Negroes within the State. In that view we cannot
regard the discrimination as excused by what is called its
temporary character.

" The judgment of the Supreme Court of Missouri is reversed
and the case is remanded for further proceedings not inconsistent with the opinion."

The importance of this judgment is enhanced by the fact
that apart from the clause about equal protection of the laws
in the fourteenth amendment, the U.S.A. Constitution
does not expressly provide for equality of educational opportunities for all citizens, irrespective of race. The express
provision contained in the fifteenth amendment is limited to
the franchise: " the right of citizens of the United States to
vote shall not be denied or abridged by the United States or
by any State on account of race, colour, or previous condition of servitude ". In this respect, the Constitution of
the U.S.S.R. is more liberal, because under article 123,
" equality of rights of citizens of the U.S.S.R., irrespective

of their nationality or race, in all spheres of economic state, cultural, social and political life, is an indefeasible law. Any direct or indirect restriction of the rights of, or, conversely, any establishment of direct or indirect privileges for, citizens on account of their race or nationality, as well as any advocacy of racial or national exclusiveness or hatred and contempt, is punishable by law ". But the Supreme Court of the U.S.S.R. has no power to disallow laws and acts which contravene the rights declared. The Presidium of the Supreme Soviet—which is a sort of joint standing committee of the Chambers of the Supreme Soviet (the Union Parliament)—interprets the laws of the U.S.S.R. and annuls decisions and orders of the governments of the Union and the constituent republics in case they do not conform to law (article 49 of the Constitution of the U.S.S.R.).

The following account, taken from the *New York Times*, of an American case is of interest in this connection:

"The U.S. Supreme Court held on June 3rd (1946) by a six-to-one decision announced by Justice Stanley F. Reed that racial segregation of bus passengers, as authorised by law in 10 States (called ' Jim Crowism, after a Negro character in an old Negro folk song), was unconstitutional on buses crossing State borders. The court dealt with the case of Irene Morgan, a Negro girl who, when travelling in a bus going from Virginia to Maryland, had been arrested and fined 10 dollars for refusing to change her seat and sit in the rear marked ' for coloured patrons ' (as is general in trolley cars, buses and trains in the South), thus violating the Virginia ' Jim Crowism ' statute. The Virginia Supreme Court of Appeal upheld the conviction and in the hearing before the Supreme Court the State of Virginia defended the segregation law as ' recognition of human nature ' arguing that it prevented racial clashes that might endanger public safety. The Supreme Court decided, however, that there being no Federal Act dealing with the separation of races in inter-State transportation, the Virginian statute interfered with the freedom of inter-State commerce which required ' uniformity ' in the seating arrangements for the different races in inter-State travel, and for this reason was unconstitutional."

16

It has already been pointed out that the " equal protection "
clause, as interpreted by the Supreme Court, does not prevent
special legislation for special classes provided the classification
is not arbitrary. It has also been pointed out that the task
of deciding whether the clause, in a given case, is arbitrary
or not, is not easy. An illustration of this difficulty has already
been given in the matter of anti-trust laws; a few others in
the sphere of taxation may now be mentioned. In 1935, in
the case *Stewart Dry Goods Co. v. Lewis* (294 U.S. 550), the
Supreme Court held invalid a Kentucky law imposing a
graduated tax upon annual gross sales of retail merchants
ranging from 1/20 per cent upon the first 400,000 dollars of
gross sales to 1 per cent on sales over 1,000,000 dollars. In
the language of the court, " the law arbitrarily classified
these vendors for the imposition of a varying rate of taxation,
solely by reference to the volume of their transactions, dis-
regarding the absence of any reasonable relation between the
chosen criterion of classification and the privilege the enjoyment of which is said to be the subject taxed ".

But in the previous year (1934), in *Fox v. Standard Oil Co.*,
of New Jersey (294 U.S. 87), the court had, by a majority of
five to four, upheld a West Virginia graduated tax running
from two dollars for one store to 250 dollars for each store
in excess of 75, saying that a series of gasoline stations maintained in a single ownership has the benefit of chain organisation and that, therefore, the graduation of the tax according
to the number of stores owned was not arbitrary. Again, in
1940, in *Madden V. Kentucky* (309 U.S. 83) the court, with two
dissentient judges, upheld a Kentucky statute imposing on
its citizens an annual *ad valorem* tax on their deposits in banks
outside the State at the rate of 50 cents per 100 dollars and
on their deposits in banks within the State at the rate of
10 cents per 100 dollars. This had been attacked on the
ground, among others, that it discriminated between those
who deposited their money in Kentucky banks and those who

deposited their money in banks outside Kentucky and thus offended against the " equal protection " clause. The court observed (1) that in taxation, even more than in other fields, the legislature possesses the greatest freedom in classification, (2) that the presumption of validity attaching to legislation can be overcome only by the most explicit proof that the classification adopted by the legislature was " a hostile and oppressive discrimination against particular persons and classes," and (3) that in this case the treatment accorded to the two kinds of deposits may have resulted from the differences in the difficulties and expenses of tax collection.

We may now turn to another clause in the fundamental rights enunciated in the Constitution of the U.S.A. In the fifth amendment, which applies to the Centre, it is declared that no persons shall be deprived of life, liberty or property, without due process of law; and in the fourteenth amendment, there is a similar declaration applying to the States: " Nor shall any State deprive any person of life, liberty or property without due process of law ". A vast volume of case law has gathered round this " due process " clause, of which it has been said that it is " the most important single basis of judicial review today ". At first it was regarded only as a limitation on procedure and not on the substance of legislation; but it has now been settled that it applies to matters of substantive law as well. In fact, the phrase " without due process of law " appears to have become synonymous with " without just cause ", the court being the judge of what is " just cause " ; and since the object of most legislation is to promote the public welfare by restraining and regulating individual rights of liberty and property, the court can be invited, under this clause, to review almost any law. The court has upheld laws providing for compulsory vaccination (1905); for compulsory sterilisation of mental defectives (1927); for commitment of persons with a " psychopathic personality " (1940); but not a law forbidding the use of shoddy in the manufacture of mattresses (1926), nor one requiring every pharmacy to be owned by a licensed pharmacist (1928). The usual issue in such cases is whether what is called the " police power " of the State—in other words, the inherent power of every State " to prescribe regulations to promote the health, peace, morals, education and good order of the people " justifies the particular law under consideration. Since there is no certain criterion in these matters, the court's verdict may vary from time to time. Thus in *Lochner v. New York* (1905, 198 U. S. 45), a New York law forbidding more than 60 hours' work in any week, or an average of more than 10 hours per day in bakeries or confectioneries, was held unconstitutional as infringing the liberty of the individual without due process of law. The judgment of the majority of the court (5 to 4) observed:

" The question whether this act is valid as a labour law, pure and simple, may be dismissed in a few words. There is no reasonable ground for interfering with the liberty of person or the right of free contract, by determining the hours of labour in the occupation of a baker. There is no contention that bakers as a class are not equal in intelligence and capacity to men in other trades or manual occupations, or that they are not able to assert their rights and care for themselves without the protecting arm of the State, interfering with their independence of judgment and of action. They are in no sense wards of the State. Viewed in the light of a purely labour law, with no reference whatever to the question of health, we think that a law like the one before us involved neither the safety, the morals, nor the welfare of the public and that the interest of the public is not in the slightest degree affected by such an act. The law must be upheld, if at all, as a law pertaining to the health of the individual engaged in the occupation of a baker. It does not affect any other portion of the public than those who are engaged in that occupation. Clean and wholesome bread does not depend upon whether the baker works but ten hours per day or only sixty hours a week. The limitation of the hours of labour does not come within the police power on that ground."

But twelve years later, in *Bunting v. Oregon* (243 U. S. 426), the court, without mentioning the Lochner case, upheld a ten-hour law for factories. Again, in 1923, *Adkins v. Children's Hospital* (261 U. S. 525), the court by a narrow majority overthrew an Act of Congress prescribing a minimum wage for women and children in the district of Columbia. But in 1937, in *West Coast Hotel Co. v. Parrish*, the court, by a bare majority (5 to 4), overruled the Adkins case and upheld a Washington Act authorising the fixing of minimum wages for women and minors. There has been similar oscillation in regard to laws providing for price-control; and Dodd's comment on this line of cases is: " The question is one as to the efficient action of the government, while at the same time protecting the essential rights of the individual. The cases printed below will indicate that the court has wavered from one position to another and may now be wavering back to its earlier position." (Dodd's *Cases and Materials on Constitutional Law*, Third Edition, *p.* 649).

We are now in a position to realise some of the difficulties of the problem of fundamental rights. To enunciate them in general terms and to leave it to the courts to enforce them will have the following consequences:

(1) The legislature not being in a position to know what view the courts will take of a particular enactment, the process of legislation will become difficult.

(2) There will be a vast mass of litigation about the validity of laws and the same law that was held valid at one time may be held invalid at another or *vice versa*: the law will therefore become uncertain.

(3) The courts, manned by an irremovable judiciary not so sensitive to public needs in the social or economic sphere as the representatives of the periodically-elected legislative body, will, in effect, have a veto on legislation exercisable at any time and at the instance of any litigant.

As against these disadvantages and compensating for them, there will undoubtedly be the advantage that racial and religious minorities will feel some security. Many European constitutions contain a declaration of fundamental rights, but there is often no court with power to pronounce an offending law unconstitutional. Even in Switzerland, where the Federal Court is competent to entertain complaints of violation of the constitutional rights of citizens, the constitution requires the court to apply the laws passed by the Federal Assembly. (See article 113 of the Swiss Constitution.)

The difference between the Supreme Court of the United States and the Swiss Federal Court in this respect is explained thus by Adams and Cunningham:

" Every judge of the Supreme Court of the United States is bound to treat as void all legislative acts, whether proceeding from Congress or from the State legislatures, which are inconsistent with the Federal constitution, or are in excess of the legislative powers which that constitution confers. The Supreme Court only inquires into the validity of Acts of Congress for the purpose of determining a question brought before it in a legal proceeding.

" The Federal Tribunal, on the contrary, cannot inquire into the constitutional character of a law or a resolution of a general nature which has been adopted by the Federal Assembly, any more than of a treaty ratified by that body. It is bound by the constitution to accept those laws and resolutions and to apply them to the cases submitted to its judgment.

" The reason is clear. The measures which, after being framed by the Federal Council and adopted by the Federal Assembly, are accepted by the people, either tacitly or through the referendum, thus obtain the sanction of the Swiss people. Hence the Federal Tribunal must bow to the decision of the people and regard all such measures as constitutional and inviolable." (*The Swiss Confederation* by Adams and Cunningham, 1889, *pp*. 267, 268.)

The Swiss Federal Court can, however, examine the constitutionality of cantonal laws.

The Irish Constitution of 1937 has followed the plan of separating "fundamental rights" from "directive principles of social policy"; the former are, to some extent, enforceable by the court, but the latter not at all. The former are set out in articles 40-44 of the constitution and the latter in article 45, which begins thus: "The principles of social policy set forth in this article are intended for the general guidance of the Oireachtas (the Irish Parliament). The application of those principles in the making of laws shall be the care of the Oireachtas exclusively and shall not be cognisable by any court under any of the provisions of this constitution." There is no similar provision in articles 40-44 expressly excluding the jurisdiction of the courts. Some of the fundamental rights appear to be couched in terms which could be enforced by the courts: *e.g.*, section 40 (6) 2° provides that laws regulating the manner in which the right of forming associations and unions and the right of free assembly may be exercised shall contain no political, religious, or class discrimination; section 44 (2) 4° prescribes that legislation providing State aid for schools shall not discriminate between schools under the management of different religious denominations; and so forth. Laws contravening these guarantees will doubtless be pronounced *ultra vires*.

But a provision such as "no citizen shall be deprived of his personal liberty save in accordance with law" occurring in section 40 (4) 1° cannot invalidate any law and is really meaningless as a guarantee against oppressive laws after enactment. Possibly it has a moral value and may afford ground for a referendum before the Bill becomes law, for under article 27, Bills may be referred to the people, if they involve proposals of national importance. There is also a provision in article 26 (1) 1° enabling the President, after consulting the Council of State (which is a sort of Privy Council), to refer any Bill to which the article applies to the Supreme Court for a decision whether the Bill or any specified provision thereof is unconstitutional.

In the Austrian Constitution of 1920, certain fundamental rights were declared (*e.g.*, article 7 declared: "All citizens of the Federation shall be equal before the law. Privileges of birth, sex, position, class and religion are abolished.") and there was also provision for a constitutional court in addition to an administrative court and the ordinary courts of law. The ordinary courts were not to inquire into the validity of any duly promulgated law [article 89 (1)], but the constitutional court was competent in certain circumstances to decide all such questions and to annul any laws, which it adjudged unconstitutional (article 140); in addition, the constitutional court was expressly given power to entertain complaints of violation by any administrative authority, of rights guaranteed under the constitution after the matter had been taken through all the stages of administrative appeal (article 144). The net result of these provisions appears to have been that the constitutional court could annul a law as unconstitutional at the instance of the Federal Government or a provincial government (as the case might be) and to annul any administrative decision as unconstitutional at the instance of any aggrieved individual. The constitutional court consisted of a President, a Vice-President and a number of other members; the President, the Vice-President and one half of the other members were elected by the Lower House and the other half of the other members by the Upper House of the Federal legislature. They were to hold office for life. Further provisions as to the organisation and procedure of the constitutional court were to be prescribed by Federal legislation.

II

We may now proceed to analyse the fundamental rights embodied in the constitutions of some of the more important countries of the world and to frame the draft of a Bill of

Rights for incorporation in the Indian Constitution. For this purpose, it is useful to recognise a distinction between two broad classes of rights: there are certain rights which require positive action by the State and which can be guaranteed only so far as such action is practicable, while others merely require that the State shall abstain from prejudicial action. Typical of the former is the right to work, which cannot be guaranteed further than by requiring the State, in the language of the Irish Constitution, "to direct its policy towards securing that the citizens may, through their occupations, find the means of making reasonable provision for their domestic needs"; typical of the latter is the right which requires, in the language of the American Constitution, that "the State shall not deprive any citizen of his liberty without due process of law". It is obvious that rights of the first type are not normally either capable of, or suitable for, enforcement by legal action, while those of the second type may be so enforced. Both classes of rights are mentioned together under the head of "fundamental rights" in certain constitutions, *e.g.*, in the Constitution of the U. S. S. R. and in the Weimar Constitution of the German Reich, possibly because neither was intended to be enforced by legal action. But the distinction is clearly recognised (though not uniformly pursued) in the Irish Constitution, which deals first with "fundamental rights" strictly so called, and then with "directive principles of social policy", the latter being expressly excluded from the purview of the courts. A similar distinction is recognised in Dr. Lauterpacht's *International Bill of Rights of Man* (1945). The substantive provisions of the Bill are in two parts, Part I dealing with rights meant to be enforced by the ordinary courts and Part II dealing with rights incapable of or unsuitable for such enforcement.

We may usefully follow this plan and separate the two classes of rights: Part A may deal with fundamental principles of State policy and Part B with fundamental rights strictly so called.* The following draft is suggested for **Part A** (it is meant to be illustrative rather than exhaustive):

PART A

" The principles set forth in this Part are intended for the general guidance of the appropriate legislatures and governments in India (hereinafter referred to collectively as ' the State '). The application of these principles in legislation and administration shall be the care of the State and shall not be cognisable by any court.

" 1. The State shall promote international peace and security by the elimination of war as an instrument of national policy, by the prescription of open, just and honourable relations between nations, by the firm establishment of the understandings of international law as the actual rule of conduct among governments and by the maintenance of justice and the scrupulous respect for treaty obligations in the dealings of organised people with one another.

" 2. The State shall promote internal peace and security by the elimination of every cause of communal discord.

" 3. The State shall, as far as possible, secure to each citizen:

    (1) the right to work,

    (2) the right to education,

    (3) the right to maintenance in old age and during sickness or loss of capacity to work,

    (4) the right to rest and leisure;

in particular, the State shall make provision for free and compulsory primary education.

" 4. The State shall promote with special care the educational and economic interests of the weaker sections of the people and, in particular, of the scheduled castes and the aboriginal tribes, and shall protect them from social injustice and all forms of exploitation.

" 5. The State shall protect the culture, language and script of the various communities and linguistic areas in India.

" 6. The State shall regard the raising of the level of nutrition and the standard of living of its people and the improvement of public health as among its primary duties.

---

* Cf. Parts IV and III of the Indian Constitution.

" 7. The State shall ensure that the strength and health of workers, men and women, and the tender age of children shall not be abused and that they shall not be forced by economic necessity to take up occupations unsuited to their sex, age or strength."

It is obvious that none of the above provisions is suitable for enforcement by the courts. They are really in the nature of moral precepts for the authorities of the State. Although it may be contended that the constitution is not the proper place for moral precepts, nevertheless, constitutional declarations of policy of this kind are now becoming increasingly frequent.* They have at least an educative value. The first clause is taken from the Declaration of Havana made in 1939 by the representatives of the governments, employers and work-people in the American Continent. The second, fourth and fifth clauses are peculiarly needed in India. The third clause embodies certain objectives of social and economic policy which are now widely recognised; see, for example, articles 118-121 of the Constitution of the U. S. S. R. and articles 42 and 45 of the Irish Constitution. The sixth clause relating to nutritional and other standards is taken from the recommendations of the United Nations Conference on Food and Agriculture, 1943, and is of special importance to India. The seventh clause is taken from article 45 (4) 2° of the Irish Constitution, 1937.

PART B

We now come to the other Part, part B, relating to fundamental rights strictly so called, that is to say, rights which are meant to be enforced by legal action. Here we enter upon controversial ground.

" There are very few countries which have fully adopted the system of judicial review enabling courts to act in that capacity

---

* (See the Introduction to the I. L. O. publication *Constitutional Provisions Concerning Social and Economic Policy*, Montreal, 1944).

in the matter of the fundamental rights of the individual guaranteed by the constitution. In the United States, by long-established practice—though not in pursuance of any express provision of the constitution—the Supreme Court has exercised that power since its decision in the historic case of *Marbury v. Madison*. This is also the position, by virtue of an express constitutional provision, in Brazil, Venezuela and some other Latin-American countries, in Czechoslovakia, Rumania and the Irish Free State. In a number of countries—such as Australia, Canada and Germany (in the constitution of 1919)—judicial review is limited largely to questions relating to the respective legislative competence of the Federation and of the member States.

" On the other hand, in many States the constitution specifically excludes the interpretation of laws—and *a fortiori* any declaration of their invalidity—from the purview of the judiciary. Judicial review of legislation is contrary to the constitutional doctrine of France and, above all, of Great Britain, where the supremacy of Parliament is absolute. Although the Constitution of Soviet Russia of 1923 gave (in article 7, sec. 43) the Supreme Court of the Union the power to render decisions, at the request of the Central Executive Committee of the Union, on the constitutionality of any regulations made by the republics of the Union, no such powers have been conferred upon it by the constitution of 1936. . . .

" The doctrine of judicial review has been defended with fervent approval by great lawyers in the United States and elsewhere. Daniel Webster and Francis Lieber praised it as a bulwark of liberty. Lord Bryce was of the view that ' there is no part of the American system which reflects more credit on its authors or has worked better in practice.' Dicey was a strong believer in the doctrine of the supremacy of Parliament in England. But he was emphatic that it was ' the glory of the founders of the United States '—in fact the doctrine of judicial review was adopted a quarter of a century after the foundation of the republic—to have established a system of protection of the constitution essential to a federal system (actually, the exercise of the power of judicial review by the Supreme Court has borne little relation to the fact of the federal structure of the United States). Tocqueville praised it as most favourable to liberty and to public order. After one hundred and forty years of operation it has the unqualified support of a large—perhaps predominant—section of American legal opinion as a bulwark of liberty of the people against the rashness and the tyranny of short-lived legislative majorities.

" On the other hand, the doctrine of judicial review has found from its very inception violent opponents and detractors in the country of its origin. Jefferson and Madison denounced it. Great teachers of constitutional law, such as J. B. Thayer, have drawn attention to the dangers of attempting to find in the Supreme Court—instead of in the lessons of experience—a safeguard against the mistakes of the representatives of the people. That criticism has grown in the last fifty years to the point of bitter denunciation as the result of the exercise of the power of judicial review in a manner which, in the view of many, has made the Supreme Court a defender of vested rights and social statics. Some French jurists, who were attempting to find a remedy for the absence of an effective guarantee of fundamental rights in their own constitution, have come to regard the experience of judicial review in the United States as a sufficient deterrent against introducing judicial review in France. In countries other than the United States, in which judicial review of legislation is recognised, it has been experienced only in rare cases for the protection of the rights of the individual." (*pp.* 186-190, *An International Bill of the Rights of Man*, 1945, by Lauterpacht).

14

SECOND CHAMBERS

ONE of the vexed questions of political science is the problem
of Second Chambers. The political thinkers of the nineteenth
century were nearly unanimous in their support of a Second
Chamber and, in the words of Sir Henry Maine, held that
" almost any Second Chamber is better than none ". But in
the present century there has been a growing opposition to it,
and even where a Second Chamber is allowed to continue or
a new one established, the general tendency has been to
restrict its powers. However, we find that almost all the important States of the modern world have Second Chambers
and only very few, *e.g.*, Turkey and Bulgaria, have dispensed
with them. It must, however, be pointed out that, though
Second Chambers are regarded as an essential element of
federal constitutions, they are the exception rather than the
rule in the constituent units of a federation. In the U.S.S.R.
and the Union of South Africa the legislatures of the constituent units are all unicameral. Of the eight provinces in the
Dominion of Canada only Quebec and Nova Scotia have
Second Chambers. In Switzerland sixteen cantons are unicameral; two cantons and four half-cantons still have their
old folk-moots or direct assemblies of all the citizens. In
Weimar Germany, half the States were unicameral. But,
except for Nebraska in the U.S.A. and Queensland in
Australia, all the State constitutions in these two countries
have Second Chambers.

The motives for creating or continuing a Second Chamber
have usually been mixed. First, there is the force of tradition.

For example, in England the representative bodies of the middle ages were organised on the basis of status: the nobles, the clergy and the commoners sat in separate chambers. The first two bodies fused to form the British House of Lords. The Lords, from being the predominant partners, gradually lost their powers to the Commoners; but even as late as the passing of the Parliament Act of 1911, the Lords had in law, and to a large extent in fact, equal powers with the Commoners.

Secondly, the propertied classes have always looked upon a Second Chamber as a protective armour for safeguarding their interests. This is true of other minority groups as well. As Herman Finer has observed, " wherever there are interests which desire defence from the grasp of the majority, a bicameral system will be claimed; for even delay of an undesirable policy is already a gratifying deliverance ". (*Theory and Practice of Modern Government* by Finer, *p.* 740). This is, for instance, seen in the framing of the French Constitution of 1875 when the monarchists, defeated at the polls, tried to entrench themselves in a Second Chamber.

Thirdly, many sincere democrats have often felt that there must be a check to prevent hasty legislation by the Lower House. They fear that a chamber directly and immediately responsible to the populace will be moved by gusts of passion of a momentary character. This is a point of view which has been forcefully expressed by Farrand in narrating an incident in the life of George Washington. " There is a tradition," he writes, " that Thomas Jefferson some two years later, upon his return from France, was protesting to Washington against the establishment of two Houses in the legislature. The incident occurred at the breakfast-table and Washington asked: ' Why did you pour that coffee into your saucer?' 'To cool it,' replied Jefferson. ' Even so,' said Washington, ' we pour legislation into the senatorial saucer to cool it '." * While the object is laudable, it has always been

* *The Framing of the Constitution, p.* 74.

found difficult to construct a Second Chamber which is responsive to public opinion and at the same time can act as a brake on the impulsive actions of the Lower House. The object is usually sought to be achieved by entrusting the work of choosing the members of the Second Chamber to a specially selected electorate as in Ireland.

Fourthly, a Second Chamber is often formed to provide representation for interests which could not be adequately provided for in the Lower House.

In federal constitutions seats are usually allotted to the constituent units in the Lower House on the basis of population and the members are elected directly by the citizens. But, in the Upper House, equality of representation of the constituent units is generally accepted, e.g., in the U.S.A. and in Australia. Even where, as in Canada, the principle of equal representation has not been strictly adhered to, the principle of allotting seats on the basis of population is considerably modified to give weighted representation to the smaller units.

Again, those who desire the representation of economic groups in the legislature but cannot agree to the abolition of the territorial principle for the Lower House, see a way out in the institution of the Second Chamber. It is said that the Upper Chamber gives scope for representation of men of status and experience who do not care to face risks of popular election. It is also supposed to avoid majority tyranny: the interests of minorities are expected to receive a more patient hearing in a Second Chamber.

Opposition to the system is, however, not inconsiderable even at the present time. The principal ground of attack is that the system is undemocratic. It is held by the advocates of this view that the legislative process in the modern world is sufficiently long drawn-out and complicated even without a Second Chamber. Every measure before being passed by the legislature is usually discussed for months and sometimes for years on the platform and by the press. Needless multiplication of checks would only make the government less dynamic. It is further held by them that the so-called impulsiveness of the Lower House is only an excuse which the propertied classes have invented to establish a Second Chamber for safeguarding their interests. They still quote Abbe Seyes that if a Second Chamber is in agreement with the first it is superfluous; and if it is not in agreement with it, it is pernicious.

Again, it is argued that experience has shown that it is very difficult to constitute a truly democratic Second Chamber on lines other than those of the first. If the franchise is fixed on a higher level than for the Lower House, power would be vested in the propertied classes; an indissoluble Second Chamber with members retiring in rotation or a Second Chamber with a life longer than that of the Lower House would not be in touch with current public opinion; the principle of equal representation to constituent units in federal constitutions often leads to minority rule; and the distribution of seats on a functional basis is at its best, to a large extent, arbitrary.

Further, the critics say, the politically backward countries suffer from insufficiency of leaders to man two chambers in small and poor countries and the expense is too heavy.

There are two main types of Second Chambers: the elective and the non-elective. Between these two types lie a variety of Upper Houses which partake of the characteristics of both. It may be convenient to consider the various Second Chambers of the world in the following order:

(1) hereditary, (2) nominated, (3) partially elected, (4) fully elected, and (5) special types.

(1) HEREDITARY SECOND CHAMBERS

GREAT BRITAIN—The British House of Lords is the only hereditary Upper House of any importance that is left now. But even this body is not, strictly speaking, wholly hereditary.

17

At present the House of Lords consists of persons who hold their seats—

(1) *by hereditary right:* the title to peerage and membership of the House of Lords are inherited according to the principle of primogeniture and the hereditary peers form the major part of the House;

(2) *by creation of the Sovereign:* the King has a prerogative right to create new peers at any time, but this power is in practice exercised by the Ministry of the day;

(3) *by virtue of office:* the Archbishops and Bishops of the realm and the Law Lords; and

(4) *by election:* the hereditary peers of Scotland elect 16 members from among themselves for the duration of each Parliament. At one time the whole body of the Irish peers also elected 28 peers for life, but this stopped with the creation of the Irish Free State.

At present the full House consists of about 740 members, but the voting strength is about 720.

Until 1911 the powers of the House of Lords were largely co-extensive with those of the House of Commons. This led to occasional conflicts between the two Houses and many important measures, such as the Reform Bill of 1832, were passed by the threat of creating new peers to overcome the opposition of the Lords. Finally, its powers were curtailed by the enactment of the Parliament Act of 1911.

At present, all money Bills, so certified by the Speaker of the House of Commons, if not passed by the House of Lords without amendment, become law without their concurrence on the royal assent being signified. Public Bills, other than money Bills or a Bill extending the maximum duration of Parliament, if passed by the House of Commons in three successive sessions, whether of the same Parliament or not, and rejected each time or not passed by the House of Lords, may become law without their concurrence on the royal assent being signified, provided that two years have elapsed

between the second reading in the first session of the
House of Commons and the third reading in the third
session. All Bills coming under this Act should reach the
House of Lords at least one month before the end of the
session.

(2) NOMINATED SECOND CHAMBERS

The main feature which distinguishes the nominated Second
Chamber from its hereditary prototype is that while the office
of the herditary peer is handed down from father to son
and cannot be resigned, the office of the nominated Senator
is terminable with death, or earlier in certain contingencies.
Of the fully nominated Second Chambers, the most interesting
instances are those of the Italian Senate under the constitution of 1848 and the Senate of Canada.

(a) *ITALY*—The Italian Senate consisted exclusively of
the Princes of royal blood and those nominated by the King
for life from certain classes, numbering 21 categories, as laid
down by the constitution of 1848. Persons who paid over
3,000 *lire* [nominally about 600 pounds] in taxes, persons
who had rendered distinguished service to the State, members
of the Lower House who had served in three parliaments or
for not less than six years, famous scientists or litterateurs and
church dignitaries were eligible for nomination. Persons
below 40 could not be nominated. There was no statutory
limit to the number of Senators, so that the Ministry of the
day, in whose hands lay the power of appointment, could utilise it for forcing laws through the Senate.

In theory, the Senate had the same powers as the Lower
House, and no Bill could become law without its consent.
But as the Ministry had the power to appoint any number
of additional members, the Senate could not effectively stand
against the Lower House, to which alone the Ministry was
responsible under the constitution.

(b) *CANADA*—The members of the Canadian Senate are nominated for life by the Governor-General, but in practice he is guided by the advice of the Ministry of the day. The constitution provides that the number of Senators should not exceed 104; but in case Newfoundland is admitted into the Union, the minimum should be 102 and the maximum 110. The present membership of the Senate is 96. According to section 22 of the British North America Act, 1867, as amended in 1915, in relation to the constitution of the Senate, Canada is deemed to consist of four divisions, namely, Ontario, Quebec, the Maritime provinces and Prince Edward Island and the western provinces, each of the divisions having equal representation consisting of 24 members. The distribution of the seats on the basis of provinces is as follows: (a) Ontario, 24; (b) Quebec, 24; (c) the Maritime provinces and Prince Edward Island, 24, *i.e.*, Nova Scotia, 10; New Brunswick, 10; Prince Edward Island, 4; (d) the western provinces, 24, *i.e.*, six members each for Manitoba, British Columbia, Saskatchewan and Alberta.

The constitution of the Senate of Canada is essentially an attempt to work the federal idea through an Upper House on the model of the British House of Lords. In giving effect to the federal idea all that has been possible to achieve is the equal representation of the four main divisions of the country and not of the provinces.

Each Senator must be at least 30 years of age, either a born or naturalised British subject and must reside in, and be possessed of property, real or personal, to the value of 4,000 dollars, exclusive of all encumbrances, within the province from which he is appointed. In the case of Quebec, he shall have his real property qualification in the electoral division from which he is appointed and shall be resident in that division. A Senator may resign his seat if he so desires. He must vacate it if he fails to attend the Senate for two consecutive sessions of the Parliament, or changes his allegiance, or becomes a brankrupt or is arraigned for treason or is convicted of felony or any infamous crime, or ceases to be qualified in respect of property or residence. The power of appointment and removal of the Speaker of the Senate is vested in the Governor-General.

The powers of the Canadian Senate are, in law, equal to those of the Lower House, excepting that money Bills must originate in the House of Commons, and convention requires that they may be rejected but not amended. There are no adequate means to adjust differences between the two Houses: all that the framers of the constitution have done for this purpose is to provide for the appointment of additional members to the Senate, but since the total strength of the House cannot exceed 104, the maximum number that can be nominated at any time to resolve differences is eight.

Thus, in theory, the Canadian Senate is a very powerful body: it has powers nearly equal to those of the Lower House; the system of nomination for life secures its independence; and it cannot be cowed down by the threat of unlimited nomination as in the case of the British House of Lords. But in practice it appears to have been lacking in vitality and Professor Lees-Smith goes to the extent of saying that Canada has had "virtually a single chamber government". This appears to have been the result of the majority of the members being, for the most part, the nominees of the party in power.

(3) PARTIALLY ELECTED SECOND CHAMBERS

Other interesting examples are the Second Chambers of South Africa and Ireland and that of Japan under its constitution of 1899.

(a) *SOUTH AFRICA*—The South African Senate consists of 40 members; eight of these are nominated by the Governor-General-in-Council and 32 elected, eight from each of the four provinces. Of the nominated Senators, four are selected mainly for their acquaintance with the reasonable wants and wishes of the coloured races. The Senators of each province are elected by an electoral college composed of the members of each Provincial Council (that is to say, the legislature of the province, which in each case consists of a single House) and the representatives of the province in the House of Assembly of the Union. Election is on the principle of proportional representation with the single transferable vote. Each Senator must be at least 30 years of age, a British subject of European descent, qualified as a voter for the election of members of the House of Assembly in one of the provinces and resident for five years within the Union. An elected Senator must be a registered owner of immovable property within the Union of the value of not less than £5,000 over and above any special mortgage. A nominated Senator holds office for ten years, both in the case of an original appointment and in the case of an appointment to fill a vacancy. An elected Senator holds office for ten years unless the Senate be sooner dissolved; but a Senator elected to fill a vacancy holds office only for the remainder of his predecessor's term.

By the Representation of Natives Act, 1936, provision has been made for the election of four additional Senators, each of whom represents one of the four electoral divisions into which the Union is divided. The Senators so elected hold their seats for five years. They should possess the qualifications prescribed for elected Senators and they enjoy all the usual privileges of Senators.

The Senate chooses its own President. He may be removed from office by a vote of the Senate, or he may resign by writing under his hand addressed to the Governor-General. Any member of the Senate may similarly resign his office. The quorum for the Senate is fixed at 12.

The South African Senate has only limited powers and is essentially a " House of review ". Money Bills must originate in the House of Assembly only. The Senate may not amend any Bill which imposes taxation or appropriates revenue or moneys for the services of the government, nor can it amend any Bill so as to increase any proposed charges or burdens on the people. In case of difference of opinion between the two Houses, the constitution provides for a joint sitting. Since the House of Assembly has three times as many members as the Senate, the will of the former generally prevails.

The South African Senate has the characteristic features of a unitary constitution. The non-elected members are appointed by the government of the Union and the members of the Union House of Assembly have a voice even in the selection of the elected members. The Parliament has also the power at any time to alter the composition of and the mode of election to the Senate.

(b) *IRELAND*—The Irish Senate (called 'Seanad Eireann') is composed of 60 members, of whom 11 are nominated by the Prime Minister and 49 elected. Of the elected members, three are elected by the National University of Ireland, three by the University of Dublin and the remaining 43 are elected from five panels of candidates containing respectively the names of persons having knowledge and practical experience of the following interests and services: (1) national language and culture, literature, art, education and such professional interests as may be defined by law for the purpose of this panel; (2) agriculture and allied interests and fisheries; (3) labour, whether organised or unorganised; (4) industry and commerce, including banking, finance, accountancy, engineering and architecture; and (5) public administration and social services, including voluntary social activities. According to the Seanad Electoral (Panel Members) Act 1937, the panel members are nominated by registered associations and by the members of the Dail Eireann, the Lower Chamber of the Irish legislature. Their election is by an electoral college composed of the members of the Dail Eireann and seven persons elected by each one of the Councils of the counties or county boroughs.

The elections to the Senate are held on the principle of proportional representation with the single transferable vote. A person to be eligible for membership of the Senate must be eligible to become a member of the Lower House.

The powers of the Irish Senate in the matter of legislation are very limited. A money Bill must originate in the Lower House; and though it has to be sent to the Senate for its "recommendation", the Senate must return the Bill within 21 days. If the Bill is not returned within this period or if it is returned with a recommendation which the Lower House does not accept, the Bill is deemed to have been passed by both Houses at the expiration of 21 days. In regard to other Bills, the Senate has, in effect, a suspensory veto for a period of 90 days. It has, however, power to ask for a reference to the people if its view has the support of one-third of the members of the Lower Chamber. This does not extend to Bills amending the constitution.

(c) *JAPAN*—Under the Japanese Constitution of 1899, the Upper House of Japan, called the House of Peers, was composed of hereditary, nominated and elected members. Under the constitution, as revised after World War II, the House of Peers will have 300 members, instead of 404 as before. These 300 will include (1) such of the Imperial Princes as are specially designated by the Emperor, (2) 30 members chosen from among the hereditary Princes, marquises, viscounts, counts and barons, (3) a maximum number of 125 members nominated by the Emperor for "meritorious service", (4) four members of the Imperial Academy, (5) 34 corporative members nominated by the Emperor to represent agriculture, commerce and industry, and (6) 120 elected members from prefectural, urban or rural, districts, who hold office for six years, with half their number to be re-elected at three-yearly intervals.

Before World War II the House of Peers was noted to be a very conservative body and more powerful than the House of Representatives. It is to be seen whether the recent changes in its constitution will reduce the House to the position of a mere revising Chamber.

(4) ELECTED SECOND CHAMBERS

Elected Upper Houses may be considered under two heads:
  (i) those in fully federalised States; and
  (ii) those in unitary States.

The Upper Houses in fully federalised States, such as the U.S.A. and Australia, present the following salient features:

  (*a*) the representation given to each of the component States is equal;
  (*b*) the Senators are elected from and in the States individually, without any interference from the central authority;
  (*c*) the term of office of the Senator is arranged in such a way as to ensure continuity of life to the Senate.

(i) SECOND CHAMBERS IN FEDERAL STATES

(*a*) *UNITED STATES OF AMERICA*—The Senate in the U.S.A. consists of 96 members, two members from each of the 48 States. They are chosen by popular vote, one-third retiring or seeking re-election every two years. A Senator must not be less than 30 years of age, must have been a citizen of the U.S.A. for nine years and a resident of the State from which he is chosen.

The United States Senate is " the only example in the world of a Second Chamber that is incontestably more powerful than the first ".* It has complete freedom in the matter

---

* Lees-Smith: *Second Chambers, p.* 154.

of initiating legislation and can amend or reject any Bill, including a money Bill, which originates in the Lower House. The consent of both the Houses is essential for the enactment of any law and there is no provision for resolving conflicts between the two Houses. In addition to its legislative functions, the consent of the Senate, by two-thirds majority, is required for the ratification of all treaties initiated by the President with foreign Powers. Its approval is also necessary for major appointments made by the President. It has further the sole power to try all impeachments.

The Vice-President of the United States of America is the President of the Senate.

(b) *AUSTRALIA*—The Australian Senate is composed of 36 members, six from each of the six States of the Commonwealth. Like the American Senate, the Australian Upper House embodies the federal idea. The Parliament may make laws, increasing or diminishing the number of Senators for each State, but only in such a way that the equality of representation of the various States is maintained and that none of the original States has less than six members. The Senators are chosen for a term of six years, half of the members retiring every three years. In the event of a prolonged disagreement between the two Houses of Parliament, the Governor-General may dissolve both Chambers, in which case the continuity of the existence of the Senate is lost and a wholly new Senate will have to be elected.

The electorate for the Senate and the House of Representatives is the same. But in the former case, the entire State forms the constituency, each voter having as many votes as there are seats to be filled. The qualifications of a Senator are also the same as those of a member of the House of Representatives. Accordingly, every Senator must be a natural born subject of the King or must have been for five years a naturalised subject under a law of the United Kingdom or of a State of the Commonwealth. He must be at least

21 years of age, must possess the electoral qualifications and must have resided for at least three years in Australia.

Unlike the American Senate, the functions of the Australian Senate are purely legislative. The Senate has equal powers with the House of Representatives in respect of proposed laws except that money Bills must originate only in the Lower House and cannot be amended (though they may be rejected) by the Senate. The Senate may, however, at any stage return to the House of Representatives any proposed law which the Senate may not amend, requesting by message the omission or amendment of any items or provisions therein. But if there is a deadlock between the two Houses, the Senate can force the dissolution of both the Houses even in regard to money Bills. If the deadlock continues even after the reconstituted Chambers meet, it is resolved by a joint sitting of the two Houses.

The Australian Senate has not allowed its powers to lapse by disuse and it is considered to be the most powerful Second Chamber in the British Dominions.

(ii) SECOND CHAMBERS IN UNITARY STATES

FRANCE—Under its latest constitution, France has a Parliament consisting of two Houses, the National Assembly and the Council of the Republic. The Assembly is constituted on a territorial basis by universal suffrage. According to the constitution, the number of members of the Council cannot be less than 250 or more than 320. The present strength is 315. Of these, 50 are elected by the National Assembly by the method of proportional representation; 65 are allotted to Algeria and the overseas territories; and 200 are elected by groups of communes and Departments. For the election of members allotted to Departments, electoral colleges based on the canton are formed. One delegate is allowed for every 300 registered voters and the delegates are elected by universal suffrage on the principle of proportional representation. Of the 200 seats allotted to Departments, 125 are filled directly by the electoral colleges, each Department forming a constituency for the purpose with one councillor for every 500,000 inhabitants. Where a Department is allotted only one seat, the candidate who obtains the greatest number of votes is elected without an absolute majority being necessary. Where more than one seat is allotted to a Department, seats are allotted to party lists according to the rule of the largest average. The remaining 75 seats are filled by a Central Commission in Paris from among the candidates who have not been returned in such a way as to make up for inequalities in the representation of parties resulting from the departmental elections.

Each of the Chambers is the judge of the eligibility of its members and the regularity of their election; it alone receives their resignations. The two Chambers hold their sittings simultaneously.

Article 14 of the constitution lays down, " the National Assembly alone votes the law. It cannot delegate this right." The President of the Council of Ministers and the members of the Parliament can initiate laws. The members of the Council submit their proposals through their own Council office and they have to be forwarded without debate to the office of the National Assembly. The latter will not accept any Bill which will result in any decrease of receipts or creation of expenditure.

A Bill is placed before the Council of the Republic after it has been voted in the first reading by the National Assembly. In the case of non-budget Bills it must give its opinion within two months after it has been transmitted by the Assembly. If it is a Bill relating to the budget, the period taken for consideration by the Council should not exceed that taken by the National Assembly. So also, where the Bill is of an urgent character and if the Assembly so decides, the Council cannot have more time than that taken by the Assembly itself. A Bill or part of a Bill rejected by the Council can be passed into law by an absolute majority of the members of the Assembly.

(5) SPECIAL TYPES

(a) *SWITZERLAND*—In Switzerland the Upper House is called Standerat or the Council of States. It consists of two members from each of the 19 cantons and one member from each of the half-cantons into which the remaining three cantons are divided. The total membership of the House is 44. There is thus equality of representation among the various units. The constitution leaves the details regarding the election and term of office of the members to the cantonal governments themselves. At the present time the people in 21 cantons or half-cantons directly elect the members; in the four remaining cantons or half-cantons the members are elected by the cantonal legislatures. The term of office of the members varies from one to four years, the term being long in the cantons with direct election of members and short in cantons where they are elected by the legislature.

The Swiss Second Chamber has in general equal powers with the first. The two Chambers sit together as one body to elect the executive, judicial and other officials, to issue amnesties and pardons and to settle administrative disputes and conflicts of jurisdiction. For all other matters they function separately. The ministers are responsible to neither House, though they must answer questions put to them equally in both. Proposals for legislation may be initiated in either House and there is no special sanctity in regard to money Bills. Everything that comes before the Federal legislature requires the concurrence of both Houses. If a difference of opinion arises between the two Chambers their respective committees try to arrive at a compromise. Normally this is not difficult and in the absence of party government there is no incentive for any section to adopt an uncompromising attitude.

The position of the Swiss Council of States is often considered to be anomalous. It is in the strict sense not a federal chamber, for it is not part of its business to safeguard the interests of the cantons as opposed to those of the Confederation; nor is it purely a Second Chamber, since it has no definite functions of legislative revision or veto.

(b) U.S.S.R.—The legislative power of the U.S.S.R. is exercised exclusively by the Supreme Soviet of the U.S.S.R. which consists of two Chambers, the Soviet of the Union and the Soviet of Nationalities. The Soviet of Nationalities is elected by the citizens of the U.S.S.R. according to Union and autonomous republics, autonomous regions and national areas on the basis of 25 deputies from each Union republic, 11 deputies from each autonomous republic, five deputies from each autonomous region and one deputy from each national area.

The Supreme Soviet of the U.S.S.R. is elected for a term of four years. Both Chambers of the legislature have equal rights, including the right to initiate legislation. A law is considered adopted if passed by both Chambers by a simple majority vote in each. The sessions of both Chambers begin and terminate simultaneously. If there is disagreement between the Soviet of the Union and the Soviet of Nationalities, the question is referred for settlement to a conciliation committee formed on a parity basis. If the conciliation committee fails to arrive at an agreement, or if its decision fails to satisfy one of the Chambers, the question is considered for a second time by the Chambers. Failing agreement between the Chambers, the Presidium of the Supreme Soviet of the U.S.S.R. dissolves the Supreme Soviet of the U.S.S.R. and orders a new election.

The Supreme Soviet of the U.S.S.R., at a joint sitting of both Chambers, elects the Presidium of the Supreme Soviet of the U.S.S.R.

(c) *WEIMAR GERMANY*—Under the Weimar Constitution of Germany there was a Reichsrat (also called the Reich Council) " formed in order to represent the German State in the legislation and administration of the Reich ". In the Reichsrat, each State had at least one vote. In the larger States one vote was assigned to each million inhabitants. Any surplus not less than the total population of the smallest State was reckoned as a full million. No State could be represented by more than two-fifths of all the votes.*

The number of votes allotted to the States could be readjusted by the Reichsrat after each general census of the population.

The States were represented in the Reichsrat by members of their governments. This was a survival of the system obtaining under the old German Empire. But unlike the old Bundersrat the Reichsrat was entirely overshadowed by the Reichstag, which was the popularly elected House.

The Reichsrat had no power to initiate legislation. The laws of the Reich were passed by the Reichstag alone, but the consent of the Reichsrat was necessary for the introduction of any Bill in the Reichstag by the government. Should the government and the Reichsrat not be in agreement, the former could nevertheless introduce the Bill; but, in doing so, it had to state the divergent view of the Reichsrat.

The Reichsrat, however, had an important and peculiar veto. It could lodge an objection with the government against a law passed by the Reichstag, within two weeks after its passage. The law was then to be reconsidered by the Reichstag, and if the two Houses could not still agree, the President of the Reich, could, within three months, order a referendum on the subject in dispute. If the President did not make use of this right, the Bill would not become law. Should the Reichstag decide by two-thirds majority against the objection raised by the Reichsrat, the President was required

* This was provided to prevent the domination of the State of Prussia.

within three months either to promulgate the law in the form approved by the Reichstag or order an appeal to the people.

The Reichsrat, under the Weimar Republic, thus occupied a peculiar position. It has been claimed that the German Parliament was not a bicameral legislature, and that the Reichstag alone constituted the German Parliament. " The Constitution of Weimar provided a one chamber system. Nor does the existence of the Reich Council (Reichsrat) disprove this fact. For the Reich Council, an Assembly of instructed representatives of the various German Lands (States) is no more an Upper Chamber similar to the United States Senate, than was the Federal Council (Bundesrat) of the Imperial Constitution." *

(d) *NORWAY*—The Norwegian Parliament, the Storting, consists of 150 members elected once in four years by universal adult suffrage by the method of proportional representation. Soon after it is constituted, it elects from among its own members one-fourth to constitute the Second Chamber, the Lagting; the remaining three-fourths constitute the first Chamber, the Odelsting. The membership of the Lagting remains unchanged for the whole life of the Parliament by which it is elected, except for the filling of casual vacancies which is done by special nomination. Provision is also made for joint sessions of the two Chambers, the Storting *in plenum*.

The constitution does not define clearly the purposes for which the two Chambers must meet separately or in joint session. By the provisions of the constitution and by usage, Bills involving questions of finance, concessions for works of public utility, the naturalisation of foreigners, amendments to the constitution and motions for controlling the executive are considered at the joint session and decisions are reached by a bare majority vote. All records of such diplomatic matters and of such matters relating to military command as are to be kept secret are laid " before a committee consisting

---

* J. H. Kraus: *Crisis of German Democracy, p.* 151.

of not more than nine members chosen from among the members of the Odelsting, if any member of the committee moves that the Odelsting gives its opinion on the subject, or that an action be brought in the High Court of the Realm ". The only purpose for which the two Chambers sit separately is in respect of ordinary legislation. Even here it is provided that " every Bill shall first be introduced in the Odelsting ", thus denying the Second Chamber any right to initiate Bills. For resolving deadlocks between the two Chambers provision is made for a joint session of the two Chambers at which two-thirds majority is required for the passage of the contested Bill.

The Lagting is vested with certain judicial powers. In con-junction with the Supreme Court of Justice, it constitutes the High Court of the Realm which pronounces judgment " in the first and last instance in such actions as are brought by the Odelsting against members of the Council ôf State (the members of the Storting) for criminal offences which they may have committed in that capacity ".

There is great diversity of opinion among scholars as to whether the Norwegian Parliament is unicameral or bica-meral. Commenting on this, Lees-Smith observes, " the best summary of her (Norway's) reply to the Second Chamber problem is that she possesses a one-Chamber system with the rudiments of a two-Chamber system. This is the broad con-clusion reached by the chief Norwegian Professors of Law ".*
Again, Marriott observes " that the Lagting fulfils some of the functions appropriate to a Second Chamber is evident; but, on the other hand, the members of it possess no differ-entiating qualifications; they are merely selected from among, and by, the members of the Storting and do not sit by virtue of any independent right conferred either by the electorate, or by official nomination or by hereditary privilege. Norway, then, must still languish in the shade of ambiguity ".†

* *Second Chambers in Theory and Practice*, p. 201.
† *Mechanism of the Modern State*, Vol. I., p. 408.

15

HEAD OF THE STATE

By "Head of the State" is meant the supreme executive authority of the State. It is now well recognised that every State must have such a chief executive. In many cases the King was originally the repository of all powers in the State. He was the law-giver, the executor of the law and the judge. But gradually, one by one, these powers were delegated by him to others and in some cases he even disappeared. Where he disappeared, the problem arose of having a suitable substitute. Even Cromwell found it necessary to evolve the office of a Lord Protector. The need was particularly felt in the international sphere. There were certain duties, *e.g.*, receiving foreign potentates and ministers which it was impossible for a body of men, like a Cabinet or a Parliament, to perform simultaneously. Thus the various types of non-hereditary executives we come across in the present day represented the various attempts made by constitution-makers to instal uncrowned kings in places which were once occupied by crowned ones.

It may be that in certain States in matters official the head of the State is no more than a distinguished "rubber stamp"; but even a rubber stamp has its use. A familiar test which is, therefore, adopted by text-book writers is to ask whether the executive is real or nominal. In some cases the real and nominal blend in one person, as in the U. S. A.; there is then really no nominal executive. But in the vast majority of cases it is possible to distinguish between the formal head of the State and the real executive. We are concerned here more with the nominal or formal executive. [The real executives of modern democracies have been dealt with in the chapter on Democratic Executives. (See Chapter 12, *pp.* 202-231 of this volume.)]

Professor J. H. Kraus in *The Crisis of German Democracy*, 1932 (*p.* 171) says that there are five possible types of State heads which, named in the sequence of their importance, can be characterised under the following terms:

(1) the representative head of the State;

(2) the head of the State bureaucracy;

(3) the guardian of the constitution;

(4) the highest equalising factor in the balance of the State machinery; and

(5) the leader of the people.

This classification reveals the various purposes for which the head of the State is constituted. The heads of the different States fall under one or more of these types according to the particular emphasis which the constitution places upon their functions.

THE UNITED KINGDOM

In the United Kingdom, there is, as everybody knows, a constitutional monarchy. Most executive authority is legally vested in the King and is exercised in his name. But every official act of the King is done on the responsibility of a minister. On this is based the doctrine that the King can do no wrong; for what he does some minister is held responsible.

The legal position of the Crown has been little affected by the passage of time. It remains nearly the same as in 1872, when Bagehot gave the following startling enumeration of the legal powers of the Crown:

"The Queen could disband the army (by law she cannot engage more than a certain number of men); she could dismiss all the officers, from the General Commanding-in-Chief downwards; she could dismiss all the sailors too; she could sell off all our ships of war and all our naval stores; she could make a peace by the sacrifice of Cornwall and begin a war for the conquest of Brittany. She could make every citizen in the United Kingdom, male or female, a peer; she could make every parish in the United Kingdom a university; she could dismiss most of the civil servants; she could pardon all offenders. In a word, the Queen could by prerogative upset all the actions of civil government, within the government, could disgrace the nation by a bad war or peace and could, by disbanding our forces, whether land or sea, leave us defenceless against foreign nations."

This passage illustrates the vast reserve of the powers vested in the King of England. The fact that no monarch in his senses would on his own even attempt to exercise these powers is another matter.

The powers of the Crown of the present day are derived from custom and from statute. The functions of the King may be dealt with briefly under three heads: (a) non-political; (b) political; and (c) formal.

(a) The Crown has been described as the pivot of the " dignified part of the constitution " and the following claims have been made for the institution of monarchy: A monarchy calls forth feelings which no republic can evoke. It appeals to the sentiments of the people more than any other form of government. It provides an " intelligible headpiece " and is valuable in excluding competition for the leadership of the society. Above all, the Crown acts as the guardian of the " invisible " constitution. It " acts as a disguise ", for " it enables the real rulers to change without heedless people knowing it ".

(b) It is not easy to describe the political functions of the Crown. A good deal depends upon the character of the monarch. The regime of Queen Victoria provides ample evidence to show how an exceptionally capable Sovereign, strong of will and greatly devoted to duty, backed up by the experience gained during a long reign, left a profound impression upon the government of the day. In the words of Gladstone, " the acts, the wishes, the example of the Sovereign in this country are a real power. An immense reverence and tender affection await upon the person of the one permanent and ever faithful guardian of the fundamental conditions of the constitution ".

(c) Of the formal prerogatives of the Crown the following are the more important, namely, (i) the right of dissolution, *i.e.*, the right to appeal from Parliament to the people; (ii) the right to refuse a dissolution, *i.e.*, the right to appeal from the Ministry to Parliament; and (iii) the right to select his chief adviser, that is, the Prime Minister. These rights are, no doubt, circumscribed by many considerations, but no one can deny that these rights exist.

Mention may also be made here of three other rights enumerated by Bagehot: the right to be consulted, the right to encourage and the right to warn. "A King of great sense and sagacity would want," he wrote, "no other." The letters of Queen Victoria afford various instances where this masterful Sovereign exercised all these rights.

CANADA, AUSTRALIA AND SOUTH AFRICA

In each of these Dominions the *de jure* head of the State is the King of England, but in every Dominion he is represented by a Governor-General.

Under the old colonial system the Governor-General represented the Crown, that is, the Home Government. He was all-powerful. Gradually, just as the power of the King at home was first checked and finally taken over by a Cabinet responsible to Parliament, so also the power of the Governor-General in the colonies passed from his hands into the hands of the people of the colonies. With the history of the transition from the colonial system to the responsible government of the present day we are not concerned. What has to be noted is that the Governor-General came to occupy in the Dominions a position similar to that of the King in England. He represented a mere formal head of the State. After the Imperial Conference of 1926, the Governor-General in a Dominion ceased to represent the government of Britain (considered as Cabinet) and became merely a representative of the King, with the result that the government of the United Kingdom had to appoint another official, called the High Commissioner, in a Dominion to act as a liaison officer between the Dominion and the Home Government.

In Canada and Australia, the Governor-General, whenever there is a vacancy in the office, is appointed by the King primarily, if not solely, on the advice of the Dominion Cabinet. But in South Africa, the Governor-General is appointed on a commission countersigned by the Prime Minister of the Union and not by a British Secretary of State. The Union Government is thus solely responsible for this appointment. The term of office of the Governor-General in all the three Dominions is five years.

The Cabinet is the *de facto* executive in the Dominion. In all political matters the Governor-General acts only on the advice of the Cabinet. He does not preside over the business meetings of the Cabinet, which are summoned in the name of the Prime Minister. The Governor-General acts merely as the constitutional head of the government advised by ministers.

IRELAND

In Ireland there is no Governor-General but a President. When the new constitution was passed in 1937, all references to the King and in the main to the Governor-General were omitted from it, but the Executive Council was authorised to avail itself, for diplomatic and consular appointments and international agreements, of any organ used for

these purposes by other members of the British Commonwealth, though that term was avoided. Therefore, it is rather
difficult to define the exact position which Ireland occupies
in the British Commonwealth. Mr. De Valera claimed that
Ireland was a republic, while His Majesty's Government
treats it as part of the British Commonwealth.

The Irish executive is of the British responsible type, that
is to say, it is a parliamentary executive. The President is,
therefore, the formal head of the State and, save as otherwise
provided in the constitution, all powers and functions
conferred on the President by the constitution are to be
exercised by him only on the advice of the government of
the day.

The President is elected by the people. The electorate is the
same as that for the Dail. The election is by secret ballot on
the system of proportional representation with the single transferable vote. He holds office for seven years from the date on
which he enters upon his office, unless before the expiration
of that period he dies or resigns or is removed from office, or
becomes permanently incapacitated, such incapacity being
established to the satisfaction of the Supreme Court consisting
of not less than five judges. A person is eligible for re-election
to that office but only once. He may not leave the State during
his term of office save with the consent of the government.
He may be impeached for stated misbehaviour. A proposal
in either House of the legislature to prefer a charge against
the President may not be entertained unless upon a notice of
motion in writing signed by not less than 30 members of that
House. And such proposal may be adopted by a House only
upon a resolution of that House, supported by not less than
two-thirds of the total membership thereof. When a charge is
preferred by one House, the other House is to investigate the
charge or cause the charge to be investigated. The President
has the right to appear and to be represented at the investigation of the charge. If, as a result of the investigation, a

resolution is passed, supported by not less than two-thirds of the total membership of the House of the legislature by which the charge was investigated or caused to be investigated, declaring that the charge preferred against the President has been sustained and that the misbehaviour, the subject of the charge, was such as to render him unfit to continue in office, the resolution operates to remove the President from his office.

FRANCE

A brief reference may be made here to the position of the French President, both under the old constitution of 1875 and under the new constitution which has just been approved by the people of France.

The President under the constitution of 1875 has been made famous by a classic aphorism of Sir Henry Maine. "There is no living functionary," he wrote, "who occupies a more pitiable position than a French President. The old Kings of France reigned and governed. The constitutional King of England, according to M. Thiers, reigns, but does not govern. The President of the United States governs, but he does not reign. It has been reserved for the President of the French Republic neither to reign nor yet to govern." This statement was substantially true; the real executive in France was the Cabinet and the President was merely a figurehead.

He was elected for seven years, not by the people but by the two Houses of the French Parliament, sitting together as a National Assembly. He was re-eligible for election any number of times. Under the previous constitution the President had been responsible to the legislature, but the inconvenience and danger of this principle soon became apparent and, therefore, when the constitution came to be revised in 1875 he was made "irresponsible" except in the case of high treason. If accused of high treason, the President could be impeached by the Chamber of Deputies and tried by the Senate. The Senate had the power to order his dismissal and to impose suitable penalties. Save as above, the President was, for the duration of his term, irremovable. In the executive sphere he could act only through his ministers who under the constitution were to countersign every decree of his. His position was, in fact, merely that of " a constitutional King for seven years ".

Under France's latest constitution the President of the republic will be elected for seven years by the two Houses of the legislature. Among his powers are the following:

He designates the Prime Minister and confirms the latter's choice of ministers. He presides over the Council of Ministers, the Council of Magistrates, now less dependent on political parties, and the Supreme Council of National Defence. He confirms the dissolution of the Assembly if the government has been outvoted twice within 18 months after the first 18 months of its existence. All his edicts must be countersigned by the Prime Minister and another minister.

THE WEIMAR CONSTITUTION OF GERMANY

Under the Weimar Constitution of 1919 the Reich President was elected by the whole German people by secret, equal and direct ballot, men and women being entitled to vote. The fathers of this constitution deliberately discarded the French system of the Parliament electing the President, as such a system was, in the words of Hugo Pruess, " false parliamentarism ". According to him, real parliamentarism postulates two organs of State which are on an equal footing, e.g., Parliament and President, and this can only be achieved if the President is elected not by the Parliament but directly by the people.

Any German over 35 years of age may be elected to the Presidency. It was not necessary, as in the U.S.A., for the

President to be born on German soil; it was sufficient if he was a German citizen. Nor was there any restrictive provision, as in the old French Constitution, prohibiting a member of one of the reigning families of Germany from becoming the President.

To be elected a President, a candidate had to receive an absolute majority of the votes cast. If at the first election no candidate received a majority of votes, a second ballot was held. This second ballot was not necessarily confined to the two candidates who obtained the highest number of votes in the first ballot; it was even permissible for a candidate to contest the election for the first time at the second ballot. For instance, in 1932, President von Hindenberg was in fact put up as a candidate only at the second ballot.

The term of office of the President was seven years, which was much longer than the term of the Reichstag which, at the most, could extend only to four years. He could be re-elected any number of times, but his term of office could be terminated prematurely by deposition. Such deposition was to be proposed by the Reichstag by a resolution which required two-thirds majority and was decided by the people. In case the verdict of the popular vote went in favour of the President, he could remain in office for a further term of seven years and the Reichstag was automatically dissolved. The President or any of his ministers could be impeached for violation of the constitution or a Reich law by two-thirds vote of the Reichstag, the trial being held in a special court, the Staatsgerichhof. In case of any temporary incapacity of the President, the Chancellor was to act as his constitutional substitute.

The President was the Commander-in-Chief of the army and navy, and represented the Reich in foreign affairs; but a declaration of war could be made only by the legislature, while alliances and treaties required its assent. The President had the power to appoint and dismiss the Chancellor and ministers as well as all the officers, civil and military. He had the right to pardon in any case decided by the German Supreme Court in the first instance or by any other court in Germany. In the sphere of legislation he promulgated the Reich laws. Under certain circumstances he could order a plebiscite to be held and, within the limits of article 48 of the constitution, could even legislate. But all his decrees and orders had to be countersigned by a minister, who thereby accepted responsibility for them. The position of the President was, therefore, strictly based on the model of a parliamentary executive.

SWITZERLAND

The executive of the Swiss Confederation is a peculiar one. The constitution provides that the supreme directing and executive power of the Confederation is exercised by a Federal Council composed of seven members. It has been said that the constitution of the Swiss Republic " confides the executive authority neither to a President nor to a Premier; neither to a Cabinet nor to an autocrat ". The Swiss executive can be classified neither under parliamentary nor under non-parliamentary executives. In fact, it appears to have succeeded in combining the merits and excluding the demerits of both the parliamentary and fixed executive systems. The Federal Council, as the Swiss executive is called, is a body consisting of seven members who are elected by the two Houses of the legislature, sitting together as a National Assembly. They are elected at the beginning of each new National Council for the duration of that Assembly, namely, three years. The Federal Council is completely renewed after every general election of the National Council. In the Federal Council power is not concentrated in any one man; it is held equally among the seven members. There is, as it were, a diffusion of executive power among a body of men. But every year the Federal Assembly nominates one of the members of the Federal Council as the President of the Confederation who presides over the Council and another as the Vice-President of the Council. The outgoing President cannot be elected President or Vice-President for the following year, nor can the same member act as Vice-President for two consecutive years. Usually the Vice-President succeeds the President and the two offices rotate among the members of the Federal Council. The President gets a salary equal to about £60 a year more than each of his colleagues during his term of office.

" By the actual arrangement, the work of the President of the Confederation has been considerably diminished. He is of course still head of a department, which may no doubt be that of foreign affairs, though he can equally direct one of the others, such, for instance, as war or finance. But his presidential functions have been lessened by relieving him of a number of matters of mere administrative procedure and of the duty of giving numerous audiences to foreign representatives and other persons. He still opens all correspondence addressed to the Federal Council, distributes the business among the different departments, presides at the sittings of the body and signs the notes and other official correspondence in its name. He still receives foreign representatives on certain occasions, such as the delivery of letters from the heads of their countries and the presentation of their letters of credence and recall. He also continues to take the first place, ranking before his colleagues, upon public occasions. It is thus clear that the President of the Confederation has not a tithe of the power entrusted to the President of the United States. He may, indeed, without any disrespect, be likened to the chairman of a board." (Adams & Cunningham: *The Swiss Confederation*, 1889).

THE UNITED STATES OF AMERICA

The American President provides a perfect illustration of a non-parliamentary or fixed executive. According to the constitution, the " executive power shall be vested in the

President of the U. S. A.," and " he shall hold office during
the term of four years . . . . together with the Vice-President
chosen for the same term ".

The method of election both of the President and the Vice-
President is provided for by the constitution with great precision. " This process of election," wrote Hamilton, " affords
a moral certainty that the office of the President will seldom
fall to the lot of any man who is not in an eminent degree
endowed with the requisite qualifications."

The constitution contemplates that the election should be
indirect. It provides first for an electoral college, the members
of which are chosen in each State to a number equal to the
number of representatives from the State to the two Houses of
Congress. The actual method of choosing these electors is
left to the discretion of each State legislature. All the State
legislatures have directed that the presidential electors shall
be chosen at the polls by the qualified voters of the State.
The electors meet in each State to nominate and cast votes
for the presidential and vice-presidential candidates. The
votes are sent to the President of the Senate and are counted
in the Houses of Congress sitting in a joint session.

The constitution intended to confer a wide discretion on
the presidential electors in the choice of a President; but, in
practice, an elector dare not cast his vote for any other than
the official nominee of his party.

" As a matter of practice, the presidential electors in each
State are nominated by the political parties, one slate of presidential electors by each party organisation. This is done at State
party conventions, or at primaries. Then at the November election in each presidential year, the qualified voters mark their
ballots for the one or the other of these party slates. The ballots
are usually arranged so that by marking a single cross the voter
can indicate his preference for the whole column of Republican
or Democratic presidential electors as the case may be.

" Thus in New York a single cross indicates the voter's choice
for the entire forty-eight presidential electors of the Republican

party or the Democratic party. Strictly speaking, therefore, the President and Vice-President are *not* elected in November. Only the presidential electors are elected at that time. The official election of President and Vice-President takes place at the hands of these electors who meet in their respective States and vote as will be explained a little later." (*The Constitution of the United States* by W. B. Munro, 1944, *p.* 74).

The author explains later that the electors meet in their respective States and cast their votes on the first Monday in the following January.

To be qualified for the office, the President must be a natural-born citizen of the U.S.A., not less than 35 years of age and resident in the country for at least 14 years. His salary (which is $75,000) shall neither be diminished nor increased during his tenure of office. In case of a vacancy in the office of the President, caused by death or any other disability during his term, his place is taken by the Vice-President; and in the event of a vacancy occurring in respect of both the President and the Vice-President, the office is to be filled *ad interim* by the various members of the government according to a settled order fixed by statute. The President, the Vice-President and all civil officers of the U.S.A., are liable to be removed from office on impeachment for, and conviction of, treason, bribery, or other crimes and misdemeanours.

As to the genesis of the office, English writers lay much stress upon the British tradition. "It is tolerably clear," wrote Sir Henry Maine, "that the mental operation through which the framers of the American Constitution passed was this: they took the King of Great Britain, went through his powers and restrained them whenever they appeared to be excessive, or unsuited to the circumstances of the United States." (*Popular Government*, p. 212).

American writers have, however, taken pains to refute this; but the historical link with the past cannot be denied. In the words of Prof. Laski, "there is no foreign institution with which in any basic sense it can be compared, because basically there is no comparable foreign institution. The President of the United States is both more or less than a King; he is, also, both more or less than a Prime Minister ". (*American Presidency*, 1943, *p.* 23).

THE UNION OF SOVIET SOCIALIST REPUBLICS

Like Switzerland the U.S.S.R. also occupies a unique position. The constitution does not provide for the office of a chief executive; on the other hand, the person who is spoken of as the President of the U.S.S.R., is the Chairman of the Presidium of the Supreme Soviet of the U.S.S.R., which is a sort of standing committee of the legislature. This rather curious state of affairs may be explained by the fact that in the Russian Constitution the demarcation between the executive and the legislature is not so clear-cut as in some of the other constitutions. It will be noticed that the Presidium of the Supreme Soviet exercises many of the executive powers which in British India are exercised by the Governor-General.

The Supreme Soviet of the U.S.S.R. elects, at a joint sitting of both Chambers, its Presidium, consisting of a Chairman, 16 Vice-Chairmen, a Secretary and 24 members of the Presidium. The Presidium is responsible to the Supreme Soviet in all its activities.

The Presidium has important functions. It convenes twice a year the sessions of the Supreme Soviet; interprets the existing laws and issues decrees, dissolves the Supreme Soviet, in case of the failure of the two Chambers to agree, and arranges for new elections; holds referendums on its own initiative or on that of one of the constituent republics; revokes the decisions and orders of the Councils of People's Commissars of the Union and of the constituent republics if they violate the law; in the intervals between the sessions of the Supreme Soviet, removes from office and appoints People's Commissars of the U.S.S.R., subject to subsequent confirmation by the Supreme Soviet; bestows decorations and honorary titles; exercises the right of pardon; appoints and dismisses the high command of the armed forces; in the intervals between the sessions of the Supreme Soviet, has the power to declare a state of war and at all times to order mobilisation, to ratify and to denounce international treaties, to appoint and recall ambassadors, to receive the credentials and letters of recall of foreign representatives.

16

SYSTEMS OF REPRESENTATION

MODERN democracy is generally representative democracy. The institutions of the Initiative and the Referendum play only a minor part in democratic decisions most of which are taken by the legislature on behalf of the people. The setting up of a truly representative legislature is, therefore, of the greatest importance for the success of democracy.

Until the late nineteenth century, however, the question of representation received little attention at the hands of statesmen and political thinkers. Political discussions centred on the merits of democracy as a form of government and the safeguards necessary for protecting the people from over-government. It is only in recent years that it has been realised that the form of representation has far-reaching political consequences, sometimes affecting the very foundations of democratic government. Here a brief account of the various forms of representation is given, with particular attention to the system of proportional representation.

SINGLE-MEMBER CONSTITUENCIES

Under this system the country is divided into as many constituencies as there are seats to be filled and each constituency returns one member. Among the candidates contesting a seat the one securing the largest number of votes is declared elected.

This system has had a long history behind it and has been adopted by most countries of the world at one time or the

19

other. While it is now losing its hold in many countries, it is still the main basis of representation in Great Britain, Canada, South Africa and the U.S.A. Although there are many front-rank political thinkers who prefer it to any of the alternatives suggested, the working of the system has brought to light many shortcomings and the volume of opposition to it has been increasing.

The system has been subjected to criticism mainly from three angles:

(1) The very assumption on the basis of which it is defended, namely, that interests within any given region are fundamentally unified and that they vary from region to region, has been questioned. It has been suggested by some that representation should be of economic groups and not of territorial groups. Others have suggested that representation should be on the basis of religion and culture.

(2) The second line of criticism is based on the principle that all minority groups, whether they be political, economic, or cultural, have a right to be represented in the legislature in proportion to their electoral strength. Under the system of the single-member constituency, the minority parties, more often than not, would be grossly under-represented. The number of seats a minority party captures depends, not upon the support it has in the country at large, but upon the concentration of its electoral strength in particular constituencies. For instance, to capture 25 per cent of the seats in the legislature, a party must have sufficient support to win seats in 25 per cent of the constituencies; but if its supporters are diffused, it may not capture even one seat, even though it polls 25 per cent of the votes in all the constituencies put together.

(3) The third line of criticism is that it does not even ensure always the success of the majority party. First, within the constituencies, if there are three or more candidates for a seat, the successful candidate is often elected only by a

relative and not an absolute majority of the votes. It is by no means certain that if the contest had been confined to the winning candidate and the most leading of the defeated candidates the former would have won. Secondly, sometimes, even when there are only two major parties, the party which has polled a smaller number of votes than the other in the country at large is returned to power. Such an anomaly would arise more frequently when there are three well-organised parties. Thirdly, when two parties are more or less equally balanced, a small group of voters who can turn the balance to the benefit of either of the parties will command power quite disproportionate to its number. The influence that Jewish votes have on the foreign policy of the U.S.A. is a case in point. The Jews form only about three per cent of the population of the country.

Recent discussions regarding the forms of representation centre on the above defects and various suggestions have been made to remedy them.*

MAJORITY PREFERENTIAL VOTING SYSTEMS

Various forms of voting are devised to ensure that every person returned to the legislature by a single-member constituency really commands the confidence of the majority in his constituency.

(1) *The Second Ballot*—Under this system two election days, with an interval of a week or two, are fixed. If in the first election one of the candidates secures a majority of the votes cast, he is declared elected. Otherwise, a second ballot is taken and voting is confined to the two candidates who in the

---

* There is another system of voting which suffers from all the shortcomings of the single-member constituency system. Under this, in a multi-member constituency, the voter is given as many votes as there are seats to be filled and he cannot give more than one vote to one candidate. This is known as the block vote or the compulsory distributive vote.

first election obtained most votes. Sometimes, as in the case of the election of candidates for the office of the President by the national conventions of the great political parties of the United States, successive elections are held with a view to eliminating the weakest of the candidates until one of them polls an absolute majority of the votes cast.

(2) *The Alternative Vote*—This seeks to achieve the same object as the second ballot without the trouble of a second election. Under this system the voter is required to mark his choice in the order of preference. The count is on the basis of the Hare System of the single transferable vote to be described later.

There is no doubt that the second is to be preferred to the first as it avoids the necessity of a second ballot. The above forms of voting generally ensure that successful candidates do command the confidence of a majority in their constituencies. But they do not remedy the other defects of the system of the single-member constituency: they do not protect the minorities; they do not prevent a party polling a lesser number of votes in all the constituencies put together from getting a larger number of the seats; they do not also prevent the major parties from being held to ransom, as it were, by small groups of voters holding the balance in the constituencies.

GERRYMANDERING AND PROTECTION OF MINORITIES

Gerrymandering may be defined as the drawing of electoral districts in such a way as to favour one political interest or the other. The term itself has unhappy associations. In 1812, in the State of Massachusetts in the U.S.A., Governor Elbridge Gerry saw that the electoral districts were drawn in such a way that his party, the old Republican party, profited most from it; as a result, his party won 29 seats in the Senate with only 50,164 votes, while the opposite party, the Federalists,

won only 11 seats with 51,766 votes. This device has sometimes been employed for quite legitimate purposes, such as
the protection of minorities. But it can be of help only to
minorities which are concentrated and not diffused. The
chances of its misuse are, however, great.

PROPORTIONAL REPRESENTATION

In general, " the term proportional representation is used
to designate the various electoral devices which aim to secure
a legislative body reflecting with more or less mathematical
exactness the strength of the groups in the electorate ". There
are different forms of it and they all aim at securing adequate
representation for the minorities. Under this system, it is
claimed that any interest or group, whether it be economic,
religious or political, would secure representation in proportion to the support it has among the electors. The system is
highly elastic and can satisfy the claims of diverse interests.
Protection will be given as long as, and only as long as, a
group of electors large enough to claim a representative wants
it. This system, it is further claimed, offers a remedy for all
the defects of the system of the single-member constituency to
which reference has already been made.

The various forms of proportional representation may now
be considered:

(1) THE NON-TRANSFERABLE VOTE

Electoral devices under proportional representation may be
classed under two broad headings: (1) proportional representation with the non-transferable vote; and (2) proportional
representation with the single transferable vote. The basis
of distinction lies in the transferability or otherwise to
others of the vote or votes cast to particular candidates.

There are mainly three types of the non-transferable vote:
(a) the limited vote; (b) the single non-transferable vote;

and (c) the cumulative vote. Multi-member constituencies are essential in all the three cases. Under the limited vote a voter has two or more votes, but less than the number of candidates to be elected by the constituency. The single non-transferable vote is a special form of the limited vote. Each voter is allowed to vote for only one candidate while there is more than one seat to be filled, and the candidates who receive most votes are declared elected. Under the cumulative vote the voter has as many votes as there are candidates to be elected from the constituency, but he may distribute them among the candidates in any manner that he sees fit: he may give all his votes to one candidate or distribute them among several candidates.

All the three systems are intended to secure protection to the minorities. In a three-member constituency, for instance, if 25 per cent of the electors *plus* one join together and vote for one candidate of their own choice, they can be sure of his being returned, both under the single non-transferable vote and the cumulative vote. Both systems, however, suffer from two defects: (1) since the votes are not transferable, votes cast on defeated candidates do not help in the return of a member; (2) it can never be said that a party secures seats in proportion to the votes cast in its favour within the constituencies and the country at large. The number of seats a party captures in an election depends on the correctness with which it has gauged the support it commands in each of the constituencies, and set up the right number of candidates on its behalf.*

As between the single non-transferable vote and the cumulative vote, the former is simpler and better suited to the needs of an illiterate electorate. But the latter is preferred by party organisers as it makes the work of organising the

---

* Harold F. Gosnell, Article on Proportional Representation in the *Encyclopaedia of Social Sciences*. Vol. XII.

electorate easier. Under the single non-transferable vote, a party which has put up candidates for more than one seat in a constituency must divide the constituency into as many geographic units as it has set up candidates and instruct the electors in each unit to vote for a particular candidate. To illustrate the point by an example: Burdwan district in Bengal, we shall say, has been formed into a multi-member constituency with four seats. A party, hopeful of securing only two seats, has to estimate the probable number of its supporters in the different parts of the district and group the sub-divisions and *thanas* into two blocks, each block being instructed to vote for one of the two party candidates. Any gross miscalculation in the estimate of the distribution of its supporters might seriously affect its electoral chances. Under the system of the cumulative vote, this difficulty of forming electoral blocks is avoided. A party will merely have to tell its followers: " Each of you has four votes: give two to candidate A and two to candidate B, both of whom have been set up by the party ". In practice the difference in the form of voting often produces different results.

(2) The Single Transferable Vote

The principle behind the single transferable vote is briefly this. Though the legislature is composed of hundreds of representatives and a constituency returns more than one representative, an elector cannot claim to have all of them as *his* representatives; he has a right to have only *one* of them as his representative. He can, therefore, have only one vote even in a multi-member constituency. But he must be sure that the person for whom he votes is returned; otherwise, he would in practice be denied one of the fundamental rights of democratic citizenship, *i.e.*, the right to be represented in the legislature. He cannot be certain of this if he has only one vote and can give this only to one candidate. If his candidate is defeated, his vote would be a waste; if his candidate gets more votes than is necessary to secure his election, his vote would be superfluous and hence again a waste. This waste could be prevented by the adoption of the system of the single transferable vote. Under this system, the elector would have only one vote; but if his vote proves ineffective for either of the above two reasons, it is transferred to another candidate to help him to get elected. The number of votes that do not help in the election of a candidate is kept very low. The transfer of votes from one candidate to another is effected in one of two ways. Under the first, the elector votes for the candidates directly and individually; he has unfettered freedom to indicate his first choice and succeeding choices. This is the well-known Hare System, popularly known as the " single transferable vote ". Under the second, each party presents a list of candidates for the acceptance of the electors. The elector votes primarily for a party; in voting for a party list, he accepts the order of preference previously determined by the party; even where he is permitted to express his preference for an individual candidate, he is not allowed to go outside the party list. This is known as the " List System of proportional representation ". Both the systems are equally in vogue and popular.

(a) *The Single Transferable Vote (Hare System)*—Under this system, " the voter indicates his preferences among the various candidates, by marking his first choice and his succeeding choices with the appropriate numerals ". For the purpose of the count all the ballots of a constituency are brought to a central place. There are four distinct stages in the count. There is, first, the fixing of the number of votes a candidate must get if he is to be considered elected beyond all reasonable doubt, or what is commonly called the fixing of the quota. There is, secondly, the counting of votes on the basis of the first choices of the electors. All those candidates who secure the quota that is fixed, or anything above it, are declared elected. Thirdly, if there are seats yet remaining unfilled, the surplus votes, or votes in excess of the quota polled by the successful candidates, are transferred to the candidates still in the run on the basis of the second or succeeding choices of the electors. All those who with the help of these votes reach the quota are declared elected. Fourthly, if there are seats yet to be filled after the surpluses have been transferred, candidates who have polled the least number of votes are eliminated and their votes transferred to the candidates still in the run on the basis of their second or succeeding choices. This is done until all the seats assigned to the constituency are filled.

These four stages of the count are common to all the forms of the single transferable vote. Various technical devices have been developed to gauge the preferences of the electors with great exactitude and give effect to their real will. The degree of exactness required depends upon the size of the electorate. Where the electorate is small the form of the count must be such as to secure the greatest possible exactness, for even minor errors might greatly affect the results. Where the electorate is large, as would be the case in respect of national and municipal elections, the form of the count could be much more simple without materially affecting the results.

(b) *The List System*—Under this system each party presents a list of candidates in the order of preference it wants them to be elected. The elector may vote for any one of the party lists, but not for more than one. In voting for a party list he tacitly accepts the order of preference fixed by the party. In many cases, however, he is allowed to express his preference for any of the candidates included in a party list. Where this is done there is really an election within an election: the elector votes for a party and also for a particular candidate within a party list. Where it is desired that the elector should have maximum freedom in selecting the party candidate, the single transferable vote (the Hare System) is adopted.

The other forms of voting, such as the single non-transferable vote, can also be used.

The most difficult problem to be faced under this system is the apportionment of seats among parties in proportion to the votes polled by them. With the known technical devices it is possible to reach any degree of exactness that is considered politically desirable.

(c) *Vacancies*—The problem of vacancies is the same under both the Hare and the List Systems. The strictly logical procedure to fill a vacancy is to have an election by the same voters who elected the member whose seat has fallen vacant. But this cannot be done even if it were possible without violating the secrecy of the ballot. Therefore, the procedure that is generally adopted is to preserve the ballot papers which helped a candidate to win a seat and, if his seat falls vacant between two general elections, to select his successor on the basis of the succeeding choices marked on those ballot papers. The defect of the system is obvious; it is based on the results of the old election and it does not indicate in any way the changes in public opinion after it.

Other methods of filling a vacancy have been advocated and practised. Vacancies are filled by election by the whole of the multi-member constituency or by election by all the rest of the members of the legislature. These would favour the majority party and are inimical to minority interests. There are a few methods which seek to protect the latter. (1) The electors of the wards in which the member whose seat has fallen vacant polled the largest proportion of first choice votes may be allowed to vote at a bye-election. (2) The party to which the member belongs or the persons who nominated him at the time of the general election may be allowed to select his successor. Sometimes, the legislature by convention elects a person to fill a vacancy from among the members of the party to which the member whose seat has fallen vacant belonged. (3) Although this suggestion does not

appear to have been made earlier, every member of the
legislature may be required to nominate two persons as his
successors in case of his death or resignation; freedom may be
given to the members to change their nominees at any time.
This procedure would be particularly useful in respect of
non-party or independent members.

(3) THE SINGLE-MEMBER CONSTITUENCY AND THE SINGLE TRANSFERABLE VOTE

Of the various forms of representation discussed above,
controversy has centred on the relative merits of the single-
member constituency with plurality voting and proportional
representation of the Hare or the List variety. The case
against the single-member constituency has been considered
already and it is strong. But the case against proportional
representation is by no means weak or unworthy of consideration. Of the objections levelled against it and the answers
given may be mentioned some.

The first objection is that the system cannot be easily
understood by the voter or easily worked by the returning
officer. Where there is a literate electorate the advocates of
proportional representation reply that there is not much
substance in this objection. As for the returning officer, he
would be educated enough to understand the rules prescribed
for the count and observe them strictly. The persons that
ought to know the full significance of the system are the
legislators; since the forms of proportional representation are
many, they must understand the political implications of
each one of the forms and select the one best suited to
the needs of the country. In a country like India the
problem of illiteracy among the electors would, however,
have to be faced.

The second objection is that constituencies under the
system are unwieldy; and as a result the electoral expenses

of candidates are very great and the personal touch between electors and their representatives is lost. To this, the advocates of proportional representation reply that electoral expenses can be reduced and the difficulty of canvassing support minimised by effective co-operation among the candidates of the same party. In the case of small minority parties much depends on the intimacy of the contact they have maintained in the period before the election. Again, they urge, unless the constituency is too big it should not be difficult for a member to keep in touch with his constituents. The press, the radio and the rapid means of communication available today should go a long way in helping the member in his task.

The third objection is that no satisfactory system of bye-election under the system has been suggested and a very valuable instrument to gauge the trend of public opinion between two general elections is lost. The advocates of proportional representation reply that this is only of minor importance and ought not to be pressed.

The fourth objection is that its effect on the party system is particularly disastrous. It gives birth to a multiplicity of parties, each party being wedded to one pet object or the other. Since the minor parties are sure of being returned with the support of their own limited following, they have no incentive to coalesce with other parties with similar ideologies. Where the system of parliamentary government prevails, the Cabinet is formed after a good deal of mutual bargaining and the association is purely temporary. There is no strong bond binding together the parties which form the coalition government. As a result, no clear-cut policies are evolved; legislation is ineffective; the executive government is weak and unstable. There is a striking contrast between the fixed determination of each of the parties to realise its objective and the unstable vacillating character of the executive government. This provides the right background for the rise of dictatorship or of a strong bureaucracy.

The advocates of proportional representation, however, observe that no such generalisation is warranted. Countries without proportional representation, such as France, have not escaped from multiplicity of parties or weak government, and countries with proportional representation like Ireland (Eire) do not suffer from these evils.

But it appears that the system of proportional representation is not an integrating force compelling the smaller units to combine together to form larger ones for the purposes of effective political action; by making it possible for small parties to function effectively, it encourages them to maintain their individuality even at a high cost. Where the social forces are strongly in favour of two parties, its disintegrating influence is not felt, *e.g.*, in Ireland, or as it might be the case in Great Britain. But where the tendency is otherwise it accentuates the situation, *e.g.*, in Germany under the Weimar Constitution. A country which has no strongly developed parties stands more to lose by the adoption of proportional representation than a country which has two strongly developed parties that cannot be easily broken up.

There is, however, general agreement even among the critics of proportional representation that the application of the system is a necessity in the case of countries with self-conscious racial or communal minorities.

17

A VISIT TO U. S. A., CANADA, EIRE AND BRITAIN

[Sri B. N. Rau was deputed by the President of the Constituent Assembly to visit the countries mentioned in the heading to this chapter for personal discussions of important features of India's draft constitution with leading constitutional experts. This is his report embodying the results of his discussions with prominent personalities.]

BETWEEN October and December 1947, I visited the U. S. A., Canada, Eire and England for personal discussions with the leading constitutional experts of these countries. I had discussions in Washington with the Chief Justice of the Supreme Court, ex-Chief Justice Hughes and Justices Frankfurter, Burton and Murphy, as well as with Mr. Boland, the Irish Secretary for Foreign Affairs; in Ottawa with Justice Thorsen, President of the Exchequer Court, Mr. John Hearne, the High Commissioner for Ireland, Mr. Wershof and Mr. Jackett, constitutional experts; in New York with Justice Learned Hand of the Federal Circuit Court of Appeals.

As the result of these discussions, I have proposed two amendments to India's draft constitution. The first of them is designed to secure that when a law made by the State in the discharge of one of the fundamental duties imposed upon it by the constitution happens to conflict with one of the fundamental rights guaranteed to the individual, the former should prevail over the latter: in other words, the general welfare should prevail over the individual right. Indeed,

Justice Frankfurter considered that the power of judicial review implied in the due process clause, of which there is a qualified version in section 16 of the Indian draft constitution, is not only undemocratic (because it gives a few judges the power of vetoing legislation enacted by the representatives of the nation) but also throws an unfair burden on the judiciary; and Justice Hand considered that it would be better to have all fundamental rights as moral precepts than as legal fetters in the constitution.

The other amendment is designed to secure that when the national interest requires that a certain matter, ordinarily falling in the exclusively provincial sphere, should be dealt with on a national basis, the Centre should have power to legislate on it on that basis.

The provision in clause 238 of the draft constitution enabling the Federal Parliament during the first three years to amend the constitution by a simple Act of its own was regarded as a wise precaution.

Two other clauses of the draft constitution were considered of particular interest. Clause 230 provides for the appointment of a Commission to investigate the conditions of the backward classes and recommend measures for improving their lot. It is interesting to note in this connection that the President of the United States appointed a committee to recommend measures for the better protection of the civil rights of the people of the United States, and the committee gave particular attention to the position of certain under-privileged classes. The committee's report amply proved the usefulness of a periodic review of this kind. Besides making a number of valuable recommendations, the committee drew attention to the remarkable work done in this sphere by the civil rights section of the Department of Justice. This section was started as an experiment in 1939, but it has already proved a most useful agency and the committee recommended that its hands should be further strengthened. Clause 229 of the Indian draft constitution provides for the appointment of similar agencies in India (they are called special officers for minorities) both at the Centre and in the provinces.

The Canadian authorities, particularly Justice Thorsen, advised me not to finalise the provisions of the constitution relating to the relations between the Centre and the provinces, especially in the sphere of taxation and finance, without a careful study of the Rowell-Sirois Commission's Report on Dominion-Provincial Relations in Canada. The Government of the United States has also issued the Magill Report on the tax structure of the Federation.

The other materials I was able to gather in the U. S. A. bore, not so much on the constitution itself as on the supplemental legislation that would be necessary under the constitution. Thus, Mr. Hearne, the Irish High Commissioner in Ottawa, was emphatically of the view that India should, as soon as possible, have a Nationality Act of her own; and Mr. Boland, the Irish Foreign Secretary, explained how Ireland had tried to solve the problem. Apparently, in future, Irish citizens will not be British subjects, even outside Ireland, as they are at present, but they will have most of the privileges of British subjects. Reciprocally, British subjects will be granted similar privileges in Ireland, although they may not be Irish citizens. This indicates a possible mode of evolving a common citizenship—or something almost equivalent thereto—even as between countries tha do not acknowledge a common allegiance, e.g., between any two members of the U.N. on a basis of reciprocity. Thus, citizens of State ' A ' will not be automatically citizens of State ' B '; but ' A ' may grant, within its own boundaries, all or any of the privileges of citizenship to the citizens of ' B ', provided ' B ' does the same to the citizens of ' A '.

Again, Justice Frankfurter was very emphatic that any jurisdiction exercisable by the Supreme Court should be exercised by the full court. His view was that the highest court of appeal in the land should not sit in divisions. Every judge, except of course such judges as might be disqualified by personal interest or otherwise from hearing particular cases, should share the responsibility for every decision of the court. Regarding the removal of judges, he drew attention to a provision which had been proposed in New York State— the provision which was lately approved and which has the support of most of the judges and lawyers in this country.

The provision is:

"9-a (1) A judge of the court of appeals, a justice of the Supreme Court, a judge of the court of claims, a surrogate, a special surrogate, a judge of the court of general sessions of the county of New York, a county judge, a special county judge or a justice of a city court of record may be removed or retired also by a court on the judiciary. The court shall be composed of the Chief Judge of the Court of Appeals, the senior associate judge of the court of appeals and one justice of the appellate division in each department designated by concurrence of a majority of the justices of such appellate division. In the absence, inability or disqualification of the Chief Judge of the Court of Appeals or of the senior associate judge of that court, the Court of Appeals shall designate a judge or judges from the Court of Appeals to act in his or their stead.

" (2) No judicial officer shall be removed by virtue of this section except for cause or be retired except for mental or physical disability preventing the proper performance of his judicial duties, nor unless he shall have been served with a statement of the charges alleged for his removal or the grounds for his retirement, and shall have had an opportunity to be heard.

" (3) The trial of charges for the removal of a judicial officer or of the grounds for his retirement shall be heard before a court on the judiciary. The affirmative concurrence of not less than four members of the court shall be necessary for the removal or retirement of a judicial officer. The court in its discretion may suspend a judicial officer from the exercise of his office pending the determination of the proceedings before the court. The action of the court shall not extend further than to removal from office, or removal from office and

20

disqualification to hold and enjoy any public office of honour, trust or profit under this State, or to retirement for disability; but any judicial officer whose removal is sought shall be liable to indictment and punishment according to law. A judicial officer retired for disability in accordance with this section shall thereafter receive such compensation as the legislature may provide.

" (4) The Chief Judge of the Court of Appeals may convene the court on the judiciary upon his own motion and shall convene the court upon written request by the Governor or by the presiding justice of any appellate division or by a majority of the judicial council or a majority of the executive committee of the New York State Bar Association thereunto duly authorised. The Chief Judge of the Court of Appeals shall act as the presiding officer of the court but in the absence, inability or disqualification of the Chief Judge, the senior associate judge of the Court of Appeals sitting on the court shall act as the presiding officer. After the court on the judiciary has been convened and charges of removal have been preferred against a judicial officer, the presiding officer of the court shall give written notice to the Governor, the President of the Senate and the Speaker of the Assembly of the name of the judicial officer against whom such charges have been preferred, of the nature of the charges, and the date set for the trial thereof, which date shall be not less than sixty days after the giving of such notice. Immediately upon receipt of such notice, the legislature shall be deemed to be in session for the purpose of this proceeding."

Mr. John Hearne, the High Commissioner of Ireland, told me—and as the Constitutional Adviser for India I was told by Mr. De Valera himself—that the system of functional representation, provided under the Irish Constitution for the election of the Senate, has proved unsatisfactory and Ireland is passing (or has just passed) new legislation for the purpose.

On November 19, 1947, I had the privilege of seeing President Truman at the White House. Almost the first thing he said was, " Whatever else you may copy from our constitution, do not copy our provision for mid-term elections ". Under the U.S.A. Constitution, the President has a four-year term and the House of Representatives a term of two years, so that there is a general election for the House in the middle of the President's term of office. This sometimes results in the return of a party opposed to the President. It was this inconvenience which the President had in mind. Since we have adopted the parliamentary system in the Indian Constitution, the point is not as important as it is in the U.S.A. Nevertheless, I was able to tell the President that we had made the President's term of office nearly the same as that of the House of the People, so that we have not copied the provision in question. President Truman then went on to say that the U.S.A. provision of an indissoluble Senate, one-third of which was renewable every two years, might well be copied: which, in fact, has been copied in the Indian Constitution.

I then mentioned that India had specially noted the step taken by him in December 1946, in appointing a committee on civil rights—particularly the civil rights of the under-privileged classes. The committee's report, which has just been published, has proved how valuable was a periodic investigation of this kind, and accordingly there has been inserted in the Indian Constitution an express provision empowering the President to appoint, from time to time, a Commission to investigate the position of the backward classes. We have gone further in India and have actually anticipated one of the recommendations of the President's committee. The committee has recommended that there should be a special section in the Department of Justice, both at the Centre and in the States, to protect the civil rights guaranteed by the constitution. We have provided in the Indian Constitution for the appointment of special officers for minorities, both at the Centre and in the provinces for a similar purpose. At the end of the interview, the President said, " I am very greatly interested and should like to have, if I may, a copy of your constitution," adding humorously that he might borrow a point or two from us. He also expressed a desire that I might stay a little longer and see some of the more prominent Senators; but my programme made that impossible. He gave the assurance that whatever assistance or material I might require from the State Department would be gladly given.

On November 20 and 21, I saw Dr. Jessup (Professor of International Law, Columbia University), Professor Mirkine (Constitutional Consultant, United Nations), Dr. Hamburger (Secretary-General, United Nations Year Book of Human Rights), and Professor Dowling (Professor of Constitutional Law, Columbia University). I had detailed discussions with each of them. Both Dr. Jessup and Prof. Dowling regarded as very important the amendment giving power to the Centre to legislate on a subject which is normally provincial if it has come to be of national importance.

I arrived in Dublin on November 26, 1947. I first saw the Attorney-General, with whom I discussed various constitutional details. He pointed out that some of the fundamental rights guaranteed in the Irish Constitution were proving very inconvenient, particularly the one relating to property. This had come under consideration in the Irish Supreme Court in connection with the Sinn Fein Funds Act. The Act related to certain trust moneys which were lying in deposit in court. The moneys belonged to the Sinn Fein organisation. While they were in court, certain persons claimed them as honorary treasurers of the organisation and while the claim was pending, the Irish Parliament passed an Act discharging the pending action (after payment of costs, etc., to the plaintiffs) and vesting the moneys in a board of which the Chief Justice of the Supreme Court was made the chairman. The Act gave the board absolute discretion to pay the moneys to the members of various armed forces and their dependants who might be in needy circumstances. The Supreme Court held that the Act was unconstitutional on the ground that it took away the property which might have belonged to the plaintiffs and vested it in the board; however desirable might be the objects of the Act, it was said to be in conflict with the rights of property guaranteed in the Irish Constitution. Certain other cases too have led to the feeling that the fundamental rights have been expressed in too broad terms.

The Attorney-General also said that the system of proportional representation, which had been provided for in various parts of the Irish Constitution, had worked very unsatisfactorily. It had resulted in multiplying groups in the legislature, often compelling coalition governments in which no one could be certain of the continued allegiance of a particular group, with the result that the administration was greatly weakened. Steps were being taken, he added, without amending the constitution, to minimise this inconvenience by reducing the number of members in each constituency to three. Some constituencies had as many as nine members, so that a small group which could command the votes of even a tenth of the electorate could secure representation in Parliament. In the proposed redistribution, 22 constituencies would have three members and the rest four each.

The Attorney-General then mentioned that the provisions relating to functional representation in the Irish Senate had also given trouble: not so much the provisions in the constitution itself as the subsidiary provisions relating to panels. Under the Irish Constitution, the Senate consists of 60 members, of whom 49 have to be elected by a system of functional representation from various panels. It appears that all the 49 members have been regarded as forming a single constituency, and the total number of voters has been between 150 and 200. This has resulted in a quota of about four, so that any member could make sure of his election by making sure of four voters. Such a system facilitates corruption and the Irish Parliament has at present under consideration a Bill for altering it: (a) to break up the existing single constituency into a number of separate constituencies, and (b) to increase the number of voters.

Finally, he observed that he was hopeful that, sooner or later, Northern Ireland and Southern Ireland would be re-united. Northern Ireland consists of six counties, in two of which the Nationalists (mainly Catholics) are already in a majority. In the other four, Nationalists form about 35 to 40 per cent of the total population; but as the Catholics are multiplying at a much faster rate than the Protestants, and as Protestant immigration has also at the same time almost ceased, it would not be long before the six counties taken together showed a Nationalist majority. He also said that although Southern Ireland had only seven per cent Protestants, the minority was treated not merely fairly but magnanimously, and that Protestants themselves had paid generous tributes to the government for the manner in which their interests had been recognised. This should facilitate re-union.

In the afternoon, I had the privilege of an interview with Mr. De Valera, who was most cordial and considerate. He remarked that if he had a chance of re-writing the Irish Constitution, he would make three changes: (i) He would do away with proportional representation in any shape or form. He preferred the British system, as it made for strong government. (ii) He would revise the provisions regarding functional representation in the Senate. (iii) He would make the right of property, guaranteed in the constitution expressly, subject to laws intended for the general welfare. So far as we have copied these provisions in the Indian Constitution, we may make similar changes.

As regards the other provisions in our draft, he had two comments to make: (1) Four years as the maximum life-time of the legislatures was far too short a period. In his experience, he had found that, under a parliamentary system of government, ministers required at least one year at the beginning of their term to acquaint themselves with the details of administration, while the last year of the term was occupied with preparations for the next general election. Thus, with a four-year term, they would only have two years for effective work which was much too short for any kind of planned administration. He would suggest a term of not less than five years for the legislatures. (2) The period of three years provided for the amendment of the constitution by a simple Act of Parliament was also far too short. Here, again, he would suggest a period of not less than five years.

Towards the end of the interview, I mentioned to Mr. De Valera (as requested by Mrs. Vijayalakshmi Pandit) that there had apparently been some misunderstanding about India's attitude on Ireland's application for membership of the United Nations. He replied that he himself was aware of the true position that the matter voted on related only to procedure, but that there had been misunderstanding in certain other quarters.*

After leaving Mr. De Valera, I saw his Secretary, Mr. Boland, and had a long discussion in the course of which, among other things, Mr. Boland said that there was likely to be practically common citizenship between Ireland and the British Commonwealth on a basis of reciprocity, and there would thus be association between Ireland and the

---

* The Eirean Prime Minister, Mr. Eamon de Valera, was asked by Mr. McBride, Republican leader, in the Dail (Parliament) on 10th December 1947 whether he could say why India opposed the admission of Eire to the United Nations.

Mr. De Valera replied that it was wrong to suggest that India opposed the admission of Eire. " I welcome the opportunity of saying this," he added, " because I know from the communications I have received from the Indian Government and from the leader of the Indian delegation at the Assembly that they are as anxious as we are that any misunderstanding that exists in this regard should be removed.

" The difficulties arose in connection with procedural matters. The fact is therefore that, far from opposing the admission of this country to the United Nations Organisation, the Indian delegates went out of their way to express friendship and goodwill towards Eire. I want to take the opportunity of assuring our Indian friends that these feelings are cordially reciprocated by us."

members of the Commonwealth on the basis of common citizenship.

I arrived in London on the 27th of November and interviewed in addition to the High Commissioner for India (Mr. V. K. Krishna Menon), Mr. Noel Baker (Secretary for Commonwealth Relations), Sir Stafford Cripps, and the Privy Councillors Sir John Beaumont and Sir Madhavan Nair. Mr. Noel Baker, discussing Commonwealth relations, mentioned that the members of the Commonwealth were now completely independent in their foreign relations and, as the latest proof of this fact, he pointed out (as stated elsewhere also) that in the voting at the meeting of the United Nations on the Palestine question that year, Canada, Australia and South Africa had voted for partition, India and Pakistan had voted against partition, while the United Kingdom had remained neutral. Whatever might have been the position at one time, it was now possible for a country to be completely independent even within the Commonwealth.

Sir Stafford Cripps was interested generally about the situation in India and Burma; there was no time for discussing any constitutional details. Sir John Beaumont and Sir Madhavan Nair desired to know exactly what India's attitude would be with regard to the appellate jurisdiction of the Privy Council. As regards pending cases, there were at least 60, possibly more, appeals already filed before the Privy Council, and Sir Madhavan Nair was anxious to know as early as possible the Constituent Assembly's decision as to their disposal. As regards the age-limit of High Court judges, Sir John Beaumont said that, in his own experience, he had at least on two occasions failed to get the best men from the Bar for appointment to the Bench, because, with the present age-limit of 60, they had no chance of earning a full pension. He thought that the age-limit should be at least 65 and observed that if a judge was not too old for the Federal Court at the age of 65, there was no reason to think that he was too old for the High Court. The volume of work before the Federal or Supreme Court, if it took over the existing Privy Council appellate jurisdiction, would hardly be less than the volume of work before any High Court. Sir Madhavan Nair had no objection to the suggestion I had in mind for empowering the Supreme Court (on the analogy of the practice in the U.S.A. and in England) to call upon any retired judge of that court (with his consent of course) to serve on any particular case. On the other hand, he thought that it would be an advantage to have the assistance of an experienced judge. A judge who was too old to be of any assistance would of course not be asked.

As the result of discussions in Washington and Ottawa, I propose the following amendments:

(1) At the beginning of clause 9 sub-clause (2) insert the words "subject to the provisions of section 10".

(2) To clause 10 add the following new paragraph:
"No law which may be made by the State in the discharge of its duty under the first paragraph of this section and no law which may have been made by the State in pursuance of the principles of policy now set forth in Chapter III of this Part shall be void merely on the ground that it contravenes the provisions of section 2, or is inconsistent with the provisions of Chapter II of this Part."

The object of these amendments is to make it clear that in a conflict between the rights conferred by Chapter II, which are for the most part rights of the individual and the principles of policy set forth in Chapter II, which are intended for the welfare of the State as a whole, the general welfare should prevail over the individual right. Otherwise it would be meaningless to say, as clause 10 does say, that these principles of policy are fundamental and that it is the duty of the State to give effect to them in its laws. In the U.S.A. Constitution there are no express directive principles of State policy, but the courts have developed what is equivalent thereto, namely, the doctrine of the " police power" which has been defined as the power " to prescribe regulations to promote the health, peace, morals, education and the good order of the people, and to legislate so as to increase the industry of the State, develop its resources and add to its wealth and prosperity ". In the exercise of this power the State may make laws for the general welfare which would otherwise be inconsistent with the American Bill of Rights. The courts in India might have been able to develop a similar doctrine but for the language of clause 9 of the draft constitution. Hence the amendments proposed :

(3) In sub-clause 1 of clause 182, add the following as item (c) :

" (c) If the Council of States had declared by a resolution supported by not less than two-thirds of the members present and voting that it is necessary or expedient in the national interest that the Federal Parliament should legislate with respect to any matters enumerated in the provincial legislative list and specified in the resolution, then, to make laws for the whole or any part of the territories of the Federation with respect to that matter."

(4) In clause 182 add the following sub-clause (3A) :

" (3A). A resolution passed under clause (c) of sub-section (1) may be revoked by a subsequent resolution passed by a similar majority by the Council of States."

(5) In sub-clause (4) of clause 182, after the words " proclamation of emergency," insert the words " or the passing of a resolution under sub-section (1) " ; and after the words " the proclamation " insert the words " or the resolution ".

(6) In clause 183, for the words " except where a proclamation of emergency has been issued under " substitute the words " except as provided in ".

The object of these amendments is to remove a defect similar to that which has disclosed itself in the Canadian Constitution.

For example, under the draft Indian Constitution, agriculture, co-operative societies and the production, supply and distribution of goods are all exclusively provincial subjects. Suppose, however, that in order to raise the standard of living of the Indian people as a whole, a system of co-operative farming and of price control of agricultural products on a national scale, and not merely in a single province, becomes desirable; in that event, the Centre should not be precluded from legislating in respect of the above subjects.

As a safeguard against unwarranted encroachment on the provincial sphere, a resolution by a special majority of the Council of States, which for the most part represents the units of the Federation, would be desirable. The provision in clause 183, depending as it does upon the consent of each of the units concerned, might prove inadequate. The essence of the matter is that where legislation is called for on a national basis, the Central legislature should have power to enact it without amending the constitution. Such legislation may be needed not only in such spheres as education, co-operative farming, or public health, but also in a matter which is coming to be regarded as one of national and indeed almost international importance, namely, the safeguarding of the civil rights of all citizens: e.g., removing the social disabilities of Harijans. A provision such as the one proposed would enable the Central legislature to enact such a measure. The Report of the President's Committee on Civil Rights published in the U.S.A. has recommended that the National Government of the United States must take the lead in safeguarding the civil rights of all Americans and that Congress must enact the necessary legislation.

18

THE PARLIAMENTARY SYSTEM OF GOVERNMENT IN INDIA

[This is the text of an address delivered by Sri B. N. Rau to I.A.S. probationers in New Delhi in June 1948.]

INDIA is now actively engaged in framing the details of her new constitution, which will be federal in structure and will embody the British parliamentary system of government, both at the Centre and in the units or States. At some of the earlier sessions of the Constituent Assembly, when the main principles of the new constitution were being laid down, there was a fairly strong current of feeling in favour of the American Presidential system, and this found expression in certain decisions of the Assembly, not only as to the mode of election of the head of the Federation and of the heads of the constituent States, but also, to some extent, as to the relations between the heads of the States and their ministers. This current is now weakening, but it may nevertheless leave some traces in the final version of the constitution. It may be interesting at this stage to take a peep into the history of India, both remote and recent, and see how far her people have been accustomed to the theory and practice of parliamentary modes of government.

ANCIENT INDIA

In ancient India, there were a number of republics, but the predominant type of polity and, for long stretches of time, the only type was the monarchical. The essence of the parliamentary system is that the monarch or King must govern the State on the advice of ministers responsible to the people. How far did this system obtain in ancient India? According to the Code of Manu, which, in its present form, may be taken to have existed in the second century A.D., the King must have colleagues or ministers with whom he must discuss and consider all matters of State: " Even what is easy to do becomes very difficult if sought to be done unaided by one man; how much more so the business of the kingdom? " *

Kautilya's *Arthaśāstra*, whose date according to some scholars is the fourth century B.C. and according to others the third century A.D., enunciates the rule, " when there is an extraordinary matter, the ministers and the Council of Ministers should be called together and informed. There, whatever the majority decides to be done should be done (by the King) ".† The *Śukranīti*, which is placed by scholars in the 12th century A.D. or even later, but which embodies the doctrines and traditions of a far more ancient time, contains the injunction: " Without the ministers, matters of State should never be considered by the King, even if he is well versed in all the sciences and in statecraft. A wise King must always follow the opinion of the members of the Council of Ministers . . . He must never stand on his own opinion. When the sovereign becomes independent, he plans for ruin; in time he loses the State and loses his subjects." ‡ The *Nītivākyāmṛta*, a work of the 10th century A.D., states that " he is no true King who acts against the advice of his ministers ".§

It is, therefore, clear that the King in ancient India was not only expected to have ministers, but also to act upon

---

* Manu, VII 30-31, 55-56; Jayaswal, *Hindu Polity* (1943), *p.* 288.
† *Arthaśāstra*, Bk. I, Ch. 15; Jayaswal, *op. cit., p.* 288.
‡ *Śukranītisāra*, II, 2-4: Jayaswal, *op. cit., p.* 289.
§ Quotation from *Nītivākyāmṛta*, X; Jayaswal, *op. cit., p.* 306.

their advice. The number of ministers varied: according to Kautilya's *Arthaśāstra*, Manu recommended 12, Brihaspati 16, Uśanas 20, while Kautilya himself did not think it necessary to fix any particular number.* As so large a council could not always be consulted in practice, Kautilya recognised a kind of informal inner council of three or four ministers for constant consultation.† This may be compared to the evolution of the Cabinet in England.

Were the ministers responsible to the people? The *Mahābhārata* (which, in its present form, existed in the second century B.C.) contains a verse to the effect that " the King must invest only that minister with jurisdiction who has lawfully earned the confidence of the *Paura-Janapada* ".‡ Even if we take the italicised word in its literal sense to mean the people of town and country,—Dr. Jayaswal interprets *Paura* as the Assembly of the Capital and *Janapada* as the Assembly of the Realm—the verse appears to embody a strikingly modern conception. More significant, however, than this general injunction is an incident in Asoka's reign recorded in the *Divyavadana*, an important Buddhist work. The city of Takshasila (Taxila) in the north became " hostile " and Asoka sent his son Kunala to pacify the people. The citizens in welcoming the Prince said: " We are not hostile to Your Highness nor are we hostile to King Asoka, but to the wicked ministers who come and insult us." § The distinction drawn between loyalty to the King and opposition to the ministers of the day is interesting and recalls the English decision of 1848 in *The Queen v. Fussell* that the expression " government by law established " in the defintion of sedition does not mean the administration of the day but the permanent government

---

* *Arthaśāstra*, Bk. I, Ch. 15; Jayaswal, *op. cit.*, *p.* 292.

† *Arthaśāstra* Bk. I, Ch. 15; Beni Prasad, *Theory of Government in Ancient India* (1927), *p.* 125.

‡ *Mahābhārata*, Śanti-Parvam, LXXXIII, 45-46; Jayaswal, *op. cit.*, *p.* 260.

§ *Divyavadana* (Ed. by Cawell and Neil), *pp.* 407-08; Jayaswal, *op. cit.*, *p.* 261.

of the country, so that it is not sedition merely to attack the Ministry of the day.* It appears from Asoka's inscriptions that the Emperor made an order that the ministers at Taxila were to go out of office every three years in order to prevent excitement or trouble among the citizens. Thus the idea that the King must change his ministers from time to time, so as to make them acceptable to the people, was not only familiar in theory but was occasionally acted upon in practice.

When we come to parliamentary procedure, we are on much surer ground, for the procedure of the Buddhist *sangha* or monastic order, of which there is ample evidence, anticipated (as stated in another chapter) to an astonishing extent the rules of business prevalent in the legislative assemblies of today. Motions, resolutions, quorum, "whips", voting by secret ballot, open voting, first, second and third readings, the right of free discussion, "tellers", the rule of decision by the majority, the appointment of committees to cut short debate and so on, were all well known.†

It would be idle to pretend that the parliamentary system in all its modern details was practised in ancient India, but we may perhaps venture to say that the essential conception was familiar.

MODERN INDIA

Modern India may be taken to date from 1858 when the Crown assumed the government of its territories in India which until then had been administered by the East India Company. From that date until the Government of India Act, 1919 came into operation, the superintendence, direction and control of the entire Government of India was, generally speaking, vested in the Secretary of State in England. The

---

* *State Trials*, New Series, Vol VI, *pp.* 723, 770.

† Jayaswal, *op. cit.*, *pp.* 90-101. Beni Prasad, *Theory of Government in Ancient India* (1927), *pp.* 324-27.

Secretary of State, along with the other ministers of the Crown, was, of course, responsible to the Parliament of the U. K., but although there were legislatures in India both at the Centre and in some of the provinces ever since 1861, no part of the Indian administration was responsible to them in the constitutional sense. An element of such responsibility was introduced, ιor the first time, by the Government of India Act, 1919, which came into full force on January 3, 1921 and so remained until April 1, 1937, when it was superseded by the Act of 1935. The scheme of the Act of 1935 was in operation, except as to certain parts of it, from April 1, 1937, to August 15, 1947, when it was largely modified by and under the Indian Independence Act, 1947. The modified scheme is still in force; but the Constituent Assembly, which has been sitting from December 9, 1946, is now in the last stages of the process of framing a new constitution.

Thus, for the purpose of studying the evolution of the parliamentary system in modern India, we may divide the years from 1858 into four periods:

(1) From 1858 to December 1920.
(2) From January 1921 to March 1937.
(3) From April 1937 to August 14, 1947.
(4) From and after August 15, 1947.

First Period

During the first period, as already remarked, no part of the Government of India was constitutionally responsible to any legislature in India. The supreme executive authority in India was vested in the Governor-General-in-Council, who was required to pay due obedience to all such orders as he might receive from the Secretary of State in England. Similarly, all provincial governments were required to obey the orders of the Governor-General-in-Council. The Governor-General and the ordinary members of his Executive Council were all appointed by His Majesty for a term which in practice extended to five years. As a rule, the Governor-General was bound by the decision of the majority of the Council, but in certain exceptional matters he could act on his own authority and responsibility.

In the provinces, executive authority was vested either in a Governor and members of his Executive Council, all appointed by His Majesty, or a Lieutenant-Governor and members of his Executive Council appointed by the Governor-General with the approval of His Majesty, or a Lieutenant-Governor similarly appointed, or a Chief Commissioner appointed by the Governor-General-in-Council. But, as already mentioned, the provincial governments were, in every case, required to obey the orders of the Central Government. It is clear that so long as the provincial governments were wholly subject to the Central Government and the Central Government wholly subject to the Secretary of State in England, neither in the provinces nor at the Centre could the executive be constitutionally responsible in any respect to any legislature in India. For, " responsibility " in this sense implies that the administration is to be conducted in accordance with the advice of persons enjoying the confidence of the legislature and not the dictates of any external authority.

This system remained in force for nearly sixty years. Then came World War I, which, among other things, intensified India's demand for " self-determination ". The demand was conceded: on August 20, 1917, His Majesty's Government announced their policy of " the gradual development of self-governing institutions with a view to the progressive realisation of responsible government in British India as an integral part of the Empire ". The Secretary of State visited India and with the Viceroy drew up a scheme of reform, which, after examination by a Joint Select Committee of Parliament, was enacted as the Government of India Act, 1919.

21

Second Period

The Government of India Act of 1919 came into full operation on January 3, 1921. Briefly, the effect of the Act (and the rules made thereunder) was (*a*) to create a number of Governors' provinces, covering almost the whole of British India (the main exceptions being British Baluchistan and Delhi and, until 1932, the North-West Frontier province), (*b*) to demarcate certain subjects—described as " provincial subjects "—for administration by the provinces, as distinguished from " Central subjects " to be administered by the Central Government, and (*c*) to sub-divide the " provincial subjects " into two classes: " reserved subjects " and " transferred subjects ". Such subjects as education, public health, and agriculture were " transferred "; while finance, police, the administration of justice and certain other subjects were " reserved ". The details of this sub-division are no longer of much importance. In each province, the Governor was to administer the " reserved subjects " with the aid of an Executive Council, the members of which were, like the Governor himself, appointed by His Majesty. In respect of these subjects, the chain of responsibility was as before the Government of India Act of 1919—that is to say, the provincial governments were subject to the Central Government and the Central Government to the Secretary of State. The position was very different in respect of the " transferred subjects ": the Governor was to administer these with the aid of ministers appointed by himself and holding office during his pleasure. No person could be a minister for more than six months, unless he was or became an elected member of the provincial legislature. In relation to the " transferred subjects ", the Governor was to be generally guided by the advice of his ministers. As the ministers were to be responsible to and have the confidence of the provincial legislature, the control of the Secretary of State and the Central Government was correspondingly relaxed; for, otherwise, the ministers would have had two masters and their position might have been impossible.

In each Governor's province, there was a legislative council consisting of elected, nominated and *ex-officio* members, at least 70 per cent of the total number being elected members and not more than 20 per cent being officials. The provincial legislature could make laws for the peace and good government of the province, subject in certain cases to the previous sanction of the Governor-General. Almost all proposed expenditure was to be laid before the legislature in the form of demands for grants, excepting loan charges, statutory expenditure and certain judicial and official salaries; but the Governor could authorise a grant, even when refused by the legislature, if it related to a " reserved subject " and, in an emergency, even if it related to a " transferred " department. He could also pass, over the head of the legislature, any Bill in respect of a " reserved subject ". Every Bill, whether relating to a " reserved subject " or a " transferred subject ", required the assent of the Governor and also of the Governor-General; and any Act, even after assent by the Governor-General, could be disallowed by His Majesty-in-Council.

Such, in broad outline, was the system of dyarchy introduced by the Government of India Act of 1919. It should be noted that the system was confined to the provincial sphere and that the Act made hardly any change in the structure of the Central Government. (It is true that the Central Legislative Assembly, consisting of about 100 elected members out of a total of about 140, was given power to refuse supplies except under certain heads of expenditure, but the Governor-General-in-Council had an overriding power, if he was satisfied that the grant refused by the Assembly was essential to the discharge of his responsibilities.) Another point to be noted is that even in the provincial sphere, it was limited to certain subjects—namely, the " transferred subjects ". And even in respect of these subjects, the ministers were responsible to a legislature which was not wholly elected and which contained an official bloc. Because of these limitations, the system failed to satisfy Indian public opinion; the Government of India Act of 1919 had provided for its examination by a Commission at the end of ten years; but in 1927, even before the end of this period, a Commission was appointed to inquire into " the working of the system of government, the growth of education and the development of representative institutions in British India and matters connected therewith ". The Commission reported in 1930, recommending full responsible government in the provincial sphere in place of dyarchy, but no substantial change at the Centre. This did not satisfy the Indian demand for reform and a new factor arose when certain Rulers of Indian States, outside British India, expressed their readiness to enter into a federation of British Indian provinces and Indian States if responsible government was extended to the Centre as well. His Majesty's Government thereupon convened a Round Table Conference in London at which most sections of Indian opinion were represented; it held three sessions in 1930-32 and, on the basis of its results, the British Government framed a scheme of reform which, after steady opposition by certain elements in Parliament, ultimately emerged as the Government of India Act, 1935.

Third Period

The greater part of this Act came into force on April 1, 1937. We are not concerned here with the details of the measure, but only with the extent to which it introduced the parliamentary system of government in India, both at the Centre and in the component units or provinces. We have already seen that the Government of India Act of 1919 introduced it only to a limited extent in a limited sphere of provincial administration, while leaving the Central executive structure unchanged. The Government of India Act of 1937 extended it, with certain qualifications, to the whole of the provincial sphere and to a part of the Central sphere.

The number of Governors' provinces, which from 1932 was nine, was increased to eleven by the separation of Sind and Orissa. Full responsible government of the British parliamentary type was provided for in each Governor's province, subject to certain reservations to be mentioned presently. The Governor was to be appointed by His Majesty and he was aided and advised in the exercise of most of his functions by a Council of Ministers who were to be appointed by him and to hold office during his pleasure, the implication—made more explicit in the instrument of instructions issued to the Governor by His Majesty—being that he must appoint only such persons to be ministers as could collectively command the confidence of the provincial legislature and must terminate their office as soon as they ceased to do so. As under the Government of India Act of 1919, a minister who for any period of six consecutive months was not a member of the provincial legislature automatically ceased to be a minister.

There were, however, certain matters in respect of which the Governor was required to act in his discretion without having to consult his ministers at all and certain other matters in respect of which he was required to exercise his individual judgment, though bound to consult his ministers. In regard to both these classes of matters, the Governor was under the general control of the Governor-General, who, in his turn, was under the general control of the Secretary of State and, therefore, of the Parliament in England. The area of responsible government in the provinces was thus restricted to some extent, though not to the same extent as under the Government of India Act of 1919.

Students of the Canadian and Australian Constitutions will remember that they also contain certain provisions calculated to distinguish between the functions of the Governor-General

and those of the Governor-General-in-Council; only in respect of the latter is the Governor-General required by the
statute to act with the advice of his Council. In practice,
however, the distinction has disappeared. The specific point
arose in Canada in connection with the removal of Letellier
de St. Just, Lieutenant-Governor of Quebec, in 1879. Under
the letter of the British North America Act, the appointment
of Lieutenant-Governors rests with the Governor-General-in-
Council, while their removal rests with the Governor-General.
Nevertheless, His Majesty's Government ruled that the
Governor-General must act on the advice of the Council in
respect of both. It was doubtless felt that if the Governor-
General insisted on the exercise of what he considered to be
his statutory power, the Ministry might resign and create a
deadlock which there was no means of resolving under the
Constitution Act.

The framers of the Government of India Act of 1935,
presumably foresaw that the distinction, which they had
attempted to draw between the matters in respect of which
the Governor was required to act on the advice of his Council
of Ministers and those in respect of which he was not so
required, would disappear in practice, unless special provision
was made to resolve any consequential deadlocks. Accordingly, the Act gave power to the Governor, acting with the
concurrence of the Governor-General and subject to certain
other safeguards, to proclaim what amounted to a suspension of
responsible government in the province that government could
not be carried on in accordance with the provisions of the Act.

It has been pointed out that under the Government of
India Act of 1919, the provincial legislatures contained a
certain number of *ex-officio* and of nominated members, so
that ministerial responsibility to the elected representatives
of the people was to that extent diluted. This defect was
almost entirely removed in the Government of India Act
of 1935. In five of the eleven Governors' provinces, the

legislature was to consist of a wholly elected single Chamber; in the other six, it was to consist of two Chambers, the Lower Chamber being wholly elected and the Upper Chamber predominantly so.

So much for the provincial part of the new Act. The part dealing with the Centre also provided for responsible government, except with respect to defence, ecclesiastical affairs, external affairs and "the tribal areas" (certain areas near the frontiers of India in the north-west and the north-east). Unfortunately, the operation of this part of the Act depended upon the establishment of the federation and this required the accession of Indian States in sufficient number to satisfy certain prescribed conditions. The necessary accessions did not take place, so that the federal part of the new Act never came into force. Consequently, the character of the Central Government remained much the same as before; and since the Government of India Act of 1919 too had made no substantial change in the Central executive structure, the net result was that that structure remained essentially the same as during the period 1858-1920. It was not to be expected that Indian public opinion would remain satisfied with this state of affairs. World War II and the events which followed it, including the advent of the Labour Government in England, led first to the establishment of a Constituent Assembly in India to frame a new constitution for the country and, later, to the passing of the Indian Independence Act of 1947.

Fourth Period

One of the main difficulties in the introduction of full responsible government at the Centre had been that of reconciling Hindu and Muslim interests. A single Central Government with a single Central legislature would ordinarily have meant the predominance of the majority community, both in the legislature and in the Cabinet; and this the

Muslims, who formed a minority of less than one-third of the entire population of India, were not prepared to accept. The Indian Independence Act of 1947 (which has been in force since August 15, 1947) has accordingly divided India into two parts, " India " and " Pakistan ", " Pakistan " comprising certain areas in the north-west and the north-east where the Muslims form the majority of the population; each part has been styled a Dominion; and full responsible government has been established in each under a provisional constitution. The provisional constitution consists mainly of the Government of India Act of 1935 with the omission of those portions which could be looked upon as subtractions from full responsible government. The permanent constitution is still to be framed, and for this purpose there is now a Constituent Assembly in session in each of the two Dominions.

19

OATHS UNDER THE DOMINION
CONSTITUTION

[This note was written at the request of the Prime Minister, who wanted the question of the oath to be taken under a Dominion constitution examined.]

I HAVE examined the question of the oath to be taken in connection with the Dominion constitution. The position seems to be as follows:

(1) So far as the members of the Constituent Assembly are concerned, no oath is required under the Assembly rules at present in force, nor is any oath required under the provisions of the Government of India Act of 1935 as proposed to be adapted. The proposed adaptations omit section 24 of the Act which prescribes the oath for members of the Central legislature. It is, of course, open to the Constituent Assembly itself, whenever it chooses to do so, to prescribe an oath, in such form as it thinks fit, for its members.

(2) With respect to the Dominion ministers, the draft adaptations to the Government of India Act of 1935 make no provision for any oath; but in some of the Dominions the Governor-General is directed, by royal instructions, to administer the oath of allegiance to the Dominion ministers. For example, paragraph 3 of the royal instructions issued to the Governor-General of South Africa in 1937 runs: " And we do authorise and require the Governor-General from time to time by himself, or by any other person to be authorised by him in that behalf, to administer to any person chosen as an

executive councillor the said oath or affirmation of allegiance, together with such other oath or affirmation of fidelity and office as he may think fit or may be prescribed by law." It is possible that similar instructions are contemplated for the Governor-General of the Dominion of India. If so, it is desirable that the form of the proposed oath should be discussed beforehand with the members of the Cabinet. The views of some of them are well known and it may be possible to meet them to some extent by adopting, *mutatis mutandis*, the form of the oath prescribed for the ministers of the Irish Free State in the constitution of 1922. It may be pointed out that the Irish Free State became a Dominion under the Statute of Westminster in 1931, so that the ministers in question were from that time Dominion ministers. If the Irish Free State form of oath is adapted to India, it would run somewhat as follows: " I etc., etc., do swear true faith and allegiance to the Constitution of India as by law established and that I will be faithful to His Majesty, his heirs and successors according to law ".

20

PANCHAYATS AS ELECTORAL COLLEGES

[An interesting proposal emerged, at the drafting stage of the Constituent Assembly's proceedings, for making village panchayats the basis of elections under the permanent constitution. The proposal was not new: the Commonwealth of India Bill of 1924, prepared by a National Convention of which Dr. Annie Besant and Sir Tej Bahadur Sapru were the joint sponsors, was based on the principle of adult suffrage at the village panchayat level and a system of indirect elections for both the Central and provincial legislatures. The President of the Constituent Assembly, Dr. Rajendra Prasad, referred it to the Constitutional Adviser, Sri B. N. Rau, for his advice. This is his note in reply.]

IT may not be easy to work the panchayat idea into the draft constitution at the present stage. Articles 67 (5) (a) and 149 (1), which, I believe, embody decisions already taken by the Constituent Assembly, provide for direct election to the Lower House, both at the Centre and in the units. These decisions will first have to be reversed if elections are to be indirect, as required by the panchayat plan. Whether this will be practicable I do not know. In all the principal federations and unions of the world, the Lower House is elected by direct election. Even the Upper House or Senate of the United States of America, which was originally indirectly elected, is now (since 1913) directly elected.

The world trend is thus strongly towards direct election for obvious reasons. It may, therefore, not be easy to reverse the decision already arrived at by the Constituent Assembly and to make indirect elections instead of direct elections obligatory.

Perhaps the best course would be so to frame the constitution as to permit either mode of election, the actual mode to be adopted in any particular case being left to the appropriate legislature. On this view of the matter, I have prepared draft amendments on the following lines:

In article 67 (5) (a), for the words "directly chosen by the voters" and in article 149 (1), for the words "chosen by direct election", substitute the words "chosen either by the voters themselves or by persons elected by the voters".

Under this amendment it will be for the Central legislature under article 290, and for the unit legislature under article 291, to prescribe whether the actual mode of election for the Lower House of the Central legislature and of the unit legislatures respectively is to be direct or indirect.

Even if the panchayat plan is to be adopted, its details will have to be carefully worked out for each province and for each Indian State with suitable modifications for towns. Apart from other difficulties, this will take time and rather than delay the passing of the constitution further, it would seem better to relegate these details to auxiliary legislation to be enacted after the constitution has been passed.

I entirely agree that legislators should have proper qualifications; the difficulty is to formulate them with any kind of precision. It would be easy enough to prescribe an educational standard which all candidates must satisfy; but this may not be considered either necessary or sufficient. The other criteria, namely, social service, character and the *sannyasin* outlook on life, do not lend themselves to precise definition, even if there was agreement about their necessity. Under the draft constitution, it would be open to the appropriate legislature to prescribe any qualifications in this behalf under articles 290 and 291 and any disqualifications under articles 83 (1) (e) and 167 (1) (e).

I have been considering the proposition that our constitution should start from the village and work upwards to the provinces and to the Centre. Let us analyse exactly what this means. A constitution deals with the organs of government, whether executive, legislative or judicial, at various levels and their relations to one another. In federal constitutions one usually—though not invariably—deals with the Centre and the units: for example, the Canadian and the South African Constitutions deal both with the Centre and the provinces, but the Constitutions of the U.S.A. and of Australia deal mainly with the Centre and hardly with the structure of the States.

Is it suggested that the Indian Constitution should deal not merely with the structure of the Centre and of the units but should go down to the village? In other words, is the Indian Constitution not merely to deal with the executive, legislative, and judicial organs of the Centre and of the provinces, but also to create and deal with similar organs for the district, the sub-division, the *thana*, the *chowkidari* union and the village?

For example, are we to have in the constitution full specifications of a district executive, a district legislature and a district judiciary? At present we have no district legislature but only certain administrative bodies, such as district boards and municipal boards, with a limited power of making by-laws for certain purposes; the district executive is provided for in-land revenue Acts or regulations, police Acts and so on; the district judiciary is provided for in Civil Courts Acts, the Criminal Procedure Code and the like. Is it suggested that these or similar provisions should be incorporated in the constitution itself? I fear that if we do this, not merely for the district but down to the village, the constitution will be of inordinate length and will be even more rigid than it is at present. It seems to me that while it may be possible to create panchayats and similar bodies to function as electoral colleges for the provincial and Central legislatures, it would be impracticable to endow them, or other bodies at the same level, with specific administrative or legislative or judicial functions by provisions inserted in the constitution itself.

21

CITIZENSHIP IN THE COMMONWEALTH
OF NATIONS

[*This is the text of a paper read by Sri B. N. Rau at the
second International Conference of the Legal Profession held at
The Hague in August* 1948.]

THE British Nationality Act is a significant piece of legislation
which deserves careful study, not only because of its actual
provisions but also of its potentialities.

The scheme of the Act can be described in a few words. Its
main principle is that the people of each of the self-governing
countries within the British Commonwealth have both a
particular status as citizens of their own country and a common status as British subjects. Accordingly, the key clause
of the Act provides that every person who under the Act is a
citizen of the United Kingdom and colonies, or who under
the law of any of the other component units of the Commonwealth, namely, Canada, Australia, New Zealand, South
Africa, Newfoundland, India, Pakistan, Southern Rhodesia
and Ceylon, is a citizen of that unit shall, by virtue of that
citizenship, be a British subject. An alternative description
of "British subjects" as "citizens of the Commonwealth"
was suggested by India and has apparently been agreed to by
the other units, and this phrase will, therefore, be used as a
synonym of British subjects in this paper. Logically there is
much to be said in its favour.

It will be remembered, for instance, that every citizen of a
Swiss canton is a citizen of Switzerland; it is, therefore, not

inappropriate that every citizen of a component unit of the British Commonwealth should be called a citizen of the Commonwealth. But the converse proposition, which is true of Switzerland and some other federations, is not yet true of the Commonwealth. Thus, a citizen of Switzerland has all the rights of a citizen of the canton where he settles; so, too, a person born in, and subject to the jurisdiction of, the United States is a citizen of the United States and also of the State where he resides; but a citizen of the Commonwealth has not necessarily all the rights of a citizen of the country where he settles or resides. From a purely legal point of view this is intelligible, because the Commonwealth is not a federation but a group of independent units, each entitled to make its own citizenship law. Nevertheless, it is to be hoped that the Commonwealth will in this respect strive for the federal ideal of having a common citizenship with no arbitrary discrimination between the citizens of one unit and those of another.

Eire (or Ireland) is in a peculiar position under the Act. It will have been noticed that it is not mentioned among the component units of the Commonwealth like Canada, Australia and the rest. Irish leaders have in the past claimed that Eire is an independent country in external association with the States of the British Commonwealth. The Act appears to give effect to this view: accordingly, under the Act, the citizens of Eire are not automatically British subjects or citizens of the Commonwealth; but the Act provides that they are to be treated as such until a further alteration is made in the law in force in the particular country of the Commonwealth concerned.

Besides citizens of the Commonwealth units, who are automatically citizens of the Commonwealth, and citizens of Eire, who though not citizens of the Commonwealth are to be treated as such for the time being, the Act deals with another class of persons called "British protected persons". A clause of the Act first defines protectorates and protected States:

" His Majesty may, in relation to the States and territories under his protection through his government in the United Kingdom, by Order-in-Council declare which of those States and territories are protectorates and which of them are protected States for the purposes of this Act ". Then follows the definition of a " British protected person " as meaning " a person who is a member of a class of persons declared by Order-in-Council made in relation to any protectorate, protected State, mandated territory or trust territory to be British protected persons by virtue of their connection with that protectorate, State or territory ".

A person who is not a British subject nor a citizen of Eire nor a British protected person is under the Act an alien.

The Act contains no definition of " British subject " except to the effect that every citizen of a unit of the Commonwealth is by virtue of that citizenship a British subject. It follows that until each of these units has a citizenship law, the persons who are at present British subjects in that unit will cease to be such upon the Act coming into force on January 1, 1949, unless special provision is made for them. The Act accordingly contains a transitional provision that during the interval they will remain British subjects without citizenship.

Such, in brief, are the provisions of the Act so far as they are material for our present purpose. Two questions arise out of the Act, one of particular importance to India and the other of general interest.

The first relates to the nationality or status of the subjects of what are known as the Indian States. What will be their position during the interval between the coming into force of this Act and the enactment of a citizenship law for India? Prior to August 15, 1947, they were under the suzerainty of His Majesty, though not forming part of His Majesty's Dominions. They had no capacity for separate foreign relations and were, therefore, not States for the purposes of international law.

On August 15, 1947, as the result of the Indian Independence Act passed by the Parliament of the United Kingdom, His Majesty's suzerainty lapsed; but certain other events have also happened. A Dominion of India comprising certain territories under the sovereignty of His Majesty has been established by the same Act and most of the Indian States, though freed by the statute from the suzerainty of the Crown, have through their Rulers executed instruments of accession, ceding to the Dominion various powers, including all powers in respect of external affairs. They have thus parted with all capacity for foreign relations in favour of the Dominion, but it cannot be said that they have parted with all their sovereignty in favour of the Crown.

In the light of these facts, let us take, for definiteness, a person born in one of these States before August 15, 1947, and consider his position with reference to the definition of " British subject " contained in the British Nationality and Status of Aliens Act, 1914. The expression " British subject " in that Act means a person who is a natural-born British subject or a person to whom a certificate of naturalisation has been granted or a person who has become a subject of His Majesty by reason of any annexation of territory. A natural-born British subject, so far as is relevant for our purposes, is defined in the same Act as any person born within His Majesty's Dominions and allegiance.

It is clear that in the case put, the person concerned was not born in territory which at the date of birth was within His Majesty's Dominions (although it was within His Majesty's allegiance). It follows, therefore, that he was not a natural-born British subject. Has he become a subject of His Majesty by reason of any annexation of territory? The instruments of accession executed by the Indian States effect, at most, a partial transfer of sovereignty in respect of certain subjects and not a complete transfer such as is implied in annexation. It is, therefore, clear that the person in question

22

is not a British subject within the meaning of the British Nationality and Status of Aliens Act and this conclusion is fortified by the provisions of section 262 of the adapted Government of India Act of 1935, which embodies India's present constitution. This section provides that the Ruler or a subject of an acceding State shall be eligible to hold any civil office under the Crown in India in connection with the affairs of the Dominion, etc., and goes on to say that, subject as aforesaid and to any other express provisions of the Act, no person who is not a British subject shall be eligible to hold any office under the Crown in India. The clear implication is that the subject of an acceding State is not a British subject.

It would also seem that after August 15, 1947, he can no longer be described even as a " British protected person " as defined in the British Nationality Act, because with the lapse of the suzerainty of the Crown, Indian States have ceased to be under His Majesty's protection through His Government in the United Kingdom as they were before August 15, 1947. It may be true in a sense that they have again come under His Majesty's protection as the result of their instruments of accession, but this would be protection through the Government of the Dominion of India and not through the Government of the United Kingdom and it is this latter protection that the Act requires for a British pro- tected person. The subject of an acceding Indian State may thus be described as a " Dominion protected person ", but not a " British protected person " as defined in the Act. Not being a British subject, nor a British protected person, nor a citizen of Eire, he would perforce be an alien under the provisions of the Act. It is a question for consideration whether a person who may be said to be under His Majesty's protection through the Government of India should be classed as an alien. It is to be noticed that the inhabitants of territories under the " mandate " or " trusteeship " of a Dominion may be British protected persons under the Act.

Of course, once India enacts a citizenship law of her own, most of the inhabitants of the acceding Indian States will probably become citizens of India and, therefore, citizens of the Commonwealth under the terms of the Act; it is during the interval that may elapse between January 1, 1949 (when the Act is due to become effective) and the enactment of a citizenship law for India that the question of the status of these persons arises. The transitional provision mentioned in an earlier paragraph does not apply to them: it applies only to those who are at present British subjects.

So much for the first question. The other matter is of more general interest and arises out of the provisions of the Act relating to Eire. Let us suppose that these provisions were widened so as to apply not only to Eire but to any "associate State of the Commonwealth", this expression being defined to mean not only Eire but also any other State that may be notified in this behalf by Order-in-Council. The result would be that any State in any part of the world, whatever may be the form of its government, could, if it so desired, become an associate State of the Commonwealth. For this purpose all that it would have to do would be to come to an agreement with the countries of the Commonwealth whereby the citizens of the associate State would be treated as citizens of the Commonwealth and reciprocally the citizens of the Commonwealth would be given a corresponding status in the associate State. Thereupon it could be notified as an "associate State". The Commonwealth would thus enter upon a new stage of development: in addition to the units that now compose it—in addition to the "component States", as we may term them, there would be a group of "associate States" linked to the Commonwealth by a form of common citizenship, but completely independent in every other respect.

There would be nothing strange or unnatural in such a development. It has been said that the Commonwealth is a growing, developing organism, subject like all vital things to change in response to change in circumstances. One of these changes has already been alluded to: since 1937, Eire has described herself in her constitution as a sovereign independent State, while preserving a link with the Commonwealth in external affairs. In other words, Eire has been seeking a looser form of association with the Commonwealth. On the other hand, there has also been in recent times an inclination on the part of certain independent States outside the Commonwealth to draw closer towards it without sacrificing their independence. These opposite but convergent tendencies point to the need for a new relationship, for the recognition of an outer group of States, associated with the Commonwealth, but not bound to it quite so closely as its inner units. In the course of the debate on the Indian Independence Act in the House of Commons in 1947, one of its supporters described the Commonwealth, not entirely in jest, as a club with various grades of members—ordinary members, county members, week-end members and even foreign members. A development of the kind indicated in the last paragraph would thus be in accordance with present-day trends.

It must, however, be remembered that a club—if one may pursue the analogy a little further—cannot grow or flourish merely by liberal rules of admission; to attract or retain members, it must give them something worth while and satisfying, not necessarily in material privileges, but at least in companionship in the pursuit of high ideals. Above all, there must be a sense of genuine equality among the members; for only then can each country be expected to give of its best and to contribute to the peace of this weary old world.

I had the honour of presenting a paper on this subject at a Conference of the International Bar Association at the Hague in August 1948 and as a result the following resolution was adopted:

" (1) That, in order to promote tolerance and good
neighbourliness among the people of different countries, as many of these as possible should secure by
mutual agreement and other appropriate means,
that the citizens of one country shall, while residing
or sojourning in another, have the incidents of citizenship of the latter; and

" (2) that this Conference would welcome, as an example, any arrangement whereby the incidents of
Commonwealth citizenship under the British Nationality Act could become available, on a reciprocal basis and under agreed conditions, to the
citizens of countries outside the Commonwealth."

It may be observed that the wording of the first part of
the resolution follows that of the preamble to the Charter of
the United Nations, which recites that the peoples of the
United Nations have determined " to practise tolerance and
live together in peace with one another as good neighbours ".
It would obviously be a step towards the accomplishment
of this aim if as many countries as possible in the world
could agree that they would not treat each other's citizens as
foreigners.

22

INDIA AND THE COMMONWEALTH—I

INDIA will before long have to decide what is to be her relationship to the British Commonwealth of Nations. This is an important but controversial question. On so momentous an issue everyone must form his own views.

Let me make it clear at the outset that any opinions which I may express here are entirely personal, coloured to a large extent by my own training and experience. Anyone whose official life has been spent mostly in the administration of justice and the study of constitutions is bound to have certain prepossessions, for in these spheres one sees English institutions and ideas at their best and is most conscious of what India owes to them. The supremacy of the law, the rule that every person must be presumed to be innocent until he is proved to be guilty, the maxim that you must hear the other side before you pronounce judgment—these and other principles which we almost take for granted in our courts of law today have come to us, at least in their present form, from England. In the working of the constitution, too, the English parliamentary system of government has become almost second nature to us. One of the most characteristic and admirable features of that system is that it not merely tolerates an Opposition, but welcomes it—indeed, regards it as so essential an element in the government of the country that the Leader of the Opposition is now paid a regular salary in England and in most of the Dominions. We have not yet copied this particular feature, but shall doubtless do so in due course. The same spirit shows itself in the administration of justice—and here India has been glad to copy the example: when an accused is undefended, the State engages an advocate to defend him lest justice should suffer.

In the last analysis, all this springs from the recognition, not merely in theory but in daily practice, of the value of the human personality—from the realisation that your opponent may be in the right as often as yourself, that the prisoner in the dock may be obeying a higher law than that which the State seeks to enforce against him, and that accordingly the best hope of the State lies not in crushing all opposition but in respecting freedom of opinion. We here touch not only one of the basic features of the English conception of what ought to be the relations between the State and its subjects but also one of the ideals embodied in the preamble to India's new constitution. Reference has already been made at some length to the way in which these conceptions or ideals were put into practice in ancient India. (See the chapter " The Parliamentary System of Government in India "). The King was not only expected to have ministers, but also to act upon their advice. Also, the idea that the King must change his ministers from time to time, so as to make them acceptable to the people, was not only familiar in theory but was occasionally acted upon in practice. Again, in the conduct of the Buddhist Sangha (monastic order) the rules of business obtaining in legislative assemblies of today have been anticipated to an astonishing extent. Indeed, in one of the *Jātaka* stories—which go back in origin to the pre-Buddhistic period—the parliamentary procedure has been caricatured thus: " A bird is repeating a motion for the election of a Raja, evidently a republican Raja; he has done so twice and the motion was opposed by another member of the assembly saying ' wait please '. The opposer of the motion begged leave to make his speech, which was granted on condition that the speaker should state his reasons on the principles of political science and law. The speaker gave his reasons and carried his opposition. The opposition was on the well-known republican ground that the proposed king (the owl) had not a pleasant presence".

Turning for a moment to another sphere, we find that the conception of the supremacy of the law was also familiar in ancient India. Never was the King placed above the law; again and again is the law declared to be above the King and as the King of Kings. The Coronation oath administered to the King ended with the promise: " I shall never be autocratic or arbitrary".

It would thus appear that the germs of the two fundamental conceptions, the supremacy of the law and the parliamentary system of government, are to be found in ancient India. They have grown up independently and are to be found today in a more developed form in England and the countries of the Commonwealth; in adopting them in her new constitution, India is not slavishly copying a foreign model, but is being true to her own best traditions.

Apart from ideological affinities, there is a powerful practical argument in favour of India's continuing to remain in the Commonwealth, at least for the present. We have not yet recovered from the formidable difficulties which followed in the wake of the partition of August 15, 1947. India has still vast and complicated problems requiring the whole of her attention—refugees, Kashmir, Hyderabad—and there are many who feel that this is no time for leaving the Commonwealth and venturing into the unknown, for she may thereby create for herself a new set of problems even more baffling. Moreover, until August 15, 1947, India had had no actual experience of what is called Dominion status in the fullest sense of the term and no opportunity of realising all that it implied; since that date the position has been entirely different. It is also a fact that the passing of the Indian Independence Act—and, one may add, of the Burma

Independence Act—has convinced many minds that the old ideas of British domination are dead and that a new chapter in Commonwealth relations is opening.

I may mention here that during my recent visit to the U.S.A. and other countries, I tried to sound several disinterested persons as to their views on this subject. None of them, of course, ventured to offer advice, but they indicated their mind sufficiently by asking the question: " What has a big country like India to fear from remaining within the Commonwealth? "

There are, however, certain points in this connection which require examination:

(1) Whether India is described as a ' Republic ', or a ' Commonwealth ', in the preamble to her new constitution—a point which is still to be decided by the Constituent Assembly—it is clear that in the actual provisions of the constitution, as already settled by the Constituent Assembly, there is no mention of His Majesty. The head of the Indian Union is an elected President in whom all executive authority is vested and in whose name all executive action is to be taken. In this sense, the constitution is of the republic type and the question arises whether there is room within the Commonwealth for a State with such a constitution.

(2) In view of the treatment of Indians in certain Dominions of the Commonwealth, would it not be better for her to sever the British connection?

(3) We have now the beginnings of a World State in the United Nations. If India adhere to a particular group or *bloc* such as the Commonwealth, would it not conflict with her loyalty to the larger organisation?

(4) Assuming that India wishes to remain within the Commonwealth, what changes in the definition of what is now called Dominion status, or in the name of the units of the Commonwealth which at present

are described as Dominions, would be necessary or desirable?

We may deal with a part of the last question first. After a long process of evolution, the Dominions have now become, to all intents and purposes, sovereign States and may well be called " sovereignties " within the Commonwealth. Amongst the recognised meanings of the term " sovereignty " is " a territory existing as an independent State ". The term " Dominion " contains a hint of domination by some outside authority and may now perhaps be replaced with advantages by the term " sovereignty " which means, or is capable of meaning, a sovereign State, whatever may be the character of its constitution. India, under her new constitution, can appropriately be described as a sovereignty.

To turn now to the other questions. First, is there room within the Commonwealth for a State with a republican form of constitution? The conception of the Commonwealth, never static, has developed considerably within the last decade. In 1937, after the republican Constitution of Eire came into operation, the British Government announced that they were prepared to treat the new constitution as not affecting a fundamental alteration in the position of the Irish Free State (which was thereafter to be described as Eire), as a member of the British Commonwealth of Nations. Indeed, Professor Keith, writing in 1938, observed: " If no place can be found in the British Commonwealth for republics, then the enduring character of the Commonwealth may well be doubted ". During World War II, when France was about to fall, she was in effect offered a place in the Commonwealth in spite of being a republic. In the course of the debate in the House of Commons on the Indian Independence Bill on July 15, 1947, the Member for Wood Green (Mr. Beverley Baxter) said:

" The one thing we have to realise is that the British Empire and Commonwealth like all vital living things is subject to change, and that no matter what side of the House we sit upon, it would be a great mistake to imagine that this is the last alteration, or that more changes will not come. I sometimes think of the Empire, and I do not mean this entirely frivolously, as a club. We here, and the Dominions and the Commonwealth countries, are the ordinary senior members. We also have county members, as one might call the colonies. We also have week-end members—Eire might almost qualify as a week-end member of the club—and I am not certain that we have not got foreign members.

    " The Argentine might be considered, or might have been considered a short time ago, as one of the foreign members of the British Empire.

    " I am not at all certain if America made application in a proper form and got a proper seconder and proposer, we may not admit her as a foreign member of the British Empire. I only say this because we should tune our minds to the fact that this is a changing organ. We should not shut our eyes to any development."

It is thus clear that the conception of the Commonwealth has been steadily growing and has now reached a stage when even States with a republican constitution may well be given a place therein. This would of course involve a change in the well-known definition of the word " Dominions " as " autonomous communities within the British Empire equal in status, in no way subordinate one to another in any aspect of their domestic or external affairs, *united by allegiance to common ideals and by a common citizenship* and freely associated as members of the Commonwealth". The italicised words require a little explanation. It has already been mentioned that there are certain fundamental conceptions or ideals which may be said to be common, both to the Commonwealth and to India: the conception of the supremacy of the law as distinct from the Fascist conception that the State is a law unto itself; the conception that opinion should be free and that the State should

be governed in accordance with public opinion freely expressed; and so on. Neither India nor any other unit of the Commonwealth should find any difficulty in rendering allegiance
to these ideals not merely in theory but in practice. The other
matter that requires to be explained is the reference to a
common citizenship. A step towards securing a common citizenship for the units of the Commonwealth has already been
taken in the new British Nationality Bill which is now (at the
time of writing) before the Parliament of the United
Kingdom. Under this Bill every person who, by the law of
any of the units of the Commonwealth, that is to say, Canada,
Australia, New Zealand, South Africa, Newfoundland, India,
Pakistan, Southern Rhodesia and Ceylon, is a citizen of that
unit, automatically becomes a British subject. As a matter of
nomenclature " Commonwealth citizen" or "citizen of the
Commonwealth " would, for obvious reasons, be a better term
than "British subject" from India's point of view. But in
any case we have here the beginnings of a common citizenship
which, when properly developed, may well become a bond of
union between the units of the Commonwealth.

It is interesting to note that in ancient India the Guptas
are said to have risen to power by their alliance with the
republican Licchavis, whose name was jointly inscribed with
that of Chandra Gupta I on the imperial coins. Thus we
have here an instance of a republic in partnership with
an empire.

We may now turn to the second question, which arises out
of the present position of Indians in some of the Dominions.
This is an issue on which India will have to fight with all her
might and main, whether she remains in the Commonwealth
or not. Many countries outside the Commonwealth are in
the same case: it is, therefore, hardly to be expected that the
position of Indians would improve by India's severance of
the British connection. Indeed, the reverse may well be the
case. If India continues in the Commonwealth, she would be

in a better position to fight for a common citizenship with full civil rights and no racial discrimination. There is a growing consciousness in England and perhaps elsewhere that the British Commonwealth, as at present constituted, consists for the most part of persons who are not of the British or any European race and that any form of racial discrimination should be strongly discouraged as being disruptive of the Commonwealth. A sign of the times may be seen in a recent incident in London, when the managing director of a restaurant refused to supply a meal to a West African lecturer of London University. The matter was raised in the House of Commons, when the Food Minister said: " The very serious character of the incident has been brought home to the managing director who now understands the grave injury done to the interests of the British Commonwealth by any form of racial discrimination ". Another sign pointing in the same direction, though not connected with the British Commonwealth, is to be found in a still more recent ruling (May 3, 1948) of the United States Supreme Court that restrictive real estate agreements which bar coloured persons from all-white neighbourhoods cannot be enforced by State or Federal Courts, as such enforcement would be contrary to the Bill of Rights. In fact the idea of human rights is on the march throughout the world and its progress can in no way be impeded by India's continuing to be within the Commonwealth.

There remains the question whether India's adherence to the Commonwealth will weaken the United Nations Organisation. Whatever may have been the position at one time of the members of the Commonwealth in respect of foreign affairs, the position now reached is that they enjoy complete freedom in this as in other respects. Eire remained neutral throughout World War II and, in spite of this, in the case *Murray v Parkes*, the Lord Chief Justice of England said in 1942 that he was not aware that Eire had ever expressly exercised its right to secede from the Commonwealth, even if there was such a right. Equally significant is the fact that even Canada remained neutral for nearly a week after the United Kingdom had declared war on Germany in September 1939: and during this week, Canadian neutrality appears to have been recognised, not only by the United States of America but even by Germany herself. Apparently, then, neutrality in a British war is compatible with continued membership of the Commonwealth. It will be remembered that the Cabinet Mission's plan of May 16, 1946, refers to " the attainment of independence by British India whether inside or outside the British Commonwealth ", implying thereby that there may be a completely independent State inside the Commonwealth. The very name " Indian Independence Act " given by Parliament to the statute establishing the Dominion of India lends further support to this view. Again, during the last autumn session of the Assembly of the United Nations on the question of the partition of Palestine, Canada, South Africa and Australia voted for partition, India and Pakistan against partition, and the United Kingdom remained neutral. It is, therefore, clear that a State, by being a member of the Commonwealth, does not sacrifice any part of its freedom in respect of its foreign affairs. Membership of the Commonwealth is now compatible with complete independence and a member is free to take whatever line it chooses on any particular question, even in the international sphere. So long as there is no doubt that the States of the Commonwealth are what they are described to be, " autonomous communities, in no way subordinate one to another in any aspect of their domestic or *external affairs* ", there is no reason for fearing that membership of the Commonwealth will weaken allegiance to the United Nations Organisation. This is a very important matter from the point of view of world security. One of Gladstone's admirers wrote to him: " We believe in no man's infallibility, but it is restful to be sure of one man's integrity." The world will not expect India, any more than any other country, to make no mistakes: but of India's integrity and her complete freedom to act as she thinks right, there should never be any doubt.

23

INDIA AND THE COMMONWEALTH—II

[*In the final stages of the drawing up of India's Constitution,
Sri B. N. Rau had discussions with the then Lord Chancellor
of Britain, Lord Jowitt, and Sir Stafford Cripps about India's
membership of the Commonwealth after independence. Early in
April, 1949, he gave Lord Jowitt the following statement out-
lining briefly the Indian and British points of view.*

Indian point of view: There is no lack of understanding in
India of the deep-seated sentiment felt for the Crown in the
U.K. and certain other countries; but there are genuine political difficulties. There are certain parties in India opposed
to membership of the Commonwealth on any terms. Recent
events in South Africa and statements of immigration policy
in Australia have made Indian public opinion peculiarly
sensitive and even suspicious just now. The Prime Minister
of India has to be very careful as to what he says and does.
Therefore, those who desire India to remain in the Commonwealth should make it as easy as possible for her to do so
and should avoid imposing conditions which, however reasonable from the point of view of British sentiment, could be
represented or even misrepresented as impairing India's
independence.

British point of view: Just as the member-States of the
U.N. are completely sovereign and yet find it possible to recognise certain organisational authorities for the purpose of
working together, so too the members of the Commonwealth
can, without impairing their sovereignty or independence in
any way, recognise the Crown as the head of the Commonwealth association. The Crown will thus be the symbol of
association for all members (" the symbol of the free association of the members of the Commonwealth," in the language

of the preamble to the Statute of Westminster) and in no sense a link of subordination for any member.

At the end of April 1949 a formal announcement was made on the subject from London. The following article was written by Sri B. N. Rau early in May, and it was broadcast * by the U. N. Radio.]

IT was announced from London that the Government of India had affirmed India's desire to continue her full membership of the Commonwealth even after she adopts her new republican constitution. This historic announcement is, of course, of deep constitutional interest, but I shall first of all deal with some of its other aspects which are of greater interest to the layman.

A few people in this country—I am speaking now from New York—appear to be somewhat puzzled by this latest development, although it has been welcomed by the press generally. They ask the question, how is it that after

---

* In a letter written by the late Lord Jowitt to Sri B. N. Rau on the broadcast, he said:

" I find your broadcast most interesting. My own belief is that we developed our present system mainly by accident; and I think one of the most important accidents was that neither George I nor George II could speak English, and to this our Cabinet system owes its origin.

" It is true that it is of the essence of our Commonwealth that all its members are equal in status. It is of course a club from which any member can resign if he is so minded. The only doubt I have is with regard to the first question you formulate: ' Is there room within the Commonwealth for a State with a republican constitution? '

" I think you deal with this in much too cavalier a fashion. I have grave doubts whether foreign countries would regard us as being in any special nexus so as to justify preferential treatment of nationals or trade preferences; and I find it difficult to formulate in my own mind what the real nexus would be.

" I realise that owing to our different history we view the institution of monarchy differently. To us it means much. We regard the King as the father of our family. To your people the existence of a monarchy may be a stumbling block.

" Yet we can help each other and we shall each need the other's help in the difficult days that confront us, and I believe this help could be better given if we both belong to the club."

23

struggling for so many years to free herself from British rule and gain complete independence, India has now voluntarily decided to remain within the Commonwealth? Why has India changed her mind? The short answer to this question is that it is not India which has changed; it is rather the Commonwealth that has changed.

Before 1947 the Commonwealth was, in Indian minds, synonymous with British rule; but since the passing of the Indian Independence Act in that year and the real and complete transfer of power to Indian hands that followed it, Indians have been feeling that the old ideas of British domination are dead and that the Commonwealth is now a really free association of nations " in no way subordinate one to another in any aspect of their domestic or external affairs ". Even the old names and labels are gradually changing: there is a growing tendency to refer to the Commonwealth as the Commonwealth of Nations instead of the British Commonwealth of Nations. Thus, the London announcement of 28th April, 1949 runs: "Accordingly the United Kingdom, Canada, Australia, New Zealand, South Africa, India, Pakistan and Ceylon hereby declare that they remain united as free and equal members of the Commonwealth of Nations freely co-operating in the pursuit of peace, liberty and progress ". Again, the same announcement avoids the use of the term " Dominion ", which contains a hint of domination, and it uses, instead, the colourless term " countries of the Commonwealth ".   Equally significant is the provision in the British Nationality Act, which came into force on January 1, 1949, and according to which " British subjects "—a name which suggests some kind of subjection to Britain—may in future be described as " Commonwealth citizens ". All these indications, trivial though they may seem, are symptomatic of a profound change in the conception of the Commonwealth and that is why I have said that it was not India so much as the Commonwealth that had changed.

There must, of course, have been other reasons also for India's decision and some of these at least it is not difficult to guess. There are deep-seated affinities between India and the United Kingdom in ideas and institutions, such as the rule of law and the parliamentary system of government; but apart from these there are cogent practical considerations. India has still vast and complicated problems requiring the whole of her attention—the problem of food for her teeming population, the problem of raising the general standard of life, the problem of re-establishing millions of refugees and so on—and her leaders must have felt that this was no time for leaving the Commonwealth and venturing into the unknown, for she might thereby create a new set of problems even more baffling. The events that have been happening in certain neighbouring countries must have emphasised this particular danger. Then, again, there were the interests of Indians overseas to consider—mainly Indians settled in various British colonies and the countries of the Commonwealth. These could be better served if India remained within the Commonwealth herself than if she went out. Finally, there was the consideration that if at any time India should find her position in the Commonwealth irksome—an unlikely contingency—it was always open to her to leave: there was no need to leave just now. All these factors must have contributed to this momentous decision.

I now come to the particular formula which has made such a decision possible. Under India's new constitution, the main principles of which have been settled by the Constituent Assembly, the head of the Indian Union is an elected President in whom all executive authority is vested and in whose name all executive action is to be taken, no powers being reserved to His Majesty the King. The constitution is thus of the republican type and in fact the preamble speaks of the resolve of the people to constitute India into a sovereign democratic republic. How is it possible to find room within the Commonwealth for a State with a republican constitution? In my own view there is no insuperable difficulty here. The formula agreed upon at the London Conference may best be explained by an analogy. The various member-States of the United Nations are completely sovereign and independent; yet they find it possible to recognise certain organisational authorities for the purpose of working together. In just the same way the members of the Commonwealth can, without impairing their sovereignty or independence in any way, recognise His Majesty as the head of the Commonwealth association.

The King is thus the symbol of free association for all members and not a link of subordination for any. Accordingly, the Government of India has declared and affirmed not only India's desire to remain within the Commonwealth, but also " her acceptance of the King as the symbol of free association of its independent member-nations and as such the head of the Commonwealth ". The declaration thus preserves the dignity of the Crown without impairing India's sovereign status. As a matter of historic interest, it may be stated (as mentioned in an earlier chapter) that in ancient India the republic of the Licchavis was in partnership with the Gupta Empire in the time of Chandra Gupta I.

I must next turn to a question which, though often answered, continues to be asked: How will India's decision affect her position in the United Nations? If she adheres to a particular group or *bloc*, such as the Commonwealth, will not her loyalty to the larger organisation be thereby impaired? The answer to this question has often been given: India does not regard membership of the Commonwealth as involving or implying adherence to any particular *bloc*. During the last two years India has been a Dominion within the Commonwealth, but that has in no way fettered her either inside the United Nations or outside. There is no reason whatever for fearing that when she becomes a republic within the

Commonwealth she will be less free. Indeed, freedom of judgment and freedom of expression of opinion may be expected to
be respected by Commonwealth countries in their relations
with each other as much as in their relations with their
own citizens.

This is a point on which I should like to dwell at some
length, because in her attempt to keep clear of *blocs*, India is
constantly misunderstood and sometimes even misrepresented.
If the world contained only two *blocs* and every country
conceived it to be its duty or interest to join one or the other,
then, what is likely to happen in the event of a dispute
between the two? According to the Charter of the United
Nations—and indeed commonsense would dictate the same
course—the parties should seek a solution by mediation,
conciliation, arbitration and so forth. But who can hope to
mediate or conciliate or arbitrate with any prospect of success
if every country is already ranged on one side or the other?
Clearly, therefore, it is necessary that there should be some
countries standing outside any *bloc* to perform this very
essential service in the community of States. Otherwise, any
dispute between the *blocs* may precipitate a world war and
that may mean the end of civilisation. It is this difficult but
indispensable function which India, in a humble way,
aspires to discharge. She may fail; it would be failure in a
good cause; but need she fail? There are chain reactions in
the moral world as much as in the physical and even a
single State may, if it is honest in its efforts, start a process
which will ultimately explode the vast mass of suspicion that
surrounds us today.

NOTE

[The following statement by the late Rt. Hon. L. S. Amery, a former Secretary of State for India in the Churchill (War) Cabinet, will be read with interest. It arose out of a discussion in London in October 1948, the participants being, apart from Mr. Amery, Mr. Eric Louw of South Africa, Mr. Vincent Massey, Governor-General of Canada and Sir Girja Bajpai, at that time Secretary-General, External Affairs Ministry, India. The main point of the discussion was whether, apart from any particular symbol of unity like the British Crown, the Commonwealth could be regarded of as a living organism.]

The essential characteristic of an organism, as contrasted with a mechanical structure, is that there is vitality in all its parts, mutual cooperation between them, and above all a general purpose to maintain its existence, whether centralised or diffused through the whole organism.

In the case of our Commonwealth of nations the basic stuff of the organism is practical cooperation and mutual aid, ranging from a wide measure of common citizenship at the base to intimate consultation and mutual understanding at the top. In between, as a natural complement and corollary, come all the various practical measures of cooperation in foreign policy, defence, trade, social welfare and culture.

As, however, we are dealing with human beings, and human beings in the mass, that abiding purpose of cooperation needs to be embodied in some sort of symbol or symbolic act. Hitherto, in the evolution of a centralised Empire to a partnership of independent equals, the Crown has served the purpose of that symbol. It means a tremendous lot to most of us, and not only to Commonwealth citizens of British origin. Mr. Vincent Massey was quite right in saying that it meant everything to the French Canadian. It means much to others too, such as the Maltese and—in spite of Mr. Eric Louw—to many Dutch South Africans of the old Cape Colony tradition. It means even more, as I know from experience, to most Africans. But I fully understand the difficulty as the symbol of Commonwealth unity which involves the head of the State in India being in any sense nominated by the King or owing allegiance to him. I know that even my suggestion that the President of an Indian republic should be automatically a representative of the Crown seemed to you to be unlikely of acceptance.

The question is whether any subsitute can be found for the Crown to serve the same purpose, or any way of associating India with the Crown so as to get rid of any notion of even theoretical subordination to something external to India. In the case of the United States allegiance is to the American Constitution. Now, we in the Commonwealth have always avoided the conception of a written constitution. Our stress has been on the principles of freedom, mutual toleration and justice which we have conceived as holding us together. Is there any reason why these principles should not be embodied in a short declaration? Even the United Nations started off with a declaration largely drafted by Smuts. As a matter of fact, the King's coronation oath towards his subjects embodies a somewhat similar conception. Might it not be possible to draft such a declaration suitable for Commonwealth purposes which could then be solemnly affirmed in future by the King on his accession and also by an Indian President on his taking office?

Again, might it not be possible for a President of India, on making such a declaration of principle, to declare his adherence to, or association with—not his allegiance to—the British Crown as the symbol in the rest of the Commonwealth of the principles of the declaration?

There is another symbol which has always meant much to mankind in the mass, and that is the flag. So far we have evolved haphazardly, using the Union Jack or some flag embodying the Union Jack, as the national flag of each part of the Commonwealth. If we are starting on a new footing, at any rate as regards some members of the Commonwealth, might it not be possible to devise a new Commonwealth flag to be flown side by side with the national flag on a few occasions and on important buildings, including the residence of the head of the State? Lastly, but also important for the masses, is the possibility of devising a Commonwealth hymn. There again " God save the King " has met the purpose of most of us and is sung alongside of a more purely national hymn like " O Canada ". There, again, the particular words, which to most of us have no real meaning apart from their broad emotional content, may very well, for India, have a specific and less welcome meaning. But would the tune itself, with new wording, be altogether unsuitable? If so, however, there might be no insuperable difficulty in finding a new tune as well as new words.

The important thing is that there should be some real symbol of moral and spiritual purpose uniting the Commonwealth, and not merely arrangements for mutual convenience devoid of any kind of spiritual content or purpose.

24

THE INDIAN CONSTITUTION

*[This was contributed as a special article by Sri B. N. Rau to
the Independence Day issue of* The Hindu *on 15th August
1948.]*

THE DRAFT of India's new constitution was released to the
public on February 26, 1948.   On a rough estimate the total
number of amendments or suggestions for amendment received
so far is nearly 500.   As the draft contains no less than 395
articles and eight schedules,* this number, though large,
cannot be said to be excessive.†   All the amendments will be

---

* By the Constitution (First Amendment) Act, 1951 the ninth schedule was
added, specifying Acts and Regulations that were validated.

† It would be of interest to reproduce here a passage from the speech of the
President of the Constituent Assembly, Dr. Rajendra Prasad, at its final session
on 26th November 1949:

"The method which the Constituent Assembly adopted in connection with
the constitution was first to lay down its ' terms of reference ' as it were in the
form of an Objectives resolution which was moved by Pandit Jawaharlal
Nehru in an inspiring speech and which constitutes now the preamble to our
constitution.   It then proceeded to appoint a number of committees to deal
with different aspects of the constitutional problem.   Dr. Ambedkar mentioned the names of these committees.   Several of these had as their chairman
either Pandit Jawaharlal Nehru or Sardar Patel to whom thus goes the credit
for the fundamentals of our constitution.   I have only to add that they all
worked in a business-like manner and produced reports which were considered
by the Assembly and their recommendations were adopted as the basis on
which the draft of the constitution had to be prepared.   This was done by
Sri B. N. Rau, who brought to bear on his task a detailed knowledge of constitutions of other countries and an extensive knowledge of the conditions of
this country as well as his own administrative experience.   The Assembly then
appointed the Drafting Committee which worked on the original draft prepared by Sri B. N. Rau and produced the draft constitution which was considered by the Assembly at great length at the second reading stage.   As
Dr. Ambedkar pointed out, there were not less than 7,635 amendments of
which 2,473 amendments were moved.   I am mentioning this only to show

considered by the Constituent Assembly at its next constitution-making session which is due to be held in the latter half of October next. Meanwhile, it may be useful to examine some of the more general criticisms levelled against the draft.

The first criticism that requires notice is that the draft borrows largely from other constitutions and in particular from the Government of India Act, 1935, and that it does not take sufficient account of India's indigenous village system. It is said that a satisfactory Indian Constitution must start from the village as the base. Let us examine this criticism in both its aspects. It is undoubtedly true that the draft has borrowed from other constitutions and notably from the Government of India Act, 1935. But so long as the borrowings have been adapted to India's peculiar circumstances, they cannot in themselves be said to constitute a defect. Most modern constitutions do make full use of the experience of other countries, borrow whatever is good from them and reject whatever is unsuitable. To profit from the experience of other countries or from the past experience of one's own is the path of wisdom. There is another advantage in borrowing not only the substance but even the language of established constitutions; for we obtain in this way the benefit of the interpretation put upon the borrowed provisions by the courts of the countries of their origin and we thus avoid ambiguity or doubt.

---

that it was not only the members of the Drafting Committee who were giving their close attention to the constitution, but other members were vigilant and scrutinising the draft in all its details. No wonder that we had to consider not only each article in the draft, but practically every sentence and sometimes every word in every article. It may interest honourable members to know that the public were taking great interest in its proceedings and I have discovered that no less than 53,000 visitors were admitted to the visitors' gallery during the period when the constitution was under consideration. In the result, the draft constitution has increased in size; and by the time it has been passed, it has come to have 395 articles and eight schedules, instead of the 243 articles and 13 schedules of the original draft of Sri B. N. Rau. I do not attach much importance to the complaint which is sometimes made that it has become too bulky. If the provisions have been well thought out, the bulk need not disturb the equanimity of our mind."

To proceed now to the other branch of the criticism, namely, that the new Indian Constitution should start with the village as the base and work upwards to the province and the Union. Let us analyse exactly what this means. A constitution deals with the organs of government, whether executive, legislative or judicial, at various levels and their relations to one another. In federal constitutions one usually, though not invariably, deals with the federal Centre and the provinces or States: for example, the Canadian and South African Constitutions deal both with the Centre and the provinces, but the Constitutions of the U. S. A. and Australia deal mainly with the Centre and hardly with the structure of the States. Is it suggested that the Indian Constitution should deal not merely with the structure of the Centre and of the provinces but should go right down to the village? In other words, is the Indian Constitution not merely to deal with the executive, legislative and judicial organs of the Centre and of the provinces or States, but also to create and deal with similar organs for the district, the sub-division, the *thana*, the *chowkidari* union and the village? For example, are we to have in the constitution itself full specifications of a district executive, a district legislature and a district judiciary? At present we have no district legislatures but only certain administrative bodies, such as district boards and municipal boards, created by provincial Acts, with a limited power of making by-laws for certain purposes; the district executive is provided for in land revenue Acts or Regulations, police Acts and so on; the district judiciary is provided for in Civil Courts Acts, the Criminal Procedure Code and the like. Is it suggested that these or similar provisions should be incorporated in the constitution itself? If we were to do this, not merely for the district but down to the village, the constitution would not only be of inordinate length but would be even more rigid than it is in the draft; for, we shall have to embody in the constitution almost all the provisions that are now spread over various local self-government Acts, land revenue Acts, police Acts, Civil Courts Acts and so forth. Any amendment of any of the provisions so incorporated would require the special procedure prescribed for amending the constitution. While it may be possible to create panchayats and similar bodies elected by adult suffrage to function as electorates for the provincial and Central legislatures, it would, to say the least, be inconvenient to endow them or other bodies at the same level with specific executive, legislative or judicial functions by provisions inserted in the constitution itself. If all that is implied in the criticism is that elections to the various legislatures named in the constitution should not be by direct adult suffrage but through intermediate bodies like the panchayats elected by the primary voters, then, all that is necessary is to insert in the constitution provisions permitting or, if the Assembly so decides, even requiring, elections to be indirect; but if the critics intend to go further, there will be the difficulties that have been pointed out already.

Another criticism that has been directed against the draft constitution relates to the part dealing with fundamental rights. It is said that these rights have been subjected to so many limitations that what is given with one hand is taken away with the other; for example, freedom of speech and expression is limited by the qualification that it shall not affect the operation of any existing law, or prevent the State from making any law, relating to libel, defamation, sedition or any other matter which offends against decency or morals or undermines the authority or foundation of the State. Critics point out that in the American Constitution there is an unqualified prohibition against any abridgement of the freedom of speech or of the press or any deprivation of liberty without due process of law and there are no irritating limitations; why, it is asked, should we not do likewise? The answer is not difficult. Although it is true that the

Constitution of the U.S.A. has not expressly imposed any limitations on free speech, the courts of the U. S. A. have done so in interpreting the constitution. The courts have developed the doctrine of what is known as the police power of the State, and in a leading case of 1925, the Supreme Court has observed:

> "The freedom of speech and of the press which is secured by the constitution does not confer an absolute right to speak or publish, without responsibility, whatever one may choose. . . . That a State in the exercise of its police power may punish those who abuse this freedom by utterances inimical to the public welfare, tending to corrupt public morals, incite to crime, or disturb the public peace, is not open to question. And, for yet more imperative reasons, a State may punish utterances endangering the foundations of organised government and threatening its overthrow by unlawful means."

Thus the limitations put on free speech in the draft constitution of India are no more than a paraphrase of those contained in this judgment. It may be asked why we cannot trust our courts to impose any necessary limitations instead of specifying them in the constitution itself. The explanation is that, unlike the American Constitution, the draft constitution of India contains an article which in terms states that any law inconsistent with the fundamental rights conferred by the constitution shall be void; unless, therefore, the constitution itself lays down precisely the qualifications subject to which the rights are conferred, the courts may be powerless in the matter. Of course, if any particular qualification has been expressed too broadly, there would be room for amendment.

To turn now to a criticism of a different kind. Certain lawyers object to the Part in the draft constitution dealing with "Directive Principles of State Policy", on the ground that since the provisions in that Part are not to be enforceable by any court, they are in the nature of moral precepts and the constitution, they say, is no place for sermons. But it is a fact that many modern constitutions do contain moral precepts of this kind, nor can it be denied that they may have an educative value. It will be remembered that under previous enactments relating to the Government of India, there used to be instruments of instructions from the Sovereign to the Governor-General and the Governors and these instruments used to contain injunctions which, though unenforceable in the courts, served a useful purpose. For example, one of them specially charged and required the Governor "to take care that due provision shall be made for the advancement and social welfare of those classes who, on account of the smallness of their number or their lack of educational or material advantages or from any other cause, specially rely on Our protection". This may be compared with the article in the draft of the new constitution which requires that the State shall promote with special care the educational and economic interests of the weaker sections of the people. The former was an instruction from the legal Sovereign to the Governors appointed by him; the latter may be looked upon as a similar instruction from the ultimate sovereign, namely, the people of India speaking through their representatives in the Constituent Assembly to the authorities set up by or under the constitution.

I must, however, notice, in conclusion, what appears to me to be a valid criticism of the amending procedure embodied in the draft constitution. The present Constituent Assembly has been elected by the provincial legislative assemblies and other bodies not based on adult suffrage and some of the members have not been elected at all but nominated. According to the draft, the constitution, as enacted by the Constituent Assembly, cannot be amended by the Parliament of the Union except by a specially difficult process, requiring special majorities and in some cases special ratifications by the legislatures of the units, although the Union Parliament will be a body almost entirely elected on the basis of adult suffrage. It seems rather illogical that a constitution should be settled by a simple majority by an assembly elected indirectly on a very limited franchise and that it should not be capable of being amended in the same way by a Parliament elected—and perhaps for the most part elected directly—by adult suffrage. The Irish Constitution, as enacted in 1937, contained a provision empowering Parliament to amend it by the ordinary law-making process during the first three years (subject to a referendum, if the President after consulting the Council of State—a kind of Privy Council—so directed). Certain Irish authorities whom I consulted on this matter in December last strongly advised that we should have a similar provision in our constitution for at least the first five years. Apart from the logical justification for such a provision, we have to bear in mind that conditions in India are rapidly changing; the country is in a state of flux politically and economically; and the constitution should not be too rigid in its initial years.

25

BHUTAN

A DELEGATION from Bhutan visited New Delhi in June 1946, shortly after the Cabinet Mission's statement on 16th May, and expressed their anxiety to learn the effect the impending constitutional developments in India might be expected to have on their country. The Foreign Secretary of the Government of India invited the delegation to prepare a statement of their case and undertook to inform the Bhutan authorities through the Political Officer in Sikkim when the appropriate moment arrived for it to be presented.

The main features of Bhutan's relationship with India may be briefly stated.

In 1924, after thorough consideration, Bhutan had been defined as a State under British suzerainty but not an Indian State; further definition was not attempted and the precise status of the territory was of purpose left undetermined.

It had been argued on behalf of the Political Department at that time that " suzerainty ", however, was itself a relationship difficult to define, possessing degrees of strength varying with the circumstances of each instance in which the relationship obtained; and it was conceivable for a State to be both suzerain of another and under the suzerainty of a third without the autonomy of any of them being affected.

Whatever the exact juridical definition of Bhutan's status might have been by treaty, Bhutan had agreed in the past to be guided in her external relations by the British Government, who for their part had expressly undertaken not to interfere in the internal affairs of the territory; and since the conduct of external relations might in the last resort involve the use of force, the British Government were responsible, by implication, for Bhutan's defence. Bhutan (according to the Political Department's view) was regarded in effect as a protectorate of Britain, but wholly autonomous so far as its internal affairs were concerned.

Bhutan was, therefore, not regarded as an Indian State, but outside India: and the treaties with Bhutan, though executed by the Governor-General-in-Council, were treaties entered into between two foreign States. Consequent on developments in India at the end of the World War II, it was felt that those treaties must either become a dead letter or be revised; and in the latter event, whatever revision there might be, it seemed evident that Britain's future relationship with Bhutan could not, for plain reasons of geography, be other than so tenuous as to have no practical meaning.

That, however, was not immediately in issue. What was in issue at the time was India's constitutional relationship in future with Bhutan and the manner in which it was to be recognised and regulated.

The logical course, it was presumed, would be for India to succeed to the British Government's position *vis-a-vis* Bhutan, a relationship which had worked satisfactorily in the past and might well be expected to work satisfactorily in the future. Such succession, however, would necessarily have had to be by agreement between the new India and Bhutan. At the same time, since Britain's withdrawal from India was the cause of the virtual abrogation of her treaties with Bhutan, it was considered reasonable that the treaty to be negotiated between India and Britain should contain provision for Bhutan's future, in common perhaps with that of any other autonomous or independent territories with which Britain had entered into treaty relations by virtue of the position she held in India.

It was assumed that India would wish to cultivate the friendliest of relations with all such countries and that she would respect their integrity in each regard. It followed that everything possible would require to be done to assist Bhutan to adjust herself easily and satisfactorily to changing circumstances.

Four questions concerning Bhutan's future have been referred to me for advice:

(1) What is the precise status of Bhutan at present? In particular, is it an Indian State?

(2) What would be its relationship to India when India becomes an independent sovereign State? In particular, what would be the effect of India's new status on the existing treaties with Bhutan?

(3) If the existing relationship between India and Bhutan is to be preserved, what is the best method of doing so?

(4) What is the position of Bhutan *vis-a-vis* the Constituent Assembly?

I discuss these questions in order:

An Indian State was defined in the Government of India Act of 1935 as meaning " any territory, not being part of British India, which His Majesty recognises as being such a State, whether described as a State, an Estate, a Jagir or otherwise ". The test is thus recognition by His Majesty. From a note of the Political Department it appears that, after thorough consideration in 1924, Bhutan was defined as a State under British suzerainty but not an Indian State. It is not clear whether this was done by means of any published document. On the other hand, in the *Memoranda on the Indian States* of 1940 (the latest Government publication on the subject), Bhutan was not only included (*pp.* 43 to 48) but also described as a State " having political relations with the Crown representative ".

Under the (1935) constitution, the Crown representative has no political relations except with " Indian States ". The main characteristic of an Indian State, from the point of view of international law, is that it has no separate external relations at all. Bhutan, on the contrary, has external relations, although by the agreement of 1910, the Bhutanese Government bound itself to be guided by the advice of the British Government in regard to them. Thus, if Britain were at war with a foreign Power, every Indian State would be automatically at war with that Power. But Bhutan would not be technically at war until the Bhutanese Government, acting on the advice of the British Government, declared war separately. The distinction between the two cases may not amount to much in practice; but it exists and is the measure of the difference between Bhutan and an Indian State.

In fact, Bhutan is, from the point of view of international law, in much the same position as the Ionian islands before their annexation to Greece in 1864. They were then under the protection of Great Britain and Great Britain could determine their foreign relations for them. But during the Crimean War it was judicially held that they were at peace with Russia, because Great Britain had not declared war for them, although she might have done so. (See the case of the Ionian Ships [1855] 2 Spinks, 212, quoted on *p.* 50 of Pitt-Cobbett's *Cases on International Law*, 1931, Vol. I.) Such a position is not possible in regard to an Indian State strictly so called; an Indian State would be automatically at war with any Power which was at war with Great Britain. I think, therefore, that Bhutan is not an Indian State strictly so called and that the *Memoranda on the Indian States* should be revised accordingly.

Strange though it may seem, Bhutan is not even a State in India; for "India", as defined in the Government of India Act, 1935, consists of British India *plus* the Indian States *plus* any territories under the suzerainty of the Ruler of an Indian State *plus* the tribal areas *plus* any other territories which His Majesty-in-Council may, from time to time, after ascertaining

the views of the Government of India and the Indian legislature, declare to be a part of India. I am not aware of any
declaration by His Majesty-in-Council including Bhutan in
India; nor does Bhutan fall in any of the other categories in
the above definition. It follows, therefore, that Bhutan is not
in India. From the point of view of geography, this may
sound strange, but such is the present legal position. If
"India" is defined differently in the new constitution, the
position will, of course, be different.

The precise legal status of Bhutan at present is that of a
semi-sovereign foreign State: "foreign", because it is not in
law an Indian State nor is it British territory; and "semi-
sovereign", because its sovereignty in external affairs is
limited by the agreement of 1910.

I next turn to question 2, "What would be the relationship
between Bhutan and India when India becomes an independent sovereign State?" This raises a very difficult question of
international law on which there may well be room for differences of opinion. The answer to the question really turns
upon the effect which India's new status would have upon the
existing treaties or agreements with Bhutan. Let us consider
some of the main provisions in these instruments. Under
article 4 of the treaty of 1865, as modified in 1910, the British
Government had agreed to make an annual allowance to the
Government of Bhutan of one lakh of rupees in consideration
of the cession of the 18 Doars by the Bhutan Government.
Under article 9 of the same treaty, there was to be free trade
and commerce between the two governments. Under article
10 of the treaty, as revised in 1910, the British Government had undertaken to exercise no interference in the internal administration of Bhutan and the Bhutanese Government, on its part, had agreed to be guided by the advice of
the British Government in regard to its external relations.

Then there were certain provisions for the surrender of
criminals upon the demand of the British Government on the

one side or the Bhutan Government on the other. It will be noticed that the term used in all these provisions is the "British Government".

The question now is, how this term is to be interpreted and what becomes of these provisions, when the British Government no longer rules in what is now British India. Will the provisions simply lapse, or will they operate to bind His Majesty's Government in the U.K. in spite of its ceasing to be sovereign in India, or will they be binding as between Bhutan and the new Government of India? It is unnecessary to go into details of the conflicting views held by different countries, or even by the same country at different times, on questions of this character; anyone interested in the subject may refer to McNair's *Law of Treaties*, 1938 (*pp.* 412-427). The conclusion to which I have been driven after studying the authorities is that when the British Government transfers the sovereignty of what is now British India, it will have to be made clear what is to be the effect of the transfer on treaty provisions of this kind; otherwise the position will remain ambiguous.

This brings me to the next question: "If the existing relationship between Bhutan and India is to be preserved, what is the best method of doing so?" The best method of removing all uncertainty on the subject and of preserving the existing relationship would be to insert an appropriate article in the contemplated Indo-British treaty which is to accompany the cession of sovereignty by the British Crown to the people of India. The article may be on some such lines as the following:

"The new Government of India engages duly to honour all the obligations of its predecessor towards any foreign State arising under any treaty, agreement, engagement or arrangements heretofore in force with that State, provided that such State—

(*a*) recognises India as an independent sovereign State, and (*b*) engages duly to honour all reciprocal obligations of its own, as if they were obligations towards the new Government of India".

Such an article would serve to keep alive existing treaties not only between India and Bhutan but also between India and any other foreign State, *e.g.*, Afghanistan or Siam. In fact, I have already suggested the insertion of an article of this kind in the Indo-British treaty. It will, of course, be open at any time to the new Government of India and the foreign State concerned to negotiate any new treaty to replace the existing treaties. The article in question is merely meant to preserve the *status quo* in the meantime.

I now come to the last question, which concerns the position of Bhutan *vis-a-vis* the Constituent Assembly. If Bhutan is not an Indian State—in my view it is not—it will not be able to have any representative in the Constituent Assembly, even by grouping with any neighbouring Indian State. Its problems will have to be dealt with in the same way as the problems of any other foreign State, such as Afghanistan, or Nepal, or Tibet or Siam: that is to say, by the insertion of an appropriate provision in the Indo-British treaty and by the negotiation, if necessary, of new treaties with the new Government of India in due course.

26

THE POWERS OF THE PRESIDENT UNDER THE CONSTITUTION *

A QUESTION of importance that will arise when India's Constitution comes into force is, " To what extent is the President under the Indian Constitution required, in the discharge of his functions, to act upon the advice of his ministers? In particular, to what extent is he required to do so in the matter of assenting to, or withholding his assent from, Bills passed by the Houses of Parliament? "

The relevant provisions of the constitution are:

Article 74 (1)—There shall be a Council of Ministers with the Prime Minister at the head to aid and advise the President in the exercise of his functions.

(2)—The question whether any, and if so what, advice was tendered by ministers to the President shall not be inquired into in any court.

Article 75 (1)—The Prime Minister shall be appointed by the President and the other ministers shall be appointed by the President on the advice of the Prime Minister.

.   .   .   .

(3)—The Council of Ministers shall be collectively responsible to the House of the People.

Article 111—When a Bill has been passed by the Houses of Parliament, it shall be presented to the President, and the President shall declare either that he assents to the Bill, or that he withholds assent therefrom:

---

* This is the text of an article by Sri B. N. Rau published in *The Hindu* (Madras), dated May 14, 1957.

Provided that the President may, as soon as possible after the presentation to him of a Bill for assent, return the Bill if it is not a money Bill to the Houses with a message requesting that they will reconsider the Bill or any specified provisions thereof and, in particular, will consider the desirability of introducing any such amendments as he may recommend in his message, and when a Bill is so returned, the Houses shall reconsider the Bill accordingly, and if the Bill is passed again by the Houses with or without amendment and presented to the President for assent, the President shall not withhold assent therefrom.

On one point the Indian Constitution leaves no doubt: article 74 (2) lays down that the question whether any, and if so what, advice was tendered by ministers to the President shall not be enquired into in any court. It follows that even if in any particular instance the President acts otherwise than on ministerial advice, the validity of the act cannot be challenged in a court of law on that ground. The constitution does not, therefore, impose any legal obligation—that is to say, any obligation that can be enforced in the courts— upon the President to act upon the advice of his ministers. The only question can be whether and to what extent it requires him to do so as a matter of convention.

In discussing this question, I shall make at the outset two assumptions, both of which are valid under normal conditions: first, that the advice tendered is that of the Council of Ministers as a whole and not merely of an individual minister; and, secondly, that the advice tendered reflects the views of the House of the People. If the advice is that of an individual minister, the President can always ask under article 78 (c) that the matter be first submitted for the consideration of the Council and the Council's decision submitted to him. The second assumption is justified by article 75 (3) of the constitution under which the Council of Ministers is collectively responsible to the House of the People.

The arguments in support of the contention that the President under the Indian Constitution is not bound, even as a matter of convention, to act upon the advice of his ministers may be summarised thus:

I. India has a written constitution, which expressly embodies some of the conventions of the British Constitution. Thus the convention that the ministers other than the Prime Minister must be appointed on the advice of the Prime Minister is expressly embodied in article 75 (1); that the ministers shall be collectively responsible to the Lower House, in article 75 (3); and so on. We must, therefore, infer that the conventions that have not to be included in this way were deliberately left out by the framers of the constitution.

By way of contrast, we may look at article 13 (9) and (11) of the Irish Constitution which provides that " the powers and functions conferred on the President by this constitution shall be exercisable and performable by him only on the advice of the government, save where it is provided by this constitution that he shall act in his absolute discretion, etc." and " no power or function conferred on the President by law shall be exercisable or performable by him save only on the advice of the government". Nothing similar to these provisions appears in the Indian Constitution. We must, therefore, infer that the omission was deliberate.

II. Article 111 of the Indian Constitution states first that the President shall declare either that he assents to a Bill passed by the Houses of Parliament or that he withholds assent therefrom, and then goes on to provide that when a Bill has been returned to Parliament for reconsideration and is passed by the two Houses with or without amendment and again presented to the President, he shall not withhold assent. Now it is unlikely, although conceivable, that ministers responsible to the House of the People would advise the President to withhold assent from a Bill passed by both Houses; but it is quite inconceivable that they would do so in respect of a Bill which has been passed, reconsidered and re-passed by both Houses. Therefore, the provisions of article 111 are intelligible only on the supposition that the functions of the President thereunder are meant to be exercised, at least in some cases, irrespective of ministerial advice.

III. The Indian Constitution differs materially from the British, not only in being a written instrument but also in its contents. The head of the State in Great Britain is a hereditary monarch; in India he is an elected President who is eligible for re-election. He is, therefore, answerable to his constituents for his acts, which implies that he should have freedom to act as he thinks right. He should not, therefore, be held to be bound by any convention to act upon the advice of others even when he considers such advice unsound.

Again, the British Constitution contains nothing corresponding to our "Directive Principles of State Policy". These directive principles are expressly stated to be fundamental in the governance of the country and " it shall be the duty of the State to apply these principles in making laws ". Suppose a Bill is passed by both Houses of Parliament which, in the opinion of the President, violates one of these principles, e.g., the principle that the State shall endeavour to foster respect for international law and treaty obligations, and suppose the ministers advise the President to assent to it. If he acts on that advice, he will be doing something which in his own view will be a violation of the constitution and may even make him liable to impeachment. It follows that he must be free to exercise his own discretion in such matters notwithstanding any conventions evolved in other parts of the world. We cannot borrow a convention from Great Britain or any other country without examining the reasons which have led to its adoption in that country or the differing circumstances that prevail in our own.

Let me now state briefly the arguments on the other side:

I. It was well understood during the framing of the Indian Constitution that the President must act on ministerial advice.

(a) In justifying the provision relating to the mode of election of the President—indirect election by the elected members of Parliament and of the State Assemblies all over India instead of direct election based on adult suffrage (now article 54 of the constitution)—the Prime Minister said: "If we had the President elected on adult franchise and did not give him any real powers, it might become a little anomalous". In other words, the intention was to emphasise that real power was vested by the constitution in the Ministry and not in the President.

(b) It will be remembered that the draft of the Indian Constitution originally contained a schedule of instructions to the President and an article one of whose clauses provided that, in the exercise of his functions under the constitution, he must be generally guided by these instructions. These instructions provided *inter alia* that he must act on ministerial advice. The relevant instruction ran: "In all matters within the scope of the executive power of the Union, the President shall in the exercise of the powers conferred upon him be guided by the advice of his ministers". Ultimately, the instructions as well as the clause were omitted as unnecessary. A number of members objected to the omission because they thought that it was not at all clear how far the conventions of the British Constitution would be binding under the Indian Constitution. But the Law Minister was emphatic that they would be. He was specifically asked, "if in any particular case the President does not act upon the advice of his Council of Ministers, will that be tantamount to a violation of the constitution and will he be liable to impeachment?" His answer was: "There is not the slightest doubt about it". That the convention about acting on ministerial advice ought to be the same in India as in England no one appears to have doubted; the only doubt voiced was whether this was sufficiently clear in the Indian Constitution. The Constituent Assembly, on the assurance of the Law Minister that the point admitted of no doubt, agreed to omit the schedule and the clause. (*Constituent Assembly Debates*, Volume 10, 1949, *pp.* 268-271.)

II. It is clear from article 74 (1) that it is the function of the Council of Ministers to advise the President over the whole of the Central field. Nothing is left to his discretion or excepted from that field by this article. By way of contrast, see article 163 which is the corresponding provision for Governors and which expressly excepts certain matters in which the Governor is, by or under the constitution, required to act in his discretion. There is no such exception in the case of the President.

Moreover, article 75 (3) makes the Council of Ministers responsible to the House of the People. If, therefore, the President acted contrary to advice, the ministers would either resign or, since the advice tendered reflected the views of the House of the People, they would be thrown out of office by the House of the People. For the same reason, no one else would then be able to form a government. The President would, therefore, be compelled to dissolve the House. Apart from the technical difficulty of carrying out the many details of a general election in such a situation— the President might have to dismiss the Ministry and instal a " caretaker " government to co-operate with him in ordering a general election—the consequences of the election might be most serious. If the electorate should return the same government to power, the President might be accused of having sided with the Opposition and thrown the country into the turmoil and expense of a general election in a vain attempt to get rid of a Ministry that had the support of Parliament and the people. This would gravely impair the position of the President.

III. If we hold that in a conflict between the Ministry and the President, the President's voice should prevail in the last resort, either generally or even in a particular class of cases, this would mean the elimination to that extent of the authority of a Ministry which is continuously subject to control or criticism by the House of the People, in favour of the authority of a President who is not so subject. It would thus result in a reduction of the sphere of " responsible government ". So important a subtraction must be justified by some express provision of the constitution. There are a few such express provisions in our constitution.

IV. If the President, in a particular case where his own views differ from those of his ministers, ultimately accepts their advice in deference to a well-understood convention, then even if the act should result in a breach of some "fundamental right" or "directive principle" enunciated in the constitution, the responsibility will be that of the ministers and not of the President.

The considerations mentioned above in the second group of arguments seem to be decisive in favour of the proposition that, in the last resort, the President should accept the advice of his ministers as in England. We are not concerned here so much with what is legally permissible as with what is politically wise; for, whether the President acts upon ministerial advice or not, the validity of his acts cannot be challenged in the law courts.

There may, however, be exceptional or border-line cases in which the President can or has to act otherwise than on ministerial advice. For example, in the choice of a new Prime Minister, he is not obliged to consult the outgoing Prime Minister: such is the position under the British Constitution also. This can hardly be called an exception, because he has necessarily to consult the incoming Prime Minister, who, as soon as he accepts office, makes himself responsible for the choice. But there may be other exceptions too, expressly mentioned in the Indian Constitution. Thus article 103 requires that if any question arises whether any member of Parliament has become subject to any of the disqualifications mentioned in article 102, the President must obtain the opinion of the Election Commission and decide the question accordingly; and that decision is final. Here there is hardly any room for ministerial advice. Article 111 affords another illustration: in certain circumstances, the President is debarred from withholding his assent to a Bill; the bar obviously applies even if the ministers should advise refusal of assent, which is hardly conceivable. But apart from a few exceptions of this kind, resting on express provisions of the constitution, the safest rule to observe appears to me to be as stated in the last paragraph.

A difficult question may sometimes arise in practice in deciding whether a particular provision of the constitution is to be construed as an express exception. By way of illustration, take the kind of case to which I have already referred: I take it, because it is of a type which has not yet occurred in practice and, therefore, need not embarrass anybody. Suppose the Houses of Parliament pass a Bill which, in the President's opinion, infringes certain treaty obligations of India. Article 51 requires "the State" to foster respect for treaty obligations; under article 36, "the State" includes the Parliament of India, of which, under article 79, the President is a component part. Article 37, therefore, requires him to apply these provisions in the making of laws. Is this to be read as an express direction ruling out any ministerial advice to the contrary? In other words, is he to refuse assent even if his ministers advise assent? The answer to my mind is this: Whether the Bill infringes treaty obligations is a matter of opinion. Presumably, the advice of the ministers is based on their considered opinion that the Bill does not infringe treaty obligations. In accepting their opinion in preference to his own, the President does not violate the constitution; therefore, he should in the last resort accept their advice. The responsibility for the result is theirs.

Does this reduce the President under the Indian Constitution to a figurehead? Far from it. Like the King in England, he will still have the right " to be consulted, to encourage and to warn". Acting on ministerial advice does not necessarily mean immediate acceptance of the Ministry's first thoughts. The President can state all his objections to any proposed course of action and ask his Ministers in Council, if necessary, to reconsider the matter. It is only in the last resort that he should accept their final advice. It has been observed that the influence of the Crown—and of the House of Lords as well—in England has grown with every curtailment of its legal powers by convention or statute. A similar result is likely to follow in India too; for, as has been well said, " the voice of reason is more readily heard when it can persuade but no longer coerce ". One can conceive of no better future for the President of India than that he should be more and more like the monarch in England, eschewing legal power, standing outside the clash of parties and gaining in moral authority.

27

THE FINANCE COMMISSION

UNDER article 280 of the constitution it is one of the duties of the Finance Commission to make recommendations to the President as to the principles which should govern " grants-in-aid of the revenues of the States " out of the Consolidated Fund of India.

Article 282 empowers the Union to make " any grants for any public purpose ".

The question has been raised as to what is the distinction between " grants " *simpliciter* and " grants-in-aid of the revenues of a State ".

One distinction seems fairly obvious. The expression " grant-in-aid of the revenues of a State " standing by itself suggests a recurring grant; a single grant for a particular year and a particular purpose can hardly, with propriety, be called a grant-in-aid of State revenues. Article 282 would cover any grants, whether single or recurring, while article 280 appears to refer to recurring grants-in-aid of the annual revenues of the States.

Is there any further implication in the use of the term " grants-in-aid of the revenues of the States " in article 280? In particular, is it implied that the grants-in-aid must or must not be for a specified purpose? I do not think that there is any such implication either way. The constitution itself mentions various types of grants-in-aid. For example, article 273 mentions grants-in-aid of the revenues of Assam, Bihar, Orissa and West Bengal, in lieu of a share of the export duty on jute and jute products. Obviously these grants-in-aid are based on the fact that these four States grow jute and the grants are, therefore, not related to any particular object of expenditure. Again, the first part of the first clause of article 275 refers to general grants-in-aid to needy States; but the provisos to the clause refer to certain grants-in-aid for specific schemes or specific areas.

It would, therefore, seem that a grant-in-aid of the revenues of a State may be conditional or unconditional; the constitution itself recognises both types of grants.

Another question which has been raised is to what extent the recommendations of the Finance Commission can be said to be binding upon the President. Supposing, for example, the Central Ministry advises the President to make some departure from the Commission's recommendations, a departure in favour of the Centre; what would be the duty of the President? Will he be bound by the recommendations of the Commission or by the advice of the Ministry? I do not think that the question is likely to arise in a court of law; for, as a matter of strict law, the recommendations of the Commission are mere recommendations and it is open to the President, if he thinks fit, to depart from them. But I venture to think that it would be unwise to depart from them except for patent error. It must be remembered that the President is elected not only by the members of the Central legislature but also by members of the various State legislatures. If, therefore, the Central Ministry should advise him to vary in favour of the Centre the recommendations of the Commission, the President might be driven to resign rather than accept the advice tendered. If he should resign and stand for re-election on the issue so raised, it is possible that he might be re-elected and a grave conflict would then arise between him and the Ministry. In the interest, therefore, of the smooth working of the constitution, I venture to think that no Ministry should advise the President to depart from the recommendations of the Finance Commission, a quasi-arbitral body whose function is to do justice as between the Centre and the States. Of course, if there are patent errors such as arithmetical mistakes, the position would be different. Even then, the best course would be for the President to return the recommendations to the Commission, if possible, for reconsideration and re-submission after rectifying proved errors. But, otherwise, I feel sure that no Ministry should advise the President to act otherwise than in accordance with the recommendations of the Finance Commission. Article 281 fortifies the same view.

28

AN INDO-BRITISH TREATY

[*The following draft of an Indo-British treaty was completed by Sri B. N. Rau in November* 1945. *In May* 1946 *the British Cabinet Mission declared:* " *It will be necessary to negotiate a treaty between the Union Constituent Assembly and the United Kingdom to provide for certain matters arising out of the transfer of power* ". *Ultimately, however, the proposal was dropped.*]

ACCORDING to the draft declaration announced by Sir Stafford Cripps in 1942, the establishment of an Indian Union with the full status and powers of a Dominion was to be subject, *inter alia*, to the signing of a treaty to be negotiated between His Majesty's Government and the constitution-making body to be set up in India. The constitution-making body, not being a government, can hardly be a party signatory to the treaty; and what is doubtless intended is that the articles of agreement for a treaty should be approved by the constitution-making body and that the actual treaty should be between His Majesty's Government in the United Kingdom and the provisional Central Government in India, to be ultimately ratified by the Government of the Indian Dominion. If this is correct, a draft of the articles of agreement will have to be got ready before the constitution-making body meets and will have to be put before that body for approval, with such amendments as it may think fit to make and as may be accepted by His Majesty's Government. The draft of the treaty must, therefore, be such as the constitution-making body, which under the Cripps plan was to consist of about 160 members elected by the various provincial assemblies *plus* about 40 members from the Indian States, can be expected to approve.

CONTENTS OF THE TREATY

According to the draft declaration, the treaty—

(a) will cover all necessary matters arising out of the complete transfer of responsibility from British to Indian hands;

(b) will make provision, in accordance with the undertakings given by His Majesty's Government, for the protection of racial and religious minorities; but

(c) will not impose any restriction on the power of the Indian Union to decide in the future its relationship to the other member-States of the British Commonwealth.

Later, in the course of a press conference, Sir Stafford Cripps added that the treaty—

(d) would not guarantee the vested rights of British interests in India;

(e) would be for a term of years in the usual form, to be continued for a further term, unless either party wished to revise it.

He also stated that the safeguards for the Services would be taken over by the British Government, which presumably means that they would not figure in the treaty.

Sir Reginald Coupland has dealt with the treaty in Chapter XIII of Part III of his report on the constitutional problem in India. (*The Future of India, pp.* 156-159). According to him, the treaty might appropriately provide for defence arrangements against external attack and in particular for such matters as—

(a) the stationing of British forces on Indian soil and their correlation with Indian forces in a joint system of defence;

(b) the provision of aerodromes; and

(c) the granting of facilities for British naval and coastal air forces at the major Indian ports.

In this connection he has suggested that, as the duty of maintaining internal security would vest solely in the Indian Government, the location of the land forces would seem naturally to lie in the neighbourhood of the north-west and north-east frontiers, just as their location in Egypt under the Egyptian Treaty of 1936 lies near the Suez Canal.

Another matter which, according to Coupland, might properly be included in the treaty is the payment of pensions, etc., to the members of the Indian defence forces and of the Secretary of State's Services whose services might be terminated at the wish of the Indian Government or their own. He is against including in the treaty any provisions for the protection of the Princes or of the minorities: such protection as may be necessary should, he thinks, be embodied in the constitution itself as the law of the land.

The British Government's view in September 1945 appeared to have been that the treaty would deal with such matters as—

(1) defence;

(2) the conduct of foreign relations;

(3) financial obligations between the United Kingdom and India;

(4) relations with the Indian States; and, possibly,

(5) minority rights and the protection of the Services.

If we take the view that the treaty is to regulate certain external relations of India, while the constitution deals with all internal matters, it will be more appropriate to put into the constitution rather than into the treaty provisions for protecting the Princes or the minorities or the Services. However, whether the provisions are ultimately put into the constitution or into the treaty, the task of preparing a suitable draft of them, to be put before the constitution-making body, cannot be evaded or put off.

The treaty between the United Kingdom and Iraq dated June 30, 1930, and the Anglo-Egyptian Treaty dated August 26, 1936, may be useful as guides. It must, however, be remembered that nothing inconsistent with full Dominion status should be proposed for inclusion in the draft, as His Majesty's Government is pledged to this. It is not possible at this stage to anticipate India's decision on the issue of complete independence involving secession from the British Commonwealth, or of remaining as a member of the Commonwealth in free and voluntary association with the other units.

According to some legal authorities in England, the procedure for the negotiation of a treaty, before the final transfer of power, on the assumption that *India would decide to secede*, would be—

(*a*) a smaller body should be set up capable of functioning at a later date as a provisional government to which power might properly be transferred. This smaller body might either be appointed *ad hoc* by the Constituent Assembly, or might be a body of acknowledged leaders of Indian opinion satisfactorily accredited as representatives of India;

(*b*) agreement for a treaty should be negotiated with this body [the treaty should include the acceptance by the Indian Government, so far as applicable, of all relevant treaty obligations];

(*c*) on the completion of negotiations, agreement should be entered into with this body, providing that the treaty would be ratified by the Government of India set up under the new constitution. If expedient, there should be simultaneous recognition of this body as the prospective provisional government of India;

(*d*) then would follow legislation in Parliament (i) conferring on His Majesty power by Order-in-Council to transfer power as and when appropriate to the provisional government; (ii) repealing the Government of India Act of 1935 as from a date to be fixed by Order-in-Council for the transfer of power; (iii) declaring that India was independent and no longer formed part of His Majesty's Dominions; (iv) giving effect to the treaty; (v) enabling His Majesty to change the style and title (preferably by a separate Act, requiring the assent of the Dominions); and (e) the treaty would in due course be concluded between His Majesty's Government and the new Government of India.

On the other hand, *should India remain in the Commonwealth—*

(A) Negotiations would have to be with an *ad hoc* body similar to (a);

(B) & (C) would roughly be the same as (b) & (c), except that the "transfer of power" would be effected differently;

(D) parliamentary legislation would (i) repeal the Government of India Act of 1935; (ii) establish the new constitution on the lines of the Commonwealth of Australia Act, 1900—*i.e.*, by annexing it as a schedule to the statute; (iii) obtain parliamentary approval and formal recognition to the agreement; (iv) declare India a Dominion; (v) empower His Majesty (by a separate Act) to change the style and title; and (vi) confer power on His Majesty to transfer power and responsibility to the new Indian Government and, pending the establishment of the new government, to a provisional body.

In either case, the treaty in its final form would be with the new government.

MEMORANDUM ON DRAFT TREATY

The following is the text of the memorandum and the notes which were circulated to certain authorities in India for their comments and opinions:

1. This treaty shall be in force for a term of — years *Term of treaty* from the commencement of the new constitution.

2. The Government of the United Kingdom (hereinafter *Co-operation in* referred to as the British Government) and *defence* the Government of India (hereinafter referred to as the Indian Government) recognise that the defence of their territories is of vital importance to the one no less than to the other, and they accordingly agree hereby to

consult and co-operate with each other to the fullest possible extent in all matters relating thereto.

3. If the British Government requests and the Indian

British forces forming part of Commonwealth strategic reserve

Government agrees that British forces (*i.e.*, armed forces raised by the Crown in the United Kingdom) be maintained at stipulated stations in India as part of a Commonwealth strategic reserve—

(i) such forces shall be under their own commanders who shall be appointed by the British Government and who, so far as training, establishments, promotions, postings and equipment are concerned, shall be responsible to the British Government, either directly or through the appropriate Commander-in-Chief in India, as may be mutually agreed between the two governments;

(ii) such forces shall be under the Supreme Commander in India for purpose of local administration and service discipline;

(iii) such forces shall be subject to the jurisdiction of the ordinary courts in India, both civil and criminal;

(iv) such forces shall at all times be at the disposal of the British Government and shall not be available to the Indian Government, except by agreement or arrangement, general or special, between the two governments.*

4. If the Indian Government requests the loan of British

British forces loaned to the Indian Government for the local defence of India

units and personnel for the local defence of India and if the British Government agrees to the request, the units and personnel so lent shall be at the disposal of the Indian Government and under the command and administration of the Supreme Commander in India.

---

* *Article 3—* (on British forces forming part of the Commonwealth reserve).

[The subject-matter of sub-clause (i) was under consideration by the Reorganisation Committee set up some time ago in India and could not, therefore, be finally drafted at this stage.

The article dealt with the position of certain British forces stationed in India *with the consent of the Indian Government.* If the Indian Government did not consent to the stationing of such forces in India, the article would not apply. If the Indian Government consented, the position created by the article would be analogous to that of " visiting forces " in certain other countries.]

5. If the British Government requests the loan of Indian

Indian forces loan-ed to the British Government for the local defence of British territory outside India

units and personnel for the local defence of any territory outside India under the control of the British Government and, if the Indian Government agrees to the request, the units and personnel so lent shall be at the disposal of the British Government and under the command and administration of the authority exercising supreme command in that territory.*

6. Subject to any modifications which the two governments may hereafter agree to introduce, the exemptions, immunities and other privileges conferred by or under any law relating to taxation, buildings and other matters in force in India at the commencement of the new constitution upon, or in respect of the personnel of, or the equipment, stores or buildings required for, the defence forces of the Crown in India shall continue to be in operation as regards British units and personnel stationed or serving in India:

Provided that similar exemptions, immunities or privileges shall be in force as regards Indian units and personnel stationed or serving in territories under the control of the British Government.†

7. Should any dispute with a third State produce a

Defensive alliance between the U. K. and India

situation which involves the risk of a rupture with that State, the Indian and British Governments will concert together, with a view to the settlement of the dispute by peaceful means, in

---

* *Article 5—*

[This article was complementary to article 4 and intended to carry out a departmental suggestion regarding Indian forces employed outside India, *e.g.*, in Burma or Aden.]

† *Article 6—*

[There were various exemptions in respect of military stores and equipment under the Sea Customs Act, 1878: there were certain immunities in respect of defence personnel and government buildings conferred by or under the Municipal Taxation Act, 1881, and the Government Buildings Act, 1899. There might be others. All these would be continued by this article, on a reciprocal basis for the term of the treaty, unless modified by mutual agreement.]

accordance with the provisions of the Charter of the United Nations and of any other international obligations which may be applicable to the case.

8. Should, notwithstanding the provisions of article 7, either of the two governments become engaged in war, the other government will, subject always to the provisions of article 9, immediately come to its aid in the capacity of an ally. The aid of either government in the event of war, imminent menace of war, or apprehended international emergency will consist in furnishing, on its own territory, to the other government, all possible facilities and assistance in its power, including the use of its ports, aerodromes and means of communication.*

9. Nothing in this treaty shall in any way prejudice the

Construction of treaty without prejudice to the United Nations Charter rights and obligations which devolve or may devolve upon either of the two governments under the United Nations Charter.†

Articles 7 and 8—

[These articles follow similar ones in the treaties with Egypt and Iraq; but the question might arise how far they were consistent with the statement in the draft declaration of 1942 that the treaty will not impose any restriction on the power of the Indian Union to decide in the future its relationship to the other member-States of the British Commonwealth. To say that if the British Government becomes engaged in war, the Indian Government will immediately come to its aid in the capacity of an ally might at first sight appear to be inconsistent with the draft declaration, because it restricts the power of the Indian Government to decide its relationship to the British Government in the event of war. If, however, the Indian Government found itself engaged in a defensive war against a great Power, it might, for at least a term of years, be compelled to seek the assistance of the British Government in repelling aggression. But India cannot obviously expect the United Kingdom to step forth to her rescue unless she undertakes a reciprocal obligation. What the proposed article, therefore, comes to is that, for the term of years for which the treaty holds, India voluntarily enters into a *defensive* alliance with the United Kingdom, the arrangement being necessarily subject to review at the end of the term. Looked at in this way, the article may, on balance, be of advantage to India. The chances of India being dragged into an aggressive war as an ally of the United Kingdom are negatived by the fact that the article in question is expressly subject to article 9 and, therefore, to the Charter of the United Nations article 2(4) which provides that all members are to refrain in their international relations from the threat or use of force against the territorial integrity or political independence of any State or in any other manner inconsistent with the purposes of the United Nations.]

† *Article 9—*

[This corresponds to similar articles in the treaties with Iraq and Egypt. It is necessitated by certain articles of the United Nations Charter, particularly

Treaties with Foreign States

10.   The Indian Government engages duly to honour the

Treaty obliga- obligations of India or the government or
tions between India any administration thereof, towards any
and foreign States foreign State (*i.e.*, a State other than an
Indian State as defined in the Government of India Act,
1935), arising under any treaty or agreement or arrangement
heretofore in force with that State, provided that such
State—

(*a*) recognises India * as an independent sovereign State and

---

those relating to regional arrangements in Charter VIII of the Charter. The
Charter is not quite clear on one point. Suppose, for instance, India has
grounds for fearing aggression from a permanent member of the Security
Council and under article 35 of the Charter brings the situation to the attention
of the Council. The Security Council will not be able to take any decision
under articles 39, 41 and 42, if the aggressor-member interposes its veto, as it
is likely to do in the circumstances. [See article 27(3)] Thus the United
Nations Organisation will be unable to act. Is action outside the Organisation permissible? The Charter does not make it quite clear whether such a
case would be covered by the liberty allowed to regional associates (articles
52 to 54) or by the reservation of " the inherent right of individual or collective
self-defence " (article 51). It may be pointed out that under article 53 no
enforcement action can be taken under regional arrangements or by regional
agencies without the authorisation of the Security Council, an authorisation
which cannot be obtained without the concurrence of every permanent member.
The precise scope and effect of the provisions of the Charter being doubtful, all
that can be said is that the provisions of the proposed treaty shall not be deemed
in any way to prejudice the rights and obligations devolving upon the parties
under the Charter.

*Article 10—

[Different views seem to have been held by different countries and even by
the same country at different times on questions of State succession. For
example:

(1) When Colombia was split up into three new States (New Granada,
Venezuela and Ecuador) in 1829-31, the question arose whether a treaty of
1825 between Colombia and the United Kingdom continued to be binding on
the three new States. The King's Advocate advised in 1834 that the treaty
of 1825 was still binding upon each of the three new States until they respectively gave due notice that they considered themselves no longer bound by it.
He qualified the opinion by stating that it would be more regular and formal
to enter into new and separate treaties with each of the three new States.

(2) When in 1905, the real Union of Sweden and Norway was dissolved,
the British Government's view as to the effect upon previous treaties was:
" Although the dissolution of the Union between Sweden and Norway undoubtedly affords the British Government the right to examine, *de novo*,
the treaty engagements by which Great Britain was bound to the dual

(*b*) engages duly to honour any reciprocal obligations of its own towards India.

---

monarchy, they gladly take note of the desire of the Swedish Government that these engagements should remain in force pending a further study of the subject."

(3) When the Republic of Finland was formed at the end of the great war and was recognised by Great Britain and other countries, the British Government defined its attitude towards Finland in the matter of treaties in the following terms:

" In the case of a new State being formed out of part of an old State, there is no succession by the new State to the treaties of the old one, though the obligations of the old State in relation to such matters as the navigation of rivers, which are in the nature of servitudes, would normally pass to the new State. Consequently, there are no treaties in existence between Finland and this country."

Thus three different views have been taken as to the effect of the splitting up of a State into two or more new States upon the treaties of the old:

(1) That the old treaties continue to be binding on the new States;

(2) that the dissolution or dismemberment gives the other party to any treaty the right to re-examine the position;

(3) that there is no succession by the new States to the treaties of the old.

Then there is another uncertainty, namely, as to the precise position of India. One view is that for treaty purposes India is even now a distinct State having been given a place in the League of Nations and that if India becomes, independent, it will not be a case of a new State coming into existence but of an existing State changing its form of government. On this view, old treaties would, at worst, be in abeyance pending the recognition of the new form of government by the other contracting party and their operation would revive automatically upon such recognition. (McNair's *Law of Treaties, p.* 384).

But Keith appears to take a rather different view of India's position: " It is not disputed that the United Kingdom and all territories dependent thereon form a single unit for purposes of international law and rank as one wholly independent and sovereign State. The position of India, indeed, is anomalous, inasmuch as India is given a place in the League of Nations and in many respects ranks as a distinct State. But to regard India as a full State in the sense of international law is impossible, because for external purposes the Government of India is no more than an agency of the Government of the United Kingdom." (*The Sovereignty of the Dominions*, 1938, *p.* 34). It results from this view that if India becomes independent, it will be in the position of a new State splitting off from an existing State (the United Kingdom and its dependencies being the existing State), and there may be no succession by the new State to the treaties of the old.

In view of the above uncertainties, a general clause on the lines of article 10 would serve to remove doubt. The article would not be necessary if India chose to remain within the Commonwealth and be a Dominion, for in that event there would be no dismemberment, but only a normal constitutional change in the form of India's Government, which would not affect treaties. (McNair's *Law of Treaties, p.* 383). Some of the instruments are called treaties and " India " is in terms one of the parties (*e.g.*, treaty for the limitation of naval armament signed in London on March 25, 1936); others are described as agreements to which the Government of India is a party (*e.g.*, agreement for the operation of regular air services over Siam and over India and Burma signed on December 3, 1937); others, again, are described as arrangements between " Administrations " (*e.g.*, arrangement for the exchange of correspondence between the postal administrations of British India and Portuguese India

POSITION OF BRITISH NATIONALS IN INDIA*

11.   Any person who immediately before the commencement of the new constitution was a British
Option to retain British nationality subject, domiciled or resident in any part of India, shall, upon its commencement and until he elects otherwise, retain his British nationality without prejudice to any other nationality or citizenship to which he may be entitled under the new constitution or any other Indian law.†

---

signed on March 19/24, 1937). Hence the use of all these terms in the article. Whether there should be a similar provision for Indian States is a matter on which they will have to be consulted.]

*These articles are not necessary if India elects to remain a Dominion within the British Commonwealth.

† *Article 11*—

[If India elects to go out of the British Commonwealth, provision will have to be made for the nationality, under the new regime, of those who at present are British subjects. From the Cabinet Mission's statement of May 16, 1946, it is clear that in due course there will be a cession of sovereignty to the people of India. One of the attributes of sovereignty being the allegiance of those persons who possess the nationality of the sovereign, it follows that a cession of the sovereignty over a particular territory involves *per se* a transfer to the acquiring State of the allegiance and nationality of those nationals of the ceding State who, at the time of the cession, are connected by a certain tie with the territory ceded. Whether that tie is residence alone or domicile alone or a combination of both is controversial and it is possible that it may depend upon the laws of the two States respectively. Dicey confines the change of nationality to nationals of the ceding State who are " resident ", the position of persons domiciled but not resident in the ceded territory at the time of the cession being uncertain. The hardship of an involuntary change of nationality has led with increasing frequency in recent years to the adoption of some form of mitigation. (McNair's *Legal Effects of War*, 1944, pp. 388-390.)

Hence the provision in this article. It creates a position analogous to that created by the Irish Constitution in Ireland, as to which the Attorney-General of England stated in the House of Commons (in 1922) " that in his judgment and in the judgment of any responsible lawyer, the fact that any person elected to accept Irish citizenship did not in any way injure or affect his status as a British subject ". The analogy is not complete, as there has been no cession of British sovereignty over Ireland.

" In all cases of the transfer of territory from one State to another, whether the event involves the extinction of a State or not, the point of chief legal interest is to determine the effect, if any, of the transfer on the international rights and duties of the States concerned. This question is often regulated by the provisions of a treaty of cession, but unless so regulated it does not admit of a simple answer, and the problems which it raises cannot be solved by assuming a general principle of ' State succession' and then proceeding to deduce its consequences." (Brierly's *Law of Nations*, Third Edition, 1942, pp. 110, 111.)

12. The Indian Government agrees to pay to the members of the family or to the servants or to the descendants of servants of former Rulers of territories in India the customary allowances referred to in section 145 of the Government of India Act, 1935, subject to the conditions applying to each.*

Payment of political pensions

PENSIONS, PROVIDENT FUND CONTRIBUTIONS, GRANTS AND OTHER SUMS DUE TO CERTAIN CLASSES OF CROWN SERVANTS

13. (1) The Indian Government agrees to pay to the British Government on account of, or in respect of, the classes of persons specified in clause (3) of this article, who were in the service of the Crown in India immediately before the commencement of the new constitution, the pensions, provident fund moneys, grants (compensatory or otherwise), leave salaries and all other sums whatsoever (whether recurring or non-recurring) that may be due to them or to members of their families under the conditions of service applicable to each case.

Payments on account of, or in respect of, certain classes of displaced Crown servants

(2) The Indian Government agrees to pay to the British Government on account of, or in respect of, the classes of persons specified in clause (3) of this article who retired from the service of the Crown in India before the commencement of the new constitution the pensions due to them or to members of their families.

Until independent India has its own ambassadors in foreign countries, Indian citizens, so long as they retain their British nationality, would be able to claim protection from the United Kingdom ambassadors as at present. The article would remove any doubt as to the nationality of Indian British subjects who were domiciled in India but who might be residing abroad at the time of the change-over. It would also remove doubts as to the nationality of European British subjects who may be residing in India, though domiciled abroad at the material date.]

* *Article 12—*

[The annual amount of these political pensions was about Rs. 20 lakhs. Almost all of them were payable because of the annexation of territories which at one time belonged to a State but were subsequently included in British India.]

(3) The classes of persons referred to in clauses (1) and (2) above are:

(i) persons appointed to any service or any post under the Crown in India by the Secretary of State;

(ii) persons holding any civil post under the Crown in India who, when first appointed to such a post, were officers in His Majesty's forces; and

(iii) British personnel, whether officers or other ranks, serving in any armed forces raised in India by the Crown.

(4) If any question arises as to the sum payable under this article in any particular case or class of cases, the question shall be determined by agreement between the two governments and, in default of agreement, by the arbitration of three persons, one to be appointed by each government and the third to be appointed by the other two arbitrators.*

FINANCIAL OBLIGATIONS BETWEEN THE UNITED KINGDOM AND INDIA

14. Any sums due from the Indian Government to the British Government under this treaty shall be set off against

---

* Article 13—

[Clause (1) of this article refers to the pensions, etc., of those who were in service immediately before the commencement of the new constitution and clause (2) to the pensions of those who retired before its commencement. The conditions of service which have been framed for recent recruits of the former class provide that if as a result of the constitutional changes, their appointments under the old regime are terminated, they or members of their families will be entitled to certain grants. Conditions not less favourable are, it has been announced, being framed for the older entrants as well. Clause (1) will implement the terms decided upon in pursuance of this announcement as well as those already granted. There is a suggestion that in both sets of conditions there should be provision for a period of notice on either side for terminating the appointment, or for exercising the option to retire, as the case may be.

A suggestion has also been made that in addition to the provisions of this article, which apply only to certain classes of Crown servants, the treaty should contain provisions to protect all other civil servants of the Crown as well. To protect all civil servants of the Crown of whatever grade is hardly necessary or practicable. What has been done in the present draft for civil servants is to provide for only those whose conditions of service have hitherto been directly under the control of the Secretary of State and in respect of whom certain commitments have already been entered into. Even so, the article will require careful scrutiny, for there is no doubt that these commitments will be closely examined by the Constituent Assembly.]

the sterling balances that may have accumulated or that may accumulate from time to time in the United Kingdom in favour of India.*

The comments on the draft treaty which was referred with the explanatory memorandum on the different articles, to certain authorities in India, were interesting. It was assumed by them that the treaty would deal with (A) defence; (B) conduct of foreign relations; (C) financial obligations between the U.K. and India; (D) relations with Indian States; and, possibly, (E) minority rights and the protection of the Services.

A—PROBLEMS OF DEFENCE

The main headings under defence would deal with (a) arrangements for Commonwealth defence, including the placing at each other's disposal of armed forces on agreed terms; (b) in time of war, the grant of necessary base and transit facilities by the contracting parties to each other; and (c) the loan of service personnel as either may require on agreed terms.

The agreed terms in (a) and (c) would include financial terms and there would be a subsidiary agreement covering them. The financial arrangements would thus be an integral part of the arrangements for defence.

What is the legal position at present? Presumably any British forces stationed in India would fall to be governed by the U. K. Army Act, unless India is formally added to the list of Dominions in the Statute of Westminster. Section 4 of

---

* *Article 14—*

[A suggestion has been made that, as in the case of Iraq, there should be a separate agreement dealing with all outstanding financial questions, including those dealt with here and in article 13 above.]

that statute prevents the annual Act of Parliament, which continues the Army Act from year to year, being extended to India without India's consent. Assuming this is to be the case, the question arises whether there is anything in the suggested treaty provisions inconsistent with Dominion status. The answer, broadly speaking, would appear to be " No ".

Both in the United Kingdom and at least in some of the Dominions, such as Canada and South Africa, there are various " visiting forces Acts " whose effect is to place such forces, for internal administration as well as discipline, under the courts and authorities constituted by their own law. As an example, we may take Act XXXII of 1932 of the South African Parliament. In that Act " Dominion " is defined as including the United Kingdom, Canada, Australia, etc. A " visiting force " is defined as any naval, military or air force at any time present in the Union with the consent of the government of the Union. Section 7(1) of the Act provides that it shall be lawful for the service courts and authorities —that is to say, the naval, military and air force courts and authorities—of the Dominion concerned to exercise within the Union in relation to the members of a visiting force of that Dominion, in matters concerning discipline and in matters concerning the internal administration of the force, all such powers as are conferred upon them by the law of the Dominion.

Then there is section 8(1) which provides that the Governor-General of the Union may, by proclamation in the gazette, authorise any government department, minister of the Crown, or other person in the Union to perform, at the request of such authority of the Dominion in question as may be specified in the proclamation, but subject to such limitations as may be so specified, any function in relation to a visiting force and members thereof which that department, minister or person, performs and could perform in relation to a Union force of like nature to the visiting force, or in relation to members of such a force; and for the purpose of the exercise of any such function, any power exercisable by virtue of any law by the minister, department, or person, in relation to a Union force or members thereof, shall be exercisable by him or them in relation to the visiting force and members thereof; provided that nothing in the sub-section shall authorise any interference with the visiting force in matters relating to discipline or to the internal administration of the force.

There are also special provisions for temporary attachment of the visiting force to a Union force, as also for occasions of joint action. The net result of these provisions appears to be that the visiting force, except when attached to, or acting in combination with, a Union force, is autonomous in matters relating to discipline and internal administration. The proposed treaty provisions make the Commonwealth strategic reserve autonomous only for purposes of training, etc., but place the force under the Supreme Commander in India for purposes of discipline and local administration. The exact scope of this subordination will have to be defined in fuller detail. The treaty assumes that there will be a Supreme Commander in India under the new regime and the assumption is doubtless based on good grounds. But time may bring about changes in this respect. The office of Commander-in-Chief was abolished in England in 1904 and his powers were transferred to the Army Council. There is an Order-in-Council defining the duties of the Army Council and, among other things, that order empowers the Secretary of State to assign specific duties to specific members of the Council: matters relating to discipline have thus been assigned to one of the military members. Presumably, the intention is that if there should be a similar development in India, then, when the treaty falls to be renewed, the clause relating to the Supreme Commander will be suitably modified.

26

The conditions of service, etc. of the loaned personnel will be determined by agreement at the time of the loan; such an agreement should define clearly, not merely the conditions of service of the personnel, including representation on headquarters staffs, but also the circumstances in which they should or should not be employed in certain contingencies, such as internal disturbance or wars in which the British Government may not be involved. If a breach of the agreement has occurred or is apprehended, representations will doubtless be made to the Dominion government through the British High Commissioner in India.

The creation of an autonomous government in India involves a radical change in the conditions of service of British officers who are in regular commission in the Indian Army and the Royal Indian Navy. If the future Government of India desires to retain them and the officers themselves are willing to continue in its service, it will be necessary to protect them, either by a treaty or by an appropriate provision in the Constitution Act. Equally, if the Government of India does not desire to retain them, or the officers themselves elect not to continue in its service, they should be given the option of transferring to the corresponding British service or, where this is not possible, suitable retiring terms. Similar arrangements for British other ranks serving in the Indian Army will also be necessary. If the officers or men elect to continue in service, provisions designed to protect them would be more appropriate in the new constitution than in the treaty, as they are concerned with internal administration. Where, however, they are discharged, or they elect to retire in consequence of the change of government, adequate compensation or suitable retiring terms might be provided for them in the treaty, as they cease to be in Indian service.

Assuming that some officers and other ranks elect to remain in the Indian armed forces after the change of government, and assuming that suitable provision is made for their protection in the new constitution, how is the provision to be enforced in the event of a breach? Similar questions will doubtless arise in connection with the working of other protective clauses. If India has full Dominion status, the remedy for any breach will, in the last resort, be diplomatic pressure through the British High Commissioner in India. In order to enable the British High Commissioner to keep in touch with what is going on around him, it has been suggested that he should have military and air force officers attached to his staff. It is said that this would not be an innovation, so that no new principle is involved.

B—THE CONDUCT OF FOREIGN RELATIONS

So far as India's external relations are concerned, it will become a matter of importance to provide for the continuance of treaties made by His Majesty's Government with countries limitrophe with India and which are only capable of fulfilment in or by India. This is not merely a question of relieving the United Kingdom of possible claims and embarrassment; but it will serve to set at rest, partially if not wholly, the very grave apprehensions which we know exist in certain capitals. And it follows that the relief of anxiety in those capitals can only be to the advantage of the new Indian State.

The British Government draws a clear distinction between—

(a) treaties signed after 1919 for India or for the Government of India specifically; and

(b) treaties concluded before or after that date in the name of the Crown, or of the Government of the United Kingdom (or even of the East India Company).

There is no doubt of the continuing validity of those in class (a) or of those parts of treaties in class (b) which relate to boundary definition. But treaties or engagements, or parts thereof, with, e.g., Afghanistan, Nepal and Tibet, which provide for consular rights exercisable in or by India, or for rights which may be grouped roughly under the commercial and economic headings, need to be tied up. For immediate purposes it would seem necessary to suggest a clause in the United Kingdom-India treaty providing that the Indian Government will regard itself as succeeding to the rights and privileges of all applicable treaties, that is to say, those of territorial and local application, with neighbouring independent States.

Regarding Indians overseas, (1) the main subjects are emigration of Indians to Empire countries and the welfare of Indians settled in those countries. It may be argued that His Majesty's Government has assumed certain responsibilities *vis-a-vis* India and Indians which should be set down in a treaty. When the emigration of indentured labour was permitted by the Government of India at the instance of His Majesty's Government, it was understood that at the end of the period of indenture the immigrants would be allowed to settle down in the country of immigration and would be accorded equality of treatment as British citizens. It should now be possible to hold His Majesty's Government to its responsibility to ensure equality of treatment for Indians settled in other parts of the British Empire, at any rate so far as those countries (colonies and mandated territories) which still continue to be under their control are concerned.

The only Dominion to which indentured labour was sent is South Africa. In respect of this part of the Empire it may not be possible to hold His Majesty's Government to any responsibility. But it may be considered whether His Majesty's Government can be got to bind itself by treaty to assume at least a neutral attitude in cases of dispute between India and South Africa on the question of Indians who have emigrated there. In the case of Ceylon, Malaya, East Africa, West Indies, Fiji, etc., His Majesty's Government should be asked specifically to bind itself to do all it can to secure equality of citizenship to Indians in those countries so long as they continue to be under the control of His Majesty's Government and are not granted self-government.

(2) If India is granting to U. K. nationals any privileges regarding entry or residence or trading or holding of office in India, a provision that similar privileges will be granted to Indian nationals in the U. K. and in countries which are under the administration of the British Government on a reciprocal basis may be included.

(3) If the British Government is given the right of appointing a representative like High Commissioner or Agent or Trade Commissioner in India, a similar right should be reserved for India to appoint similar officers, both in the U. K. and in territories directly administered by the British Government like colonies, mandated territories, etc.

C—FINANCIAL OBLIGATIONS BETWEEN THE U. K. AND INDIA

Any revision of the existing arrangements regarding the sharing of expenditure between India and the U.K. in respect of Persia and the Persian Gulf, etc., it was suggested, might suitably be included in a separate agreement.* In fact, it might be desirable to regulate the matter by convention and agreement from time to time rather than by rigid provision in the treaty or a supplementary agreement. The possibilities are that India will have to shoulder larger expenditure on her own representation than at present.

Here, again, the Iraq precedent should be followed, *i.e.*, the main treaty itself should not be burdened with these details; but provision should be made in the notes to be exchanged with the treaty that the contracting parties agree that all outstanding financial questions should form the subject of a

---

* *Cf.* para 2 of the summary of notes exchanged in the treaty between Iran and the U.K.

separate agreement, to be concluded as soon as possible and to form an integral part of the main treaty.

So far as the financial implications of the protection of the Services are concerned, the broad details to be provided for in the agreement would be the following:

(*a*) *Matters in which the U.K. is interested:*

(1) The redemption of any sterling loans together with their interest charges; (2) pensions, including family pension and provident funds, both current and prospective, of officers payable in (i) sterling, (ii) rupees; (3) compensation payable to such protected personnel as might like to retire voluntarily, or may be compelled to retire as a result of the new constitutional arrangements.

(*b*) *Matters which interest India:*

These will chiefly relate to the sterling assets held by India, with particular reference to their liquidation and the value of the sterling itself during the currency of the sterling holdings. It is probable, however, that the question of sterling assets will have been settled before the new treaty comes to be signed, in which case there will be no necessity for any special provision in the treaty beyond making such reference as may be required for the due fulfilment of the agreement. As regards the value of sterling, it may be assumed that the entire international monetary arrangements will be governed by the Bretton Woods Agreement, and no specific provision would seem to be indicated in the proposed treaty beyond, possibly, a statement that the two countries will be bound by such agreement as had already been entered into mutually in this regard.

As regards the various obligations which interest the U.K., India's sterling obligations have now attenuated to something like ten million. So long as the existing obligations remain unliquidated, it will be necessary to guarantee their redemption and interest in the agreement to be made under the treaty.

As regards India's borrowing in the sterling market, this is an unlikely contingency for a considerable time. In any case, this will be a matter for negotiation as and when the necessity arises and will be governed by India's credit in the London market.

(c) *Pensions*: Sterling pensions may be divided into three classes:

(1) current pensions for retired personnel,

(2) pensions payable to persons on the termination of services voluntarily or compulsorily,

(3) pensions for those who elect to continue under the new dispensation after the control of the Secretary of State over the Services ceases.

If before the conclusion of the treaty, a decision is taken to implement the pensions remittance scheme now in cold storage, the problems as regards (1) above would have been solved, as the necessary capitalised value would have been paid to the U.K. in the form of sterling, although if the legal liability remains with India, a formal acceptance of the liability and an undertaking to honour it might be necessary. If, however, the scheme does not become operative, a suitable provision will have to be made in the agreement under the treaty.

As regards (2) above, if arrangements can be made for payment of the capitalised value, no provision would be necessary in the agreement under the treaty. Otherwise, suitable provision will have to be made.

As regards (3), the position is somewhat complicated. There will be two elements, the protected element till the date when the Secretary of State's control disappears from the constitutional picture, and an unprotected portion pertaining to service under a self-governing India. The latter will be purely contractual and no provision in the treaty or agreement would be necessary.

The payment in respect of the protected portion may be capitalised and dealt with in the general financial settlement or an appropriate obligation entered in the agreement under the treaty.   The precise treatment will depend upon the ultimate administrative decision taken.

There are some British personnel who are entitled to receive their pensions in rupees at a privileged rate. It is presumed that they are to be treated as " protected " officers. In their case, it may be worth while considering whether the liabilities in their regard should not be commuted in terms of sterling and dealt with either by a capital payment to the British Government or a provision in the agreement. The British Government will thereafter be responsible for payment if the officers choose to take pensions in rupees.

The only remaining point to be considered is the compensation payable to retiring or discharged protected personnel. Here, again, a lump payment will be made and suitable provision may have to be made in the agreement if the payment is not made before the treaty is concluded.

To conclude, the view expressed in general terms is that it may be found convenient to capitalise as many commitments as possible and make lump payments rather than cumber the agreement with obligations to meet a variety of claims in respect of protected Services and pensions.

D—RELATIONS WITH INDIAN STATES

(a) The first point concerns the continued payment, after the transfer of power to an autonomous Government of India, of what are known as political pensions.*

A succession government which inherits the assets of its predecessor presumably inherits also its liabilities. While

---

* Details of these pensions to which specific reference is made in section 145 of the Government of India Act, 1935, are contained in the departmental handbook *Details of the Appropriation* under "Payments to Crown representative" for 1945-46.

there is no reason to suppose that the new Government of India would decline to accept responsibility for continuing the payment of these historic pensions, it is for consideration whether an undertaking to this effect should be included in the proposed treaty between the United Kingdom and India, or whether other means could more appropriately be adopted to ensure the continued payment of the pensions.

The second point relates to States' rights in the territory now administered as part of British India. In a number of cases [vide Chapter IV of the Report of the Indian States Enquiry Committee (Financial) 1932] States ceded sovereignty over territory in return for specific promises of protection, or assigned territory in trust to ensure payment of the agencies required to give protection. It has now been accepted that when the Crown ceases to be in a position to fulfil its obligations of protection, paramountcy will lapse and the rights surrendered by the States to the paramount Power in return for protection will revert to the States. The States will thus be entitled to claim retrocession of territory ceded or assigned as the price of protection.

It is possible that in the interim period which must elapse before the new autonomous Government of India comes into being, some States will, in return for a promise of protection from the authorities who will form the new government, waive their claim to the retrocession of ceded territory. But there will inevitably be other cases in which negotiations will still be incomplete when the time for the transfer of authority arrives. The position, so viewed, is this: The British Government has received territory as consideration for a guarantee of protection. When it is no longer able to fulfil the obligation to protect, it is politically and legally bound to surrender the consideration which it received in return for the guarantee of protection. It may, in practice, prove impossible to give a State de facto possession of ceded territory which has for a century or more been administered as part of British India; but if such restoration is not made, the British Government will render itself liable to claims for compensation from the aggrieved State.

In the circumstances, the only solution seems to be that, when the time comes for sovereignty over British India to be transferred from the Crown to a succession government, the Act of Parliament or other instrument effecting the transfer should make it clear beyond the possibility of dispute that only those rights which vest in the Crown absolutely are transferred, thus saving to the States those rights over territory administered as part of British India which only vest in the Crown temporarily or conditionally. Alternatively, appropriate articles saving the States' rights might be included in the treaty between the United Kingdom and the new Government of India.

A tentative view in regard to these two points is that provision should be made in the treaty for continued payment of the political pensions, but that reservation of States' rights in territory administered as part of British India should be secured in the Act of Parliament or other instrument transferring sovereignty from the Crown to the new Government of India.

(b) The question whether any special provisions relating to finance would be required under this heading really depends upon the following factors:

(i) The arrangements to be made for the transfer of the existing relations of the Crown with Indian States to the Indian Union; (ii) the nature and extent of such transfer; (iii) the guarantees, if any, given by the Indian Union to the British Government in the treaty for the maintenance of such relations as the Indian Union may assume under the new constitution.

In dealing with these matters, it will be necessary to discuss the theoretical possibility of there being two classes of Indian States—

(i) States which will adhere to the Indian Union, and
(ii) non-adhering States.

According to the British Government's declaration of 1942
and subsequent pronouncements by the British Prime Minister
and the Secretary of State, the position seems to be that
whether or not an Indian State elects to adhere to the constitution, it will be necessary to negotiate a revision of its
treaty arrangements so far as this may be required in the
new constitution. Indian Princes have been assured that
the fulfilment of the fundamental obligations arising out of
their treaties and *sanads* remain an integral part of British
policy. Assurances have also been given that there would
be no denunciation of treaties under the Union, and that the
treaties of non-adhering States would not be revised without
their consent. Presumably, this can be taken to mean that
the Crown's obligations to States will continue, unless and
until they are replaced by relations forged between Indian
States and the Union which are acceptable to the Rulers. It
is, however, doubtful whether an Indian Union of the Dominion type can ever be established if an Indian State attempts
to stand out of the Union, of which it is geographically and
economically an integral part, and insists upon the maintenance of its existing treaty relations with the Crown. The
only States that could conceivably stand out would be those
outside the frontiers of the Union.

The relations of the Crown with Indian States are in fact
relations between British India and Indian States with which
they are interlaced and have so many matters of common
interest of everyday importance. It is inconceivable that
any authority extraneous to the Indian Union would be able
to implement the Crown's obligations to Indian States without such considerable detraction from the internal autonomy
of the Union as to make self-government a fiction. Professor Coupland has also stated in his *Future of India*
(Part III, *p.* 144) that " paramountcy and Dominion status

are manifestly incompatible ". It is not, therefore, relevant to discuss at this stage the problems that will arise in the event of non-adherence of any Indian State, *i.e.*, for the continuance of any provision, as in section 145 of the Government of India Act, for payments by the Indian Union to the Crown for the exercise of the relations of the Crown with Indian States.

As regards the adhering States, the rights and obligations of the Crown may be classified broadly under the following headings:

(1) The guarantee of the integrity of an Indian State.

(2) The protection of the State and the Ruler thereof against external aggression and internal uprisings.

(3) The rights of States in the economic and fiscal spheres in respect of the levying of sea customs, production and taxation of salt, rights to receive free grants of salt or cash compensations, postal rights, *e.g.*, free service stamps and free carriage of mails, customs immunities, right to issue currency notes, coinage rights, etc.

(4) The right of the Crown to receive certain payments from States, *e.g.*, cash contributions.

As regards (1), the matter is so fundamental that the Rulers would not be satisfied with anything less than a provision in the treaty guaranteeing the territorial integrity of individual States and making a provision for the just disposal of disputes by the Union relating to succession. No financial issues are involved here.

As regards (2), this is covered at present in a few cases by specific military guarantees of the Crown, *i.e.*, the obligation to maintain troops at the expense of the Crown (in practice the Central Government) in the States concerned; and in other cases it is only a general obligation to afford military protection against external aggression or internal uprisings. These are matters to be settled in the treaty of accession of the States to the Union and do not require any provision in the Union's treaty with the British Government other than a general provision as is referred to below.

The obligation of protection involves on the part of the Ruler the counter-obligation of good government and the right of the Crown to intervene in the affairs of any Ruler, for which purpose the machinery of the Political Department exists at present. If any authority extraneous to the Union is out of the question, the only safeguard for the subjects of Indian States against oppression will presumably be the introduction of responsible government in the States, which the Rulers are likely to prefer to intervention by a party government of the Indian Union. Presumably, this question will be settled in the course of negotiations. The question of provision in the treaty for the expenses of any external authority may, therefore, be left out for the present.

As regards the fiscal and economic rights and obligations of States, including treaty payments, here again the instruments of accession of the States will have to settle the matter in a manner acceptable to both parties. It is not relevant for the purposes of the treaty with the British Government to go into details of the nature of the settlement between individual States and the Indian Union.

The general conclusion would, therefore, appear to be that if arrangements acceptable to the Indian States be made for the transformation of the existing relations of the Crown with them into relations with the Indian Union and embodied in the relevant instruments of accession, the only provisions which would be necessary in the treaty between the British Government and the Union, besides the one providing for the agreement by the Union to maintain the territorial integrity and dynasties of States, will be in general terms stating that the rights and obligations of the Crown are transferred to the Indian Union and will be regulated in future in accordance with the terms of accession of the States to the Union.

E—MINORITY RIGHTS AND THE PROTECTION
OF THE SERVICES

(a) The draft declaration of 1942 contemplated a treaty which, among other things, would make provision " in accordance with the undertakings given by His Majesty's Government for the protection of racial and religious minorities ". Coupland had pointed out that for various reasons this part of the declaration should be considered (*The Future of India*, *pp.* 156, 163). Presumably, the treaty was intended to deal with matters external to the Union and the constitution with matters internal. On this view, it would be difficult to justify any provisions in the treaty relating to the protection of minorities, as this was a matter entirely internal to the Union.

(b) The protection by treaty should extend to all officers appointed by the Secretary of State, whether to a service or to a post under a province or any other authority.

It is also considered that the protection should be extended to all British subjects serving the Crown in India for the following reasons: (i) this is a treaty between two sovereign States and it is desirable to protect all the nationals of each, in so far as there may be grounds for presuming a possible case for protection; (ii) all Crown servants are at present protected by the Secretary of State through section 52 (c) of the Government of India Act, 1935 (Governor's special responsibilities).

TREATY OBLIGATIONS

Some legal authorities in Britain examined in detail two questions:

(1) To what extent treaty obligations towards foreign States entered into by the East India Company, the Crown, the Government of the United Kingdom and the Governor-General of India-in-Council and how those observed by India will devolve upon a future Indian Government which succeeds, by regular constitutional means, to the powers

now exercised in relation to Indian external affairs by the existing authorities;

(2) whether any and, if so, what action should be taken with regard to this matter.

From a legal point of view the question belongs to the sphere of State succession in the matter of treaties. Further, seeing that distinctions have to be made according to the different circumstances in which the State succession arises, it belongs in essence to the class of cases where a real union (such as Norway and Sweden, Denmark and Iceland, and Colombia which became New Granada, Venezuela and Ecuador) is split up into separate States as opposed to cases where one State conquers another and absorbs it; or there is a cession of part of the territory of one State to another as the result of war. Since even within this class distinctions are made, it is relevant to point out that the case in question is one where the division is made peacefully, as in the case of Norway-Sweden and Denmark-Iceland, and with the full consent of both parties, as opposed to cases where the division is made forcibly by a successful revolt of part of a territory and against the will of the original State and per-haps remains unrecognised by that State *de jure* for a number of years after it has taken place. Finally, this is a case where it can be said that the identity of the original State remains (*i.e.*, the United Kingdom) and not a case where it can be said that, as a result of the decision, the original State really disappeared (as for instance in the case of Austria-Hungary).

Though we are only considering the question in 1946, from the point of view of international law, the division really took place in 1919. In 1919-20, as a result of the manner in which the Treaty of Versailles was signed and of the admission of India as an original member of the League of Nations, India became, from the point of view of international law, a separate international person on the same footing as Canada and the other Dominions. It is quite true that from the internal and constitutional aspect India was not fully self-governing and that the Government of the United Kingdom was able to control the action of India in the matter of foreign affairs. This does not, however, alter the position from the point of view of international law, and it may be said at once that there are other instances outside the British Empire of what may be considered to be the same anomaly.

Thus, the Sultan of Morocco is an international person concluding treaties which are binding on Morocco, although in fact he is entirely controlled by the French. Similarly, for a period, Egypt was an international person also concluding treaties and so forth, when in fact the Egyptian Government was controlled in foreign affairs by His Majesty's Government. On the other hand, Southern Rhodesia and Newfoundland have never had any international status at all or any power to conclude treaties, although they are, or were, fully self-governing. In other words, complete political independence and status as members of the family of nations are not two things which always go together.

The question only arises in a practical form as regards India now, because from 1919 up to the present time the United Kingdom has been able to control the foreign relations of India and, therefore, to ensure that all these treaties were observed in India. From the point of view of international law, however, the fact that during this period of 25 years, since India became a separate member of the family of nations, all these treaties have continued to be observed and treated by India as being binding, naturally makes it all the more difficult, if there were otherwise any possibility of doing so, of denying their continued applicability to India merely because of a change in the internal constitutional position which has no effect on India's already separate international status. In other words, the problem that we are considering now in relation to India is the same problem which arose in the case of the Dominions in the years 1919-20. It is probable that Canada and South Africa form the closest analogy to the present case, just because there was a number of treaties made by the Crown or by the Government of the United Kingdom regulating matters between Canada and the United States, and some treaties regulating local matters between South Africa and the neighbouring Portuguese colonies.

It follows from the above that a clear distinction can be drawn in the first place between (A) treaties signed after 1919 "for India" or for the Government of India specifically, and (B) treaties concluded before or after * this date simply in the name of the Crown or in the name of the Government of the United Kingdom (or in the name of the East India Company, the Government of the United Kingdom or the Crown having admitted their inheritance from the Company). In the case of treaties in the first class, no possible question can arise. They were specifically concluded for India as a separate international person and must, on any possible view, continue to be binding on India. International engagements in this category include (a) obligations accepted by India as a member of the League of Nations; (b) provisions of various bilateral and multilateral treaties and conventions to which India is a party; and (c) commercial and similar treaties concluded by the United Kingdom with foreign countries to which India was a separate signatory or to which she has subsequently acceded. In this category are of course included the San Francisco Charter, the Chicago Air Agreements and the Bretton Woods Agreements as well as instruments (such as the Ottawa Trade Agreements) concluded between the component States of the British Commonwealth which have never been regarded by the United Kingdom Government as international treaties registrable

---

* It was probably an error (it was in any case anomalous) that after 1919 treaties should have been made applying to India which were not made specifically for India, but it is clear that this in fact was done once or twice.

with the League of Nations or the United Nations Organisation.

Thus it may be said that, apart from the security provisions of the San Francisco Charter, this category of obligations relates, broadly speaking, to matters falling within the economic and social, rather than the political, field of international relations. It is perfectly irrelevant from the point of view of international law that India may have been under the control of foreign affairs of the United Kingdom at the time and that the full powers for signature or instruments of ratification may have issued on the advice of the Secretary of State for India.

It is, therefore, in regard to treaties in category *B* only that any question can arise. It may be repeated here that the observation already made earlier that from the point of view of international law, even if there were any of them which India could otherwise say were no longer binding on her, it would be more difficult for her to do so when in fact they have continued to be observed 25 years after India achieved her international status. It may be desirable, however, to consider the legal position as it would be apart from this fact. Authority is to be found in the books and in the recorded practice in States in parallel situations. Annexe I contains information about the practice followed in regard to the Dominions in 1919-20. Annexe II contains some references to the authors and short statements of their opinions, and Annexe III some information as to the practice followed in cases where foreign States were concerned and where the circumstances are as near as possible analogous.

The deductions which I draw from this review by the various authorities in India and Britain are as follow:

(*a*) There is a certain class of treaties which always pass to the successor, whatever the circumstances which give rise to the succession may be. The class is described by Oppenheim as "such international rights and duties as are locally connected with the part of the territory" and fiscal obligations connected with that territory. The expression "locally connected" is not very precise and it is clear that some authors interpret it more widely than others. Undoubtedly, all arrangements connected with boundaries and with the regime of rivers are included, but some authors bring within this class treaty rights for foreign nationals to enjoy a certain treatment in the territory.

(b) The class of treaties which pass to the new State is wider where the division takes place as the result of a friendly arrangement and by constitutional means than it is where the separation is the result of war or successful revolt.

(c) The practice in the case of the creation of the Dominions as separate international persons and in the case of separations such as Norway-Sweden or Denmark-Iceland, was that the continued application of virtually all treaties was accepted, except, of course, those of a general political character which could not be said to have any particular territorial or local application. Similarly, in the case of the separation of the old Republic of Colombia into what is now Colombia, Venezuela and Ecuador, His Majesty's Government maintained that their commercial treaty rights could be invoked against all the three new republics and this claim seems to have been admitted.

(d) There is considerable precedent for regulating the position as regards the succession to treaties by express steps taken at the time to avoid doubts and disputes, as in the case of Norway and Sweden, Denmark and Iceland.

(e) If it is not clearly agreed by both parties to the division (in this case India and the United Kingdom, or in 1919 the Dominions and the United Kingdom) that all applicable treaties, i.e., all those which have any territorial or local application) will be observed, the United Kingdom will be in danger of receiving claims and complaints from foreign States which it would not be in a position to satisfy. The Crown as represented by the Government of the United Kingdom would be in a position of having accepted obligations which could only be fulfilled in India and then at the time when, by the action of the United Kingdom itself, India became free to pursue its own way in international affairs, of having failed to take those steps that were necessary, either to secure the agreement of the foreign country in question to the annulment of the obligation, or its continued observance by the now wholly independent India. The point is put concisely by Keith in his *Theory of State Succession* on *p.* 23, when discussing a hypothetical cession of Newfoundland by the United Kingdom to the United States of America. Keith, while disputing the contention of other authors that the United Kingdom's treaty obligation towards France in respect of Newfoundland would necessarily and automatically pass to the United States (Keith may not be right about this, but he represents, so to speak, the low water-mark in his views about the obligations which pass), goes on to say, " politically and legally Great Britain was bound either to satisfy France's claim in Newfoundland or, if not, only to cede Newfoundland to the United States of America subject to the French rights ".

Unless, therefore, His Majesty's Government can feel certain that the future Government of India will accept and observe without question all those treaties concluded in the name of the Crown or the Government of the United Kingdom (including those of the East India Company) which can only be fulfilled in India or only wholly fulfilled if India observes them (as the Dominions did in 1919), it is clear that His Majesty's Government would do well, in order to guard themselves against legitimate claims from foreign States, to come to some specific agreement on this subject with whatever Indian provisional government a treaty may be made for the future of India. Such a treaty should contain provisions to the effect that this agreement shall be accepted in some binding form by the future fully constitutional Indian Government.

In this connection, attention may be called in particular to certain treaties which may be considered to be important illustrations of category *B*. The first is the treaty between " the British Government and the Government of Afghanistan signed in November 1921 and ratified in February 1922". It is a good example because it contains so many diverse provisions. Thus, article 1 is merely a mutual recognition of internal and external independence. Article 2 reaffirms a frontier agreement with small modifications and at the same time gives a right to Afghanistan to draw water from the British side of the boundary; this is a provision which must pass to India in any possible circumstance. Article 3 deals with the exchange of diplomatic representatives and can be observed between the United Kingdom and Afghanistan without reference to India at all. On the other hand, article 4 provides for the establishment of Afghan consulates in India. Article 5 deals with the treatment of diplomatic and consular representatives and, therefore, is one which can only be fully fulfilled both in the United Kingdom and in India. Article 6 deals with the import of goods into Afghanistan through India; article 7 with the question of customs duties to be levied in British Indian ports on goods for Afghanistan; article 8 with the establishment of Afghan trade agents in three towns in India; and article 9 with goods imported into Afghanistan through India. The treaty ends with a clause providing that it can be denounced at twelve months' notice, so that any difficulties arising out of this particular treaty could be got rid of by denunciation. However, not all the obligations in category *B* are thus terminable, and in any case the denunciation of such a treaty with Afghanistan would require careful consideration from the political point of view.

There is also a convention between Great Britain and Tibet of 1914 which, amongst other things, continues as binding a series of other previous agreements which are inserted in a schedule and is followed by Anglo-Tibetan agreed trade regulations of the same date. While the effect of these agreements is too complicated to summarise here, it seems to be evident that the possibilities of political difficulties and complications are considerable, if it is not clear that the future Government of India will also observe and recognise these arrangements. There is also an agreement of 1923 between Great Britain and Nepal providing for, among other things, freedom for the Nepal Government to import arms and munitions from or through British India into Nepal.

The conclusions, therefore, are—

(1) that there should be no doubt as regards the treaties in category *A*. If they were the only category of treaties in question, there should be no need for any action;

(2) that diplomatic claims and political difficulties of a grave character will be likely to arise, placing His Majesty's Government in the United Kingdom in a most difficult position if the continued observance by India of the treaties in category *B* is not made perfectly plain so that any foreign governments interested can be informed officially of the fact;

(3) that if His Majesty's Goverment could be sure that the future Indian Constitutional Government would adopt consistently the same view that the governments of the Dominions did in 1919, matters might be left on the basis of some agreed assurance. But in the case of a future Indian Government it seems questionable whether it is prudent to leave the matter on such an informal basis. One could imagine, for instance, that the future Indian Government might possibly be activated by a wish to assert its new independence by stressing its freedom from everything the Government of the United Kingdom had done

for it in the international sphere before. In this case, arguments based on the international law with regard to State succession or the practice might not be sufficient. In any case, it must be admitted that this branch of international law is by no means one of the clearest;

(4) that, consequently, there are probably good reasons for dealing with this matter of treaties in the manner indicated above and having a schedule specifying precisely those treaties which India will continue to observe and the binding precedents for drawing up this scheme should be the practice followed by the Dominions after 1919 and by Norway-Sweden and Denmark-Iceland.

ANNEXE I

In the case of the Dominions (other than the Irish Free State) there seem to have been no precise arrangements. Both the United Kingdom and the Governments of the Dominions and foreign governments seem to have accepted without question the position that the Dominions inherited all treaty rights and obligations of every kind which had any possible local or territorial application to them. Not only were treaties which referred in terms to Canada and the other Dominions as the case might be held to pass, but the Dominions accepted the obligations and claimed the benefits of treaties, such as commercial treaties and the like, whose provisions applied territorially to the whole Empire and from which *all* British subjects benefited in foreign countries.* In

* In 1930 there was a question of a convention with the U.S.S.R. which was *inter alia* to specify what treaties concluded with the Czarist Government should continue and what should be regarded as abrogated. The United Kingdom Government had correspondence with the Dominion Governments on this matter, in which they pointed out that some of the treaties applied to the Dominions as being of Empire-wide application and gave the fur seals convention of 1911 as an example. His Majesty's Government asked the

other words, the only treaties which did not pass were
(a) treaties which, by their terms or by necessary implication,
were locally limited to the United Kingdom or some non-
Dominion territory, or (b) those of a general political character which had no local or territorial application at all. In
fact, some Dominions had in their constitutions already
provisions with regard to treaties concluded by the Crown
and considered these provisions applicable to the new
situation.*

2. In the case of the Irish Free State, however, the matter
was raised in a letter from the Colonial Office to the provisional Government of Ireland of 2nd May, 1922. It was
stated that " international conventions already in force will
continue to apply to the Irish Free State when it is established
unless or until they are modified. The necessary steps will
be taken at the instance of the Free State Government with
a view to putting the Free State in the same international
position as the other self-governing Dominions in accordance
with the treaty ". This letter was acknowledged without
comment.

3. In 1933, a question was asked in the Dail whether, in
respect of treaties between the Government of the late United
Kingdom of Great Britain and Ireland and of the United
States of America, the United States Government contended
that such treaties were, since 1922, no longer in force between
the United States and the Irish Free State. Mr. De Valera
replied that " the Government of the United States have
never contended that treaties referred to in the Deputy's
question are not in force between the Irish Free State and

Dominions if they agreed that their position should be placed on record as
being the same as that of the United Kingdom. Canada, Australia and New
Zealand agreed. The Union of South Africa did not agree, because it wished
to have no relations with the U.S.S.R. The Irish Free State did not agree
because it wished to conduct its own negotiations with the U.S.S.R., but *no*
Dominion Government questioned the continued application to them of the
treaties referred to.

* [Canada 132 British North America Act, 1867.]

the United States. Such treaties have been acted upon by the two countries as occasion has arisen ". He further said: " The present position of the Irish Free State with regard to treaties and conventions concluded between the late United Kingdom and other countries is based upon the general international practice in the matter when a new State is established. When a new State comes into existence, which formerly formed part of an older State, its acceptance or otherwise of the treaty relationships of the older State is a matter for the new State to determine by express declaration or by conduct (in the case of each individual treaty) as considerations of policy may require. The practice here has been to accept the position created by the commercial and administrative treaties and conventions of the late United Kingdom until such time as the individual treaties and conventions themselves are terminated or amended. Occasion has then been taken, where desirable, to conclude separate engagements with the States concerned."

In 1934, there was some semi-official correspondence between the Foreign Office and the Secretariat of the League of Nations as to the position of the Irish Free State in relation to League conventions which had been ratified in respect of the United Kingdom before the Irish Free State came into being. It appeared that in the early stages the Free State Government had taken the line that the Irish Free State was to be regarded as having ratified these conventions, but that in 1931, when the question came up on a particular convention, the representative at Geneva of the Irish Free State orally expressed the opinion that " the view of the Free State was that it was not bound by the treaties prior to the establishment of the Free State unless it, in some form or other, adopted them ".

Later in the same year, the Irish Free State definitely notified their accession to the white slave traffic convention of 1910 which had been ratified at the time by the United

Kingdom. It was considered, however, that it would be undesirable to arouse controversy with the Free State on this point and that no communication should be made to them on the subject. In any case, the action of the Irish Free State only had the effect of continuing the obligations in question, while putting the Irish Free State in the position of a separate independent contracting party.

ANNEXE II

In reviewing the works of the authors mentioned in the note below, it has been borne in mind that in the case of India we are not dealing with a cession of territory to another State, but with what may be considered either as the formation of a new State by dismemberment of the old or as the creation of two independent States from a pre-existing real union.

Many of the writers on international law do not discuss in detail either the different circumstances which may give rise to the problem of succession to treaty rights and obligations or the different types of treaties. The earlier authors reason from first principles and lean towards a theory of general succession. A few authors reject this theory and deny the existence of any rule of international law by which new States succeed to the treaty rights and obligations of the State out of which they have been created. The tendency of authors during the last 35 years has been to uphold the view that there is succession to certain types of treaties, to recognise the difficulty of clear definition of the types which pass, and to consider the problem objectively, emphasising the need for examining each case individually.

However, whatever general theory the various authors adopt, on closer examination their views do not differ as widely as their theories indicate. They all recognise, either expressly or by implication, that some treaty rights and obligations pass to the new States and some do not. On the one hand, are treaties such as those which define boundaries, river navigation and port rights and which may be considered as creating rights in the nature of property. On the other hand, are what may be called political treaties, such as those of guarantee or of alliance, which are only of significance so long as the old State remains and clearly could not apply to a new one. The difficulty arises in relation to those treaties which do not fall clearly into either of these two classes: this third class includes commercial, customs, extradition and other treaties of an administrative character.

It is in relation to these administrative treaties that opinions really differ. However, even in these cases, those authors who consider the problem agree (i) that, if the parent State does not lose its identity, it will continue to be bound by a treaty even after part of its territory has broken away and formed a new State; and (ii) that the new State will continue to be bound by the treaty if it accepts it either expressly or by acquiescence.

Bearing in mind all these considerations, it is not surprising that modern practice shows a strong tendency in favour of settling by international agreement any possible doubts as to which treaties do or do not pass to the new State.

I. *Writers who support the theory of general succession*—The following works support the theory of general succession to treaty rights and obligations:

(1) Kent: *International Law* (Abdy), 1866, *p.* 107.

(2) Halleck: *International Law*, Vol. I, 1878, *pp.* 76, 77.

(3) Phillimore: *International Law*, Vol. I, 1879, *paragraph* 137, *p.* 212.

(4) Calvo: *Le Droit International Theoretique et Pratique*, Vol. I, 1887, article 106, *p.* 262.

These authors use almost identical language and base their views upon short statements by Grotius and Story. A quotation from Abdy's Kent will serve as an example of the opinion of these authors. He says at *p.* 107: "But in the event of a State being divided into two or more independent sovereignties, the obligations which had accrued to the whole before the division are rateably binding on the two parts; for, as Story says, ' the division of an empire creates no forfeiture of previously vested rights of property '."

It may be observed that the statement is general in character and shows no close or careful consideration of the practical problems involved. Furthermore, the quotation from Story suggests that the analogy of rights attaching to property is really being applied.

II.   *Writers who hold that there is no State succession to treaty rights or obligations:*

(1) Pradier-Fodere: *Traite de Droit International Publique*, Vol. I, 1885, article 157, *p.* 275 and article 162, *p.* 278.

(2) Keith: *Theory of State Succession*, 1907, Chapters 4 and 12.

While Pradier-Fodere is quoted by Keith as denying succession in cases of a State becoming independent, he does discuss what he thinks ought to be done in various cases. Though he may not go so far as to say that there is any succession (by international law) to treaty rights and obligations in the absence of some special arrangement, his treatment is similar to that of authors who distinguish between different types of treaties.

Keith reviews most of the books written before 1907 and concludes that there is no succession to treaty rights and obligations. He says at *p.* 20: "On the other hand, Huber and everyone else have to admit that many treaties are in some way too personal to pass over and they must maintain the thesis of a general succession for the sake of the other treaties which do seem to persist, but whose persistence can easily be explained by the doctrine of tacit or informal renewal." The reference in this sentence to " tacit or informal renewal " is of course of considerable significance in view of the position of India with regard to treaties since 1919, and Keith makes great use of this idea to square his theory with international practice. Further, all these writers to a greater or lesser degree admit that there is a class of treaty which passes with the land, *e.g.*, boundary treaties.

III. *Writers who distinguish between different types of treaties:*

(1) Huber: *Staaten Succession*, quoted by Keith at *p.* 17.

(2) Vattell: *Le Droit des Gens*, 1863, Vol. II, Ch. 12, articles 183-197.

(3) Rivier: *Principe du Droit des Gens*, 1896, *pp.* 70 and 141.

(4) Westlake: *International Law*, 1900, Part I, *pp.* 60-63 and 84.

(5) Wheaton: *International Law*, 1916, *p.* 45.

(6) Hyde: *International Law*, 1922, Vol. II, *p.* 86.

(7) Hall: *International Law*, 1924, *p.* 114 *et seq.*

(8) Smith: *Great Britain and the Law of Nations*, 1932, Vol. 1, Ch. V, Secs. 4 and 5.

(9) Oppenheim: (edited by Lauterpacht) *International Law*, 1937, Vol. I, *p.* 153, 154.

(10) McNair: *The Law of Treaties*, 1938, *p.* 412 *et seq.*

Vattell and Wheaton distinguish between real and personal treaties but do not really discuss succession in the type of cases which we are now considering.

Vattell's distinction also is a curious one, being between treaties which are personal to the Rulers and all other treaties.

According to Rivier, agreements conferring private rights and those conferring public rights which have real character will be effective after separation, but other treaties will come to an end.

Huber distinguishes between personal and territorial treaties. He explains that the personal element consists in the fact that the exercise of the power in the territory belongs to a certain State. On the other hand, treaties that have their effect at once produce real rights and remain as objects of succession: such treaties include those regulating boundary relations, streams, river navigation, railway conventions and, perhaps, such treaties as concern classes of person, *e.g.*, free exercise of religion, use of schools, hospitals, etc., which are mainly local in character. (See Keith, *p.* 17).

Westlake's view is that there is no succession except in the case of transitory or "dispositive" treaties; that is, those which dispose of or create rights in the nature of property and servitudes or easements.

The more modern books make the test of succession whether or not the treaties are locally connected to the territory of the new State. Thus Hyde says: "When a new State is formed out of the territory formerly belonging to another, as Panama or the Republic of Texas, or when a State comes into being as the result of separation from another, as in the case of Sweden and Norway, the treaties of the old State are regarded as still binding upon the new one, at least in so far as they relate to matters of peculiarly local concern".*

Hall considers the question carefully and says (*pp.* 114, 115):

"The fact of the personality of a State is the key to the answer. With rights which have been acquired and obligations which have been contracted by the old State as personal rights and obligations, the new State has nothing to do. On the other hand, rights possessed in respect of the lost territory, including rights under treaties relating to cessions of territory and demarcations of boundary, obligations contracted with reference to it alone, and property which is within it and has, therefore, a local character, or which, though not within it, belongs to State institutions localised there, transfer themselves to the new State person. Conversely, of course, the old State person remains in sole enjoyment of its separate territory, and of all local rights connected with it.

"Thus treaties of alliance, of guarantee, or of commerce are not binding upon a new State formed by separation, and

---

* See Hackworth's *Digest of International Law*, Vol. V, *p.* 360.

it is not liable for the general debt of the parent State; but it has the advantages of privileges secured by treaty to its people as inhabitants of its territory or part of it, such as the right of navigating a river running through other countries upwards or downwards from its own frontier; it is saddled with local obligations, such as that to regulate the channel of a river, or to levy no more than certain dues along its course; and local debts, whether they be debts contracted for local objects, or debts secured upon local revenues, are binding upon it. If debts are secured upon special revenues derived from both sections of the old State—if, for example, they are secured upon the customs or excise—they are evidently local to the extent that the hypothecated revenues are supplied by the two sections respectively; they must, therefore, be proportionately divided. Property which becomes transferred by the fact of separation consists in domains, public buildings, museums and art collections, communal lands, charitable and other endowments connected with the State and the like. When a portion of the lands belonging to a commune or to an endowment lies without the boundary of the new State, it is only considered that a right to the value of the property is transferred. Convenience may dictate expropriation from the property itself, and it is only then necessary to pay its full value by way of compensation."

Perhaps the most concise and most convenient statement of the "locally connected" theory is that given by Oppenheim. The treatment of the subject by Smith and McNair is objective. It points to the difficulty of applying general principles to particular cases and different types of treaties and leads to the conclusion that where possible the effect on treaty obligations of the separation of a State into two or more independent States is a matter that, according to modern practice, should be settled by international agreement.

McNair, in his book on treaties, quotes opinions in certain cases. He mentions the separation of Colombia in 1829-31 into three new States of New Granada, Venezuela and Ecuador.

The King's Advocate, advising on the effect of this separation on a treaty between His Majesty's Government and Colombia governing diplomatic relations, said that so far as it related to anything which was stipulated to be done under the treaty and which had not been done or any obligations contracted during the union, the new States remained bound by it, but that the treaty as such would not be binding after separation.

He advised that the treaty of commerce of 1825 with Colombia was still binding upon each of the new States so as to entitle His Majesty's Government to require its observance as to subjects of His Majesty's Government resident in any part of the territories which had constituted the Republic of Colombia.

On the other hand, he advised that Venezuela would be entitled to the navigation privilege under the treaty of 1825 only, " provided that either by a new treaty or convention, or by some solemn act, accepted by this country (*i.e.* Great Britain), she shall declare that she adopts as binding upon her the stipulation of the treaty of 1825 ".

In 1834, Great Britain and Venezuela made a treaty to "adopt and confirm " the treaty of commerce of 1825. In 1851, the Anglo-Ecuadorian treaty of friendship, commerce and navigation recited the desire to maintain the relations of amity, commerce and navigation which had "subsisted up to the present time between them " and was stated to "replace." the treaty of 1825.

When Brazil was separated from Portugal but remained under the same personal sovereign, the King's Advocate advised that *prima facie* Brazil would be " subject to, and entitled to the benefit of, former treaties in all things not otherwise regulated by stipulation or mutual declaration, or not essentially distinguishable from the nature of the subject ".

However, he added that the principle was of great nicety and might involve questions of considerable difficulty in its operation. He again emphasised this difficulty of application in a further opinion on a treaty of guarantee of 1813 between Portugal and Algiers. In this case he advised that the treaty was framed with special reference to Portugal proper and, therefore, did not extend to Brazil after the severance.

At *p*. 427, McNair says: " It appears to be the view of the U. K. Government (and also of Austria and Hungary themselves) that, apart from any provision to the contrary in the peace treaties or in other treaties, they are respectively the direct successors of the Austro-Hungarian Empire and are entitled to the benefit, and subject to the liabilities, of the treaties to which it was a party, and both Austria and Hungary have made declarations to this effect."

ANNEXE III

Norway and Sweden—After the dissolution in 1905, the position as regards treaties between the U. K. and the united monarchy was regularised by exchanges of notes with both countries. [For the texts, see State papers, Vol. 98, *pp*. 833-836.] (It may be assumed that Norway and Sweden addressed similar notes to other countries with which they were in treaty relations.) By the notes exchanged between the U. K. and Norway and Sweden, treaties concluded in common by Norway and Sweden were to be considered as valid by each government separately until further notice. However, it was stated that the dissolution gave His Majesty's Government the right to examine, *de novo*, the treaty engagements by which Great Britain was bound to the dual monarchy. In 1907, in a letter to the French Ambassador in London, the British Secretary of State for Foreign Affairs expressed the view that

28

a treaty of 1855 with the "King of Sweden and of Norway", by which Her Britannic Majesty and His Majesty the then Emperor of the French made certain promises of armed assistance, automatically lapsed on the dissolution of the Union.

Austria-Hungary—After the break-up of the Empire in 1918, matters were settled as far as Austria and Hungary were concerned (without their having much choice in the matter) by the relevant peace treaties.

[Saint-Germain: Articles 234-247 (with article 241 dealing with bilateral treaties between Austria and the other signatories). Trianon: Articles 217-224 (article 224 dealt with bilaterals).]

Finland and Russia—The question whether India's treaties with Russia continued in force between the U. K. and Finland after the establishment of the latter's independence was examined in 1920. The Foreign Office consulted the Board of Trade, who expressed no views on the legal aspect, but considered it desirable to arrive at some understanding with Finland, based on a recognition of the existing treaties with Russia, pending the preparation of new instruments.

For a number of reasons His Majesty's Government did not wish all the instruments to remain in force (and was getting on with the negotiation of new ones, *e.g.*, extradition) and the Government of India advised His Majesty's Minister at Helsingfors in December 1920 that "in the case of a new State being formed out of part of an old State, there is no succession by the new State to the treaties of the old one, though the obligations of the old State in relation to such matters as navigation, which are in the nature of servitudes, would normally pass to the new State. Consequently, there are no treaties in existence between Finland and this country".

Sweden and Finland arranged, by an exchange of notes in November 1919, for the continued validity of certain named instruments pending their replacement.

Iceland and Denmark—The case of Iceland/Denmark is most analogous to that of India/U. K. since before the dissolution of the Union there was a separate Icelandic Government. The Icelandic Government agreed to the continued validity, pending their revision, of the instruments in force at the time of the dissolution of the Union. The line which His Majesty's Government took then was not the same as in the case of Finland in 1920, but was based on the Norway/Sweden precedent of 1905; in any case, the circumstances were somewhat different as Iceland under the union with Denmark was a free and sovereign State—which was not the case of Finland under Russia—and the Act of Union provided for application to Iceland of Denmark's treaties prior to the union and arranged for their application, with Icelandic consent, after the union.

The relations between free India and the Princely States are another problem of great importance and complexity.

It has been suggested that this should be one of the matters to be dealt with in the proposed treaty between the United Kingdom and India. Professor Coupland * prefers that any guarantees required in this connection should be embodied in the constitution itself as the law of the land, rather than in any treaty. Whether they are ultimately to be embodied in the treaty or in the constitution, we have now to consider the question what the provisions themselves should be.

For our purposes it may be postulated that there should be established as soon as possible an Indian Union with the full status and powers of a Dominion and consisting, initially, of some or all of the existing British Indian provinces; but that the Indian States, or at least some of them, will initially stand out of the Union. The subject to be discussed is the relations of these Indian States *vis-a-vis* the proposed Indian Dominion.

---

* *The Future of India, p.* 152.

Under the 1935 constitution the relations of the Indian States are with the Crown, discharging its functions in this behalf (which may for brevity be referred to as the " paramountcy functions ") through the Crown representative and his officers of the Political Department. The office of the Crown representative is at present distinct from that of the Governor-General, although both offices are held by the same person. In abstract theory it will be possible to maintain the same position under the proposed Dominion constitution; that is to say, it will be theoretically possible to vest the paramountcy functions in an authority distinct from the head of the Dominion; but there will be formidable and indeed insuperable difficulties in practice. For example, if this external authority, whom we may continue to call the Crown representative, desired to implement certain paramountcy obligations, he would find himself without the means of doing so except with the co-operation of the Dominion government, a co-operation which is not likely to be forthcoming if the Dominion is kept out of the paramountcy field. Thus, if the Crown representative required troops to be sent to a particular State to quell disorder, the Dominion might refuse to supply him with the necessary troops; and even if he were, in some way, furnished with troops of his own, the Dominion might refuse the use of its railways or other means of transport for the movement of the troops to the required place.

Again, there may be a treaty obligation by which customs duties levied by the Dominion at British Indian ports on goods imported from a foreign country for consumption in a particular Indian State are to be credited to that State; if the Crown representative sought to enforce this obligation, the Dominion government might not agree. Similarly, there may be agreements in connection with railways or posts and telegraphs which the Crown representative will be unable to implement without the assistance of the Dominion government. Under the existing constitution the Crown representative is in a position to discharge his functions because (*a*) in several important matters the Central Government and the Central authorities are required by the constitution to obey the Crown representative's requisitions, and (*b*) both the Crown representative and the Central Government are at present subject to the control of the Secretary of State. For examples of (*a*) see section 145 of the Government of India Act of 1935, which requires the Federation to pay to His Majesty such sums as may be required by the Crown representative for the discharge of paramountcy functions; section 198 which requires the "Federal Railway Authority" to discharge such functions in relation to railways in an Indian State as the Crown representative may entrust to that authority; section 286 which requires the Governor-General to furnish such armed forces as the Crown representative may require for the discharge of his functions, and so on.

We cannot expect that provisions of this kind will find place in the Dominion constitution (for they will be serious subtractions from "Dominion powers"), nor will the Dominion authorities, under the proposed constitution, be subject to the control of the Secretary of State. It will, therefore, be impossible in practice to maintain the existing position and continue to keep all paramountcy functions outside the Dominion field. On the other hand, any transfer of the paramountcy functions to the Dominion without the consent of the Princes may be resisted by them on grounds familiar to most students of this subject—see, for example, paragraph 58 of the Report of the Indian States Committee, 1928-29 (the Butler Committee).

We have, therefore, to discover some way of reconciling this conflict. A *via media* that suggests itself may be detailed here.

The first step is to transfer all the paramountcy functions to the Dominion government, to be exercised, in the usual way, by the head of the Dominion government upon the advice of a responsible minister, who for brevity may be

referred to as the paramountcy minister. Whatever qualifications and safeguards may be suggested by way of softening
the blow, this step seems inevitable. As a necessary consequence of this step, the constitution will have to provide
that the rights and obligations of the Crown under the
treaties, agreements and *sanads* with Indian States (all of
which may conveniently be referred to as "treaties"), will
be the rights and obligations of the Dominion. There is,
constitutionally speaking, no difficulty or inappropriateness
in such a provision: for example, section 132 of the British
North America Act, 1867, which is the Constitution Act of
Canada, provides: "The Parliament and Government of
Canada shall have all powers necessary or proper for per-
forming the obligations of Canada or of any province thereof,
as part of the British Empire, towards foreign countries
arising under treaties between the Empire and such foreign
countries".

Even assuming that all the treaties with the Indian States
were on behalf of the Crown, there can be no objection to the
Crown discharging its obligations through one agent rather
than through another, so long as the obligations are discharged. In the well-known case *Williams v. Howarth*, [1905]
A. C. 551, the plaintiff claimed 10sh. a day as his pay on
a contract between him and the New South Wales Government, out of which he had received only 5sh. 6d. a day from
the colony and he accordingly brought an action for the
balance. It transpired that he had received the balance of
4sh. 6d. a day from the Imperial Government. It was held
in effect that both governments were agents of the Crown
and the Crown had satisfied its obligations through one or
the other of them. From the point of view of the Princes,
therefore, it is immaterial whether the treaty obligations are
carried out by the Crown through the Dominion government
or through a Crown representative distinct from the Dominion government.

From the point of view of the Dominion, too, there should be no objection to accepting the treaty obligations, just as Canada accepted them in the provision quoted above. In this connection, it is worth while noting that in clause 85 of the recommendations contained in the report of the All Parties' Conference, 1928 (often referred to as the Nehru Report) it was provided that the Commonwealth of India " shall exercise the same rights in relation to, and discharge the same obligations towards, Indian States arising out of treaties or otherwise, as the Government of India has hitherto exercised and discharged them ".

The Princes may not, however, agree to such a transfer as is proposed in the last preceding paragaraph owing to a fear of the unknown. By way of assuaging their fears the following safeguards may be granted to them:

(A) *A safeguard on the lines of that contained in the schedule to the South Africa Act of* 1909.

It may be observed, at the outset, that South Africa is a full-fledged Dominion and the schedule in question is, therefore, no subtraction from Dominion status. The schedule deals, *inter alia*, with certain arrangements for the government of any protectorate that may be transferred to the South African Dominion. Broadly speaking, it provides that the territory so transferred shall be administered by the Prime Minister, advised by a Commission of not less than three members. The Governor-General, of course, acts upon the advice of the Prime Minister but the Prime Minister is not bound by the advice of the Commission. Whether he accepts the advice of the Commission or not, he is bound in any matter, other than routine, relating to the administration of the territories to consult the Commission. If he does not accept the recommendation of the Commission, he has to place the case before the Governor-General-in-Council with the views of the Commission as well as his own, and then the

Governor-General-in-Council decides the matter; but even then the Commission can demand that the entire case should be laid before both Houses of the legislature. It may be possible to have a similar provision in India with respect to Indian States: the paramountcy functions will be exercised by the head of the Dominion on the advice of the paramountcy minister; but it may be provided that, in all except routine matters, the minister must consult a Commission of prescribed composition and in case of a difference of opinion it may be laid down that the case must be considered by the Dominion government as a whole, and possibly even reported to the legislature, if so required by the Commission. It will not be possible to carry this safeguard any further without subtracting from Dominion responsibility. The exact composition of such a Commission is a matter for discussion, if the principle is accepted.

(B) *A safeguard with regard to the interpretation of treaties.*

One of the complaints of the Princes even under the present constitution has been with regard to the interpretation of their treaties. They have represented from time to time that when there is a dispute as to the meaning of a treaty provision falling within certain categories, the Crown representative must, if so requested by a Ruler, refer the matter to arbitration. These representations have not so far been accepted, but we can go some way towards accepting them in connection with the establishment of the new Dominion.

Hitherto, the Crown, that is to say, the Crown representative, subject to the control of the Secretary of State, has been the final interpreter of the treaties with Indian States. The principles of interpretation are now fairly established. The text of the treaty has of course to be followed; but in addition to the text due regard has to be paid to usage and sufferance, changes of circumstance and the paramount interests of the subjects of the State and of India as a whole. So long as these principles (and any others that are at present being observed) are clearly laid down, their application to a particular case can safely be entrusted to judicial authority such as the Federal Court. Indeed, the Federal Court will be in a better position to give an opinion because it will have the advantage of hearing both sides. It is sometimes said that courts are not a proper tribunal for interpreting treaties, but courts do interpret them sometimes even now.

For example, in *Forester v. the Secretary of State* (L. R. Supplementary Volume I. A. 10) the Privy Council had to construe a treaty or agreement with Begum Summroo made in 1805 for the purpose of deciding whether she was a sovereign Princess or a mere tenure-holder. It was decided that she was a mere tenure-holder. Again, in the case of *Muhammad Yusuf-ud-din v. Queen Empress* (1897) 24 I. A. 137, the Privy Council had to construe an agreement contained in some correspondence between the British Government and the Nizam of Hyderabad. Perhaps the best example of a court interpreting a treaty, not merely in the light of the text of the treaty, but also of usage and of national interests, is furnished by the American case *Whitney v. Robertson* (1887) 124 U. S. 190. In this case the Supreme Court of the United States had to interpret a " most favoured nation clause " contained in a treaty between the United States and San Domingo. The court departed from the literal meaning of the clause, after considering a similar treaty made with Denmark and the injurious consequences upon the national interests of the United States that would result from a literal interpretation. In a recent English case *Stoek v. Public Trustee* (1921) 2 Ch. 67, the court did not hesitate to interpret certain provisions of the Treaty of Versailles in spite of a suggestion from the Solicitor-General that as the treaty was an international document, the interpretation should be left to the high contracting parties.

These examples might suffice to show that a court like the Federal Court would not be an inappropriate authority to advise the head of the Dominion government upon the interpretation of disputed treaty provisions. All that would be required for this purpose would be a provision, on the lines of section 213 of the present Government of India Act, enlarged so as to cover disputes relating to treaties with Indian States. Such a provision would not detract from Dominion status in the least, while at the same time it might go a long way towards reconciling the Princes to the new order. A similar provision occurs in clause 85 of the recommendations in the Nehru Report which has already been referred to. The provision runs as follows: " In case of any difference between the Commonwealth and any Indian State on any matter arising out of treaties, engagements, *sanads* or similar other documents, the Governor-General-in-Council may, with the consent of the State concerned, refer the said matter to the Supreme Court for its decision ". It will be noticed that this provision goes even further than has now been suggested, inasmuch as it vests the power of final decision in the Supreme Court, whereas what is now suggested is that the Federal Court should be asked for an advisory opinion.

29

THE CONSTITUTION OF BURMA

[In framing the constitution of independent Burma, Sri B. N. Rau played a significant part. General Aung San, the young and brilliant head of the post-war Burma Government, passed through New Delhi in the closing weeks of 1946 *on his way to London for a discussion of his country's future with the Labour Government. In New Delhi he showed a keen interest in the procedure and mechanism of the Indian Constituent Assembly and consulted Sri B. N. Rau on the practicability of setting up in Burma similar machinery for framing her constitution. Following the discussion, General Aung San appointed a Constitutional Adviser for Burma early in* 1947. *The latter visited New Delhi and had prolonged consultations with Sri B. N. Rau, as a result of which the first draft of the constitution was prepared and taken to Rangoon in May* 1947. *It was adopted by Burma's Constituent Assembly on the* 24th *September of that year—a most creditable achievement despite the severe shock to the administration in consequence of the assassination of General Aung San and some of his Cabinet colleagues in July* 1947. *The article reproduced below was originally written by Sri B. N. Rau for the* India Quarterly, *the journal of the Indian Council of World Affairs. It is included in this volume with the permission of the Council.]*

THE Constitution of Burma, which came into force on January 4, 1948, has many features of great interest to the constitution-maker. In form and content, in magnanimous treatment of special regions and racial groups, and in speed of enactment, it provides an example well worth our attention at the present time.

I had the honour of being associated closely with the framers of the constitution at almost every stage. The Constitutional Adviser of Burma came to Delhi in April 1947, for discussion and collection of material; a first draft of the new constitution was then prepared and he took it back with him to Rangoon in May. There it underwent certain modifications and its provisions, as so modified, were accepted in substance by the Constituent Assembly of Burma. A drafting committee was then appointed to give it final shape. The committee sat for about a fortnight in August and September. The Constituent Assembly passed it on September 24, 1947, with a provision that it would come into operation on such date as the provisional President might announce by proclamation. On December 10, 1947, the Parliament of the United Kingdom passed the Burma Independence Act, recognising Burma as an independent country with effect from January 4, 1948. Accordingly, this date was proclaimed for the commencement of the new constitution. Thus the whole process from start to finish, including the enactment of the constitution and of auxiliary legislation (such as the Burma Judiciary Act) by the Constituent Assembly and of the Independence statute by the British Parliament, occupied no more than about eight months, in spite of the interruption caused by the assassinations of July 1947.

The constitution is bilingual in form as required by section 217; that is to say, two copies of it have been made, one in Burmese and the other in English, both of them signed by the President of the Constituent Assembly and kept for record in the office of the Registrar of the Supreme Court. Both are said to be " conclusive evidence " of the provisions of the constitution, so that neither by itself is the authoritative version and each will have to be interpreted in the light of the other.

Let us proceed to glance briefly at the contents of the new constitution. The preamble runs:

> WE, THE PEOPLE OF BURMA including the Frontier Areas and the Karenni States, determined to establish in strength and unity a SOVEREIGN INDEPENDENT STATE, to maintain social order on the basis of the eternal principles of JUSTICE, LIBERTY AND EQUALITY and to guarantee and secure to all citizens JUSTICE, social, economic and political, LIBERTY of thought, expression, belief, faith, worship, vocation, association and action; EQUALITY of status, of opportunity and before the law, IN OUR CONSTITUENT ASSEMBLY this tenth day of Thadingyut waxing, 1309 B.E. (twenty-fourth day of September 1947 A.D.), DO HEREBY ADOPT, ENACT AND GIVE TO OURSELVES THIS CONSTITUTION.

The phrasing is taken from the Objectives resolution of the Indian Constituent Assembly passed in January 1947, while the final words are borrowed from the preamble to the Constitution of Ireland.

Chapter I relates to the form of the new constitution. Burma is described as a sovereign independent republic to be known as the Union of Burma, with sovereignty residing in the people. Symbolic of this Union is the national flag described in section 215: a rectangle of red with a canton of dark blue displaying a five-pointed large white star, with five smaller similar stars between the points. Each of the small stars represents a special region of the Union: there are five such regions, namely, the Shan State, the Kachin State, the Karenni State, the Chin Division, and the rest of Burma which forms the central region. The large star stands for the entire Union. The constitution contains special provisions for the administration of each of the peripheral regions as well as of the entire Union.

Chapter II deals with citizenship and fundamental rights. The citizenship provision is somewhat complicated, Burmese blood rather than birth on Burmese soil being the main test. As regards persons of non-Burmese blood, the conditions for citizenship are:

(1) they must have been born in territory which at the date of their birth was British;

(2) they must have resided in Union territory for a period of at least eight years in the ten years immediately preceding the commencement of the constitution, or immediately preceding January 1, 1942, this latter alternative being for the benefit of those who had to leave Burma during the Japanese occupation;

(3) they must intend to make Burma their permament abode;

(4) they must signify their election of Burma citizenship in the manner and within the time prescribed by law.

Most of the Indians now in Burma were either born in pre-partition India or in Burma and their position needs attention. If the place where they were born was at the time of their birth British territory, *e.g.*, Chittagong or Madras, but not Travancore or Mysore, the first of the above four conditions is satisfied; if they satisfy the other three conditions as well, one of them being that they must elect Burma citizenship within a prescribed time, then, and not otherwise, they become Burma citizens. If they do not elect to become Burma citizens, their nationality remains what it was. But if they do become Burma citizens, the position will be different. They will cease to be British subjects by virtue of section 13 of the British Nationality and Status of Aliens Act. And we may anticipate that they will not be eligible for initial citizenship of the new Indian Union either. For, under the draft Indian Constitution, a person who, before the date of commencement of the new Constitution of India, acquires the citizenship of a foreign State is not an Indian citizen; it follows that if he has elected Burma citizenship, he cannot be an Indian citizen at the inception of the Indian Union, although it may be possible for him to become one later by naturalisation. There is a demand among Indians in Burma that even if, for the time being, they elect to be Burma citizens, India should provide a specially easy mode of naturalisation for them, if owing to changed circumstances they find it necessary later to migrate back to India. This is a matter which the framers of the naturalisation law of India will have to bear in mind. Another matter worth notice concerns persons who, though born, say, in Chittagong (of parents and grandparents also born in the same place) and having their permanent abode in Burma at present, do not elect to become Burma citizens. What is their nationality? They will retain their status as British subjects; but, assuming that India and Pakistan remain within the British Commonwealth, will such persons, besides being British subjects, be citizens of India or of Pakistan, their birthplace being now in Pakistan? Under the draft Indian Constitution they can become citizens of India, provided they acquire a domicile in India before the commencement of the new constitution, the principle adopted being that, in order to qualify for citizenship of the Indian Union at its inception, a person must have some kind of territorial connection with the Union, whether by birth or descent or domicile. In the case put above, there is no such connection by birth or descent—the birthplace of the persons concerned and their parents and grandparents being in Pakistan territory—and, therefore, at least domicile in Indian territory must be established. For this purpose, the draft Indian Constitution provides special facilities in view of the existing difficulties. If the place of birth in the above case was, say, Madras instead of Chittagong and the persons concerned did not elect to become Burma citizens, they would, besides remaining British subjects, be citizens of India by birth.

The fundamental rights in the Burma Constitution follow closely, both in form and content, those recommended by the

Advisory Committee of the Indian Constituent Assembly: rights of equality, rights of freedom, rights relating to religion, cultural and educational rights, economic rights and rights to constitutional remedies. Occasionally the phrasing is more cautious than that of the corresponding recommendation of the Advisory Committee; for example, the right to personal liberty is put in the form: "No citizen shall be deprived of his personal liberty save in accordance with law". This follows the provision in the Irish Constitution. It is open to the criticism that it leaves the legislature free to make any law to curtail personal liberty. But we have to remember that Burma has a very difficult law-and-order situation to face and that conditions in the country, as evidenced by the assassinations of July 1947, are far from normal; they may have to be dealt with by exceptional measures; to fetter the discretion of the legislature in these circumstances may well have seemed to the framers of the constitution to be unwise.

Freedom of religion is circumscribed by the salutary warning, "The abuse of religion for political purposes is forbidden; and any act which is intended or is likely to promote feelings of hatred, enmity or discord between racial or religious communities or sects is contrary to this constitution and may be made punishable by law".

Among the economic rights guaranteed is that of private property, but it is subject to the following important limitations:

No person shall be permitted to use the right of private property to the detriment of the general public.

Private monopolist organisations, such as cartels, syndicates and trusts formed for the purpose of dictating prices or for monopolising the market or otherwise calculated to injure the interests of the national economy, are forbidden.

Private property may be limited or expropriated if the public interest so requires, but only in accordance with law which shall prescribe in which cases and to what extent the owner shall be compensated.

The right to move the Supreme Court by appropriate proceedings for the enforcement of any of the fundamental rights guaranteed by the constitution is also guaranteed, except in times of war or insurrection.

Chapter III deals with the relations of the State to peasants and workers and contains the interesting provision that the State is the ultimate owner of all land. There is nothing revolutionary in this doctrine, because even in England all land is ultimately held by the Crown. More striking is the provision: "There can be no large land holdings on any basis whatsoever. The maximum size of private land holding shall, as soon as circumstances permit, be determined by law".

Chapter IV contains certain directive principles of State policy which are recommended for the general guidance of the State, but are not enforceable in any court of law. They correspond to the instrument of instructions with which we are familiar in the Indian Constitution; only, instead of being addressed to the Governor-General or the Governor, they are addressed to all State authorities, legislative or executive. The directive principles embodied in the Burma Constitution are on the lines indicated in one of the pamphlets prepared for the Indian Constituent Assembly with certain significant additions. Among the main additions are the following:

The State shall ensure disabled ex-Servicemen a decent living and free occupational training. The children of fallen soldiers and children orphaned by war shall be under the special care of the State.

The economic life of the Union shall be planned with the aim of increasing the public wealth, of improving the material conditions of the people and raising their cultural level, of consolidating the independence of the Union and strengthening its defensive capacity.

The State shall direct its policy towards giving material assistance to economic organisations not working for private

29

profit. Preference shall be given to co-operative and similar economic organisations.

The State shall direct its policy towards operation of all public utility undertakings by itself or local bodies or by people's co-operative organisations.

The State shall direct its policy towards exploitation of all natural resources in the Union by itself or local bodies or by peoples' co-operative organisations.

Chapter V deals with the President's office. The head of the Union is the President, elected by both Chambers of Parliament in joint session by secret ballot. He holds office for five years and is eligible for re-election, but no person may be President for more than two terms in all. He must be a citizen of the Union, who was, or both of whose parents were, born in Union territory. He may be impeached for high treason, violation of the constitution, or gross misconduct. The charge is to be preferred by one of the two Chambers and investigated by the other; the resolution preferring the charge as well as the resolution declaring it proved requires a two-thirds majority; the latter resolution operates to remove the President from office.

The President is intended to be a constitutional head, acting for the most part on the advice of the Union Government, which consists of the Prime Minister and his colleagues. There are, however, certain exceptional matters in which the advice of the government is not required or is not sufficient. Among these exceptional matters are the following:

(1) The President has to appoint the Prime Minister on the nomination of the Chamber of Deputies.

(2) When the Prime Minister has ceased to retain the support of a majority in the Chamber of Deputies, the President may refuse to prorogue or dissolve the Chamber on his advice; but, in that event, he must forthwith call upon the Chamber to nominate a new Prime Minister and if the Chamber fails to do so within fifteen days, it must be dissolved.

(3) The President cannot declare war except with the assent of the Parliament; but the government may take preliminary steps for the protection of the Union, and the Parliament, if not sitting, must be summoned to meet at the earliest possible date.

(4) All the judges of the Supreme Court and the High Court have to be appointed by the President with the approval of both Chambers of Parliament in a joint sitting.

There is no Vice-President for the Union. Should the office of the President fall vacant, his functions are to be exercised by a Commission consisting of the Chief Justice of the Union, the Speaker of the Chamber of Nationalities and the Speaker of the Chamber of Deputies.

The legislative power of the Union is vested in the Union Parliament which consists of the President, the Chamber of Deputies (the Lower House), and the Chamber of Nationalities (the Upper House). Parliament must meet at least once in every year and at intervals of less than twelve months. There is an enabling provision for payment of members. Any property qualification for membership of Parliament or for the parliamentary franchise is prohibited; so, too, any disqualification on the ground of sex, race, or religion, except that members of any religious order may be debarred by law from standing for election or voting. Every citizen who has completed the age of twenty-one years and who is not placed under any disability or incapacity by the constitution or by law is eligible for membership of Parliament. Every citizen who has completed the age of eighteen years and who is not disqualified by law (e.g., on the ground of insolvency or unsoundness of mind or crime) has the right to vote at parliamentary elections. Voting is to be by secret ballot. Electoral districts are to be equal as far as possible; more precisely, " the ratio between the number of members to be elected at any time for a constituency and the population of that constituency as ascertained at the last preceding census shall, so far as practicable, be the same for all constituencies throughout the Union, except in the case of the constituencies of the special Division of the Chins and the Karenni State, in respect of which the ratio may be higher ". Polling at every general election must be on the same day throughout the Union.

The Chamber of Nationalities consists of 125 members and the Chamber of Deputies about twice that number. Representation to the Chamber of Deputies is on the basis of population. The population of Burma being about 17,000,000, a total membership of 250 would mean one member for every 68,000 of the population, which is about half-way between the maximum and minimum limits laid down in the constitution. The normal life of the legislature is four years, a dissolution of the Chamber of Deputies operating also as a dissolution of the Chamber of Nationalities. The composition of the Chamber of Nationalities is prescribed in a schedule to the constitution. Of the 125 seats in that Chamber, 25 are allotted to the Shan State, 12 to the Kachin State, eight to the special Division of the Chins, three to the Karenni State, 24 to the Karens, and the remaining 53 to the remaining territories of the Union. All the representatives from the Shan State in the Chamber of Nationalities are to be elected by the Saophas or Chiefs of the Shan State from among themselves: the Saophas are not eligible for membership in the Chamber of Deputies. There are similar provisions for the Karenni State.

Money Bills can be initiated only in the Chamber of Deputies. Every such Bill, after being passed by the Chamber of Deputies, is to be sent to the Chamber of Nationalities for its recommendations. If it is not returned by the Chamber of Nationalities to the Chamber of Deputies within 21 days, or is returned within that period with recommendations which the Chamber of Deputies does not accept, it is deemed to have been passed by both Chambers at the expiration of that period. Other Bills may be initiated in either Chamber; if one Chamber passes it and the other Chamber rejects or fails to pass it, or passes it with amendments to which the Chamber where the Bill originated will not agree, the President has to convene a joint sitting of the two Chambers, and if it is passed by a majority of the total number of members of both Chambers present and voting, it is deemed to have been passed by both Chambers.

Chapters VI and VII deal respectively with the Union Parliament and the Union Government. The Burma Constitution follows the Constitution of Ireland in seeking to reduce to statutory form the conventions of responsible government. The provision relating to the appointment of the Prime Minister has already been mentioned, as also one of the provisions relating to dissolution; the former certainly differs from the convention in England and so too, probably, the latter. The following provisions may also be noticed in this connection:

115. The government shall be collectively responsible to the Chamber of Deputies.

117. (1) The Prime Minister may resign from office at any time by placing his resignation in the hands of the President.

(2) Any other member of the government may resign by placing his resignation in the hands of the Prime Minister for submission to the President and the resignation shall take effect upon its being accepted by the President under the next succeeding sub-section.

(3) The President shall accept the resignation of a member of the government other than the Prime Minister, if so advised by the Prime Minister.

118. The Prime Minister may, at any time, for reasons which to him seem sufficient, request a member of the government to resign; should the member concerned fail to comply with the request, his appointment shall be terminated by the President if the Prime Minister so advises.

119. The Prime Minister shall resign from office upon his ceasing to retain the support of a majority in the Chamber of Deputies, unless on his advice the President dissolves the Parliament under section 57 and, on the re-assembly of the Parliament after the dissolution, the Prime Minister secures the support of a majority in the Chamber of Deputies.

120. (1) If the Prime Minister at any time resigns from office, the other members of the government shall be deemed also to have resigned from office, but the Prime Minister and the other members of the government shall continue to carry on their duties until their successors shall have been appointed.

The distribution of legislative power between the Union and the units is, subject to certain exceptions, on the Canadian model; that is to say, there are only two legislative lists, a Union list and a State list, any matter not enumerated in the latter being allocated to the former. Thus what is called the residuary power belongs to the Centre. Broadly speaking, the subjects which in the present Indian Constitution fall in the provincial legislative list fall under the Burma Constitution in the State list and the rest in the Union list. Any State Council (which is the name of the State legislature) may, by resolution, surrender any of its powers or territories to the Union.

Chapter IX deals with the States and other semi-autonomous areas. There are at present three States with special Councils for legislating on State subjects: the Shan State, the Kachin State and the Karenni State. For the rest of the Union, comprising by far the larger part of its area, the Union Parliament is the only legislature, whether the subject be in the Union list or not. It is as if the larger part of India, under the present constitution, consisted of Chief Commissioners' provinces, or as if the larger part of the United States of America consisted of "territories" instead of "States". Another noteworthy feature of the Burma Constitution is that each State Council consists entirely of the representatives of the particular State concerned in the Union

Parliament. In other words, what may be called the State Committee of the Union Parliament is the legislature of the State for purely State subjects. It will be remembered that in the British Parliament, Bills relating exclusively to Scotland are referred to a Grand Committee including all the Scots members; the Burma Constitution has adopted the same idea. And just as there is a Secretary of State for Scotland in the British Cabinet to deal with Scottish affairs, each of the above States in Burma has a special minister in the Union Cabinet to deal with the affairs of the State. Thus, section 160, which relates to the Shan State, provides:

> A member of the Union Government to be known as the Minister for the Shan State shall be appointed by the President on the nomination of the Prime Minister acting in consultation with the Shan State Council from among the members of the Parliament representing the Shan State.

The minister so appointed is also the executive head of the State. In other words, just as the representatives of the State in the Union Parliament constitute the legislature for the State, the minister for the State in the Union Cabinet is the executive head of the State in such matters. The head of the State is required to consult the State Council in all matters relating to the State and in order to facilitate this consultation, the State Council is required, at its first meeting after a general election, to elect from among its members or otherwise a Cabinet of State ministers to aid and advise the head of the State in the exercise of his powers.

Besides the State legislative list, the constitution contains a State revenue list, the object of which is to indicate what sources of revenue are to be allocated to the States. It may happen that although for purposes of legislation a subject falls in the Union list, the revenue arising from it must be allocated to the States, as in the case of forests. Besides the revenues allocated to the States, the Union may make grants

to the States out of its own revenues upon the recommendation of any board or other authority appointed for the
purpose.

In addition to the three States named above, there are
two special areas known respectively as the Kaw-thu-lay
Region and the Chin Division. Each of these areas, though
not a regular State with powers of legislation, has a considerable measure of regional autonomy. Thus, section
197 provides:

> 197. (1) A Chin Affairs Council shall be constituted con-
> sisting of all the members of the Parliament representing the
> Chins.
>
> (2) A member of the Union Government to be known
> as " the Minister for Chin Affairs " shall be appointed by the
> President on the nomination of the Prime Minister, acting in
> consultation with the Chin Affairs Council, from amongst the
> members of the Parliament representing the Chins.
>
> (3) Subject to the powers of the Union Government—
>
>> (i) the general administration of the Special Division,
>> and in particular all matters relating to recruit-
>> ment to the Civil Services in the Special Division,
>> to postings and transfers and to disciplinary
>> matters relating to these Services, and
>>
>> (ii) all matters relating to schools and cultural insti-
>> tutions in the Special Division,
>
> shall be under the superintendence, direction and control of
> the Minister for Chin Affairs.
>
> (4) The Chin Affairs Council shall aid and advise the
> minister in the discharge of his duties.
>
> (5) Any member of the Council who shall have ceased
> to be a member of the Parliament shall be deemed to have
> vacated his seat in the Council, but he may continue to carry
> on his duties until his successor shall have been elected.

One significant limitation on the autonomy, whether of
States or of the other special areas mentioned, is expressly
prescribed in the constitution:

No military, naval or air forces, or any military or semi-military organisation of any kind (not being a police force maintained under the authority of any unit solely for duties connected with the maintenance of public order) other than the forces raised and maintained by the Union with the consent of the Parliament shall be raised or maintained for any purpose whatsoever.

It is important to distinguish the Karenni State from the Karen State, of which one often reads in the daily press. The Karenni State consists of three small principalities which in the old days were non-British territory, rather like the smaller Indian States in India; these principalities now form a single State and a unit of the Burma Union. But the constitution also provides for the ultimate creation of a larger State to be known as the Karen State; this is to consist of the existing Karenni State and the special region of Kaw-thu-lay which was part of British Burma. This larger State is to be constituted if the majority of the people of these areas and of the Karens living in Burma outside these areas so desire. The demand for the larger State is, therefore, not to be regarded as an attempt to disrupt the Union; on the other hand, it is something which is recognised and provided for in the constitution itself.

The procedure for amendment of the constitution is laid down in Chapter XI. Every proposal for the amendment of the constitution has to be in the form of a Bill.

209. (1) Such Bill may be initiated in either Chamber of the Parliament.

   (2) After it has been passed by each of the Chambers of the Parliament, the Bill shall be considered by both Chambers in joint sitting.

   (3) The Bill shall be deemed to have been passed by both Chambers in joint sitting only when not less than two-thirds of the then members of both Chambers have voted in its favour.

(4) A Bill which seeks to amend—
   (*a*) the State legislative list in the third schedule, or
   (*b*) the State revenue list in the fourth schedule, or
   (*c*) an Act of the Parliament making a declaration under paragraph (iv) of sub-section (1) of section 74 removing the disqualification of any persons of membership of the Parliament as representative from any of the States shall not be deemed to have been passed at the joint sitting of the Chambers, unless a majority of the members present and voting, representing the State or each of the States concerned, as the case may be, have voted in its favour.

(5) A Bill which seeks to abridge any special rights conferred by this constitution on Karens or Chins shall not be deemed to have been passed by the Chambers in joint sitting, unless a majority of the members present and voting, representing the Karens or the Chins, as the case may be, have voted in its favour.

Thus the interests of the States and other special areas are sufficiently safeguarded.

The judiciary is dealt with in Chapter VIII of the constitution, which provides for a Supreme Court and a High Court. The Supreme Court is the court of final appeal and exercises appellate jurisdiction over the High Court and such other courts as the Union Parliament may by law prescribe. The High Court is the highest court of original jurisdiction, but may also exercise appellate jurisdiction over subordinate courts. The mode of appointment of judges has already been mentioned. Qualifications are prescribed in the constitution similar to those in the existing Indian Constitution. The age of retirement is not prescribed in the constitution, but has been left, along with other matters such as remuneration and pension, to be prescribed by a separate law to be made by the Parliament. A judge may be removed by the President for proved misbehaviour or incapacity, but only upon a resolution of both Chambers at a joint sitting after the charge has been investigated by a special tribunal of three members, including the Speakers of the two Chambers.

The Supreme Court has, in addition to its appellate jurisdiction, an advisory jurisdiction in respect of important questions of law referred to it by the President. The constitution specifically provides that while the High Court may sit in the capital city of the Union, one or more judges of the High Court must sit in such place in the Shan State as the President may, after consultation with the Chief Justice of the Union, from time to time appoint. Here, again, the solicitude of the framers of the constitution for the interests of the State is evident.

It will be noticed from what has been said that the relationship between the Union and the units in Burma is very close, closer than in Canada and much closer than in the U.S.A.; for, not only are the residuary powers vested in the Centre, but even the legislatures and the executive heads of the States are drawn from the Central legislature and the Central Cabinet.

We now come to an unusual feature of the constitution: the Union is not indissoluble. The Shan State and the Karenni State—but not the Kachin State—have been given the right to secede, but the right is not to be exercised during the first ten years of the Union. The procedure for secession is laid down in Chapter X thus:

> 203. (1) Any State wishing to exercise the right of secession shall have a resolution to that effect passed by its State Council. No such resolution shall be deemed to have been passed unless not less than two-thirds of the total number of members of the State Council concerned have voted in its favour.
>
> (2) The head of the State concerned shall notify the President of any such resolution passed by the Council and shall send him a copy of such resolution certified by the Chairman of the Council by which it was passed.

204.   The President shall thereupon order a plebiscite to be taken for the purpose of ascertaining the will of the people of the State concerned.

205.   The President shall appoint a Plebiscite Commission consisting of an equal number of members representing the Union and the State concerned in order to supervise the plebiscite.

The first general election under the new constitution is to be held within eighteen months from the date of its coming into operation (January 4, 1948). In the meantime, the Constituent Assembly will itself function as the provisional Union Parliament and there is also a provisional President as well as a provisional government.

In all these different ways—by constitutional experiments, by sympathetic understanding and treatment of the problems of special areas, by generous dealing with sensitive minorities— Burma has not only averted any partition of her territories, but has fashioned them all into a close-knit unity. The 36 Shan States, the two Wa States, the three Karenni States, the Karen Region and the Chin Division, some of which threatened to break away at one stage and were a source of considerable anxiety, have been quietly and without fuss integrated along with the rest of Burma into a close Union. It is true that there is a qualified right of secession, and other difficulties, not yet suspected, may arise; but the magnanimity with which the Constituent Assembly elected one of the Shan Chiefs, first as its President and then as the provisional President of the new Union, augurs well for the future. The credit for this achievement belongs in large measure to Burma's great leader, the Bogyoke, whose assassination in July last filled the country with grief and anxiety. But the tragedy has only served to bind the Burmese people closer together and he rules them from the grave even more than he did during life.

And so the new Union has been launched. The captain and the crew are all young men full of high ideals and eager hope; and India, which may claim in a sense to be their spiritual home, will watch their progress with sympathy and goodwill.

APPENDIX

APPENDIX—A

STATEMENT OF THE CABINET MISSION AND THE
VICEROY, MAY 16, 1946

1. On March 15th last, just before the despatch of the Cabinet Delegation to India, Mr. (now Earl) Attlee, the British Prime Minister, used these words:

> *My colleagues are going to India with the intention of using their utmost endeavours to help her to attain her freedom as speedily and fully as possible. What form of government is to replace the present regime is for India to decide; but our desire is to help her to set up forthwith the machinery for making that decision. . . . I hope that India and her people may elect to remain within the British Commonwealth. I am certain that they will find great advantages in doing so. . . . But if she does so elect, it must be by her own free will. The British Commonwealth and Empire is not bound together by chains of external compulsion. It is a free association of free peoples. If, on the other hand, she elects for independence, in our view she has a right to do so. It will be for us to help to make the transition as smooth and easy as possible.*

2. Charged in these historic words we—the Cabinet Ministers and the Viceroy—have done our utmost to assist the two main political parties to reach agreement upon the fundamental issue of the unity or division of India. After prolonged discussions in New Delhi we succeeded in bringing the Congress and the Muslim League together in conference at Simla. There was a full exchange of views and both parties were prepared to make considerable concessions in order to try and reach a settlement; but it ultimately proved impossible to close the remainder of the gap between the parties and so no agreement could be concluded. Since no agreement has been reached we feel that it is our duty to put forward what we consider are the best arrangements

30

possible to ensure a speedy setting up of the new constitution. This statement is made with the full approval of His Majesty's Government in the United Kingdom.

3. We have accordingly decided that immediate arrangements should be made whereby Indians may decide the future constitution of India and an interim government may be set up at once to carry on the administration of British India until such time as a new constitution can be brought into being. We have endeavoured to be just to the smaller as well as to the larger sections of the people; and to recommend a solution which will lead to a practicable way of governing the India of the future and will give a sound basis for defence and a good opportunity for progress in the social, political and economic fields.

4. It is not intended in this statement to review the voluminous evidence that has been submitted to the Mission; but it is right that we should state that it has shown an almost universal desire, outside the supporters of the Muslim League, for the unity of India.

5. This consideration did not, however, deter us from examining closely and impartially the possibility of a partition of India; since we were greatly impressed by the very genuine and acute anxiety of the Muslims lest they should find themselves subjected to a perpetual Hindu-majority rule.

This feeling has become so strong and widespread amongst the Muslims that it cannot be allayed by mere paper safeguards. If there is to be internal peace in India it must be secured by measures which will assure to the Muslims control in all matters vital to their culture, religion and economic or other interests.

6. We, therefore, examined in the first instance the question of a separate and fully independent sovereign State of Pakistan as claimed by the Muslim League. Such a Pakistan would comprise two areas; one in the north-west consisting of the provinces of the Panjab, Sind, North-West Frontier and British Baluchistan; the other in the north-east consisting of the provinces of Bengal and Assam. The League were prepared to consider adjustment of boundaries at a later stage, but insisted that the principle of Pakistan should first be acknowledged. The argument for a separate State of Pakistan was based, first, upon the right of the

Muslim majority to decide their method of government according to their wishes; and secondly, upon the necessity to include substantial areas in which Muslims are in a minority, in order to make Pakistan administratively and economically workable.

The size of the non-Muslim minorities in a Pakistan comprising the whole of the six provinces enumerated above would be very considerable as the following figures show: *

NORTH-WESTERN AREA	MUSLIM	NON-MUSLIM
Panjab ...	16,217,242	12,201,577
North-West Frontier Province ...	2,788,797	249,270
Sind ...	3,208,325	1,326,683
British Baluchistan ...	438,930	62,701
	22,653,294	13,840,231
	62·07%	37·93%

NORTH-EASTERN AREA	MUSLIM	NON-MUSLIM
Bengal ...	33,005,434	27,301,091
Assam ...	3,442,479	6,762,254
	36,447,913	34,063,345
	51·69%	48·31%

The Muslim minorities in the remainder of British India number some 20 million dispersed amongst a total population of 188 million.

These figures show that the setting up of a separate sovereign State of Pakistan on the lines claimed by the Muslim League would not solve the communal minority problem; nor can we see any justification for including within a sovereign Pakistan those districts of the Panjab and of Bengal and Assam in which the population is predominantly non-Muslim. Every argument that can be used in favour of Pakistan can equally in our view be used

* All population figures in this statement are from the census taken in 1941.

in favour of the exclusion of the non-Muslim areas from Pakistan. This point would particularly affect the position of the Sikhs.

7. We, therefore, considered whether a smaller sovereign Pakistan confined to the Muslim majority areas alone might be a possible basis of compromise. Such a Pakistan is regarded by the Muslim League as quite impracticable because it would entail the exclusion from Pakistan of (a) the whole of the Ambala and Jullundur divisions in the Panjab; (b) the whole of Assam except the district of Sylhet; and (c) a large part of Western Bengal, including Calcutta, in which city the Muslims form 23.6% of the population. We ourselves are also convinced that any solution which involves a radical partition of the Panjab and Bengal, as this would do, would be contrary to the wishes and interests of a very large proportion of the inhabitants of these provinces. Bengal and the Panjab each has its own common language and a long history and tradition. Moreover, any division of the Panjab would of necessity divide the Sikhs, leaving substantial bodies of Sikhs on both sides of the boundary. We have, therefore, been forced to the conclusion that neither a larger nor a smaller sovereign State of Pakistan would provide an acceptable solution for the communal problem.

8. Apart from the great force of the foregoing arguments there are weighty administrative, economic and military considerations. The whole of the transportation and postal and telegraph systems of India have been established on the basis of united India. To disintegrate them would gravely injure both parts of India. The case for a united defence is even stronger. The Indian armed forces have been built up as a whole for the defence of India as a whole; and to break them in two would inflict a deadly blow on the long traditions and high degree of efficiency of the Indian Army and would entail the gravest dangers. The Indian Navy and the Indian Air Force would become much less effective. The two sections of the suggested Pakistan contain the two most vulnerable frontiers in India and for a successful defence in depth the area of Pakistan would be insufficient.

9. A further consideration of importance is the greater difficulty which the Indian States would find in associating themselves with a divided British India.

10. Finally, there is the geographical fact that the two halves of the proposed Pakistan State are separated by some seven hundred miles and the communications between them both in war and peace would be dependent on the goodwill of Hindustan.

11. We are, therefore, unable to advise the British Government that the power which at present resides in British hands should be handed over to two entirely separate sovereign States.

12. This decision does not, however, blind us to the very real Muslim apprehensions that their culture and political and social life might become submerged in a purely unitary India, in which the Hindus with their greatly superior numbers must be a dominating element. To meet this the Congress have put forward a scheme under which provinces would have full autonomy, subject only to a minimum of Central subjects, such as foreign affairs, defence and communications.

Under this scheme, provinces, if they wished to take part in economic and administrative planning on a large scale, could cede to the Centre optional subjects in addition to the compulsory ones mentioned above.

13. Such a scheme would, in our view, present considerable constitutional disadvantages and anomalies. It would be very difficult to work a Central executive and legislature in which some ministers, who dealt with compulsory subjects, were responsible to the whole of India, while other ministers, who dealt with optional subjects, would be responsible only to those provinces which had elected to act together in respect of such subjects. This difficulty would be accentuated in the Central legislature, where it would be necessary to exclude certain members from speaking and voting when subjects with which their provinces were not concerned were under discussion.

Apart from the difficulty of working such a scheme, we do not consider that it would be fair to deny to other provinces, which did not desire to take the optional subjects at the Centre, the right to form themselves into a group for a similar purpose. This would indeed be no more than the exercise of their autonomous powers in a particular way.

14. Before putting forward our recommendation we turn to deal with the relationship of the Indian States to British India.

It is quite clear that with the attainment of independence by British India, whether inside or outside the British Commonwealth, the relationship which has hitherto existed between the Rulers of the States and the British Crown will no longer be possible. Paramountcy can neither be retained by the British Crown nor transferred to the new government. This fact has been fully recognised by those whom we interviewed from the States. They have at the same time assured us that the States are ready and willing to co-operate in the new development of India. The precise form which their co-operation will take must be a matter for negotiation during the building up of the new constitutional structure, and it by no means follows that it will be identical for all the States. We have not, therefore, dealt with the States in the same detail as the provinces of British India in the paragraphs which follow.

15.   We now indicate the nature of a solution which in our view would be just to the essential claims of all parties, and would at the same time be most likely to bring about a stable and practical form of constitution for all-India.

We recommend that the constitution should take the following basic form:

(i) There should be a Union of India, embracing both British India and the States, which should deal with the following subjects—foreign affairs, defence and communications—and which should have the powers necessary to raise the finances required for the above subjects.

(ii) The Union should have an executive and a legislature constituted from British Indian and States representatives. Any question raising a major communal issue in the legislature should require for its decision a majority of the representatives present and voting of each of the two major communities, as well as a majority of all the members present and voting.

(iii) All subjects other than the Union subjects and all residuary powers should vest in the provinces.

(iv) The States will retain all subjects and powers other than those ceded to the Union.

(v) Provinces should be free to form groups with executives and legislatures, and each group could determine the provincial subjects to be taken in common.

(vi) The constitutions of the Union and of the groups should contain a provision whereby any province could, by a majority vote of its legislative assembly, call for a reconsideration of the terms of the constitution after an initial period of ten years and at ten-yearly intervals thereafter.

16.   It is not our object to lay out the details of a constitution on the above lines, but to set in motion the machinery whereby a constitution can be settled by Indians for Indians.

It has been necessary, however, for us to make this re-commendation as to the broad basis of the future constitution because it became clear to us in the course of our negotiations that not until that had been done was there any hope of getting the two major communities to join in the setting up of the constitution-making machinery.

17.   We now indicate the constitution-making machinery which we propose should be brought into being forthwith in order to enable a new constitution to be worked out.

18.   In forming any assembly to decide a new constitutional structure, the first problem is to obtain as broad-based and accurate a representation of the whole population as is possible. The most satisfactory method obviously would be by election based on adult franchise; but any attempt to introduce such a step now will lead to a wholly unacceptable delay in the formulation of the new constitution. The only practicable alternative is to utilise the recently elected provincial legislative assemblies as the electing bodies. There are, however, two factors in their composition which make this difficult. First, the numerical strengths of the provincial legislative assemblies do not bear the same proportion to the total population in each province. Thus, Assam with a population of 10 millions has a Legislative Assembly of 108 members, while Bengal, with a population six times as large, has an Assembly of only 250. Secondly, owing to the weightage given to minorities by the Communal Award, the strengths of the several communities in each provincial legislative assembly are not in proportion to their numbers in the province. Thus, the number of seats reserved for Muslims in the Bengal Legislative Assembly is only 48% of the total, although they form 55% of the provincial population. After a most careful consideration of the

various methods by which these inequalities might be corrected, we have come to the conclusion that the fairest and most practicable plan would be—

(*a*) to allot to each province a total number of seats proportional to its population, roughly in the ratio of one to a million, as the nearest substitute for representation by adult suffrage;

(*b*) to divide this provincial allocation of seats between the main communities in each province in proportion to their population;

(*c*) to provide that the representatives allotted to each community in a province shall be elected by the members of that community in its legislative assembly.

We think that for these purposes it is sufficient to recognise only three main communities in India: 'General', Muslim and Sikh, the 'General' community including all persons who are not Muslims or Sikhs. As the smaller minorities would, upon the population basis, have little or no representation since they would lose the weightage which assures them seats in the provincial legislatures, we have made the arrangements set out in paragraph 20 below to give them a full representation upon all matters of special interest to the minorities.

19. (i) We, therefore, propose that there shall be elected by each provincial legislative assembly the following numbers of representatives, each part of the legislature (General, Muslim or Sikh) electing its own representatives by the method of proportional representation with the single transferable vote:

TABLE OF REPRESENTATION

SECTION—A

Province		General	Muslim	Total
Madras	...	45	4	49
Bombay	...	19	2	21
United Provinces	...	47	8	55
Bihar	...	31	5	36
Central Provinces	...	16	1	17
Orissa	...	9	0	9
Total	...	167	20	187

SECTION—B

Province	General	Muslim	Sikh	Total
Panjab ...	8	16	4	28
Noth-West Frontier Province ...	0	3	0	3
Sind ...	1	3	0	4
	9	22	4	35

SECTION—C

Province	General	Muslim	Total
Bengal ...	27	33	60
Assam ...	7	3	10
	34	36	70

Total for British India   ...   292

Maximum for Indian States ...   93

Total   ...   385

[*Note:* In order to represent the Chief Commissioners' provinces there will be added to *Section-A* the member representing Delhi in the Central Legislative Assembly, the member representing Ajmer-Merwara in the Central Legislative Assembly and a representative to be elected by the Coorg Legislative Council.

To *Section-B* will be added a representative of British Baluchistan.]

(ii) It is the intention that the States should be given in the final Constituent Assembly appropriate representation which would not, on the basis of the calculations adopted for British India, exceed 93, but the method of selection will have to be determined by consultation. The States would in the preliminary stage be represented by a negotiating committee.

(iii) The representatives thus chosen shall meet at New Delhi as soon as possible.

(iv) A preliminary meeting will be held at which the general order of business will be decided, a Chairman and other officers elected, and an Advisory Committee (see paragraph 20 below) on the rights of citizens, minorities and tribal and excluded areas set up. Thereafter the provincial representatives will divide up into the three sections shown under A, B and C, in the Table of Representation in sub-paragraph (i) of this paragraph.

(v) These sections shall proceed to settle the provincial constitutions for the provinces included in each section and shall also decide whether any group constitution shall be set up for those provinces and, if so, with what provincial subjects the group should deal. Provinces shall have the power to opt out of the groups in accordance with the provisions of sub-clause (viii) below.

(vi) The representatives of the sections and the Indian States shall re-assemble for the purpose of settling the Union constitution.

(vii) In the Union Constituent Assembly resolutions varying the provisions of paragraph 15 above or raising any major communal issue shall require a majority of the representatives present and voting of each of the two major communities.

The Chairman of the Assembly shall decide which (if any) of the resolutions raise major communal issues and shall, if so requested by a majority of the representatives of either of the major communities, consult the Federal Court before giving his decision.

(viii) As soon as the new constitutional arrangements have come into operation, it shall be open to any province to elect to come out of any group in which it has been placed. Such a decision shall be taken by the new legislature of the province after the first general election under the new constitution.

20. The Advisory Committee on the rights of citizens, minorities and tribal and excluded areas should contain full representation of the interests affected, and their function will be to report to the Union Constituent Assembly upon the list of fundamental rights, the clauses for the protection of minorities and a scheme for the administration of the tribal and excluded areas, and to advise whether these rights should be incorporated in the provincial, group, or Union constitution.

21. His Excellency the Viceroy will forthwith request the provincial legislatures to proceed with the election of their representatives and the States to set up a negotiating committee. It is hoped that the process of constitution-making can proceed as rapidly as the complexities of the task permit, so that the interim period may be as short as possible.

22. It will be necessary to negotiate a treaty between the Union Constituent Assembly and the United Kingdom to provide for certain matters arising out of the transfer of power.

23. While the constitution-making proceeds, the administration of India has to be carried on. We attach the greatest importance, therefore, to the setting up at once of an interim government having the support of the major political parties. It is essential during the interim period that there should be the maximum of co-operation in carrying through the difficult tasks that face the Government of India. Besides the heavy task of day-to-day administration, there is the grave danger of famine to be countered; there are decisions to be taken in many matters of post-war development which will have a far-reaching effect on India's future; and there are important international conferences in which India has to be represented. For all these purposes a government having popular support is necessary. The Viceroy has already started discussions to this end, and hopes soon to form an interim government in which all the portfolios, including that of war member, will be held by Indian leaders having the full confidence of the people. The British Government, recognising the significance of the changes in the Government of India, will give the fullest measure of co-operation to the government so formed in the accomplishment of its tasks of administration and in bringing about as rapid and smooth a transition as possible.

24. To the leaders and people of India who now have the opportunity of complete independence we would finally say this: We and our government and countrymen hoped that it would be possible for the Indian people themselves to agree upon the method of framing the new constitution under which they will live. Despite the labours which we have shared with the Indian parties and the exercise of much patience and goodwill by all, this has not been possible. We, therefore, now lay before you

proposals which, after listening to all sides and after much earnest thought, we trust will enable you to attain your independence in the shortest time and with the least danger of internal disturbance and conflict. These proposals may not, of course, completely satisfy all parties, but you will recognise with us that at this supreme moment in Indian history statesmanship demands mutual accommodation.

We ask you to consider the alternative to acceptance of these proposals. After all the efforts which we and the Indian parties have made together for agreement, we must state that in our view there is small hope of peaceful settlement by agreement of the Indian parties alone. The alternative would, therefore, be a grave danger of violence, chaos and even civil war. The result and duration of such a disturbance cannot be foreseen; but it is certain that it would be a terrible disaster for many millions of men, women and children. This is a possibility which must be regarded with equal abhorrence by the Indian people, our own countrymen and the world as a whole.

We, therefore, lay these proposals before you in the profound hope that they will be accepted and operated by you in the spirit of accommodation and goodwill in which they are offered. We appeal to all who have the future good of India at heart to extend their vision beyond their own community or interest to the interests of the whole four hundred millions of the Indian people.

We hope that the new independent India may choose to be a member of the British Commonwealth. We hope in any event that you will remain in close and friendly association with our people. But these are matters for your own free choice. Whatever that choice may be, we look forward with you to your ever increasing prosperity among the great nations of the world and to a future even more glorious than your past.

APPENDIX—B

BRITISH PRIME MINISTER'S STATEMENT IN THE HOUSE OF COMMONS ON 20TH FEBRUARY 1947

1. It has long been the policy of successive British governments to work towards the realisation of self-government in India. In pursuance of this policy, an increasing measure of responsibility has been devolved on Indians, and today the civil administration and the Indian armed forces rely to a very large extent on Indian civilians and officers. In the constitutional field, the Acts of 1919 and 1935 passed by the British Parliament each represented a substantial transfer of political power. In 1940 the coalition government recognised the principle that Indians should themselves frame a new constitution for a fully autonomous India, and in the offer of 1942 they invited them to set up a Constituent Assembly for this purpose as soon as the war was over.

2. His Majesty's Government believe this policy to have been right and in accordance with sound democratic principles. Since they came into office, they have done their utmost to carry it forward to its fulfilment. The declaration of the Prime Minister of 15th March last, which met with general approval in Parliament and the country, made it clear that it was for the Indian people themselves to choose their future status and constitution and that, in the opinion of His Majesty's Government, the time had come for responsibility for the Government of India to pass into Indian hands.

3. The Cabinet Mission which was sent to India last year spent over three months in consultation with Indian leaders in order to help them to agree upon a method for determining the future constitution of India, so that the transfer of power might be smoothly and rapidly effected. It was only when it seemed clear that without some initiative from the Cabinet

Mission agreement was unlikely to be reached that they put forward proposals themselves.

4. These proposals, made public in May last, envisaged that the future constitution of India should be settled by a Constituent Assembly composed, in the manner suggested therein, of representatives of all communities and interests in British India and of the Indian States.

5. Since the return of the Mission, an interim government has been set up at the Centre composed of the political leaders of the major communities, exercising wide powers within the existing constitution. In all the provinces Indian governments responsible to legislatures are in office.

6. It is with great regret that His Majesty's Government find that there are still differences among Indian parties which are preventing the Constituent Assembly from functioning as it was intended that it should. It is of the essence of the plan that the Assembly should be fully representative.

7. His Majesty's Government desire to hand over their responsibility to authorities established by a constitution approved by all parties in India in accordance with the Cabinet Mission's plan. But unfortunately there is at present no clear prospect that such a constitution and such authorities will emerge. The present state of uncertainty is fraught with danger and cannot be indefinitely prolonged. His Majesty's Government wish to make it clear that it is their definite intention to take necessary steps to effect the transference of power to responsible Indian hands by a date not later than June 1948.

8. This great sub-continent now containing over four hundred million people has for the last century enjoyed peace and security as a part of the British Commonwealth and Empire. Continued peace and security are more than ever necessary today if the full possibilities of economic development are to be realised and a higher standard of life attained by the Indian people.

9. His Majesty's Government are anxious to hand over their responsibilities to a government which, resting on the sure foundation of the support of the people, is capable of maintaining peace and administering India with justice and efficiency. It is

therefore, essential that all parties should sink their differences in order that they may be ready to shoulder the great responsibilities which will come upon them next year.

10. After months of hard work by the Cabinet Mission a great measure of agreement was obtained as to the method by which a constitution should be worked out. This was embodied in their statement of May last. His Majesty's Government there agreed to recommend to Parliament a constitution worked out in accordance with the proposals made therein by a fully representative Constituent Assembly. But if it should appear that such a constitution will not have been worked out by a fully representative Assembly before the time mentioned in paragraph 7, His Majesty's Government will have to consider to whom the powers of the Central Government in British India should be handed over on the due date, whether as a whole to some form of Central Government for British India, or in some areas to the existing provincial governments, or in such other way as may seem most reasonable and in the best interests of the Indian people.

11. Although the final transfer of authority may not take place until June 1948, preparatory measures must be put in hand in advance. It is important that the efficiency of the civil administration should be maintained and that the defence of India should be fully provided for. But, inevitably, as the process of transfer proceeds, it will become progressively more difficult to carry out to the letter all the provisions of the Government of India Act, 1935. Legislation will be introduced in due course to give effect to the final transfer of power.

12. In regard to the Indian States, as was explicitly stated by the Cabinet Mission, His Majesty's Government do not intend to hand over their powers and obligations under paramountcy to any government of British India. It is not intended to bring paramountcy, as a system, to a conclusion earlier than the date of the final transfer of power, but it is contemplated that for the intervening period the relations of the Crown with individual States may be adjusted by agreement.

13. His Majesty's Government will negotiate agreements in regard to matters arising out of the transfer of power with the representatives of those to whom they propose to transfer power.

14. His Majesty's Government believe that British commercial and industrial interests in India can look forward to a fair field for their enterprise under the new conditions. The commercial connection between India and the United Kingdom has been long and friendly and will continue to be to their mutual advantage.

15. His Majesty's Government cannot conclude this statement without expressing, on behalf of the people of this country, their goodwill and good wishes towards the people of India as they go forward to this final stage in their achievement of self-government. It will be the wish of everyone in these islands that notwithstanding constitutional changes, the association of the British and Indian peoples should not be brought to an end; and they will wish to continue to do all that is in their power to further the well-being of India.

APPENDIX—C

STATEMENT MADE BY HIS MAJESTY'S GOVERNMENT ON JUNE 3, 1947

INTRODUCTION

1. On 20th February 1947, His Majesty's Government announced their intention of transferring power in British India to Indian hands by June 1948. His Majesty's Government had hoped that it would be possible for the major parties to co-operate in the working-out of the Cabinet Mission plan of 16th May 1946, and evolve for India a constitution acceptable to all concerned. This hope has not been fulfilled.

2. The majority of the representatives of the provinces of Madras, Bombay, the United Provinces, Bihar, Central Provinces and Berar, Assam, Orissa and the North-West Frontier Province, and the representatives of Delhi, Ajmer-Merwara and Coorg have already made progress in the task of evolving a new constitution. On the other hand, the Muslim League party, including in it a majority of the representatives of Bengal, the Panjab and Sind, as also the representative of British Baluchistan, has decided not to participate in the Constituent Assembly.

3. It has always been the desire of His Majesty's Government that power should be transferred in accordance with the wishes of the Indian people themselves. This task would have been greatly facilitated if there had been agreement among the Indian political parties. In the absence of such agreement, the task of devising a method by which the wishes of the Indian people can be ascertained has devolved upon his Majesty's Government. After full consultation with political leaders in India, His Majesty's Government have decided to adopt for this purpose the plan set out below. His Majesty's Government wish

31

to make it clear that they have no intention of attempting to frame any ultimate constitution for India; this is a matter for the Indians themselves. Nor is there anything in this plan to preclude negotiations between communities for a united India.

Issues to be Decided

4. It is not the intention of His Majesty's Government to interrupt the work of the existing Constituent Assembly. Now that provision is made for certain provinces specified below, His Majesty's Government trust that, as a consequence of this announcement, the Muslim League representatives of those provinces, a majority of whose representatives are already participating in it, will now take their due share in its labours. At the same time, it is clear that any constitution framed by this Assembly cannot apply to those parts of the country which are unwilling to accept it. His Majesty's Government are satisfied that the procedure outlined below embodies the best practical method of ascertaining the wishes of the people of such areas on the issue whether their constitution is to be framed:

(*a*) in the existing Constituent Assembly; or

(*b*) in a new and separate Constituent Assembly consisting of the representatives of those areas which decide not to participate in the existing Constituent Assembly.

When this has been done, it will be possible to determine the authority or authorities to whom power should be transferred.

Bengal and the Panjab

5. The provincial Legislative Assemblies of Bengal and the Panjab (excluding the European members) will, therefore, each be asked to meet in two parts, one representing the Muslim-majority districts and the other the rest of the province. For the purpose of determining the population of districts, the 1941 census figures will be taken as authoritative. The Muslim-majority districts in these two provinces are set out in the appendix to this announcement. [*Vide p.* 488.]

6. The members of the two parts of each legislative assembly sitting separately will be empowered to vote whether or not the province should be partitioned. If a simple majority of either part decides in favour of partition, division will take place and arrangements will be made accordingly.

7. Before the question as to the partition is decided, it is desirable that the representatives of each part should know in advance which Constituent Assembly the province as a whole would join in the event of the two parts subsequently deciding to remain united. Therefore, if any member of either legislative assembly so demands, there shall be held a meeting of all members of the legislative assembly (other than Europeans) at which a decision will be taken on the issue as to which Constituent Assembly the province as a whole would join, if it were decided by the two parts to remain united.

8. In the event of partition being decided upon, each part of the legislative assembly will, on behalf of the areas they represent, decide which of the alternatives in paragraph 4 above to adopt.

9. For the immediate purpose of deciding on the issue of partition, the members of the Legislative Assemblies of Bengal and the Panjab will sit in two parts according to Muslim-majority districts (as laid down in the appendix) and non-Muslim majority districts. This is only a preliminary step of a purely temporary nature, as it is evident that, for the purposes of a final partition of these provinces, a detailed investigation of boundary questions will be needed; and, as soon as a decision involving partition has been taken for either province, a Boundary Commission will be set up by the Governor-General, the membership and terms of reference of which will be settled in consultation with those concerned. It will be instructed to demarcate the boundaries of the two parts of the Panjab on the basis of ascertaining the contiguous majority areas of Muslims and non-Muslims. It will also be instructed to take into account other factors. Similar instructions will be given to the Bengal Boundary Commission. Until the report of a Boundary Commission has been put into effect, the provisional boundaries indicated in the appendix will be used.

SIND

10. The Legislative Assembly of Sind (excluding the European members) will, at a special meeting, also take its own decision on the alternatives in paragraph 4 above.

NORTH-WEST FRONTIER PROVINCE

11. The position of the North-West Frontier Province is exceptional. Two of the three representatives of this province are already participating in the existing Constituent Assembly. But it is clear, in view of its geographical situation and other considerations, that if the whole or any part of the Panjab decides not to join the existing Constituent Assembly, it will be necessary to give the North-West Frontier Province an opportunity to reconsider its position. Accordingly, in such an event, a referendum will be made to the electors of the present Legislative Assembly in the North-West Frontier Province to choose which of the alternatives mentioned in paragraph 4 above they wish to adopt. The referendum will be held under the aegis of the Governor-General and in consultation with the provincial government.

BRITISH BALUCHISTAN

12. British Baluchistan has elected a member, but he has not taken his seat in the existing Constituent Assembly. In view of its geographical situation, this province will also be given an opportunity to reconsider its position and to choose which of the alternatives in paragraph 4 above to adopt. His Excellency the Governor-General is examining how this can most appropriately be done.

ASSAM

13. Though Assam is predominantly a non-Muslim province, the district of Sylhet which is contiguous to Bengal is predominantly Muslim. There has been a demand that, in the event of

the partition of Bengal, Sylhet should be amalgamated with the Muslim part of Bengal. Accordingly, if it is decided that Bengal should be partitioned, a referendum will be held in Sylhet district under the aegis of the Governor-General and in consultation with the Assam Provincial Government to decide whether the district of Sylhet should continue to form part of the Assam province or should be amalgamated with the new province of Eastern Bengal, if that province agrees. If the referendum results in favour of amalgamation with Eastern Bengal, a Boundary Commission with terms of reference similar to those for the Panjab and Bengal will be set up to demarcate the Muslim-majority areas of Sylhet district and contiguous Muslim-majority areas of adjoining districts, which will then be transferred to Eastern Bengal. The rest of the Assam Province will in any case continue to participate in the proceedings of the existing Constituent Assembly.

REPRESENTATION IN CONSTITUENT ASSEMBLIES

14. If it is decided that Bengal and the Panjab should be partitioned, it will be necessary to hold fresh elections to choose their representatives on the scale of one for every million of the population according to the principle contained in the Cabinet Mission plan of 16th May 1946. Similar elections will also have to be held for Sylhet in the event of it being decided that this district should form part of East Bengal. The number of representatives to which each area would be entitled is as follows:

PROVINCE	GENERAL	MUSLIMS	SIKHS	TOTAL
Sylhet District	1	2	nil	3
West Bengal	15	4	nil	19
East Bengal	12	29	nil	41
West Panjab	3	12	2	17
East Panjab	6	4	2	12

15. In accordance with the mandates given to them, the representatives of the various areas will either join the existing Constituent Assembly or form the new Constituent Assembly.

ADMINISTRATIVE MATTERS

16. Negotiations will have to be initiated as soon as possible on the administrative consequences of any partition that may have been decided upon—

(*a*) between the representatives of the respective successor authorities about all subjects now dealt with by the Central Government, including defence, finance and communications;

(*b*) between different successor authorities and His Majesty's Government for treaties in regard to matters arising out of the transfer of power;

(*c*) in the case of provinces that may be partitioned, as to the administration of all provincial subjects such as the division of assets and liabilities, the police and other services, the High Courts, provincial institutions, etc.

TRIBES OF NORTH-WEST FRONTIER

17. Agreements with the tribes of the North-West Frontier of India will have to be negotiated by the appropriate successor authority.

THE STATES

18. His Majesty's Government wish to make it clear that the decisions announced above relate only to British India and that their policy towards Indian States contained in the Cabinet Mission memorandum of 16th May 1946 remains unchanged.

NECESSITY FOR SPEED

19. In order that the successor authorities may have time to prepare themselves to take over power, it is important that all the above processes should be completed as quickly as possible. To avoid delay, the different provinces or parts of provinces will proceed independently as far as practicable within the conditions of this plan. The existing Constituent Assembly and the new Constituent Assembly (if formed) will proceed to frame

constitutions for their respective territories: they will of course be free to frame their own rules.

IMMEDIATE TRANSFER OF POWER

20. The major political parties have repeatedly emphasised their desire that there should be the earliest possible transfer of power in India. With this desire His Majesty's Government are in full sympathy, and they are willing to anticipate the date of June 1948, for the handing over of power, by the setting up of an independent Indian Government or governments at an even earlier date. Accordingly, as the most expeditious and indeed the only practicable way of meeting this desire, His Majesty's Government propose to introduce legislation during the current session for the transfer of power this year on a Dominion status basis to one or two successor authorities, according to the decisions taken as a result of this announcement. This will be without prejudice to the right of the Indian Constituent Assemblies to decide in due course whether or not the part of India in respect of which they have authority will remain within the British Commonwealth.

FURTHER ANNOUNCEMENTS BY GOVERNOR-GENERAL

21. His Excellency the Governor-General will from time to time make such further announcements as may be necessary in regard to procedure or any other matters for carrying out the above arrangements.

APPENDIX

[To His Majesty's Government's Statement on June 3, 1947.]

Muslim-Majority Districts of the Panjab and Bengal
according to the 1941 Census

THE PANJAB

Lahore Division—Gujranwala, Gurdaspur, Lahore, Sheikhu-
pura, Sialkot.

Rawalpindi Division—Attock, Gujrat, Jhelum, Mianwali,
Rawalpindi, Shahpur.

Multan Division—Dera Ghazi Khan, Jhang, Lyallpur,
Montgomery, Multan, Muzaffargarh.

2.   BENGAL

Chittagong Division—Chittagong, Noakhali, Tippera.

Dacca Division—Bakerganj, Dacca, Faridpur, Mymensingh.

Presidency Division—Jessore, Murshidabad, Nadia.

Rajshahi Division—Bogra, Dinajpur, Malda, Pabna, Rajshahi,
Rangpur.

INDEX

INDEX

INDEX TO PROPER NAMES

INDEX—GENERAL

INDEX TO AUTHORITIES CITED